The idea of a dialogue – sometimes harmonious, sometimes divisive – between the centre and periphery of the early modern European state stands at the heart of much of John Elliott's historical writing. It is the fulcrum around which his *Imperial Spain* revolves, and it lies at the heart of his analysis of the causes of the revolt of the Catalans against the centralizing policies of the Madrid government, directed by the charismatic but insensitive count-duke of Olivares, in 1640. Elliott subsequently extended the concept of centre *versus* periphery beyond Spanish shores. 'Revolution and continuity in early modern Europe', his inaugural lecture as Professor of History at King's College, London, in 1968, perceived the various revolts of mid-seventeenth-century Europe as essentially conflicts between the loyalties owed to one's *patria* – representing a province or a principality more often than a nation – and those owed to one's monarch. His writings on the Americas, such as *The Old World and the New, 1492–1650* (1970), likewise stressed the relationship between centre and periphery. Finally, in the balance between Castile (which declined in the seventeenth century) and the other Spanish kingdoms (which did not) Elliott found the secret of the survival of Spain as a great power long after its economic and demographic base had been eroded.

This collection of essays by a group of Elliott's former students examines different aspects of this important theme and develops them. Taken together with the 'personal appreciation' of Elliott (Regius Professor of Modern History at Oxford), it forms an important examination of the work of the greatest living historian of Spain as well as a major contribution to early modern European history.

Spain, Europe and the Atlantic world

Sir John Elliott

Spain, Europe and the Atlantic world

Essays in honour of John H. Elliott

Edited by Richard L. Kagan
The Johns Hopkins University

and Geoffrey Parker
Yale University

CAMBRIDGE
UNIVERSITY PRESS

PUBLISHED BY THE PRESS SYNDICATE OF THE UNIVERSITY OF CAMBRIDGE
The Pitt Building, Trumpington Street, Cambridge, United Kingdom

CAMBRIDGE UNIVERSITY PRESS
The Edinburgh Building, Cambridge CB2 2RU, UK
40 West 20th Street, New York NY 10011–4211, USA
477 Williamstown Road, Port Melbourne, VIC 3207, Australia
Ruiz de Alarcón 13, 28014 Madrid, Spain
Dock House, The Waterfront, Cape Town 8001, South Africa

http://www.cambridge.org

First published 1995
First paperback edition 2002

A catalogue record for this book is available from the British Library

Library of Congress Cataloguing in Publication data
Spain, Europe, and the Atlantic world / Richard L. Kagan & Geoffrey Parker [editors].
p.   cm.
Includes index.
ISBN 0 521 47045 5
1. Spain – History.   2. Elliott, John Huxtable.
I. Kagan, Richard L., 1943–   .   II. Parker, Geoffrey, 1943–
DP161.S63   1995
946–dc20   94-42370   CIP

ISBN 0 521 47045 5 hardback
ISBN 0 521 52511 X paperback

Contents

Notes on contributors		*page*	ix
Acknowledgements			xiii
List of abbreviations			xiv

Sir John Elliott: an appreciation   I

Introduction   14

PART I Power and propaganda: the world of the court   25

1   Twin souls: monarchs and favourites in early seventeenth-century Spain   27
  Antonio Feros

2   Taxation and political culture in Castile, 1590–1640   48
  Charles J. Jago

3   Clio and the crown: writing history in Habsburg Spain   73
  Richard L. Kagan

PART II The pattern of society: community and identity in Habsburg Spain   101

4   *Toledanos* and the kingdom of Granada, 1492–1560s   103
  Linda Martz

5   Castile, Spain and the monarchy: the political community from *patria natural* to *patria nacional*   125
  I. A. A. Thompson

vii

6 Aragonese constitutionalism and Habsburg rule: the varying
   meanings of liberty   160
   Xavier Gil
7 Patriotism in early modern Valencia   188
   James Casey
8 The mental world of Jeroni Pujades   211
   James Amelang
9 Centring the periphery: the Cerdanya between France and
   Spain   227
   Peter Sahlins

PART III   **Spain and its empire**   243
10 David or Goliath? Philip II and his world in the 1580s   245
   Geoffrey Parker
11 Olivares, the Cardinal-Infante and Spain's strategy in the
   Low Countries (1635–1643): the road to Rocroi   267
   Jonathan I. Israel
12 Conquest after the conquest: the rise of Spanish domination
   in America   296
   Peter Bakewell
13 Heeding Heraclides: empire and its discontents, 1619–1812   316
   Anthony Pagden
14 Why were Spain's special overseas laws never enacted?   334
   Josep M. Fradera

Index   350

Notes on contributors

James S. Amelang is Professor of Early Modern History at the Autonomous University of Madrid (Spain). While a graduate student at Princeton University he studied with John Elliott, and in 1980–1 worked as his assistant at the Institute for Advanced Study. He is the author of *Honored citizens of Barcelona: patrician culture and class relations, 1490–1714* (Princeton, 1986), and *A journal of the plague year: the diary of the Barcelona tanner Miquel Parets, 1651* (New York, 1991). He is presently completing a study of artisan autobiographies in early modern Europe.

Peter Bakewell is Professor of History at Emory University, Atlanta. He wrote his doctoral dissertation under John Elliott's direction at Cambridge, receiving his doctorate in 1969. The revised dissertation was published as *Silver mining and society in colonial Mexico, Zacatecas 1546–1700* (Cambridge, 1971). His other main publications are *Miners of the Red Mountain: Indian labor in Potosí, 1545–1650* (Albuquerque, 1984); and *Silver and entrepreneurship in seventeenth-century Potosí: the life and times of Antonio López de Quiroga* (Albuquerque, 1988). He is currently at work on *Middle and South America*, a general history of Latin America from the late pre-conquest to the present, for Basil Blackwell.

James Casey is Senior Lecturer in the School of History at the University of East Anglia, Norwich. His interest in Spanish history began after reading John Elliott's *The Revolt of the Catalans* (1963). After graduating from the

Queen's University of Belfast in 1965, he went to Cambridge to research under Professor Elliott's supervision on the kingdom of Valencia in the time of Olivares. The resulting doctoral thesis (1968) was later expanded into a book-length study of *The kingdom of Valencia in the seventeenth century* (Cambridge, 1979). Since then he has worked on Spanish family history in the early modern period, and has published a general introduction to the theme, *The history of the family* (Blackwell, Oxford, 1989).

Antonio Feros is Assistant Professor of History at New York University. After studying in the Autonomous University of Madrid, he served as research assistant to Professor Elliott at the Institute for Advanced Study, Princeton, from 1988 to 1990. He joined the graduate programme of the Department of History at The Johns Hopkins University, Baltimore, in 1990, and received his doctorate in 1994 for his dissertation *The king's favorite, the duke of Lerma: power, wealth and court culture in the reign of Philip III of Spain, 1598–1621*. He has published articles on Spain in the reign of Philip III, the governments of the duke of Lerma and the count-duke of Olivares, and theatre and politics in Golden Age Spain.

Josep M. Fradera i Barcelo was born in Mataro, Spain, and is currently Associate Professor of Early Modern and Modern History at the Universitat Pompeu Fabra, Barcelona. He worked as John Elliott's research assistant at Princeton in 1987–8. His major publications include *Industria i mercat. Les bases comercials de la industria catalana moderna, 1814–1845* (Barcelona, 1987), and his present research concerns the political, economic and cultural relations between Spain and its colonies in the nineteenth century.

Xavier Gil, Associate Professor of Early Modern History at the University of Barcelona, was John Elliott's research assistant at the Institute for Advanced Study in 1981–2 and 1984–5. He obtained his doctorate at the University of Barcelona in 1989 with a thesis on the central government and local élites in Aragon, 1585–1648, soon to be published as a book. He is also the author of a number of essays on early modern political history, including various contributions to volumes edited by John Elliott.

Jonathan Israel is Professor of Dutch History and Institutions in the University of London. He began his career as a historian of the Spanish empire, after being introduced to Mexican colonial history in a documents course taught by John Elliott at Cambridge in 1966–7. His first book, *Race, class and politics in colonial Mexico, 1610–1670*, was published in 1975. It was followed by *The Dutch Republic and the Hispanic world, 1606–1661* (1982) and *Dutch primacy in world trade* (1989). His latest book is *The Dutch Republic: its rise, greatness and fall, 1477–1806* (1995). He is a Fellow of the British Academy and was also elected a Fellow of the Royal Netherlands Academy of Arts and Sciences in 1994.

Charles J. Jago entered Cambridge University in 1965 after completing his undergraduate studies at Huron College, The University of Western Ontario, in Canada. He commenced his doctoral studies in 1966 under the supervision of Professor Elliott, graduating in 1969 following successful completion of his thesis, 'Aristocracy, war and finance in Castile, 1621–1665'. He has held two academic appointments during his career: from 1970 to 1987 at McMaster University in Canada where he advanced to the rank of professor, and from 1987 to the present as the President of Huron College, his alma mater. He has published numerous articles in *Past and Present*, *The American Historical Review*, *The Economic History Review* and elsewhere on both the seventeenth-century Castilian aristocracy and, more recently, on the Cortes of Castile during the Habsburg era.

Richard L. Kagan first became interested in Spanish history during his final year of undergraduate studies at Columbia University in 1964–5. He completed his doctorate at Cambridge University under John Elliott's direction in 1968. Currently, he is Professor of History at The Johns Hopkins University. His publications include *Students and society in early modern Spain* (Chapel Hill, 1974); *Lawsuits and litigants in Castile, 1500–1700* (Chapel Hill, 1981); *Spanish cities of the Golden Age: the views of Anton van den Wyngaerde* (Berkeley, 1989); and *Lucrecia's dreams: politics and prophecy in sixteenth-century Spain* (Berkeley, 1990). He is presently collaborating with the Spanish art historian, Fernando Marías, on the volume *Urban images of the Hispanic world 1500–1800*.

Linda Martz, a freelance writer, editor and researcher, began her doctoral studies with John Elliott at King's College, University of London, in 1970. She completed her dissertation in 1974 under the direction of H.G. Koenigsberger following Elliott's departure in 1973 for the Institute for Advanced Studies at Princeton. The research was later published as *Poverty and welfare in Habsburg Spain: the example of Toledo* (Cambridge, 1983). Other books include (with Julio Porres) *Toledo y los toledanos en 1561* (Toledo, 1974). She is currently completing *A network of Toledo families: the assimilation of a minority*.

Anthony Pagden is Reader in Modern Intellectual History at Cambridge University, and Fellow of King's College. His first publication was an edition and translation of Hernán Cortés' *Cartas de relación*, for which John Elliott wrote an historical introduction (Oxford, 1971, new edition New Haven and London, 1986). He was a Member of the Institute for Advanced Study between 1979 and 1980 and, together with Nicholas Canny organized, under John Elliott's auspices, a conference on Colonial Identity in the Atlantic World, 1500–1800. The proceedings of this meeting were published, with an introduction by John Elliott, by Princeton University Press in 1987. His other publications include *The fall of natural man* (Cambridge, 1982), *Spanish imperialism and the political imagination* (New Haven and London, 1990) and *European encounters with the New World* (New Haven and London, 1993).

Geoffrey Parker is Robert A. Lovett Professor of Military and Naval History at Yale University. He completed his doctorate under John Elliott's direction at Cambridge in 1968. It was later published as *The Army of Flanders and the Spanish Road, 1567–1659: the logistics of Spanish victory and defeat in the Low Countries' wars* (Cambridge, 1972). His other publications include *The Dutch revolt* (London, 1977); *Philip II* (Boston, 1978), dedicated to John Elliott; *The military revolution: military innovation and the rise of the West, 1500–1800* (Cambridge, 1988); and (with Colin Martin) *The Spanish Armada* (London, 1988). He is currently completing *The grand strategy of Philip II* for Yale University Press. In 1984 he was elected a Fellow of the British Academy, and in 1987 a Corresponding Fellow of the Royal Spanish Academy of History.

Peter Sahlins studied with John Elliott at Princeton University and was his research assistant at the Institute for Advanced Study in 1986–7. He is the author of *Boundaries: the making of France and Spain in the Pyrenees* (Berkeley and London, 1989) and *Forest rites: the war of the demoiselles in nineteenth-century France* (Cambridge, Mass., 1994), and is currently working on immigration and nationality in early modern France.

I. A. A. Thompson, now Fellow of the University of Keele in the Department of History, was John Elliott's first research student in Spanish history. His PhD was completed in 1965 and forms the basis of his *War and government in Habsburg Spain 1560–1620* (London, 1976). His other publications include *War and society in Habsburg Spain* (Variorum, 1992) and *Crown and Cortes: government, institutions and representation in early-modern Castile* (Variorum, 1993).

Acknowledgements

The editors would like to thank Oonah Elliott for providing the frontispiece; Jonathan Brown, Brian Pullan and Orest Ranum for helpful advice; James Amelang for invaluable assistance in finalizing the volume; and William Davies for seeing it through the Press.

Abbreviations

Archives and libraries

ABZ	Archivo y Biblioteca de Zabálburu, Madrid
ADPO	Archives Départementales des Pyrénées-Orientales
ADZ	Archivo de la Diputación de Zaragoza
AGR	Archives Générales du Royaume, Brussels
	SEG Secrétairerie d'Etat et de Guerre
AGS	Archivo General de Simancas
	CC Cámara de Castilla
	CJH Consejo y Juntas de Hacienda
	CM Contaduría de Mercedes
	CMC Contaduría Mayor de Cuentas
	CR Consejo Real
	Est. Estado
	GA Guerra Antigua
	PR Patronato Real
AHN	Archivo Histórico Nacional, Madrid
	Cons. Consejos Suprimidos
	Est. Estado
AHP	Arxiu Històric de Puigcerdà
AHPT	Archivo Histórico de Protocolos, Toledo
AM	Archivo Municipal
AMLL	Arxiu Municipal de Llívia

List of abbreviations

BL   British Library
          Add.   Additional Manuscripts
BNM   Biblioteca Nacional, Madrid
BSLE   Biblioteca del Real Monasterio de San Lorenzo de El Escorial
IVDJ   Instituto de Valencia de Don Juan, Madrid
RAH   Real Academia de Historia, Madrid
          CSC   Colección Salazar y Castro

Other abbreviations

ACC   *Actas de las Cortes de Castilla* (60 vols., Madrid, 1877–1914)
CLC   Cortes de los antiguos reinos de León y Castilla (5 vols., Madrid, 1861–1903)
CSP   Calendar of State Papers, Venetian, 1534–80 (9 vols., London, 1873–90)
leg.   *legajo*
lib.   libro
prot.   protocolo

Sir John Elliott: an appreciation

RICHARD L. KAGAN AND GEOFFREY PARKER

Sir John Huxtable Elliott was born in Reading, England, on 23 June 1930. After winning a scholarship to Eton, and national service, he graduated with first class honours in history from Cambridge and then earned a doctorate in history from Cambridge in 1955. He remained at Cambridge, first as a fellow of Trinity College (from 1954) and later as a university lecturer in history, until 1967 when he became Professor of Modern History at King's College, University of London. In 1973 he left King's to become professor in the School of Historical Studies at Princeton's Institute for Advanced Study where over the next seventeen years he welcomed and inspired scholars from all parts of the world. In 1990 he was named Regius Professor of Modern History at Oxford University.

A complete account of Professor Elliott's scholarly publications and a list of his awards and honours would fill many pages. To mention but a few, he has received honorary doctorates from several universities (including the Autonomous University of Madrid, the University of Genoa and the University of Barcelona). In addition, he is the recipient of Spain's Order of Isabella la Católica (1987), the Grand Cross of the Order of Alfonso the Wise (1988) and the Gold Medal of Fine Arts (1990). His prizes include the American Historical Association's Gershoy Prize for his book, *Richelieu and Olivares* (1985), the Wolfson Prize for his monumental biography, *The count-duke of Olivares: the statesman in an age of decline* (1986) and the Antonio de Nebrija prize for the Spanish edition of this same work (1993). In 1994, he was knighted by Queen Elizabeth II.

But how did a child from Reading become the world's foremost historian of Spain? The English tradition of writing about Spain and its history began centuries ago, but suffered disruption during and after the Spanish Civil War. General Franco's Spain enjoyed little foreign support and remained taboo for those British intellectuals sympathetic to the Republic that Franco defeated – a pariah state to be attacked and criticized, but never visited, and definitely not a suitable terrain for serious historical research. Consequently, outside the language faculties, Spain's history and culture were scarcely taught in British universities, and Elliott himself knew little about the country until, in the summer of 1950, with a group of students from Cambridge University he went to Spain for the first time. As he later wrote,

Like so many others from the North who make contact for the first time with the civilization of Southern Europe, I was immediately enthralled. Here was a society which, amidst all the sadness of the post-war period, gave the impression of possessing an extraordinary basic vitality amid its austerity which had a profound effect on me; and I felt an immediate desire to pursue my own exploration of these mysteries.

A visit to the Prado Museum formed the highlight of the trip.

I was left overwhelmed by the variety and the quality of the collection, and I was particularly affected by the work of Velázquez, of which I had until then seen very little. All of his portraits fascinated me; but my attention was particularly attracted to the great equestrian portrait of the count-duke of Olivares, for reasons that even now I cannot entirely explain. I stood before a historical figure of outstanding importance who, in the hands of Velázquez, had acquired extraordinary stature – and yet I had heard nothing about him in Cambridge during my courses on European history. When I got back to England I found I was not the only one. Even the basic text books on seventeenth-century Europe had little or nothing to say about the count-duke.

So even before he graduated, Elliott had found his dissertation topic – even though he had only a 'rudimentary knowledge of Spanish, which I had never studied formally'.[1]

Elliott's strong attraction to the study of seventeenth-century Spain stemmed at least in part from the interesting parallel with the situation of the country in which he lived.

---

[1] *Discurso de investidura de Doctor 'Honoris Causa'. Profesor John H. Elliott* (Madrid, 1984), pp. 23f.

I suspect that my choice ... [was] influenced at some level by my sense, as an Englishman living in the aftermath of the Second World War, that the collective predicament of the last great imperial generation of Spaniards after the triumphs of the sixteenth century was not entirely dissimilar to the collective predicament of my own generation after the triumphs of the nineteenth and early twentieth. At least this may have given me a certain sympathy across the centuries with the aspirations and dilemmas of men who, as heirs to a glorious historical legacy, were seeking for national renewal in the midst of perceived decline.[2]

Therefore, under the genial direction of Herbert Butterfield, in 1952 John Elliott began reading about early modern Spain both in printed works and in the documents which abounded in the British Library, thus improving his command both of Spanish and of seventeenth-century palaeography. He provisionally entitled his thesis 'Olivares' policy of centralisation' and, in the summer of 1953, aged just 23, he arrived at the archives of Simancas full of enthusiasm and high expectations. However, as the days and then the weeks passed, it became increasingly clear that the *legajos* which he had confidently requested did not contain the information for which he searched. He had hoped to find important memorials and correspondence of the count-duke on different aspects of his plans for the future of Europe; but he found nothing. 'I must confess', he wrote thirty years later,

that those weeks of fruitless research in 1953 are among the most desolate of my life. And when I found out by chance, during these very weeks, that the personal archive of the count-duke had been destroyed by a fire in the palace of the dukes of Alba in the late eighteenth century, my sense of desolation brought me close to suicide. The worst fate that awaits a research student had befallen me: I had lost my topic.[3]

But Elliott reacted fast. Perhaps, he speculated, it might be possible to rescue something from the wreckage of his plans by looking at Olivares as a reformer and statesman. Clearly, in terms of domestic policies, the most important event of his ministerial career occurred in 1640 with the rebellions first of Catalonia and then of Portugal; and so a detailed study of the antecedents of one of those two revolts might provide the material for a useful thesis, yet still leave open for later the original project of studying the policies of the count-duke.

I could either go to Lisbon, or to Barcelona. Fortunately, influenced by the fact that I had already been to Barcelona and had met there Jaume Vicens Vives, I chose to go east. Since the basic documentation on the origins of the Portuguese revolt has still

---

[2] John H. Elliott, *Spain and its world 1500–1700: selected essays* (New Haven, 1989), p. ix.
[3] *Discurso de investidura*, pp. 25f.: 'mi desolación llegó poco menos al borde del suicidio'.

not come to light, and possibly no longer exists, this decision proved to be my salvation.[4]

The fact that Elliott knew not a word of Catalan did not deter him, and from September 1953 until spring 1954 he worked in the rich archives of the crown of Aragon and put together not only a doctoral thesis but also a dissertation which won him a fellowship at Trinity College. He then returned for almost a year, autumn 1955 to summer 1956, learning not only about the Catalan past, but also about the Catalan present, and spending 'what was for me, although not, I fear, for Catalunya, a golden age'. He lived with Catalan families and met with Catalan historians – one of whom remarked 'how completely I was part of Catalan society without being part of it' – so that he 'felt for the first time, emotionally rather than intellectually, the power of national sentiment'.[5] He also came under the influence of Jaume Vicens Vives, who

exercised a greater influence on me than any other living historian. I think I was impressed above all by his vigour, his sheer historical intelligence, and the intensity of his commitment to history as a serious intellectual enterprise ... His mission, as he saw it, was to demythologize the history of Catalonia, and indeed of Spain, and put in its place a history which combined intense archival work with the approaches and the insights of the most up-to-date historical scholarship.

'Those years taught me', Elliott later recalled, 'the obligation of the historian to follow what he believes to be the truth, however uncomfortable the consequences may be. All societies need their myths; but all societies also need their historians to question those myths, and to ensure that the past does not become fossilized in the minds of the present.'[6]

From this comprehensive historical education in Barcelona came Elliott's first masterpiece, *The revolt of the Catalans: a study in the decline of Spain, 1598–1640*, published in 1963. The relatively long delay between accumulating the sources and the publication of this work is partially explained by the rather more leisurely pace at which printers then operated (the book took over a year to be published by Cambridge University Press). But even more it reflected the heavy teaching burden which Elliott assumed from 1957, when he was appointed an assistant lecturer in the Cambridge history faculty. It was the burden of not just lecturing on his specialty, early modern European history, but also of supervising undergraduates on a wide

---

[4] Ibid., p. 26.
[5] *Solemne investidura de Doctor Honoris Causa al Profesor Sir John Elliott* (Barcelona, 1994), p. 23.
[6] Ibid., pp. 25, 29.

range of subjects. Elliott now had to give tutorials to undergraduates on such topics as English economic history and the history of political thought from Plato to Rousseau. (The pedagogical philosophy of Cambridge University's history faculty in those days held that instructors should not teach undergraduates subjects in which they themselves had detailed expertise.)

Two other important developments occurred in these years. First, in 1958, John Elliott married Oonah Butler, who has loyally supported and assisted all his projects and who has accompanied him in almost all his professional duties. They welcomed students to their house in Long Road, Cambridge, with its spectacular wisteria and magnificent garden; she prepared the indexes of his early books; she accompanied him on lecture tours; she visited with him the places about which he wrote – including a memorable horseback tour of the Alpujarras in 1973 which saw the exhausted Elliotts obliged to groom their horses every night before collapsing on to their spartan beds. Second, while still completing *The revolt of the Catalans*, Elliott accepted an invitation to write a general textbook on early modern Spain. Again, his teaching provided the stimulus:

I now shudder to remember it, because of the presumption involved in writing a textbook of that sort at the beginning of one's career. I was completely ignorant of whole areas of the subject, but I needed such a book for my own courses at Cambridge and, since none seemed to exist, I was almost forced to write my own. I suspect that today I would not be able to do it.

The task forced him to 'abandon the labyrinth of details that threatened to drown my study of the count-duke of Olivares and Catalonia and helped me to identify and analyse those themes which seemed to me most important in the history of Spain from the accession of the Catholic kings to the succession of the Bourbons'. Thanks to his distinctive perspective, both as a foreigner aware of the major historiographical currents that flowed elsewhere in Europe and as an expert on Catalonia rather than on Castile, *Imperial Spain 1469–1716* (also published in 1963) bristled with new questions and research topics – many of them taken up, in due course, by his own students. It was then, and it still remains, a marvellous textbook: a model of its kind.[7]

The appearance of Elliott's first two academic books in 1963 did much to

---

[7] *Discurso de investidura*, p. 28. Geoffrey Parker's first contact with John Elliott occurred as a freshman in Michaelmas term 1962, when he attended a lecture course given in a room immediately after Elliott had ended and found discarded stencilled handouts on such matters as the conciliar structure of government in Habsburg Spain. The idea of handouts was then novel; the material later appeared in *Imperial Spain*.

demythologize Spanish history, just as Vicens Vives had wished.[8] Tired questions of national character – was the Spanish temperament compatible with modernity? – had long dominated its domestic historiography, while foreign historians found it difficult to escape the Black Legend and a certain fascination with what was perceived as Spanish bigotry, cruelty and backwardness. Both treated Spain as a world apart and wrote its history as if it had occurred in a vacuum, both isolated from and impervious to the broad currents of the European past.

Tentative steps to alter these stereotypes had already been taken by the French scholars Fernand Braudel, whose path-breaking *The Mediterranean and the Mediterranean world in the age of Philip II* first appeared in 1949, and Pierre Vilar, whose magnificent three-volume *Catalonia and modern Spain* came out in 1962. But in his two books of 1963 Elliott managed to re-attach Spain to Europe by demonstrating that its history, for all of its individuality, generally reflected phenomena evident in other European states. In Elliott's hands, the age-old issue of Spain's seventeenth-century decline, traditionally interpreted (especially by protestant scholars) as the result of weaknesses inherent in Spanish national character and religion, became part of the general crisis of the seventeenth century, that congeries of economic, demographic, social and political setbacks from which no European state emerged unscathed. Likewise, Elliott's understanding of other European monarchies enabled him to interpret what historians had traditionally decried as the decadence of the court of Philip IV as but one expression of the seventeenth century's penchant for princely magnificence and display. In other words, by refocusing the prism through which Spanish history was traditionally viewed, Elliott established a new research agenda grounded upon the premise that Spain was not, in the phrase of Franco's Ministry of Tourism, 'different' and, consequently, comprehensible only in purely national terms; rather, by inserting Spain into a broad European – and indeed Atlantic – context, he succeeded in rendering the study of its past susceptible to the same methods and questions posed by historians elsewhere.

In my opinion, every Hispanist runs the risk of becoming a narrow antiquarian unless he looks at more than Spain. I am convinced that, to gain the maximum yield from his knowledge of Spain and its history, politics and culture, the Hispanist must be capable of tracing the links between the peninsula and events in the wider world

---

[8] Elliott's very first book, illustrated by Julian Slade, was written for children: *Nibble the squirrel* (London, 1946).

and to draw parallels and comparisons which will themselves help to clarify the Spanish situation.[9]

Between 1963 and 1973 Elliott wrote two more books which, without specifically concentrating on the history of Spain, allowed him to highlight this mutual interaction between Spain and the rest of the world. *Europe divided, 1559–1598* (1969) which covered the whole of Europe during the forty years in which Philip II and Spain enjoyed political pre-eminence, came out in 1968 as a volume in the prestigious Fontana History of Europe series. *The Old World and the New, 1500–1650* (1970), based upon the Wiles Lectures delivered the previous year at the Queen's University, Belfast, allowed him to compare and contrast the achievements and nature of various societies established on both sides of the Atlantic. Each displays a breath-taking erudition and, although brief, has remained the best work available on its subject.

In 1973, however, John Elliott moved from England to the United States to become a professor at the Institute for Advanced Study in Princeton, where (in his own words) 'I enjoyed the incomparable privilege of living the life of the university professor without any obligation to teach'. For the first time, he had the chance to stand back and make some long-term plans, free from the interruptions of administration and instruction. After so many years of writing under pressure, with little leisure and less archive time, he decided that he would undertake a much broader project, one that would have no deadline, one that he would be able to pursue for as long as necessary. He thus at last had the opportunity to realize the ambition that had taken hold of him in 1950 before the equestrian portrait of Olivares: to write a complete study of his ministerial career. First, however, he had to overcome the problem encountered earlier: the almost total absence of the crucial planning documents produced by the count-duke. Hence he compiled, with José Francisco de la Peña, two volumes of *Memorials and letters of the count-duke of Olivares* (1978–81), publishing not only an important selection of documents, but also an extensive and erudite commentary on the texts.[10]

Elliott's next book was also a product of collaboration. In conversations with Jonathan Brown, a professor of the history of art at New York University's Institute of Fine Arts and a distinguished specialist in Spanish

[9] *Discurso de investidura*, p. 29.
[10] They decided not to proceed with a planned third volume, which would have covered the extensive surviving correspondence of the count-duke with Philip IV's brother, the Cardinal-Infante.

art during the seventeenth century, the idea arose of combining the disciplines of history and the history of art in order to explore a particular subject. At first they chose 'The surrender of Breda', painted by Velázquez to celebrate a major victory by Philip IV's forces in 1625. Almost at once this topic seemed too narrow, however, because the painting belonged to a whole series of battle pictures commissioned around the same time to decorate the same room – the Hall of Realms in a new palace, the Buen Retiro, built for the king by Olivares. Finally, the two authors decided that they should discuss not only the room but rather the whole palace in which the paintings were to hang; and the result was that scintillating work of scholarship, *A palace for a king: the Buen Retiro and the court of Philip IV* (1980).

Next, while completing his biography of Olivares, an invitation from Cambridge University to deliver the Trevelyan Lectures in 1983 offered an opportunity to set the count-duke's problems in an international context. Elliott would have preferred to undertake a comparative study of France under Louis XIII with Spain under Philip IV; but 'clearly the state of historical studies at the time did not permit such an ambitious comparison. What we know of the first so far exceeds what we know of the second that it would be quite impossible to compare the two societies at an equivalent level of research.' He therefore compared the two statesmen who directed those countries and who wrestled with remarkably similar problems: royal indebtedness, challenges to the royal authority, reconstruction of the fleet, crippling defence costs and the revitalization of the economy at a time when both the French and the Spanish élites were reluctant to become merchants. By this historical Wimbledon he showed that problems that used to be considered specific to Spain were in fact common to the whole of Europe in the first half of the seventeenth century. An entire generation of politicians, subject to the same pressures and educated in the same intellectual environment, adopted common solutions to identical problems. 'We are predisposed to think of Richelieu's rule as a success and that of Olivares as a failure; but from the comparative point of view the terms success and failure become highly ambiguous.'[11]

Elliott's masterpiece, *The count-duke of Olivares: the statesman in an age of decline*, a book which has sold spectacularly well both in the Anglo-Saxon world and in Spain, appeared in 1986. The reasons for its success are not hard to find: the limpid, elegant style for which Elliott has become justly famous, enlivened by translated extracts from the original sources so vigor-

---

[11] *Discurso de investidura*, pp. 37f.

ous (and yet so accurate) that they brought the past alive, applied to a major problem of permanent relevance – how political leaders with aspirations from a former age struggle to achieve the impossible with diminished resources. Elliott had visited almost every archive in Europe in search of papers, opinions and insights; and the result, as all reviewers said, was a triumph – not least because it virtually turned the tables on the count-duke's old rival: historians (at least those who read only English) now know and understand far more about Olivares than about Richelieu.

The success of *Olivares*, coming on top of so many other major works of European history (as well as over fifty articles and chapters in books, plus a host of reviews), made Elliott the obvious candidate for the Regius Chair of Modern History at the University of Oxford, to which he returned from Princeton in 1990. His inaugural lecture at Oxford in May 1991 called on his colleagues, and particularly his colleagues in British history (in effect) to adopt his own approach to Spanish history and to introduce an awareness of European developments into their researches and writings on the past. On the one hand, he deprecated the tendency of British historians to see their national history in isolation: 'British history', he reminded his listeners, 'need not be, and should not be, insular history.' On the other, he went on to express concern that

we do not have more historians on the faculty whose prime specialism is in the history of a country other than their own. I am concerned, too, by the fact that the structure of our syllabus makes it too easy for undergraduates to leave this university with only the narrowest and most chronologically limited knowledge of continental European history. Finally, I am concerned, as we must all be concerned, by their widespread inability to read historical works in any language other than English, and by their reluctance to choose subjects requiring the study of foreign-language texts.[12]

These principles had long been familiar to John Elliott's own graduate students – often referred to by Spaniards as the 'Anglo-Saxon School' of Spanish historical studies.[13] In fact, no such school ever existed; and even if it did, it could hardly be labelled 'Anglo-Saxon'. For one thing, Elliott's disciples, first in England and then at the Institute, included several Spaniards, several of whom are contributors to this volume. For another,

---

[12] John H. Elliott, *National and comparative history: an inaugural lecture delivered before the University of Oxford* (Oxford, 1991), p. 15.
[13] The Dutch scholar P. B. M. Blaas, in a special issue of an Italian journal devoted to Netherlands historiography since 1945, even referred to a 'scuola di Elliott' for Dutch history: see *Rivista storica italiana*, 95 (1983), 613.

John never required his research students to favour particular topics over others, nor even to utilize a particular historical method: rather, to borrow a Spanish expression, he generally gave his pupils enough rope to hang themselves. A prime example of this occurred in 1965 when no fewer than six research students simultaneously appeared on the doorstep of his rooms in Trinity College.[14] Elliott had directed four doctoral dissertations previously – by Brian Pullan, Edward Cooper, Tony Thompson and the late Peter Brightwell – but the advent of a sizeable group of young researchers posed a challenge of a different sort. To help them, John convoked what amounted to Cambridge's first research seminar devoted to early modern history, to which he invited any visiting Hispanists and in which each of his students had to present some account of the dissertation they hoped to write. He also arranged for this seminar to pay collective visits to touch the hem of the robes of other Cambridge dons with research interests – and methodologies – different from his own: Harry Hinsley and Herbert Butterfield for international relations; Tony Wrigley for demography and quantification; Charles Wilson for economic history; George Kitson Clark for social issues. John's aim, of course, was to encourage his students to work together as well to broaden their intellectual horizons. The technique worked splendidly: we all still correspond and share information; and the advice we received in those early visits has left its mark – the bar graphs and tables in our various books came from Wrigley, the willingness to use much-despised ambassadorial reports ('poor for interpretation, good for circumstantial details, excellent for dates') from Butterfield and so on.

The visits also served as one more way of encouraging students to write the kind of history to which they were personally attracted. All that John insisted on, with rigour and without compromise, was that good history required clear, simple prose; a broad framework; and, most important, a bold theme. Small wonder, then, that his students eventually ranged from sixteenth-century Bohemian cultural history, through rich and poor in Renaissance Venice, to silver mining in colonial Mexico, as well as concentrating on imperial Spain.

---

[14] The sudden influx seems to have been fortuitous: three had just graduated from the Cambridge History Faculty and one from the Department of Spanish; the others came from the Queen's University, Belfast and from Columbia University, New York. But three more research students (one from Cambridge, one from Canada and one from the United States) soon joined the team and in July 1967 Elliott received a note from Don Ricardo Magdaleno, director of the archives of Simancas, to say that although all Elliott's students had behaved 'con la mayor corrección' he would be 'grateful if their visits could, as far as possible, be staggered' in order to leave some space for others in the archive reading room. Elliott passed this request on to those in the *Sala de Investigadores* with only a hint of self-satisfaction.

Elliott's distinctive combination of common sense and relaxed direction with uncompromising scholarly rigour also characterized his undergraduate teaching. Brian Pullan recalls that, even in his tutorials on English economic history in 1957–8, John gave his students skilfully chosen pamphlets and articles and discussed these items 'lucidly and amiably in the spirit of someone who is only a few years further down the road'. He was affable, 'but very firm about the need to write, readably, elegantly and coherently'. And he had 'scant sympathy for anyone who claimed to be suffering from writer's block; to him this was just weakmindedness and disorganization'. Nothing had changed a decade later: graduates who possessed telephones would dread a call early on Monday morning ('John Elliott here. . .') requiring their presence the following Friday with another chapter; the rest never collected their mail in college free of the fear of finding an envelope with the Trinity College crest enclosing a similar summons. How John found the time to read through and critique innumerable drafts of six theses simultaneously in 1967–8, while he was also carrying a full undergraduate teaching load and writing *Europe divided* remains a mystery; but every dissertation was submitted within three years of being started.

John Elliott has always devoted enormous time and effort to his pupils. Although he never technically 'gave' a student a subject for study, many of them picked up one of the innumerable ideas he threw out, either in presentations, in letters or in conversation, as worthy of further investigation. For example, in his lecture on the Dutch Revolt, in his undergraduate course on Europe 1494–1715 at Cambridge in 1964, Elliott pointed to the map behind him and observed: 'One of the aspects of the Eighty Years' War that no one has yet explained is just how Spain managed to maintain an army of 80,000 men, 1,000 miles away. How did she recruit and move the men? How did she supply them? How did she pay them?' Geoffrey Parker, who heard the lecture, trailed Elliott back to his rooms just off Trinity's Great Court to ask for some reading on the subject. He was directed to Lucien Febvre's *Philippe II et Franche-Comté*, a book that had exercised a strong influence on Elliott himself; the idea thus became flesh and, under Elliott's firm guidance, eventually turned into a thesis.[15]

This pattern could be repeated for almost all of Elliott's students: a challenging idea, a well-chosen spontaneous bibliography, followed by careful solicitude. Later, while they served out their year of research abroad, Elliott would write an immediate reply, often holograph and always full of good advice and sympathy, to every letter he received. Once again the

[15] For the influence of Febvre on Elliott, see *Solemne investidura*, p. 25.

burden that this imposed must have been almost intolerable; but he never complained (although one letter in August 1967, when eight of his graduate students were abroad researching, briefly noted that 'the demand on my 9d stamps has been fantastic over the last few months'). In students' final year Elliott constantly emphasized the need to write up research already done before moving on to gather more, and always warned against accumulating so much material that one became overwhelmed. Then, once the drafts came in, he spent as much time on the presentation and the style as on the content and the structure ('It's not the matter but the manner that worries me...'). The need to be aware of the audience always remained prominent. 'My doubts about 250 pages on Alba's march', he warned Geoffrey Parker, eager to write a monograph on the odyssey of the duke and his 10,000 Spaniards to the Netherlands in 1567, 'relate particularly to (a) who will publish it? and (b) who will read it?'

Nor did the solicitude end with graduate studies. John made sure that his protégés met his colleagues and other historians, attended conferences (four went as his guests to Belfast for a week to hear his Wiles Lectures in 1969 and to enjoy the legendary hospitality that accompanies them), and knew what others in the field were doing. He developed job strategies with them – weighing the pros and cons of a short-term research fellowship against those of a permanent job – and did his best to 'place' them advantageously. He also helped them with subsequent projects and, just as many good ideas grew out of Elliott's conversation and correspondence, so (mercifully) many bad ideas died there. As he once admitted, 'Anybody who knows me will be well aware that I tend to be harder on my pupils than on anyone else'.[16] And when something worthwhile finally emerged, he strove to ensure the publication of both books and articles in appropriate locations.

But Elliott's efforts to promote students and to introduce them to the historical principles he advocates is by no means a thing of the past. As Regius Professor at Oxford, his own research – which currently focuses on a comparative examination of British and Spanish colonization in the New World – embodies one of the themes of his 1991 inaugural lecture: the necessity to avoid making 'national' history into 'insular' history. Meanwhile, Elliott's interest in comparative history is reflected in Oxford's proposed new Centre for Atlantic Studies (which he is helping to create) as well as in his recent efforts to broaden the geographical scope of Oxford's undergraduate history requirements. The research students presently working under Elliott's direction at Oxford are also gravitating towards

[16] Letter to Geoffrey Parker, 3 December 1983.

subjects (among them, one on Mexican viceroys and another on the history of Spain's Trinitarian Order) that incorporate his belief that history should be written in something other than a purely national mode. Should this trend continue (and given Elliott's energy and inspiration, there is little reason to believe otherwise), the long-imagined *scuola di Elliott* may one day become a reality.

John Elliott once said 'I hope I shall never become a *grand maître* like Braudel';[17] but, through his own tireless efforts and his unflagging encouragement of the productivity of others, this wish has been denied. He has already played the decisive role in the research career of some twenty students and he is currently supervising the work of several more. On a wider scale, his work has influenced a whole generation of scholars, both in Europe and America. Although even more can be expected from him in the future, several of his ideas have already proved central to the history of Spain and its world; others have influenced the evolution of scholarship in adjacent fields. Perhaps his most notable contribution to date, however, has been the suggestion that the tension between centre and periphery lies at the heart of the political development of early modern Europe; and for that reason we have chosen it as the theme of this volume in honour of John Elliott's sixty-fifth birthday.

[17] Letter to Geoffrey Parker, 12 April 1976, after a conference at The Johns Hopkins University at which Braudel (as was his custom) called without warning upon Elliott to comment on a paper which the Master had just given.

Introduction: the centre and the periphery

RICHARD L. KAGAN AND GEOFFREY PARKER

The history of Spain in the late fifteenth and early sixteenth centuries was to consist of a continuing, and fruitful, dialogue between periphery and centre.[1]

The idea of a dialogue – sometimes harmonious, sometimes divisive – between the centre and periphery of the early modern European state stands at the heart of much of John Elliott's historical writing. It is the fulcrum around which his *Imperial Spain* revolves, and it lies at the core of his analysis of the causes of the revolt of the Catalans in 1640 against the centralizing policies of the Madrid government, directed by the charismatic but insensitive count-duke of Olivares. Elliott subsequently extended the concept of centre versus periphery beyond Spanish shores, notably in 'Revolution and continuity in early modern Europe', his inaugural lecture as Professor of History at King's College London, in 1968, which perceived the various revolts of mid-seventeenth-century Europe as essentially conflicts between the loyalties owed to one's *patria* – representing a province or a principality more often than a nation – and those owed to one's monarch.[2] In his writings on the Americas, too, the relationship between centre and periphery plays a vital role. Elliott's Wiles Lectures of 1969 on *The Old World and the New, 1492–1650*, the classic statement on the intellectual

[1] John H. Elliott, *Imperial Spain, 1469–1716* (London, 1963), p. 32.
[2] Originally published in *Past and Present* (1969), and reprinted in John H. Elliott, *Spain and its world 1500–1700: selected essays* (New Haven and London, 1989), pp. 92–113, see especially pp. 104–11.

interchange set in motion by Columbus' voyage, cited the perceptive memorandum of the humanist Hernán Pérez de Oliva to the city of Cordoba in 1524, drawing attention to the way in which the discovery and exploitation of America had affected the relative position of Spain, 'because formerly we were at the end of the world, and now we are in the middle of it, with an unprecedented change in our fortunes'.[3]

Finally, in the balance between centre and periphery Elliott found the secret of the survival of Spain as a great power long after its economic and demographic base had been eroded. Charles II, the last of the Spanish Habsburgs, undoubtedly ruled a smaller empire than his great-grandfather Philip II, and the decisions that affected its future were taken in Paris, London and Turin rather than in Madrid: 'Nobody', Elliott has written, 'would dispute that the seventeenth century saw a *relative* decline of Spanish power, when compared with its principal European rivals.' But the paradox of survival amid this decline may be explained by two distinct developments. On the one hand, the experience of Castile (the heart of the empire) differed from that of the rest. 'Other parts of the Iberian peninsula, especially along the periphery, either suffered less than Castile from the seventeenth-century recession, or even made modest gains, so that, over the course of the century, there was some shift in the internal balance of economic forces, to Castile's detriment.' 'It would seem that we are faced with a diminution of Castile's capacity to bear the cost of empire, and consequently with the problem, in the first instance, not so much of the decline of Spain as of the *decline of Castile*.' On the other hand, the Iberian experience proved far from unique: many other societies in Western Europe experienced severe economic and social problems in the mid-seventeenth century: 'Seventeenth-century Spain needs, therefore, to be set firmly back into the context of contemporary conditions, and particularly conditions in the Mediterranean world.'[4]

Instead of dismissing Spain's decline as either the inevitable result of some deeply rooted flaw in the Spanish character, the consequence of the personal shortcomings of its rulers, or the inexorable outcome of 'strategic overstretch', Elliott viewed it as a process that might have been reversed with the right combination of economic, political and social reforms. Instead of irreversible decline, then, the key questions became how could the great empire best be managed and how could its power and reputation best be maintained. That is how the count-duke of Olivares, the statesman to whom he has devoted so many years of research, conceived the problem;

[3] John H. Elliott, *The Old World and the New, 1492–1650* (Cambridge, 1970), p. 73.
[4] Elliott, *Spain and its world*, pp. 215, 222 and 221.

and that is how Elliott succeeded in offering a new and original way of understanding the history of seventeenth-century Spain as a great power.

Like Olivares, moreover, Elliott recognized that political power in the seventeenth century did not simply come out of a gun. It was also a function of image and of *reputación*. From the 1590s to the 1650s, Spain's leaders consistently refused to adjust their foreign policy in line with the declining resources available to sustain it.

Throughout these years, the principal objectives of Spain's [foreign] policy remained unchanged: the maintenance of the catholic cause, the defence of the dynastic interests of the two branches of the House of Austria, the retention of the loyal provinces of the southern Netherlands, and the exclusion of foreigners from Spain's empire of the Indies.

Admittedly, these aims sound modest; but, as Elliott noted, 'a defensive mentality ... does not necessarily imply a defensive posture. Attack may, after all, be the best form of defence.' During the reign of Philip IV, many of Spain's political leaders came to believe that the monarchy could only be maintained by taking an assertive stance whenever Spanish interests were perceived to be at risk, if only to preserve 'reputation'. However 'an excessive commitment to upholding "reputation" precludes a flexible response to changing situations, and casts its exponents, at least in their own eyes, as men in a heroic mould, battling gallantly against the oncoming tide'. Thus, in a letter of 1625 to a veteran diplomat who had suggested that the ship of state was about to founder, Olivares replied with characteristic hyperbole that 'as the minister with paramount obligations it is for me to die unprotesting, chained to my oar, until not a fragment is left in my hands'. Eight years later, when Spain's domestic and international situation had deteriorated even further, the count-duke asserted that the best policy in adversity was to '"die doing something"'. It was a not inappropriate response for a great power whose days of greatness were numbered.'[5]

The tension between centre and periphery, the nature of patriotism and community, the costs of empire, the need to conserve – and to justify – the assets conferred on Castile by providence: these form the interlocking themes of John Elliott's work on Spain and its world during the early modern period, and they have been taken up in this collection of essays by his students and disciples. Each derives, in some way, from an idea or assertion in Elliott's work, and each has benefited from his perceptions and path-breaking research.

[5] Quotations taken from 'Foreign policy and domestic crisis: Spain 1598–1659' in *Spain and its world*, pp. 114–36, at pp. 134, 115 and 135–6.

Part I, 'Power and propaganda: the world of the court', centres on the organization and projection of government authority. In 'Twin souls', Antonio Feros focuses on the 'language of friendship' in the early seventeenth century in an effort to explain the political power acquired by Francisco Gómez de Sandoval y Rojas, duke of Lerma and favourite of Philip III between 1598 and 1618. Where Elliott studied Philip IV's favourite, the count-duke of Olivares, Feros focuses on Lerma's political career, endeavouring to understand how Lerma and his followers justified the unusual degree of trust and confidence the monarch bestowed upon him, and how he transformed this trust into political power. Lerma's key position was that of *sumiller de corps* (groom of the stole), who accompanied the king on all occasions – at public audiences and ceremonies, when visiting the queen's chambers and when retiring to his privy chamber. Indeed, palace etiquette required that the king 'should never withdraw from the sight' of the *sumiller*, whom some saw as the king's 'companion and friend, whom [he] will ask for advice on all matters' (see pages 37–8 below). Feros offers a better understanding not only of Lerma – a historical figure whom most historians, Elliott included, have simply dismissed as a corrupt opportunist – but also of the 'peculiar institution' of the favourite, which flourished at the courts of many early modern monarchs.

Power, in the sense of fiscal power – the ability to tax – is central to the essay of Charles Jago. What limits, if any, restrained the Habsburg monarchs' power to tax their subjects? What arguments were utilized to justify their right to exact tribute, and what arguments were deployed in opposition? Jago demonstrates that these issues received serious and sustained consideration between the 1590s and the 1630s. In the sixteenth century they had been central to the School of Salamanca, a group of canon lawyers, philosophers and theologians whose writings examined numerous aspects of what would later become known as 'political economy'; in the seventeenth century, as the burden of taxation inexorably rose, they became a subject for national debate. Countless pamphlets and treatises addressed the morality of the Habsburgs' efforts to extract more and more money from their subjects, while theologians all over Spain were asked to assess the legality of each major request for more taxes. In this context, 'the periphery' becomes the harassed taxpayer and 'the centre' a monarchy whose demands proved almost insatiable.

In the final essay of this section, Richard L. Kagan addresses yet another facet of royal power: the right to control knowledge of the past, the power to write history itself. History for Habsburg Spain becomes a struggle between accounts written at the royal court by a sequence of royal chroniclers as opposed to those elaborated in the provinces as well as in specific cities and towns. To whom did Spain's history belong? What was to be included in the record of Spain's past and what left out? Was history simply a list of princely *gestae*, and thus an instrument of royal propaganda; or should it focus on the achievements of individual town and cities, many of which commissioned histories written from a distinctive local perspective designed as a corrective to the work of scholars in the monarchy's employ? The lively debate on this issue sparked new interest in historical writing and served as the catalyst for Spanish chorography, one of the most vibrant (if misunderstood) historical genres of the sixteenth and seventeenth centuries.

Because Elliott conceived the tensions between centre and periphery primarily in political terms, he was sensitive to the fact that the Habsburg monarchy was a 'composite state', an amalgam of separate polities – each with its own laws, institutions and traditions – that owed allegiance to a single ruler. Within this amalgam, obvious differences abounded. Catalonia spoke Catalan, Castile spoke Castilian and so on; but language was not the only division among the Habsburgs' Iberian subjects. Customs barriers, distinctive economies, profound differences in topography and temperament, and racial and religious divisions – notably the centuries-old cleavage between Christian and Muslim, Jew and Gentile, New Christian and Old – also inhibited the development of a strong, centralized state. Competing but vigorous notions of local and regional identity based upon these differences complicated matters yet further so that the underlying patterns of Spanish society, as the essays in Part II of this volume ('The pattern of society: community and identity in Habsburg Spain') make clear, militated against the emergence of a unitary state.

The incorporation of a sizeable population of converted Jews (*conversos*) and their descendants into a profoundly catholic society constituted a central episode in the evolution of early modern Spanish society. The *conversos* of Castile by and large dwelt in the cities, and the challenges they posed to the Old Christian majority represents an important, albeit conflictive chapter in the history of many Spanish towns. Linda Martz explores this particular cleavage in her study of the place of Toledo's *converso* merchants in the kingdom of Granada, which fell under Castilian dominion in 1492. Here the question of centre versus periphery is examined from a novel perspective because Toledo, in the heart of Castile, represents the centre, with Granada, only recently conquered, a periphery brimming with opportunities for land, office and riches (notably the profits derived from the cultivation and manufacture of silk). Toledo's *converso* merchants proved quick to take advantage of these opportunities, and many migrated to Granada soon after its conquest and annexation to the crown of Castile. In doing so they became wealthy but, as they soon discovered, riches brought their own embarrassments, and provoked not only resentment among Toledo's Old Christians but also local statutes which progressively excluded the *conversos* from the exercise of municipal and religious office. Granada in this sense helped to marginalize Toledo's *conversos* at the very moment when this 'periphery' was itself in the process of becoming integrated into Castile.

But what was Castile? And how did the centre of the empire view itself? This is the question addressed by I. A. A. Thompson, harking back to Elliott's essay 'Revolt and continuity in early modern Europe', which recognized the vital role played by the concept of *patria* in early modern revolts. *Patria* defies easy definition, but it can be linked to the concept of homeland, *Heimat* or *patrie*, with the attendant meanings of identity, loyalty and self-definition. Kagan's discussion of Spanish chorography addressed the issue of local identity, which proved central to the manner in which early modern Spaniards situated themselves in the world. But how, and to what degree, did the concept of *patria* function on a wider scale? In other words, to what extent – and under what circumstances – did Castilians view themselves as Castilians, Catalans as Catalans and Valencians as Valencians? Thompson's essay goes a long way in providing an answer to this set of questions for the kingdom of Castile, the centre of the Spanish monarchy but one which nevertheless felt itself alienated and apart from the monarchy for most of the early modern era. He argues that whereas at the beginning of this period Castilians understood themselves as constituting a 'natural' community as distinct from, and often in opposition to, other such communities (Catalan, Portuguese, French), by the eighteenth century they conceived of themselves principally as Spaniards – that is, as members of the 'political community' that Spain's new Bourbon monarchy in the eighteenth century endeavoured to construct.

Xavier Gil deals with many of these same issues, but from the perspective of the crown of Aragon. Focusing on sixteenth- and early seventeenth-century Aragonese constitutionalism, he offers a detailed analysis of the various meanings of the term 'liberty' as elaborated by a series of Aragonese jurists and political theorists. The word 'liberty' could be heard in the streets of Saragossa during the uprising of 1590–1, for it provided a rallying cry for those Aragonese opposed to the Inquisition and to the policies of Philip II and in essence embodied the laws and privileges which distinguished the government of Aragon from that of Castile. At issue here was the Aragonese *patria*, which was conceived largely in legal-jurisdictional terms and defined in opposition to the laws and policies elaborated by the monarch in Madrid.

James Casey reaches similar conclusions regarding the meaning of *patria* from the perspective of Valencia, whose history was the focus of his study *The kingdom of Valencia in the seventeenth century* (Cambridge, 1979). There, Casey's concerns were primarily demographic and economic; in this essay, he turns to the subject of Valencian patriotism as manifested in the writing of local history, various commemorative celebrations, and the defence of the Valencian *furs* (customs) – the legal embodiment of the Valencian *patria*. Valencian identity stood apart from loyalty to the king; but, unlike Catalonia, which rose in revolt against the monarchy in defence of its own sense of *patria*, Valencia remained quiescent, largely because its élite was far better integrated into the world of the court than its Catalan equivalent.

The question of Catalan identity – a central concern of Elliott's *Revolt of the Catalans* – is the subject of James Amelang's essay on the journal kept between 1600 and 1630 by the Catalan lawyer and chronicler, Jeroni Pujades. Elliott himself discovered the missing sections of this important diary while conducting research in Barcelona in 1956 ('"Sensacional, Elliott, sensacional", cried Vicens [Vives] when I told him of my find.')[6] Amelang uses this document, still rated the most important first-person source for the history of Catalonia in the decades leading up to the revolt, less as an autobiographical document than as a tool for understanding what it meant to be Catalan. Pujades, who also wrote an important history of the principality, emerges as a Catalan patriot. But he was not the only Catalan to keep a diary or to write an autobiography: almost eighty 'first-person documents' from Catalonia have so far been discovered for the sixteenth to the eighteenth centuries. Indeed, the relatively democratic régime of the principality encouraged citizen participation in government, so that auto-biographical writing became a public as well as a private act, an expression of citizenship itself. The anti-castilianism expressed in Pujades' diary there-fore offers an interesting insight into the views of the centre held on the periphery, and a way of understanding the cultural forces that frustrated Olivares' attempts to erode the barriers that existed between the states of the peninsula.

Identity, both local and national, also figures in the essay by Peter Sahlins, which examines how the national frontier separating France and

---

[6] *Solemne investidura de Doctor Honoris Causa al Profesor Sir John Elliott* (Barcelona, 1994), p. 28.

Spain came to be delineated in the Cerdagne, a valley high in the Pyrenees. In his view, the emergence of this boundary had less to do with politicians at the centre, in Paris and Madrid, than with peasants and village communities on the periphery, in the Cerdagne itself. Although central governments might negotiate the boundaries at international conferences, it was 'the dialectical interplay of centre and periphery in the borderland [that] structured the emergence of distinct state territories and national identities of France and Spain between 1659 and 1868' (pages 228–9 below). National identities, Sahlins argues, were not imposed from 'above' or the 'centre' but developed out of local disputes in a local context in which opposing groups (both French and Catalan speakers) only occasionally appealed for help from their respective 'nation-states'. The formation of national identity was thus essentially local: it did not emerge – as some have argued – at the expense of local identity, but rather complemented, and in some cases actually reinforced it.

The dialogue between centre and periphery, albeit in a somewhat different sense, arises in the third part of this volume: 'Spain and its empire'. Following Philip II's annexation of Portugal in 1580, Spain became a truly global monarchy, with responsibilities that ranged through Mexico, Peru, Brazil and the Philippines, to Macao, Malacca and Goa and back through Mozambique, and Angola to the European heartland. As the English traveller James Howell observed in 1623, King Philip IV 'hath dominions in all parts of the world ... so the sun shines in all the four-and-twenty hours of the natural day upon some part or other of his countries'.[7] But an empire of such unprecedented size brought numerous problems in its wake: how to conceptualize it, how to organize and harness its energies, and how to defend it against other Europeans.

The first two essays in this section examine issues of imperial defence at two crucial junctures. Geoffrey Parker examines the 1580s, and questions whether the acquisition of the Portuguese empire strengthened or weakened Spain. Initially, it is true, it made Philip II seem to many a new David, a warrior-king chosen by God to reunite His people and subdue His enemies. But the spectre of Iberian domination alarmed other European powers. The scale and riches of the combined Spanish–Portuguese empire also served as an invitation to those who simply wished to live off the crumbs Philip II left behind. But what began as piracy and privateering quickly evolved into full-scale armed attack, as it was discovered that the Spanish empire could

---

[7] J. Jacobs, ed., *Epistolae Ho-elianae: the familiar letters of James Howell* (2 vols., London, 1890), I, p. 198, letter to Lord Colchester from Madrid, 1 February 1623.

only respond to such challenges slowly, and with disproportionate expenditures of both men and money. The costs of defending this new worldwide empire, Parker argues, proved to be Spain's Achilles' heel and led ultimately to the ruin of that part of the empire that paid most of the bills: the kingdom of Castile.

By the 1630s, the difficulties of defence had become acute. Jonathan Israel's essay, 'Olivares, the Cardinal-Infante and Spain's strategy in the Low Countries (1635–1643): the road to Rocroi', demonstrates that the central government had resolved to turn the Low Countries, a thousand miles to the north and far removed from the Mediterranean–Madrid–Seville–Indies axis, into its principal military theatre, or *plaza de armas*. Even after France declared war in 1635, Olivares and his ministers continued to concentrate their forces against the Dutch and (in a remarkable piece of detective work) Israel shows that the celebrated invasion of France in 1636, which penetrated as far as Corbie, was undertaken in contradiction of express orders from Madrid. The military commander in Brussels, Philip IV's brother the Cardinal-Infante, responded on his own initiative and at short notice to a request from the Holy Roman Emperor for a campaign in support of his own attack on France (pages 278–9 below). Only the outbreak of rebellion, first in Catalonia and then in Portugal, forced a major shift in strategy: after 1640, the principal task of the Spanish Army of Flanders was to pin down French forces in order to prevent them from sending support to the rebels in the Iberian peninsula. At first the new strategy worked well, with several striking successes; but it led to disaster in 1643 at the battle of Rocroi which, more than any other single event, undermined Spain's international position abroad and caused anguish at home. In the words of Don Luis de Haro, Olivares' successor as chief minister:

The defeat of Rocroi has been followed in all areas by the consequences we had always feared. It was a terrible outcome, and one for which most observers have failed to find any military or political cause. I must tell you that it is something that can only be recollected with great pain, because although the losses inflicted by God must be accepted, those which seem to stem from the hand of Man are always harder to bear.[8]

Nevertheless, in spite of rebellions and defeats in Europe, Spain retained control of its dominions in America almost intact. Peter Bakewell focuses on the way in which the Spanish *máquina* – as the empire was sometimes known – successfully harnessed the resources of the vast American territories that Cortés, Pizarro and other *conquistadores* had vanquished in the king's name.

[8] Bibliothèque publique et universitaire, Geneva, Collection manuscrite Edouard Favre, 39/88-9, Haro to the marquis of Velada, 17 November 1643.

These territories covered an area initially four times as large as the kingdom of Castile, and contained a population seven times as great. But how were they to be managed? Bakewell surveys the establishment of the mining operations, the technology and the trading networks created by the Spaniards to tap El Dorado's riches, along with the administrative, judicial and religious institutions designed to keep these new enterprises and those who managed them – both indigenous and European – under close scrutiny and control. But, as Spanish officials and churchmen soon learned, it was easier to control the bodies of the *indios* than their minds. Bakewell thus raises the important question of the limits of Spanish domination in regions far removed from the centre of the empire in Madrid: the 'conquest after the conquest' remained – and was doomed to remain – incomplete.

Many *conquistadores*, of course, regarded such matters as irrelevant. For them, empire was a simple matter of exploration, conquest and exploitation, or as the crude motto of one of them read: 'A la espada y el compás. Mas y mas y mas y mas' ('To the sword and the compass, more and more and more and more').[9] Many Spanish lawyers and theologians thought differently, however, and recognized that all empires had their limits. Anthony Pagden considers these 'opponents of empire', who asked how it was possible to defend an empire which was already over-extended, and debated the ultimate aim of imperial conquest: more territory or more wealth? Initially, as he shows, the Habsburgs opted for land, but by the eighteenth century the Bourbons stood this policy on its end. Their new policy was to extract more from less, mainly in the form of commercial developments of mutual benefit to both colony and metropolis.

In the end, however, that too created its own set of problems, which form the subject of the last essay in the volume, by Jusep Fradera. The issue here is the integration of Spain's last colonies – Cuba, Puerto Rico and the Philippines – into Spain itself. From the sixteenth century onwards, the colonies were, both juridically and politically, a world apart: a periphery in every sense of the word. The delegates gathered at the famous liberal Cortes of Cadiz in 1810, however, envisioned an empire in which the division between metropolis and colony would be erased. Their idea was to abandon the laws which made the Americas into colonies, replacing them with others that would create 'a single, united monarchy, a single, united nation, a single, united family' and guarantee all Spanish Americans, natives and creoles alike, the same rights and privileges as Spaniards themselves. Yet the legal equality promised by the Cortes proved elusive. As Fradera

---

[9] Bernardo de Vargas Machuca, *Milicia y descripción de las Indias* (1599), frontispiece.

demonstrates, Spanish officials in Havana resisted all legislative efforts to transform Cuba from colony to province, and in Madrid even intense lobbying by wealthy Cuban sugar merchants was unable to break the juridical status quo. Self-interest, of course, accounted for much of the resistance, but so too did engrained habits of mind. Colonies had helped to define Spain for centuries – they had literally made it into a centre – and the thought of relinquishing that status was too much even for Spain's liberal governments to contemplate. At a time when world events were already making Spain into a periphery, the Spaniards proved reluctant to do anything to speed that process along.

By the end of the nineteenth century, Spain, after considerable soul-searching on the part of many intellectuals, surrendered to the forces that moved it to the periphery of world affairs. Yet, for over three hundred years, 'the empire upon which the sun never set' served as the fulcrum around which much of world history had turned. Fundamental questions about how and why this vast empire survived for so long still defy easy answer. The essays gathered in this volume provide some clues – among them, the unusual combination of a strong centre in the guise of a centralized royal bureaucracy with a periphery characterized by an entrenched yet flexible set of local and provincial identities and institutions. Although both centre and periphery always wanted more for themselves, over time a bargain was struck: each agreed to tolerate the other so long as they were accorded their slice of the imperial pie. As John Elliott put it:

The clue to this [the empire's] surprising resilience is to be found in the structure of the monarchy. Loosely tied together by dynastic arrangements, it was not, as Olivares discovered to his cost, amenable to rapid and drastic change. Essentially it relied on its own inertia – on a system of equilibrium by which Madrid, the viceroys and the local aristocracies all enjoyed a share of power. So long as the equilibrium was not unduly disturbed, there was no great inducement in the provinces to make a bid for independence ... [By and large] the local élites in the different parts of the monarchy found that they could do better for themselves within the framework of the monarchy than if they struck out on their own.[10]

Although, as Elliott himself pointed out, the same could be said of almost all early modern states, it proved a particular source of strength for the Spanish monarchy, which possessed a far larger 'periphery' than any other. In a system in which the strength of the periphery enhanced that of the centre, a quasi-federal empire on which the sun never set was, paradoxically, superbly equipped to survive.

[10] John H. Elliott, 'Monarchy and empire (1474–1700)', in P. E. Russell, ed., *Spain: a companion to Spanish studies* (London, 1973), pp. 107–44, at p. 142.

Part I

Power and propaganda:
the world of the court

I

Twin souls: monarchs and favourites in early seventeenth-century Spain

ANTONIO FEROS

In 'Of friendship', one of his most fascinating essays, Francis Bacon refers to what seemed to him a general phenomenon in Europe during his time: the existence of royal favourites.[1] Writing in the early seventeenth century, Bacon asserted that every man needs a friend and the same is true for monarchs. Certainly, monarchs have higher qualities and more important roles in the community than the rest, which in theory could deny them the opportunity to have friends, unless 'they raise some persons to be as it were companions and almost equals to themselves. . . The modern languages give unto such persons the name of *favourites*, or *privadoes*, as if it were matter of grace, or conversation.' Not only weak monarchs had favourites, but

also the wisest and most politic that ever reigned; who have oftentimes joined to themselves some of their servants, whom both themselves have called friends, and allowed others likewise to call them in the same manner, using the word which is received between private men.

Unlike Francis Bacon, modern historians have not paid particular attention to the language of friendship as it pertains to monarchs and their favourites in early modern Europe. In our own time, the notion of friend-

I would like to thank Professors Richard L. Kagan, J. G. A. Pocock, Orest Ranum and Sir John Elliott for their support and advice. I also owe a great deal to Irma T. Elo for her assistance, comments and inexhaustible support. All translations are mine unless otherwise attributed.

[1] Francis Bacon, 'Of friendship', in his *Essays*, ed. John Pitcher (Harmondsworth, 1985), p. 139. Written ca. 1607, 'Of friendship' first appeared in print in 1612. This paper represents a summary of parts of my doctoral dissertation, 'The king's favorite, the duke of

ship refers to a private association between individuals and the language used to describe it does not encompass the political connections these individuals have with the state and the society. Friends should be creatures of a private world, and when friendship and politics combine the result is usually perceived as corruption, the infringement of private interests on the public good.

Analysis of political culture must avoid what Dena Goodman describes as 'rigidly oppositional thinking that assumes two spheres or two discourses, one public and the other private'.[2] In seventeenth-century Spain, as elsewhere, various languages were used to talk and act politically. The language of friendship was among them and, as we shall see, it was central not only to Bacon's understanding of England's political reality, but also integral to Spanish political discourse during the first half of the seventeenth century.

I

In early modern Europe friendship referred to what we now know as a patron–client relationship,[3] or to what was then defined as 'common friendship'. Such a friendship was one in which individuals helped each other as allies, protectors and advisers in an effort to improve their opportunities for advancement at court.[4] In contrast, 'ideal friendship' was understood as 'the permanent union of the lives of two men' and as the perfect state towards which all men should strive.[5] 'Nothing else in the whole world is so

Lerma: power, wealth and court culture during the Reign of Philip III', The Johns Hopkins University, 1994.

[2] Dena Goodman, 'Public sphere and private life: toward a synthesis of current historiographical approaches to the Old Regime', *History and Theory*, 31 (1992), 14.

[3] On the increasing importance paid to the language of love and friendship to analyse patron–client relationships, see Maurice Aymard, 'Friends and neighbors', in *A history of private life*. III: *Passions of the Renaissance*, ed. Roger Chartier, trans. Arthur Goldhammer (Cambridge, Mass. and London, 1989), pp. 447–92; Sharon Kettering, 'Friendship and clientage in early modern France', *French History*, 6 (1992), 139–58; and Jonathan Dewald, *Aristocratic experience and the origins of modern culture: France, 1570–1715* (Berkeley, 1993), chapter 3.

[4] Baldassare Castiglione, *El Cortesano* [Spanish edition by Boscán, 1534] (facsimile edition, Madrid, 1985), I, pp. 148–9. For an English translation see *The book of the courtier*, ed. George Bull (London, 1967), pp. 137–9.

[5] Marsilio Ficino, to Giovanni Cavalcanti, in *The letters of Marsilio Ficino*, ed. Oskar Kristeller (London, 1975), I, letter 51, p. 96. In the following pages, I draw my argument and quotations from Spanish authors, or from authors who influenced Spanish ideas during the sixteenth and seventeenth centuries. There are many others who also addressed this topic, but I have attempted to keep the number of quotations to a minimum. On early modern

completely in harmony with nature', wrote Cicero, 'and nothing so utterly right, in prosperity and adversity alike.'[6] The intimate and exclusive nature of the ideal amity made it, as Michel de Montaigne put it, 'indivisible: each one gives himself so wholly to his friend that he has nothing left to distribute elsewhere'.[7] A friend was to share with the other his feelings and ideas and 'the occupation (whatever it is) that constitutes his existence, or makes life worth living'.[8] True friendship was thus viewed as the communion of wills, a complete sharing of feelings and ideas, a fusion of the souls that transformed friends into 'one soul in two bodies'.[9] This fusion of the souls, the human element that determines personality and outer image, allowed classical and early modern authors alike to assert that friends were identical. Seeing one's friend was akin to seeing one's own image in a mirror.[10]

This ideal friendship needed to be nourished through shared experiences and intimacy. Thomas Aquinas, for example, assured that 'living together is required for friendship as its proper act'. He added that friends tended to live together because of the 'likeness of friendship to sensual love, in which we observe that lovers desire most of all to see the persons they love. They prefer this sense, sight, to the other external senses because the passion of love begins especially by seeing ... and is preserved by this sense.'[11] In addition, friends had several obligations towards each other. In contrast to a flatterer (false friend), whose sole reason 'to court' the other is to obtain an

---

theories on ideal friendship, see Mark Morford's excellent book *Stoics and neostoics. Rubens and the circle of Lipsius* (Princeton, 1991), chapter 2.

6 Cicero, 'Laelius: on friendship', in *Cicero: on the good life*, ed. Michael Grant (London, 1971), p. 185. Cicero's essay on friendship was one of the most influential works in early modern Europe, including Spain; for the numerous editions of Cicero's 'On friendship' in Spain, see José Simón Díaz, 'Autores extranjeros traducidos al castellano en impresos publicados durante los siglos XV-XVII', *Cuadernos bibliográficos*, 40 (1980), 23–52.

7 Michel de Montaigne, *Essays*, ed. Donald M. Frame (Stanford, 1958), book I, 28, pp. 140–1; on the influence of Montaigne in Spain, see Juan Marichal, 'Montaigne en España', *Nueva revista de filología hispánica*, 7 (1963). For similar remarks, see Juan Pérez de Moya, *Comparaciones o símiles para los vicios y las virtudes* (Alcalá, 1584), fos. 69r–73r.

8 Aristotle, *The nicomachean ethics*, trans. J. A. K. Thomson (London, 1976), book IX, xii, p. 310.

9 Juan Luis Vives, *De anima et vita* [1538], in Juan Luis Vives, *Obras completas*, ed. Lorenzo Riber (Madrid, 1948), II, p. 1260; see also Cicero, 'On friendship', p. 187.

10 See, for example, Leone Ebreo, *Dialoghi di amore*, Spanish trans. by Garcilaso de la Vega, el Inca, in 1590 (facsimile edition, Seville, 1989), fo. 20v. On Ebreo's influence in Spain, see M. Menéndez Pelayo, *Historia de las ideas estéticas* (Madrid, 1974), chapter 6.

11 Thomas Aquinas, *Commentary on the nicomachean ethics of Aristotle*, trans. C. I. Litzinger (Chicago, 1964), II, pp. 726, 854. See also Seneca, *Epistolae morales*, trans. Richard M. Gummere (London and New York, 1925), I, letter IX, p. 49; Vives, 'Of both loves indistinctly', *De anima et vita*, II, p. 1261. In Spanish the words *amigo* and *amiga* also have the meaning of 'lover'; see Sebastián de Covarrubias Orozco, *Tesoro de la lengua castellana o española* [1611] (facsimile edition, Madrid, 1984), pp. 109–10.

immediate benefit for himself, true friends offer trust and support at times of trouble.[12] A true friend is straightforward: he always tells the truth; he is companionable and congenial; he will not criticize or listen to other's criticism; and he will always defend his friend.[13]

These characteristics made true friends ideal companions at the court, which was often viewed as the locus of vicious feuds, a place where individuals depended on 'their faith in God's mercy and the help of loyal and prudent friends'.[14] Even monarchs, it was said, needed the support of those who loved them, their friends, to help them weather moments of tension and frustration. During the sixteenth century, however, monarchs had two types of friends, a distinction that resulted from the theory of the king's two persons. 'Every Prince has two persons', wrote Fadrique Furió Ceriol in 1559, 'the first, the *natural person*, is a simple product of nature and its essence is the same as in other human beings. The other, the *public person*, is a reward of fortune and heaven created to govern and protect the public good.'[15] This division helps to explain references to specific types of royal friends, among them, the royal counsellors, who – as expressed originally by Aristotle – 'must be friends of the monarch and of his government; if not his friends, they will not do what he wants'.[16] Following Aristotle, sixteenth-century Spanish political writers attributed to royal counsellors some of the qualities that characterized ideal friends – truthfulness, loyalty to the interests of the monarch, et cetera. Yet the same writers recognized the obstacles that prevented these counsellors from becoming the monarch's true friends. For one thing, they were too many; for another, counsellors were supposed to be friends of the kingdom and obliged to defend its interests, even if they conflicted with those of the king. The council, states Furió Ceriol, is 'for the people as a father, as a tutor and curator. *Both, the king and the council, are God's vicars upon earth.*'[17]

---

[12] Cicero, 'On friendship', p. 191. See also Antonio de Guevara, *Avisos de privados y doctrina de cortesanos* (Valladolid, 1539), 'Introduction', which is a discourse on friendship.

[13] Cicero, 'On friendship', p. 210.

[14] Pedro de Ribadeneira, *Tratado de la tribulación* [1589], in *Obras escogidas del padre Pedro de Ribadeneira*, ed. Vicente de la Fuente (Madrid, 1944), p. 384.

[15] Fadrique Furió Ceriol, *El concejo y consejeros del príncipe* [1559], ed. D. Sevilla Andrés (Valencia, 1952), p. 95; emphasis added.

[16] Aristotle, *The politics*, ed. S. Everson (Cambridge, 1988), 1287b12–36; on Aristotle's presentation of the royal counsellors as the king's friends and *participes curarum*, see Frederick W. Conrad, 'A preservative against tyranny: the political theology of Sir Thomas Elyot' (doctoral thesis, The Johns Hopkins University, 1988), esp. pp. 34–45. For a summary of the theories of Spanish writers about the role of the royal counsellors, see Feros, 'The sacred council', in 'The king's favorite'.

[17] Furió Ceriol, *El Concejo*, p. 108, emphasis added; see also Juan López de Hoyos, *Real aparato y suntuoso recibimiento con que Madrid recibió a la serenisima reyna doña Ana de*

Better suited than the counsellors for the role of the king's ideal friend was the royal favourite or *privado*. In theory, his devotion to the monarch enabled him to defend the king's interests even against those of the kingdom. Moreover, by spending his time in the company of the monarch the *privado* developed an almost exclusive intimacy with the king that automatically transformed him into the friend of the king's natural person. It was this relationship between a king and his favourite, or *mignon*, that Johan Huizinga referred as 'sentimental friendship', a relationship that sixteenth-century monarchs liked to boast about in public, as Emperor Charles V did at the time of his abdication.[18]

Despite the apparent importance of this relationship, sixteenth-century political writers rarely refer to the royal favourite in terms of the king's ideal friend. Their reluctance to do so is difficult to explain, but it seems to have been connected with the notion that ideal friendship could not exist between two unequal individuals. If, as noted above, friendship led to equality between friends, how could a king have a friend and thus create another king? Thomas Aquinas made a similar point when he wrote that friendship was impossible between gods and humans as well as between kings and 'people in humbler walks of life'.[19] In *The courtier*, Castiglione also recognized both the possibilities and the limitations of the *privado*'s role as the king's friend. The perfect courtier's main goal was to attract the attention of the prince in the hope of gaining 'the love of his master in such a complete way as to become his *privado*'.[20] But Castiglione was also aware that his prescription for the role of the *privado* touched upon the question of equality between two unequal individuals. I know, he wrote, 'that to talk of a courtier being conversant with his prince in this way *implies a certain equality that can hardly exist between a ruler and his servant*, but for the time being we shall let this go'.[21]

The difficulties of envisioning the existence of an individual equal to the monarch deterred political writers from depicting the relationship between the king and the favourite as a relationship between two ideal friends. Another hurdle impeding the portrayal of the favourite as the king's friend was the tendency of sixteenth-century monarchs to have more than one

Austria [1572] (facsimile edition, Madrid, 1976), fo. 28v, where the author called the counsellors 'fathers of the common-wealth'.

[18] Johan Huizinga, *The waning of the Middle Ages* [1924] (English translation, New York, 1954), p. 54.

[19] Thomas Aquinas, *Commentary on nicomachean ethics*, II, p. 738.

[20] Castiglione, *El Cortesano*, II, p. 115; *The book of the courtier*, p. 287.

[21] Ibid., I, p. 132; *The book of the courtier*, p. 125. Emphasis added.

favourite. As a result, writers tended to view royal favourites as counsellors of the king and sometimes, given their closeness with their masters, as the monarch's chief counsellors. In fact, during the reign of Philip II the word favourite or *privado* took on the meaning of chief counsellor.[22] Marco Antonio Camos, for instance, could refer to 'the *privado*'s office' (*el oficio de privado*) in 1592, and claim that the royal favourite's privileged position rested on 'having been selected and approved by the King' to help him govern the monarchy.[23] The variety of meanings associated with the word *privado* at the end of sixteenth century is evident in Luis Cabrera de Córdoba's description of Cristóbal de Moura, Philip II's most influential minister and favourite during the 1590s. Cabrera de Córdoba refers to Moura as a member of the king's 'privy chamber', as a 'favourite', and also as 'a minister of higher authority (who assisted) the Prince out of love and fidelity...so that the King might enjoy respite from the responsibility of dealing with persons and affairs'.[24]

How these different images of the royal favourite intermingled with the theory of the king's two persons and theories of friendship can be seen in Luis de Zapata's *De la amistad y amigos grandes de estos tiempos* ('On friendship and great friends of these times'), a chapter in his *Miscelánea*, written at the end of the sixteenth century.[25] After reviewing current theories on friendship, Zapata expresses his own ideas concerning the characteristics of the king's friend, using Emperor Charles V as an example. The emperor, Zapata wrote (pp. 184–5):

had Don Luis de Avila ... as his *privado* ... and this friendship (because love made them equal), that among princes is called *privanza*, lasted until they were old ... Charles also had another great *privado*, Don Francisco de los Cobos ... but this *privado* was different. Charles was like Alexander who also had two *privados*, Hephaestion and Craterus. During Alexander's time it was said that Craterus was the King's friend, and Hephaestion Alexander's friend. Thus, Cobos was the King's friend, and Don Luis de Avila was Charles' friend.

Zapata's ideas no doubt were rooted in the political culture of the sixteenth century, but his treatment of the two kinds of royal favourites – one the friend of the king's natural person, the other the friend of the king's

---

[22] On this topic, see Feros, 'A new kind of favorite', in 'The king's favorite'.

[23] Marco Antonio Camos, *Microcosmia y gobierno universal del hombre christiano* (Barcelona, 1592), pp. 120–1. Emphasis added.

[24] Luis Cabrera de Córdoba, *Felipe segundo, rey de España* [1609] (4 vols., Madrid, 1876), II, p. 144; III, p. 217 and IV, pp. 65–6.

[25] Luis de Zapata, *Miscelánea*, in *Memorial histórico español*, XI (Madrid, 1859), pp. 182–7 I am grateful to Dr Fernando J. Bouza Alvarez for bringing Zapata's work to my notice.

public person – distinguished him from previous writers on this topic. Zapata also parted from his predecessors by making a clear distinction between the king's friend, who should be *one*, and the king's counsellors, who should be *many* (pp. 182–3). In other words, Zapata defended the idea that the king should have just *one* favourite and that this favourite could be depicted – despite the different qualities between the monarch and his subjects – as the king's sole friend.

II

After the turn of the century other writers also began to refer to the possibility of a friendship between two unequal individuals, and specifically to that between the monarch and the favourite, suggesting at the same time that such a friendship would benefit the whole kingdom. Juan Fernández de Medrano, for example, wrote that the king's many responsibilities required him to have 'a faithful friend [*amigo fiel*] ... whose duties are to moderate the prince's passions, help him support the weight of government and tell him the truth'.[26] This redefinition of the political discourse concerning the royal favourites did not come about simply as the result of a linguistic evolution; it mirrored a changing political reality. As J. G. A. Pocock has reminded us, 'history consists of actions, events, and processes'.[27] Hence, in the analysis of the past we need not only to reconstruct different political languages and their evolution, but also to comprehend how political acts 'modify the contexts they are performed in, and how some of these modifications lead to the creation and diffusion of new languages and new contexts'.[28] In the case of the Spanish monarchy one political act definitely modified the political context, and thus the political discourse on royal favourites: Philip III's announcement, in September 1598, that he had a royal favourite, Francisco Gómez de Sandoval y Rojas, duke of Lerma (1552?–1625), and that the duke would play an important role in palace and governmental matters.

The duke of Lerma rose to power at the moment when one of the most

---

[26] Juan Fernández de Medrano, *República mixta* (Madrid, 1602), p. 83. Medrano dedicated his book to the duke of Lerma.

[27] J. G. A. Pocock, 'Texts as events: reflections on the history of political thought', in *Politics of discourse: the literature and history of seventeenth-century England*, ed. Kevin Sharpe and Steven N. Zwicker (Berkeley, 1987), p. 22.

[28] J. G. A. Pocock, 'The concept of a language and the *métier d'historien*: some considerations on practice', in *The languages of political theory in early-modern Europe*, ed. Anthony Pagden (Cambridge, 1987), p. 30. See also Gabrielle M. Spiegel, 'History, historicism, and the social logic of the text in the Middle Ages', *Speculum*, 65 (1990), 59–86.

important characteristics of the Spanish kings, 'their invisibility, and indeed their sheer inaccessibility', was solidly established.[29] In this sense, Philip III was as invisible and inaccessible as his father Philip II. Educated in the grave court ceremonial imposed by his predecessor, Philip III preferred 'solitude, with very little court',[30] and he made it clear that access to his person and privy rooms was going to be even more difficult than during his father's reign.[31] The political importance of Philip III's privacy was perfectly captured by an anonymous adviser who in 1598 affirmed that Philip II 'was obeyed and feared even when he had locked himself into his rooms', and that Philip III should do the same to establish his authority.[32]

Philip III, however, did more than simply model himself after his father. During his lifetime, the king's inaccessibility evolved into an enduring political axiom, a veritable religion of state that distinguished the Spanish monarchy from its European counterparts. In effect, although other European monarchs tried to isolate themselves from public view and political pressure by retreating into an aristocratic milieu, this practice hardly replaced the accepted principle that good monarchs were public monarchs, accessible to their subjects and open to the advice of the body politic.[33] The French writer Pierre Mathieu, a contemporary of Philip III, observed the uniqueness of the Spanish monarchy when he noted that the French needed a visible and accessible king because otherwise they will believe that there is

---

[29] John H. Elliott, 'The court of the Spanish Habsburgs: a peculiar institution?', in his *Spain and its world, 1500–1700* (New Haven and London, 1989), p. 148. See also, Fernando Checa Cremades, 'Felipe II en El Escorial. La representación del poder real', in *El Escorial. Arte, poder y cultura en la corte de Felipe II* (Madrid, 1989), pp. 17–20; Javier Varela, *La muerte del rey. El ceremonial funerario de la monarquía española (1500–1885)* (Madrid, 1990), pp. 44–8; M. J. Rodríguez-Salgado, 'The court of Philip II of Spain', in *Princes, patronage, and the nobility: the court at the beginning of the modern age, c.1450–1650*, ed. Ronald G. Asch and Adolf M. Birke (Oxford, 1991), pp. 212–19; Fernando J. Bouza Alvarez, 'La majestad de Felipe II. Construcción del mito real' in *La corte de Felipe II*, ed. José Martínez Millán (Madrid, 1994), pp. 37–72; and Feros, 'The invisible king', in 'The king's favorite'.

[30] Simeone Contarini to the Venetian Senate, 1605; cf. Elliott, 'The court of the Spanish Habsburgs', p. 148.

[31] On this topic, see Feros, 'Looking for intimacy', in 'The king's favorite'.

[32] BNM, ms. 18275, 'Memorial que dieron al Duque de Lerma, cuando entró en el valimiento del sr. Rey Felipe III', fo. 2r.

[33] On this topic see, R. Malcom Smuts, 'Public ceremony and royal charisma: the English Royal Entry in London, 1485–1642', in *The first modern society: essays in English history in honour of Lawrence Stone*, ed. A. L. Beier, David Cannadine and James M. Rosenheim (Cambridge, 1989), p. 85; Orest Ranum, 'Courtesy, absolutism, and the rise of the French state, 1630–1660', *Journal of Modern History*, 52 (1980), 426–451. For the Russian case, see Valerie A. Kivelson, 'The devil stole his mind: the tsar and the 1648 Moscow uprising', *The American Historical Review*, 98 (1993), 733–56.

no king, while the Spaniards believed that the power of the royal majesty will increase when the king is invisible and inaccessible.[34]

In the early seventeenth century Spanish political writers also wrote about this distinctive character of the Spanish kingship. Juan Fernández de Medrano, for example, advised the king not to let himself be seen by his subjects: 'it is a certain kind of religion to retire from your subjects. You should not become familiar with anyone, except with the person who is your oracle, because *Continuus aspectus verendo minos magnus homines ipsa societate facit.*' There were many historical examples to support this viewpoint, but Medrano selected the Emperor Tiberius as his model because he had lived '*Occultum, ac subdolum fingendis virtutibus*'.[35] As suggested by these precepts, the king's invisibility meant that the monarch should speak only with a small group of selected individuals. The author of *Discurso de las privanzas* suggested, for example, that if the king were to talk with all of his subjects he would lose their respect and obedience and, again using Tiberius as a model, further noted that 'in [Tiberius'] times the only permitted way to address the prince was by writing, even when the prince was present'.[36] Silence rather than rhetoric was considered the ideal way for the Spanish king to establish his pre-eminence, because 'the death of a man is hidden under the tongue; for this reason, the king has to regard silence as the true guardian of his life'.[37] That Philip III understood the value of 'regal silence' is demonstrated by the advice he gave to his daughter Anne of Austria – queen of France through marriage to Louis XIII – 'speak as little as possible ... because with words you can win a reputation but also lose it'.[38]

---

[34] BNM, ms. 9078, 'Breve compendio i elogio de la vida del rey Don Phelipe segundo de felicíssima memoria escrito en francés por Pierre Matiu choronista mayor del Reyno de Francia', fos. 32r–v; cf. Bouza Alvarez, 'La majestad de Felipe II', p. 51.

[35] Medrano, *República mixta*, p. 32. See also Baltasar Alamos de Barrientos, *Aforismos al tácito español* [1614], ed. J. A. Fernández-Santamaria (Madrid, 1987), I, pp. 99–100, and Lorenzo Ramírez de Prado, *Consejo y consejeros de príncipes* [1617], ed. José Beneyto (Madrid, 1958), p. 24. These three books were dedicated to the duke of Lerma.

[36] 'Discurso de las privanzas', in Francisco de Quevedo, *Obras completas*, ed. Felicidad Buendía (Madrid, 1960), II, p. 1393.

[37] Francisco de Gurmendi, *Doctrina phísica y moral de príncipes* (Madrid, 1615), Book I, chapter 6: 'De la importancia y excelencia del silencio', fo. 22v; Francisco de Gurmendi dedicated his book to the duke of Lerma.

[38] 'Instrucción que el rey Don Felipe III dio escrita de su mano a su hija la infanta doña Ana, cuando fue a ser Reina de Francia', in Antonio Rodríguez Villa, ed., 'Cartas autógrafas de Felipe III a su hija Doña Ana, Reina de Francia', *Revista de archivos, bibliotecas y museos*, I (1897), 17. On the silence of England's Charles I as a way to rule his monarchy during the period of 'personal rule', see Kevin Sharpe, 'The king's writ: royal authors and royal authority in early modern England', in *Culture and politics in early Stuart England*, ed. Kevin Sharpe and Peter Lake (Stanford, 1993), pp. 131–4.

The reclusiveness of the Spanish monarchs and the principles that justified it helped to transform the king's chamber (or as the Spaniards called it
at the time, the *retrete*, 'the most secret part of the house'), into 'a dreadful
place where [the invisible] Power lurks'.[39] For those fighting for power and
influence, however, the monarch's chamber was also the place to be. The
monarch's invisibility had irrevocably altered the old meaning and function
of the royal palace as 'the place where the king exercises justice personally,
where he eats and talks with his subjects'.[40] Increasingly, the monarch's
chamber came to be seen as the monarch's private space, a place where the
monarch could withdraw accompanied only by a small, select group of
servants. These servants were by definition intimate with the king; individuals who talked with the monarch, shared his thoughts, his ambitions,
and ultimately his power.

Physical intimacy with the monarch became thus the key to success at
court, and a political commodity that favourites and other palace officials
used to their own advantage, transforming court politics into 'a politics of
intimacy'.[41] To gain intimacy with the monarch, however, one needed a
palace office, especially one that offered to its holder access to the king's
privy chamber. To understand these palace officials' potential for influence
and power, it is important to consider how Spaniards themselves viewed the
individuals commonly known as *palaciegos*. From our point of view, many
palace servants carried out quite menial tasks, but – as pointed out by David
Starkey – 'the numinous powers of a king – that god upon earth – trans-
muted the humblest act of personal attendance into something worthy of the
best blood in the kingdom. With the king, the ordinary social conventions
were actually inverted, and the more minutely personal the attendance, the
more honourable it was.'[42] To serve in the king's chamber, to have the

---

[39] These are the words used by Roland Barthes in his analysis of Racine's plays; see *On Racine*,
trans. Richard Howard (Berkeley and Los Angeles, 1992), pp. 3–4. On the importance of the
court etiquette to limit access to the king's chamber and as instrument of distance, see
Elliott, 'The court of the Spanish Habsburgs', pp. 146–54. On the meaning of the word
retrete in seventeenth-century Spain, see Covarrubias, *Tesoro de la lengua castellana*,
'Retrete'.

[40] For the old view of royal palace, see *Las siete partidas*, part II, tit. IX, law. xxix, 'Qué cosa es
palacio'.

[41] This term comes from David Starkey, 'Intimacy and innovation: the rise of the privy
chamber, 1485–1547', in David Starkey *et al.*, *The English court from the Wars of the Roses to
the Civil War* (London, 1987), p. 118.

[42] David Starkey, 'Representation through intimacy', in *Symbols and sentiments*, ed. Ioan
Lewis (London, 1977), p. 213. This was exactly the meaning of Luis de Zapata's assertion:
'to serve the monarchs, help them dress and put on their spurs is something that belongs
only to great lords and princes', in Zapata, *Miscelánea*, p. 97.

opportunity to help the king in his most intimate actions, was for the philosopher Juan Luis Vives the same as 'to be invited to eat at the gods' table'.[43] For many Spaniards, in fact, palace offices were far more important and coveted than those of royal secretaries and council presidents, as is illustrated by the count of Portalegre's advice to his son:

As far as peacetime offices go, be advised that palace offices have an advantage over the rest. They might seem less weighty, but they do not hinder, indeed they nourish and facilitate, possibilities of advancement ... because the prince has more knowledge of those who are in his presence.[44]

No one was in a better position to discern the importance of the palace offices than Philip III's favourite, the duke of Lerma, who arranged to be appointed *sumiller de corps* (groom of the stole) in December 1599.[45] The *sumiller de corps*, as the head of the privy chamber and thus as the king's closest servant,[46] had as his most important practical function – and certainly the one that gave this office its eminence – to assist the king during the *lever* and *coucher*, and while the king ate in his privy chamber.[47] Palace etiquette explicitly established that the king 'should never withdraw from the sight' of the *sumiller de corps*, who must always accompany the king in public audiences, visits to the queen's chamber, public ceremonies, and when the king retires to his privy chamber.[48] Hence, the *sumiller de corps* was viewed as the most important of the palace functionaries because he was 'more continuously in the king's presence and conversed with the king more frequently than others, and he was always the king's most secret counsellor'.[49] Some seventeenth-century authors even likened the *sumiller de corps*, or the *camarero mayor*, to the king's 'brother' with whom the monarch

---

[43] Vives, *Exercitatio linguae latiane* [1538], dialogue xviii, 'Regia', in his *Obras completas*, ii, p. 945.

[44] 'Instrucción de don Juan de Silva, conde de Portalegre, quando envió a don Diego, su hijo, a la corte' (n.p., n.d.), fo. 17r. The original manuscript was written in 1592; on this instruction and in general on Portalegre, see Bouza Alvarez, 'Corte es decepción. Don Juan de Silva, conde de Portalegre' in *La corte de Felipe II*, pp. 451–502.

[45] Archivo General del Palacio Real (AGPR), Expedientes Personales, 548/4.

[46] Officially the titular of the privy chamber was the *camarero mayor* (the grand chamberlain), but from the second half of the sixteenth century Spanish kings never appointed a grand chamberlain, passing the responsibility of the privy chamber to the groom of the stole.

[47] On the palace etiquette and offices, see Antonio Rodríguez Villa, *Etiquetas de la casa de Austria* (Madrid, 1913), and Elliott, 'The court of the Spanish Habsburgs', pp. 143–7.

[48] Villa, *Etiquetas*, p. 48.

[49] Gonzalo Fernández de Oviedo, *Libro de la cámara real del príncipe don Juan*, ed J. M. Escudero (Madrid, 1870), p. 14.

shared everything and also the king's 'companion and friend, whom [the king] will ask for advice on all matters'.[50]

As *sumiller de corps* Lerma was both the closest person to and the principal servant of Philip III's natural person; but as the king's favourite he also became the closest person to and the principal minister of Philip III's public person. Lerma's political power became evident when, immediately after his confirmation as the king's favourite, he was given responsibility to control the day-to-day administration of the monarchy. Lerma became in fact the vital conduit between Philip III and his councils, and he alone had the right to consult in person with the king. In turn, Philip III's other servants could only communicate with the king on paper, through written *consultas*.[51] Lerma's role as an intermediary between Philip III and the royal institutions transformed the way in which affairs of state were managed. Hence, if until Philip III's reign the royal institutions received their orders through communiqués signed by the monarch, during Lerma's *privanza*, from September 1598 to October 1618, debates in the royal institutions began only upon the receipt of Lerma's *billetes*, the notes through which the duke transmitted Philip III's orders.[52] In October 1612 Philip III made this practice, which had operated informally until then, explicit in an order sent to the council of State, and most likely to others as well:

Since I have known the duke of Lerma, I have always seen him serve the king my lord and father [Philip II], and me with much contentment from both. Every day I am more satisfied with how he handles all matters I ask of him, and how well-served I feel. Given this and how much he has helped me sustain the weight of state affairs, I order that you obey the duke in all matters. All members of the council are obliged to tell him all he wants to know, and although this system began from the moment I inherited these kingdoms, I have decided explicitly to tell and order you now.[53]

---

[50] Miguel Yelgo de Vázquez, *Estilo de servir a príncipes, con ejemplos morales para servir a Dios* (Madrid, 1614), fo. 15v. As *sumiller de corps*, Lerma was also in charge of controlling entry to the king's chamber, a role perfected thanks to his functions as *caballerizo mayor* (master of the horse), an office he obtained in August 1598. See AGPR, Expedientes Personales, 548/4. Thus, inside and outside of the royal palace it was impossible to see or talk with Philip III without first confronting the figure of the duke of Lerma, the shadow of the king.

[51] On the government of the monarchy during Philip III's reign and the role of Lerma, see Feros, 'The art of ruling', in 'The king's favorite'.

[52] There are thousands of *billetes* Lerma sent to the councils and other royal institutions among the papers produced during the reign of Philip III. The last *billete* with these characteristics I have found was written on 30 September 1618, just a few days before Lerma's dismissal from power on 4 October 1618. Lerma always began his *billetes* with the phrase: 'The king orders ...', and the royal institutions responded accordingly: 'Complying with what the King has ordered through the duke of Lerma'.

[53] AGS, Est., *leg.* 4126, fo. 59: 'Copia de lo que Su Majd. ordenó al Consejo de Estado por Octubre 1612 tocante al Duque de Lerma'. This document has been published by Francisco

The political problem that Lerma and his supporters had to confront was how to justify the duke's role. At the time, many political writers found it difficult to defend the fact that a royal favourite was managing the affairs of state with the blessing of the monarch himself. Most early seventeenth-century writers believed that royal power 'had to be exercised personally' by the king,[54] and considered the notion of a king delegating his sovereignty to one of his subjects a contradiction in terms. The Jesuit Francisco Suárez noted in the same year, 1612, that a monarch could not delegate sovereignty to another individual. To do so, he wrote, the king would create two monarchs, it would be 'like having a body with two heads, a monstrous result that could only harm the government of the realm'. Suárez also claimed that the monarch could not even delegate the daily administration of the kingdom to others, because '[t]he crown is the responsibility of the monarch ... and [he] cannot neglect that responsibility or delegate it to someone else; he cannot separate the power of sovereignty from his duty to rule the kingdom'.[55]

Confronted with such ideas, Lerma's supporters found other ways to justify the duke's role in the government of the monarchy, turning in particular to the language and concepts of friendship. An important milestone in this regard was a pamphlet, *Discurso del perfecto privado*, written in 1609 by Lerma's confessor, Pedro de Maldonado.[56] Dedicating the first few paragraphs of his pamphlet to the concept of friendship, Maldonado asked whether common precepts of friendship could describe the relationship between a king and his favourite. Maldonado believed strongly in the importance of friends for monarchs and argued vehemently against those who claimed that the king should not have a friend. The rest was relatively easy because, given the hierarchy of the court at the time, if the monarch could have a friend this could only be the royal favourite. 'The *privado*', Maldonado wrote, '[is] a man whom [the king] has chosen among the rest for a particular kind of equality based on love and friendship, and with whom the king discusses all matters' (fo. 2r).

Tomás y Valiente, *Los validos en la monarquía española del siglo XVII* (Madrid, 1982), p. 157. On the political context of Philip III's decree, see Feros, 'Losing control', in 'The king's favorite'.

[54] Richard Bonney, 'Absolutism: what's in a name?' *French History*, 1 (1987), 99.

[55] Francisco Suárez, *De Legibus* [1612], ed. L. Pereña *et al.* (Madrid, 1971–7), v, pp. 119–21.

[56] BNM, ms. 6778, Pedro de Maldonado, *Discurso del perfecto privado* [1609]; Maldonado presents himself as Lerma's confessor to whom he dedicated his work. Maldonado's *Discurso* was never printed, but it had an enormous influence on all subsequent works on royal favourites; on the influence of Maldonado's 'Discurso', see Tomás y Valiente, *Los validos*, pp. 131 ff. Further references in the text.

In a few brief pages, Maldonado revolutionized the way others wrote about royal favourites and it greatly helped those who wanted to legitimize the political role of the royal favourite. Maldonado's definition of the favourite, for instance, deeply influenced many of the plays written after 1609. 'Great friend of mine', 'particular friend', 'confidant of the secrets of my soul', and 'I will make you my equal', are only a few examples of how kings addressed their favourites in many of these plays. A typical example of this kind of dialogue is found in Mira de Amescua's *Comedia famosa de Ruy López de Avalos, o primera parte de Don Alvaro* in which the characters are King John II of Castile (1406–1454) and his favourite Alvaro de Luna (1385?–1453). After promising each other 'their most loyal and pure friendship', King John asks Alvaro de Luna: 'If you were the king what would you give me as a proof of your love?'

Alvaro de Luna: My *potestas* would be yours,/ you would be king;/ I would be a mute statue/ following your will,/ my being would unite with yours,/ and both together our two natures would look like one/ and thus, I would not give you anything,/ because already you would be the absolute master of the kingdom and me.[57]

The opinions of Mira de Amescua on the absolute equality between monarchs and favourites were more extreme than those of other contemporary political authors. Most of Lerma's supporters in fact refrained from such language in order to avoid charges that Lerma was usurping the king's prerogatives. They simply wanted to demonstrate that a special relationship between the monarch and his favourite did not necessarily imply that the latter should be viewed and treated as another king. Gil González Dávila used this particular concept of the royal favourite as the king's unequal partner in a mutual friendship to define the relationship between the duke of Lerma and Philip III. In explaining Lerma's rise to power, for example, González Dávila noticed that:

the King declared his grace to the marquis-duke, and asked Lerma to help him with affairs of state given that Lerma was his Friend, which is the major honour that a king can give to one of his subjects. In all the papers of the King answering Lerma's

---

[57] Antonio Mira de Amescua, *Comedia famosa de Ruy López de Avalos (Primera parte de don Alvaro de Luna)*, ed. N. E. Sánchez-Arce (Mexico, 1965), p. 61. For plays on favourites, see Mary Austin Cauvin, 'The *Comedia de Privanza* in the seventeenth century' (doctoral thesis, University of Pennsylvania, 1957); Raymond MacCurdy, *The tragic fall: don Alvaro de Luna and other favorites in Spanish golden drama* (Chapel Hill, 1978), and Luis Caparrós Esperante, *Entre validos y letrados. La obra dramática de Damián Salucio del Poyo* (Valladolid, 1987).

reports, and I have seen many, the King always signs *Your Friend*, and the duke always responds with these words, *Humble Slave of Your Majesty*.[58]

But, if the favourite was a lesser partner in relation to the monarch, that did not discourage political writers from present a quite appealing view of the roles reserved to the favourite in the ruling of the monarchy. Maldonado, for example, claimed that the favourite was 'the best part of the king' (*la más rica parte del Rey*) (fo. 2r.), and that an honourable favourite was more crucial than a good king for the well-being of the community. This is why the *privado* should be helped by good advisers since 'the favourite has the same duties as the king [towards the kingdom]' (fo. 3v). The *privado* in fact appeared as the essential intermediary between the king and the kingdom,[59] 'the neck through which the king (the head) communicates his virtues and goodness to other members of this *corpus mysticum*' (fo. 7r). He became the monarch's chief counsellor or prime minister, a kind of 'philosopher-favourite' modelled after the 'Philosopher Plato' in his role as Dionysus' counsellor.[60] In this role, Pedro de Maldonado noted, the favourite's task was not only to help the king govern the monarchy, but also to make certain that the monarch did not shrink from his obligations towards the community (fos. 7r–16r).

More important is that in using the concept of the favourite as the king's friend, political writers could present new images in support of the royal favourite that would have been inconceivable in former times. All humans had the right to have a friend and the monarch as a private individual also possessed this right, explained the duke of Uceda, Lerma's oldest son, in 1622. But, because the monarch was also a public person, the head of the community, his friend-favourite could also speak in the king's name, because:

in all matters the favourite, we have to suppose, is only a mere executor of the king's will, and thus no one can limit the favourite's actions in public life [*en lo exterior y público*] because every time the favourite leaves the king's chamber [*retrete*] he is an incarnation of the prince [*viene su príncipe transformado en él*].[61]

The favourite 'is his master's voice in all matters concerning the community, not because of his office but because he is the incumbent of his master's favour', and no one has the right to interfere with the favourite's activities

---

[58] Gil González Dávila, *Historia de la vida y hechos del inclito monarca, amado y santo Don Felipe Tercero* (Madrid, 1771), p. 40. This book, although published in 1771 was completed in the 1620s to 1630s.

[59] 'Discurso de las privanzas', II, p. 1393.   [60] Ibid., II, p. 1396.

[61] BNM, ms. 11569, 'Memorial del pleito contra el duque de Uceda', fo. 220r.

just as no one has the right to interfere with the king's actions.[62] Hence, when the favourite recommended a course of action or when he ordered something, it was not because he had usurped the king's power but because he was the king's other self. The monarch and his favourite – as one of Lerma's supporters noted in a reference to Philip III and Lerma – just had similar wills and natures because 'they are joined together as if they were only one'.[63]

III

This new conception of the favourite as the monarch's ideal friend did not go unchallenged. The *privanza* of the duke of Lerma, especially after 1614, was in fact threatened by the attempts of Lerma's foes to recast and control the political discourse on favourites with arguments aspiring to demonstrate that the existence of a royal favourite depicted as the king's friend undermined the integrity of the Spanish political system itself. Fray Juan de Santa María's *República y policia christiana* (1615) was the finest example of these efforts.[64] Given that favourites were products of the king's pleasure, Santa María noted that the mere fact of being selected as a favourite transformed the individual into a friend of the king. 'But, friendship can only exist between two equals and for this reason it seems to me impossible that one of the king's subjects could be his friend' (pp. 281–2). If a king has a friend-favourite, the king and the kingdom face two dangers, both with deadly consequences. In having a friend, the king 'lowers himself to the level of his subject making him his equal. The king is and should be the head of the body politic, and he cannot diminish the sovereignty God has given him by becoming equal with one of his subjects' (p. 282). Alternatively, if the king has a friend-favourite he may 'aggrandize his friend' and thus create a monster, a body politic with two heads. To avoid this horrifying fate, Santa María advised the king to have *many* favourites who could help him. But do not let them, Santa María advised, have any say in matters of justice and government, and always remember that the advice of your favourites is not as important as that of 'your wise counsellors and councils' (p. 295).

---

[62] Ibid.

[63] Francisco Fernández de Caso, *Oración gratulatoria al capelo del ilustrísimo y excelentísimo señor cardenal duque* (n.p., 1618).

[64] Fray Juan de Santa María was an active player in the opposition against Lerma before and after 1618. His book became a best-seller with editions in Madrid (1615), Barcelona (1617, 1618, 1619), Valencia (1619), Lisbon (1621) and Naples (1624), and was translated into English in 1632, during Charles I's personal rule, under the title *Christian Policie*. I used the edition published in Naples in 1624; further references in the text.

Not surprisingly, Lerma tried to impede the distribution of Santa María's book, although in the end his efforts to do so were counterproductive because they only increased attention on Santa María and his ideas.[65] But, even if Lerma had managed to silence Santa María, he still had to confront a series of books and pamphlets which also claimed that the existence of *one* friend-favourite was detrimental to the well-being of the community. This was certainly the case with Francisco de Quevedo's *Política de Dios y gobierno de Cristo* (1617), which explicitly attacked weak monarchs and 'evil favourites'.[66] All monarchs, claimed Quevedo, and especially weak monarchs, should remember that Jesus did not let 'one of his followers be superior to the rest'. Jesus did not have 'favourites but disciples'; the king should not have favourites but simply subjects (pp. 602–3, 623). Moreover, a monarch has to remember that 'he is a public person and that his crown represents his duty towards his kingdom' (pp. 635–6). Recalling the temptations suffered by Jesus when he retired to the desert, Quevedo assures that the king who is alone becomes dominated by one of his subjects, by one Satan who soon will ask the monarch 'to kneel before him, to adore him . . . He will try to change his role of a servant for that of the master, and transform his master into a simple servant' (p. 649).

These arguments, sharpened after Lerma's downfall in October 1618 and again after Philip III's death in March 1621, convinced the new king, Philip IV, and the new favourite, the count of Olivares (soon to be count-duke), that they needed to approach the topic of royal favourites from a new perspective.[67] An illustrative example of this new approach was *Discurso sobre los privados y cómo se ha de gobernar el príncipe con ellos* ('Discourse on the *privados* and how the prince should behave towards them'), a pamphlet written by an anonymous author in the last months of 1621.[68] Focusing on the monarch's need to rule with the advice of his subjects, the author noted that in former times those who counselled the monarch were known as the king's friends, but that in modern times these counsellors are called *privados* (151r–v). There were, however, various kinds of *privados*. Because the monarch has two persons, as the *king* he should have a 'political or civil' *privado* with whom he has to discuss all matters of government. This

[65] See Juan de Vitrián, *Las memorias de Felipe de Comines con escolios propios* (Antwerp, 1643), II, p. 414. I am grateful to Julio A. Pardos Martínez for bringing Vitrián's book to my notice.
[66] Francisco de Quevedo, *Política de dios y gobierno de Cristo*, in his *Obras completas*, I, pp. 599–655; the first part of this work was written in 1617, although it was not published until 1626 when it was dedicated to Philip IV and the count-duke of Olivares.
[67] On how criticism against Lerma affected Olivares, see John H. Elliott, *Richelieu and Olivares* (Cambridge, 1984), pp. 34–5.
[68] BNM, ms. 17772/6. References to folios in the text.

'political *privado*' was no doubt the best kind of favourite, although he should never become the monarch's sole source of counsel. As a *man*, the king could also have a *'familiar'* favourite, whom the king should love and esteem but with whom he should not discuss matters of government. The final type of favourite, and the worst, was 'the *personal* favourite', a favourite who played both roles, the friend of the king's two persons and who – due to his enormous power and influence over his master – could destroy the king and the kingdom, as had happened during the reign of Philip III (151v–2152r).[69]

Adhering to these principles during the first years of his *privanza* Olivares kept himself as Philip IV's familiar favourite, while Olivares' uncle, Baltasar de Zúñiga, occupied the role of chief minister.[70] Even more revealing is that from 1622, following Zúñiga's death in October, Olivares 'had every inducement to disclaim for himself the title of favourite'. Olivares' desire was to be identified as 'a "minister" – the king's "faithful minister" – emphasizing the official, and not the personal, character of the high position' he had assumed.[71] To understand Olivares' approach to the topic of favourites and how his ideas affected the political discourse, one needs only to compare Mira de Amescua's *Comedia famosa de Ruy López de Avalos*, in which the favourite is depicted as an ideal friend of the king, his equal, and Francisco de Quevedo's *Cómo ha de ser el privado*, in which the royal favourite Valisero – an anagram of Olivares – is characterized as the king's faithful minister, his humble and obedient servant fully cognizant of his lesser stature.[72]

This is not to say that during Olivares' *privanza* all things changed. If anything, both political practice and discourse under Olivares showed more continuity than discontinuity.[73] For instance, many of the theories and

---

[69] The Flemish author Carolus Scribani defended similar theories in his *Politico-christianus* (Antwerp, 1624), a book he dedicated to Philip IV; see Robert Bireley, *The Counter-Reformation prince: anti-machiavellianism or catholic statecraft in early modern Europe* (Chapel Hill and London, 1990), pp. 174–5.

[70] See John H. Elliott, *The count-duke of Olivares: the statesman in an age of decline* (New Haven and London, 1986), pp. 42–3.

[71] Elliott, *The count-duke of Olivares*, p. 169; see also Elliott's *Richelieu and Olivares*, pp. 39–40.

[72] On Francisco de Quevedo's *Cómo ha de ser el privado*, see Elliott, 'Quevedo and the count-duke of Olivares', in Eliott's *Spain and its world*, pp. 189–209.

[73] For a comparison between Lerma's and Olivares' behaviour, see Antonio Feros, 'Lerma y Olivares: la práctica del valimiento en la primera mitad del seiscientos', in *La España del conde-duque de Olivares*, ed. John H. Elliott and Angel Garcia Sanz (Valladolid, 1990), pp. 197–224; for the continuity of the theories on royal favourites during Olivares' *privanza*, see 'Epilogue' in Feros, 'The king's favorite'.

concepts used by Lerma's supporters to describe the royal favourite were used by Olivares' supporters, and in 1641 Olivares received a book entitled *El privado christiano* which reproduced, word by word, Maldonado's definition of the *privado*.[74] Continuity also characterized the rhetoric of the opposition that emerged against the count-duke of Olivares, who – after trying to disassociate himself from the negative elements linked to royal favourites – had to contend with criticisms similar to those that Lerma had previously endured. Their opponents agreed, for instance, on the favourites' desire not only to control the monarchs but also to become monarchs themselves. Hence, Lerma was often accused of being 'the real king', while Philip III was urged to become 'the king' and imitate his father Philip II.[75] Similarly, Olivares was denounced as a tyrant and usurper, as 'a count who is a king', while Philip IV was depicted as 'a person whom the count-duke seeks to conserve in order to make use of the office of king – a mere ceremonial ruler'.[76]

These attacks against Lerma and Olivares uncovered the Achilles' heel of those theories which likened royal favourites to protective shields that enabled their masters to remain aloof from political controversy. As pointed out by numerous seventeenth-century political writers and as practice itself demonstrated, attacks against royal favourites had immediate repercussions for their masters.[77] Even worse, royal favourites became, as the duke of Rohan, a French aristocrat, put it 'the pretext for all the quarrels that occur' in a monarchy.[78] During the last years of his *privanza* Olivares was in fact depicted as the root of all evils, and his policies and attitudes were denounced as the spark that initiated the revolts of Catalonia and Portugal against Philip IV.[79]

The picture of a monarchy crumbling into pieces forced many royalist writers to assert that the preservation of personal monarchy – what Juan de Vitrián called 'the despotic government of the monarchy' – required monarchs to redefine the public role of the royal favourite.[80] Early modern political writers were aware of the importance of reputation for monarchical rule and they consequently advised princes to be mindful of how their

---

[74] José Laynez, *El privado christiano* (Madrid, 1641), p. 25.
[75] On condemnations of the Duke of Lerma and criticism against Philip III, see Feros, 'The king's favorite', chapter 6 and epilogue.
[76] Elliott, *The count-duke of Olivares*, p. 316, and *Richelieu and Olivares*, p. 101.
[77] See, for example, Barrientos, *Aforismos al tácito español*, I, p. 312.
[78] Cf. J. H. M. Salmon, 'Rohan and the reason of state', in Salmon, *Renaissance and revolt* (Cambridge, 1987), p. 106.
[79] See Elliott, *The count-duke of Olivares*, chapters 14–15.
[80] Vitrián, *Las memorias de Felipe de Comines*, I, p. 284.

subjects perceived them.[81] As the Jesuit Juan de Mariana had reminded Philip III in 1599, 'in government, as in public life, the opinions of the people have more influence than the reality. When prestige dies, so does power.'[82] Similarly political writers in the 1630s and 1640s believed that Philip IV had to present himself as a flawless 'divinity', a paragon of perfection, if he wanted to avoid weakening his authority. True, no one – not even a king – was totally free of weaknesses, but in those circumstances the best attitude was to conceal them.[83] Perhaps the monarch, like other human beings, needed favourites-friends to support him in moments of frustration and help him to cope with his duties, but to have favourites invariably brought forth contempt. The monarch could solve this dilemma, however, if he relegated his favourites to the shadows of the royal palace, by keeping them as friends and *bon compagnons* of the king's natural person. For his part, the monarch had to monopolize the public sphere as the glorious head of his kingdoms. As Vitrián alleged, in the universe there was only one God, in each household one master, in each body one soul; the monarch 'as a human god, the master and the soul of the body politic' can only be one.[84]

Philip IV, after the experience of Olivares' *privanza*, understood that a public favourite was a political liability, a sign of personal weakness and an invitation for anyone seeking to challenge his authority. Yet it was not a question of eliminating royal favourites entirely, but of determining how favourites were to be presented in public and their roles in the monarch's public affairs. Philip IV referred to these matters in a letter to Sor María de Agreda, one of his spiritual counsellors, in January 1647. Reminding her that even the wise and prudent Philip II had a select group of servants to help him rule the monarchy, Philip IV assured her that 'this kind of government has taken place in all monarchies – ancient and modern – since in all of them monarchs have had a principal minister or a close servant', who helped their masters to rule the kingdom because it could not be done without assistance. Philip also acknowledged that he still had a favourite. After Olivares, he asserted, 'it is true that I gave my confidence and approval to one of my servants [don Luis de Haro] who grew up with me'.

[81] See Quentin Skinner's introduction to Machiavelli's *The prince*, ed. Quentin Skinner and Russell Price (Cambridge, 1988), pp. xx–xxiii.

[82] Juan de Mariana, *De rege et regis institutione*, ed. Luis Sánchez Agesta (Madrid, 1981), p. 44.

[83] Baltasar Gracián, *The art of worldly wisdom* [1647], trans. Martin Fischer (New York, 1993), p. 23.

[84] Vitrián, *Las memorias de Felipe de Comines*, I, p. 31, and II, p. 114.

But he qualified this admission by claiming that 'I always *refused to give him [Haro] the character and name of minister* to avoid the past troubles.'[85]

Philip IV's words signalled the beginning of a new era marked by the disappearance of favourites perceived both as the king's ideal friend and as the king's chief minister. The era of omnipotent favourites such Lerma and Olivares was over.[86] Similar developments occurred in other European monarchies, notably in France where opposition to Louis XIV's chief minister, Cardinal Mazarin, helped to trigger the Fronde.[87] Chastened by this experience, Louis XIV promised himself never to permit the emergence of figures similar to Cardinals Richelieu and Mazarin. What 'makes for the greatness and the majesty of kings', he wrote in his *Mémoires*, 'is not so much the sceptre that they bear as the manner in which they bear it ... [and thus there is] nothing more shameful than to see on the one hand all the functions and on the other the mere title of king'.[88]

---

[85] Philip IV to Sor María de Agreda, January 1647; cf. Tomás y Valiente, *Los validos*, pp. 172–3. Emphasis added.

[86] After Olivares' fall there were royal favourites in Spain, but none of them reached the power and influence enjoyed by Lerma and Olivares. See I. A. A. Thompson, 'The government of Spain in the reign of Philip IV', in his *Crown and Cortes: government, institutions and representation in early-modern Castile* (Aldershot, 1993), chapter 4, pp. 57 ff., and Tomás y Valiente, *Los validos*, pp. 15–31. See also Robert Stradling, *Philip IV and the government of Spain, 1621–1665* (Cambridge, 1988), chapters 9 and 10.

[87] On the Fronde, see now Orest Ranum, *The Fronde: a French revolution* (New York and London, 1993).

[88] Louis XIV, *Mémoires for the instruction of the dauphin*, ed. and trans. Paul Sonnino (New York, 1970), p. 31; see also pp. 238–40.

2

Taxation and political culture in Castile 1590–1640

CHARLES J. JAGO

On 12 June 1635, the count of Castrillo, a member of the council of Castile and nephew of the count-duke of Olivares, composed a hastily scribbled note to his confessor.[1] In his note Castrillo had a number of pressing questions to ask. Can the king require his subjects to serve him personally in arms? What obligation do they have to serve him with their wealth, especially the members of the aristocracy and the bishops? What is the obligation of the Cortes to concede taxes? Does it matter whether the war which serves to justify the taxes is fought at home or abroad? On what grounds can a member of parliament, a proctor (*procurador*), vote for taxes in good conscience? What is the extent of the Cortes' obligation to approve new taxes when it is obvious to all that the kingdom is impoverished? In short, 'how, given the widest latitude possible, might His Majesty best be served within the limits of conscience?' These questions, along with the confessor's careful response, provide a unique and valuable insight into the political culture of Olivares' Castile – a culture in which theology and a preoccupation with informed conscience significantly shaped the context in which political decisions were made.

At the time Castrillo raised his questions, the atmosphere at the royal court in Madrid was tense. Spain had recently declared war on France and

---

All translations are by the author unless otherwise attributed.
[1] BL, Add. 9936, fos. 287–92.

military preparations were in high gear.[2] Castrillo's own preoccupations were financial. To wage war successfully the government needed money, and he, along with other leading ministers, including Olivares, had become involved in a series of emergency meetings for the purpose of identifying new sources of government revenue.[3] Castrillo had a particular interest in these meetings: as the minister responsible for conducting negotiations with the Cortes of Castile, it was he who would ultimately have to persuade the proctors to approve the tax proposals adopted.[4] Such approval was never easy, but the relations between the crown, the Cortes and the leading Castilian cities – those with parliamentary representation – had become severely strained in the 1620s and early 1630s as a result of Olivares' aggressive attempts to initiate major fiscal reforms.[5] Thus, faced with the prospect of a new round of tax demands, Castrillo was justifiably apprehensive and sought the counsel of his confessor to assuage his conscience troubled by vexing questions of political ethics.

For a senior statesman to approach his confessor in such circumstances was entirely consistent with the practice of the age. Theologians, along with jurists, were expected to apply their intelligence and learning to serve as 'legitimizers and rationalizers of power' – 'to find, largely through scholastic debate, and the collective wisdom of learned men, convincing arguments within the theological and humanistic cultural traditions of the time' for

---

[2] John H. Elliott and José F. de la Peña, *Memoriales y cartas del conde duque de Olivares* (2 vols., Madrid, 1978–81), II, p. 69. The authors note that in June 1635 the count-duke of Olivares, Philip IV himself, and a number of court nobles began to take classes on fortifications from the Jesuit Francisco Antonio Camassa in preparation for the war.

[3] AHN, Est. lib. 871, 'Consultas y Votos tocantes al desempeño de la Real Hacienda en el año de 1633'; ibid., Consejo de Castilla, 'Consulta del Medio que se deve usar para sacar del Reino este año 3 Millones de ducados para las urgencias presentes', 6 February 1634; ibid., Junta del Aposento del Conde Duque, 16 May 1635; ibid., Junta del Aposento del Conde Duque, 24 December 1635; AHN, Est. lib. 853, fos. 1–68, consulta, Consejo de Estado, 22 September 1634; AHN, Cons. *leg.* 7131 consulta, Consejo de Hacienda, 30 April 1635; AHN, Cons. *leg.* consulta, Consejo de Hacienda, 14 May 1634; AGS, CJH, *leg.* 730/158 consulta, Consejo de Hacienda, 16 March 1635; AGS, CJH, *leg.* 730/178 consulta, Consejo de Hacienda, 5 May 1635.

[4] Elliott and la Peña, *Memoriales y cartas*, II, pp. 114–15.

[5] Felipe Ruiz Martín, 'La Banca de España hasta 1782', in *El Banco de España. Una historia económica* (Madrid, 1970), pp. 73–96; Charles Jago, 'Habsburg absolutism and the Cortes of Castile', *American Historical Review* 86 (1981), 317–22; P. Fernández Albaladejo, 'La Resistencia en las Cortes', in John H. Elliott and A. García Sanz, eds., *La España del conde duque de Olivares* (Valladolid, 1990), pp. 317–37; I. A. A. Thompson, 'El reinado de Felipe IV', in José Andres-Gallego (ed.), *Historia general de España y América.* VIII: *La crisis de la hegemonía española, siglo XVII* (Madrid, 1986), pp. 443–92.

public policy decisions.[6] As Francisco de Vitoria, the leading Spanish theologian of the first half of the sixteenth-century, notes: 'all men are compelled to consult the wisest and best-informed persons they can find before reaching a decision on any issue where matters of conscience are involved'.[7] Spanish monarchs assiduously followed this advice. So frequently did Philip II consult with academic theologians and jurists that he has been aptly described as the 'perfect realization of the School of Salamanca' – the dominant school of theological, juridical, ethical, political and economic thought in sixteenth-century Spain.[8] Philip III and Philip IV followed suit, the latter forming a Great Council of Theologians, chaired by his own confessor, Fray Antonio de Sotomayor, to advise him on fiscal proposals.[9] An even more striking example of this desire for confessional guidance is Philip IV's extensive correspondence with Sor María de Agreda during the latter years of his reign.[10] Why these consultations? Anthony Pagden contends that in order to fulfil 'its self-appointed role as the guardian of Christendom' the Spanish crown found it essential on all occasions to be seen to act 'in strict accordance with Christian ethico-politico principles'. 'The task of theologians and jurists under Habsburg rule', he continues, 'was to establish just what these principles were.'[11] Somewhat more cynically, Juan Linz considers the consultations to have served a 'legitimizing' function, but one that was 'directed more towards the subject than towards

[6] Juan J. Linz, 'Intellectual roles in sixteenth- and seventeenth-century Spain', *Daedalus* 101 (1972), 89–90.

[7] Anthony Pagden, 'Dispossessing the barbarian: the language of Spanish Thomism and the debate over the property rights of the American Indians', in Anthony Pagden, ed., *The languages of political theory in early-modern Europe* (Cambridge, 1987), p. 79.

[8] Luciano Pereña Vicente, *La Universidad de Salamanca, forja del pensamiento político español en el siglo XVI* (Salamanca, 1954), p. 92.

[9] BNM, ms. 2367, 'Discurso sobre la pragmática del papel sellado ...', fos. 274–299 lists the members of this Junta Grande consisting of 'los theólogos mas insignes que entonces se allaron en esta corte'. See also John H. Elliott, *The count-duke of Olivares: the statesman in an age of decline* (New Haven, 1986), pp. 416–18. The creation of this *junta* was merely a formalization and extension of previous practice. For example, Philip III consulted a special *junta* of twelve royal confessors at the commencement of his reign to seek their advice on continuing negotiations with the Castilian cities over the ratification of a subsidy conditionally approved the Cortes in 1596: *ACC*, XVI, pp. 568–70. Both Philip III and IV also included their confessors in consultations on lesser matters. The former included his confessor on a *junta* created to oversee the collection of the *millones* in 1602: *ACC*, XX, pp. 220–1. When the latter in 1624 wanted an opinion on his right to approve the export of hides from Castile in contradiction of a condition of the *millones*' contract, he consulted a *junta* consisting of the President of the Council of Castile, the Inquisitor General, and his confessor: AHN, Cons. *leg.* 1427, consulta, 3 February 1624.

[10] D. Francisco Silvela, ed. *Cartas de la Venerable Sor Maria de Agreda y del Señor Rey Don Felipe IV* (2 vols., Madrid, 1885–6).

[11] Pagden, 'Dispossessing the barbarian', pp. 79–80.

satisfying the conscience of the ruler'.[12] But it also bears noting that seventeenth-century Spaniards operated within a conception of the state that was still theocratic – a conception in which basic issues of social and political action were inextricably tied to principles of divine and natural justice as explicated by theology.[13] Theirs was a world in which theology enjoyed a central role in politics even as political thought was becoming increasingly secularized. 'It was precisely at this point', argues Fernández Santamaría, when politics started to be regarded as 'an art ... with limited goals and limited functions' that 'the moralists' entered the picture reinforcing the place of politics as 'the bailiwick of theology'.[14]

When it came to questions of taxation, the need to seek theological guidance extended to all those directly involved in the process, from the king and his counsellors who formulated policy, to the proctors in the Cortes and aldermen (*regidores* or *veintiquatros*) in the cities whose responsibility it was to approve subsidy proposals. The deference shown to expert opinion – not only theological but also legal and political – is amply testified. In 1598, for example, at the time when Philip II's proposed annual subsidy of 500,000 ducats was encountering severe opposition in the Castilian cities, Melchor de Avila, the *procurador* from Toledo, proposed to the Cortes the creation of a *junta* (committee) of six theologians, six jurists, and six 'good men, statesmen (*republicanos*) of conscience and intelligence' to draft guidelines for an alternative parliamentary subsidy.[15] Likewise, in the mid-1630s when the crown's financial situation was equally desperate, Philip IV sought the best political, legal and theological advice available by consulting his council of State, council of Castile and Great Council of Theologians on issues of taxation.[16] The belief that questions relating to taxation required such august expertise is further evidenced by a consulta of the council of Finance of 5 May 1635.[17] All four councillors present on that occasion refrained from voting on a proposal to tax income from state annuities, the first because 'the final resolutions belong to the members of the Council of State, the Royal Council of Justice and to theologians', the second because 'the justification for this important matter is proper to His Majesty's royal

---

[12] Linz, 'Intellectual roles', pp. 88–90.
[13] Carmelo Viñas y Mey, ed., *Pedro de Valencia. Escritos sociales* (Madrid, 1945), p. 23.
[14] J. A. Fernández-Santamaría, *Reason of state and statecraft in Spanish political thought, 1595–1640* (Lanham, Md., 1983), p. 169.
[15] *ACC*, XVIII, pp. 460–9. The theologians, he noted, 'are knowledgeable in divine law and in the human will', the jurists 'in human, civil and canon law' and the *republicanos* 'in the state of the Realm and its members'.
[16] See above, note 3.
[17] AGS, CJH, *leg.* 730/178, consulta, Consejo de Hacienda, 5 May 1635.

conscience and to the Royal Council of Justice', the third who declared that he would vote in favour 'if approved by the council of Castile and theologians', and the fourth, Bartolomé Espinola, a Genoese financier, who stated simply that the matter was 'not of his profession'.

There was one obvious benefit to this pooling of political, legal and theological expertise: the tax proposals that resulted were easier to justify to the proctors in the Cortes and to the city aldermen. In 1624, for example, when the king's local representatives (*corregidores*), following the instructions issued by the crown, presented the text of a new subsidy proposal to their respective city councils, they emphasized that the subsidy carried the approval of the Cortes, the king's leading ministers, and 'the theologians of greatest stature in these realms'. They drew from this observation the obvious conclusion that 'when anyone finds himself differing in whole or in part he ought to consider that his opinion cannot be as certain or sure as that which has been established and determined by such eminent persons versed in these matters'.[18]

But to assuage their own consciences, individual proctors and aldermen tended to seek their own independent counsel, thereby creating the conditions for a clash of theological expertise. To avoid this eventuality the ministers of the crown, both at court and in the cities, routinely briefed leading ecclesiastics to ensure that they gave proper advice. In 1594, for example, Philip II assigned to the members of the *Junta de Asistentes*, the committee which oversaw the Cortes, responsibility for speaking to court theologians to ensure that when the proctors eventually sought their advice 'they might be well-instructed and edified in what to counsel them'.[19] Parallel practices occurred in the cities. In 1597, for example, the *corregidor* in Jaén formed a local *junta* of theologians 'to assure the consciences of the scrupulous'.[20] His counterpart in Valladolid, facing a hostile and resistant council, turned for support to the bishop of the city saying 'that although I give a thousand reasons to persuade them . . . as I am a weak theologian they do not want to believe me'.[21] These practices continued well into the seventeenth century. In 1625, for example, the *corregidor* in Cordoba

---

[18] AM Valladolid, Libros de Acuerdos, 1623–24, 11 March 1624. This claim was standard procedure. In 1608, for example, the *corregidor* of the city of Cordoba, in urging the *veintiquatros* to approve the renewal of the *millones*, noted that the Cortes in recommending it had consulted with 'great theologians and legists': AM Cordoba, Libros Capitulares, 1608, fo. 109.

[19] *ACC*, XVI, pp. 209–11, consulta, Junta de Asistentes, 15 January 1594. The ecclesiastics were also charged with reporting back to the *junta* indicating the intentions of their advisees.

[20] AGS, PR, 85/72, carta del corregidor de Jaén, 21 April 1597.

[21] AM Valladolid, Libro de Acuerdos, 1597–99, fos. 483–5.

reported that he took a copy of the proposed new subsidy agreement to three monasteries 'which are the three where everyone generally goes to seek counsel'.[22] And in 1637 the *corregidor* in Segovia, when seeking the city's approval for the sale of annuities on the *millones*, spoke 'with all the grave clerics of this city which have the greatest influence on the aldermen'.[23]

But theological opinion was not easily amenable to external control. In 1609, for example, the *corregidor* in Avila summoned a '*junta* of theologians and religious' only to have them decline to issue a statement in support of the proposed new *millones* subsidy. Their silence was generally interpreted as disapproval leaving the *corregidor* to lament that his strategy had done 'more harm than good'.[24] In the same year the *corregidor* in Cordoba urged the patriarch to punish several local priests because, 'due to their misdeeds and bad opinions toward His Majesty's service, Cordoba has determined not to vote money for the King'.[25] Sometimes priests moved into open opposition and encouraged resistance to what they saw as an unjust tax. This was the case in Granada in 1619 when the aldermen suspended the collection of *sisas* immediately upon the expiry of the current *millones* agreement. They claimed that they had been 'urged' to take this action 'by our confessors' who argued that by allowing the taxes to continue they were not properly fulfilling their service to God or the king, or indeed remaining 'in good state' personally.[26] And there were even occasions when local priests took their opposition to the general public. In 1598, for example, the *corregidor* in Jaén accused dissident preachers and aldermen of 'raising the spirits of the vulgar people by presenting themselves as their defenders and those who favour the subsidy as the enemies of the republic'.[27] This was also the situation in 1631 when the agitation of local priests stirred popular protests against the introduction of a salt tax, particularly in Seville.[28]

Evidence abounds, therefore, that theologians played a significant role in late sixteenth- and seventeenth-century Castile in advising kings, government officials and local authorities on taxation, as well as in forging public opinion. Written examples of the type of advice given by both theologians and jurists survives in printed and manuscript copy. These discourses

---

[22] AGS, PR, 91/155, carta del corregidor de Córdoba, 21 May 1625.
[23] AHN, Cons. *leg.* 513/41, carta del corregidor de Segovia, 30 April 1637.
[24] AGS, PR, 88/106, carta del corregidor de Avila, 12 August 1609.
[25] AGS, PR, 88/135, carta del corregidor de Córdoba, n.d.
[26] *ACC*, xxxiii, pp. 294–302.
[27] AGS, PR, 85/37, carta del corregidor de Jaén, 21 August 1598.
[28] Antonio Domínguez Ortiz, *Política y hacienda de Felipe IV* (Madrid, 1960), p. 265 and Quintín Aldea, *Iglesia y estado en la España del siglo XVII* (Comillas, Santander, 1961), p. 38.

subdivide into three general categories: those directed exclusively to the king and his senior officials; those supportive of specific tax initiatives and directed primarily toward parliamentary proctors and city aldermen, and finally those written in opposition to taxation. Representative of the first category are several learned treatises submitted to Philip II in the mid-1590s on the subject of the flour tax.[29] These treatises are carefully crafted and academic in character; as Philip II said of one, 'more appropriate for learned men, theologians and *corregidores* ... than for the proctors and cities'.[30]

Discourses directed toward the parliamentary proctors and aldermen were designed to persuade. Typically written by theologians or jurists, they appeared strategically whenever subsidy proposals were referred to the Cortes or the cities for approval. For example, in the late 1590s, several tracts, all in favour of Philip II's proposed subsidy of 500,000 ducats, circulated among the cities. Their titles reveal their authorship: 'The opinion of some theologians of Segovia', 'The opinion given by some theologians in Burgos', 'The proposition made by don Joan de Gaviria, *corregidor* in the city of Granada' and 'Discourse by *licenciado* Antonio Sirvente de Cárdenas, president of the *Chancilleria* [or High Court] of Granada'.[31] In 1601 'The opinion of father Ildefonso de Castro of the Company of Jesus, provincial of the province of Andalusia, over the concession of the 18 *millones*' circulated to encourage urban support for Philip III's proposed renewed subsidy.[32] Likewise, the renewal of the *millones* proposed in 1619 was supported by the 'Discourse of *licenciado* Jerónimo de Ceballos, alderman of Toledo'.[33] On occasion the crown released its own papers to justify subsidy proposals, such as 'The letter and political discourse written to the cities of the kingdom' in 1624, which carried the explicit requirement that it was not to circulate outside of the city councils (*ayuntamientos*).[34]

Tracts written in opposition to new taxes were intended for a wider audience and were, consequently, more polemical in character. Pre-eminent

---

[29] BNM, ms. 1749, fos. 346–8, Juan de Sigüenza, 'Parecer del Rector de la Compañia de Jesús de Madrid acerca de la imposición de la harina', 5 May 1594. BNM, ms. 1479, fos. 351–2, Doctor [Elecciones?], no title, 4 June 1594. For a detailed discussion of the debate over the flour tax in the 1590s see José Ignacio Fortea Pérez, *Monarquia y cortes en la corona de Castilla. Las ciudades ante la política fiscal de Felipe II* (Valladolid, 1990), pp. 418–28.

[30] *ACC*, XVI, pp. 265–8.   [31] AGS, PR, 85/85, 149 and 347.

[32] BNM, ms. 3207, pp. 529–42.

[33] BL, 1323.k.13.24, 'Discurso del lic. Gerónimo de Cevallos, regidor de Toledo, y su comisario, para la determinación de la concessión de millones deste año de mil y seiscientos y diez y nueve ...'

[34] BL, Add. 9936, fos. 283–6.

among them during the Olivares period were Mateo Lisón y Biedma's *Discursos y apuntamientos* – containing various of his tracts from 1622 to 1628 – and his *Desengaños de rey y apuntamientos para su Govierno* (1623).[35] A favourite literary device employed by oppositional writers was the dialogue. In his *Desengaños*, for example, Lisón y Biedma records a three-way debate between 'a powerful king, an afflicted kingdom, and a dispassionate counsellor'. Likewise in *La hora de todos*, Francisco de Quevedo includes a vignette involving a discussion on taxation between an anonymous minister of the crown and 'the voice of the people'.[36] Such dialogues also circulated locally. In 1624, coinciding with the debate over the renewal of the *millones*, there appeared two dialogues, one from Granada, the other from Seville.[37] In both cases the discussants were an alderman and a powerful minister of the crown. In the Seville manuscript the minister is specifically identified as the count-duke of Olivares.[38] Theological opinion figured significantly in these oppositional tracts. For example, one undated tract, entitled 'Questions on the imposition of tributes raised for the security of conscience of a *procurador* with a vote in the Cortes', sets out the arguments advanced by an anonymous confessor to dissuade a parliamentary proctor from approving a subsidy.[39] Likewise in the 1624 Seville and Granada dialogues, the discussion between the royal minister and the local alderman turns into a proxy debate between their respective confessors. The alderman in the Granada dialogue, in refusing to support the subsidy, attributes his decision to persons 'of great learning and sound Christianity'. The fictitious royal minister, in rebuttal, attempts to overcome his adversary's scruples by inviting him to consult the king's confessor, 'a person of much authority, saintliness and letters', or his own, 'a great counsellor of blameless life'. In the Seville manuscript, a similar invitation advanced by Olivares prompts the alderman to decline the offer in favour of the advice of his own

---

[35] For a surviving example of Lisón y Biedma's *Discursos y apuntamientos*, see BL 5384. aaa. 47; for the *Desengaños de rey y apuntamientos para su govierno, diálogo entre rey poderoso, reino aflixido, consejero desapasionado...* see BL, Add. 9935, fos. 37b–105b.

[36] Francisco de Quevedo, *La hora de todos y la fortuna con seso*, ed. Luisa López-Grigera (Madrid, 1975), pp. 126–9 and Conrad Kent, 'Politics in *La hora de todos*', *Journal of Hispanic Philology*, 1 (1976), 99–119.

[37] BL, Add. 9935, fos. 106–13b, 'Discursos y plática entre cierto ministro faborecido y un veintiquatro sobre la concession de los millones' and AM, Seville, Papeles del Conde de Aguilar, LIX.

[38] Philip IV and Olivares visited a number of the Andalusian cities with representation in the Cortes in 1624, including Seville: see Jago, 'Habsburg absolutism and the Cortes of Castile', p. 320, and Elliott, *The count-duke of Olivares*, pp. 153–8.

[39] BNM, ms. 6754, 'Preguntas que se hacen sobre la seguridad de conciencia del voto en Cortes que da al Procurador dellas para imponer tributos en el Reyno', n.d.

confessor, a man of incomparable virtue 'who is not concerned with private gain but only in trying to please God'. He clinches his case in opposition to the tax by claiming that 'he who absolves me, assures me that I cannot do what Your Excellency orders'.

The role assigned to confessors in these political debates was a direct product of the centrality of theology to the intellectual culture of early modern Spain in general, and to the commanding influence of the sixteenth-century School of Salamanca in particular.[40] It has been argued that the greatest contribution made by the theologians of Salamanca to Spanish political thought was their theory of political power – a theory that had a direct influence on the School's fiscal thought.[41] According to this theory, both the state and its authority originated in God; nevertheless the actual right of governments to exercise political power came to them by delegation from the people they governed. In the words of Luis de León:

Kings, if they be true kings, have received all of their power and all of their right to command from the people. Thus kings do not have their right to reign over others by nature, rather it is the express or tacit consent of the people that makes it possible for one to gain ascendancy over others and to administer justice.[42]

To rule well, kings were expected to rule justly. They were also expected to dedicate their energies to attaining the public good – a concept defined by Luis de León as 'a situation of tranquillity in justice and in the abundance of goods'.[43] According to the more radical members of the School, kings who pursued self-interest and failed to work unselfishly toward justice and the public good – the proper ends of the state – could, in extreme cases, be legitimately deposed or assassinated as tyrants.[44]

The School of Salamanca also embraced the principle of private property, another basic ingredient of their fiscal theory.[45] Their belief in the inherent

---

[40] For general works on the School of Salamanca see Bernice Hamilton, *Political thought in sixteenth-century Spain: a study of the political ideas of Vitoria, Soto, Suárez and Molina* (Oxford, 1963); Pereña Vicente, *La universidad de Salamanca*; Luis Sánchez Agesta, *El concepto del estado en el pensamiento español del siglo XVI* (Madrid, 1959); Restituto Sierra Bravo, *El pensamiento social y económico de la escolástica, desde sus orígenes al comienzo del catolicismo social* (2 vols., Madrid, 1975).

[41] Pereña, *La universidad de Salamanca*, p. 123.

[42] Fray Luis de León, *De legibus o tratado de las leyes, 1571*, ed. Luciano Pereña (Madrid, 1963), p. 29.

[43] Ibid., p. 25.

[44] Guenter Lewy, *Constitutionalism and statecraft during the golden age of Spain: a study of the political philosophy of Juan de Mariana* (Geneva, 1960), pp. 66–79.

[45] For the importance of the concept of private property in early modern Spanish political thought see José Antonio Maravall, *Estado moderno y mentalidad social. Siglos XV a XVII* (Madrid, 1972), I, pp. 345–56.

freedom of the individual included each person's right to own property. They did not, however, regard this as an unqualified right. Because private property was considered to be a social construct – a condition of human existence in the fallen state of nature – they held it to be legitimately subject to social constraint. Taxation was one such constraint. They agreed that kings had the right to impose taxes when such taxes were proper to the ends of the state and for the public good. To cite Diego de Covarrubias:

Princes put up with a great deal of work on behalf of their subjects when they care for their well-being and for the common good, when they apply themselves to the administration of justice, to giving to each what is properly his due, and to ensuring that no-one's rights are violated, and when they look out for the security of their states through arms to ensure that their subjects are not oppressed by neighbouring peoples. For these reasons, [kings] justly exact taxes from their people, as the labourer is due his daily wage . . .[46]

In the thought of the School of Salamanca, taxation involved fundamental principles of justice. Borrowing heavily from Thomas Aquinas, Roa Dávila in the second part of his *De Regnorum Iustitia*, formulates six criteria for a just tax.[47] First, the prince or government imposing a tax has to possess legitimate authority and be properly constituted. A tyrant by usurpation, consequently, could never impose a just tax. Secondly, the prince has to show cause, for it was held that 'the sovereign cannot take from his subjects the dominion they hold over their possessions except for just causes'.[48] Thirdly, to be just taxes have to be moderate, sufficient to meet the expressed needs of the state but not so heavy as to exceed the ability of the subjects to pay. Fourthly, taxes have to be equitable, falling upon all those who stood to benefit from their expenditure but burdening them only in proportion to their wealth. Fifth, justice requires that tax revenues be spent strictly in accordance with the causes for which the tax was approved. Finally, justice also requires that once these causes are removed, the tax be revoked. Because Roa Dávila considers taxation to be a matter of justice, he also considers it to be a matter of individual conscience. The king is morally obliged to ensure that any tax imposed fully meets the requirements of justice, otherwise he is obliged to make restitution.[49] Similarly, those who are responsible for approving taxes are also morally obliged to refuse an

---

[46] Diego de Covarrubias y Leyva, *Textos jurídico-políticos*, intr. Manuel Fraga Iribarne, trans. Atilano Rico Seco (Madrid, 1957), p. 18.
[47] Roa Dávila, *De Regnorum Iustitia*, pp. 57–65.
[48] Quoted in Pereña, *La universidad de Salamanca*, p. 115.
[49] Roa Dávila, *De Regnorum Iustitia*, p. 48.

unjust tax. In the words of Diego de Covarrubias, who also held this opinion:

> If taxes are unjust, either because their imposition emanates from one who does not possess the right to them, or because they are taxes imposed by the prince which far exceed what is necessary for the exigencies of government, there is no obligation in the liberty of conscience [*el fuero de la conciencia*] to pay them and one can, without any blame, refuse to hand them over ...[50]

The discussions that took place around these various criteria exposed some fundamental differences among the members of the School of Salamanca. One issue on which debate occurred was whether public consent for taxation was necessary and, if not, in what circumstances it could be waived. The dominant strain within the School was constitutionalist or 'republican'.[51] The constitutionalists held firmly to the principle of consent and affirmed the right of parliamentary institutions to approve taxation. But there was a contrary strain of thought within the School favourable to royal absolutism. Juan de Mariana, the leading constitutionalist of the late sixteenth-century, condemned the pro-absolutists when he denounced those who claimed that 'it is a great subjection for kings to have to depend on the will of their vassals, thereby making the people the master, not the king'.[52] For his part, Philip II favoured the pro-absolutist doctrine which, however, appears to have been only of modest significance during his reign.[53] But given the divided state of scholarly opinion Philip wisely refrained from promoting open philosophical debate on taxation. For example, he refused the publication of Alvarez de Toledo's treatise in defence of the flour tax in 1595 because the author 'puts into question whether I can impose taxes, in what amount, with what qualities and for what period', questions which, he argued, despite the author's advocacy of the king's authority to tax, 'will give some dissidents [*no bien intencionados*] cause to find other texts ... to dispute it'.[54]

The polarities within the School of Salamanca on the subject of taxation

---

[50] Diego de Covarrubias, *Textos jurídico-políticos*, pp. 22–3.

[51] Pereña, *La universidad de Salamanca*, p. 86; Hamilton, *Political thought in sixteenth-century Spain*, p. 36; Maravall, *Estado moderno*, p. 353; and J. L. Castellano, *Las Cortes de Castilla y su diputación (1621–1789). Entre pactismo y absolutismo* (Madrid, 1990), pp. 41–2.

[52] Mariana, *Tratado y discurso sobre la moneda de vellón*, in Biblioteca de autores españoles (BAE), 31 (Madrid, 1854), p. 578.

[53] Pereña, *La universidad de Salamanca*, p. 86. With reference to a 400 page treatise by Dr Oñate y Sagastizabal which defended the divine right of kings and the absolute subordination of the people to the monarch, Pereña notes that the book was published, but like other writings of its type, ignored.

[54] *ACC*, XVI, pp. 265–8.

are captured in the contrasting ideas of two late sixteenth-century scholastics, Juan Roa Dávila and Juan de Mariana. Roa Dávila accepts the opinion that, ideally, kings should live off their own, but he recognizes that this condition no longer applies.[55] Consequently, he argues that it is both necessary and legitimate for kings to tax as long as their taxes are required by the circumstances, serve the public good, and meet the criteria for justice as established by Aquinas and subsequent theologians and jurists. Furthermore, he considers parliamentary consent to be conditional, not essential. In times of adversity, he maintains, kings can legitimately dispense with consent and impose taxes entirely on their own authority. And in the specific case of Castile, he disputes that a clear tradition exists to justify the opinion that the consent of the Cortes for the introduction of new taxes is absolutely required.

Mariana rejects these conclusions, both in general and specifically with reference to Castile.[56] He considers consent to be a necessary condition for taxation and maintains that the king 'should never believe himself to be the master of the republic nor of his vassals ... [rather] he should believe himself to be the chief of state receiving a certain pension as determined by the citizens which he should never dare to increase unless it has been approved by them'. He defines the good king as one who

never has the need to impose great and extraordinary taxes on his communities [*pueblos*]; but if sometimes inevitable problems or new and unexpected wars oblige him to do so, he raises them with the consent of the same citizens to whom, far from talking with terror, threats and bribes on his lips, he will explain frankly the dangers that exist, the harms that threaten, and the needs of the treasury.

Mariana finds his 'proof' for the proposition that 'the authority of the republic is greater than that of princes ... in our own Spain [by which he means Castile] where the king cannot impose taxes without the consent of the communities'.

These divisions within the School of Salamanca were bequeathed to the seventeenth century where they were perpetuated, if not accentuated, in the works of the Spanish political and economic writers of the period. There exists an abundant literature on taxation for the first half of the seventeenth century. Political treatises where taxation receives substantial treatment include: Juan Márquez, *El governador christiano* (1612), Pedro Fernández Navarrete, *Conservación de monarquías y discursos políticos* (1621), Eugenio Narbona, *Doctrina política y civil* (1621), Jerónimo de Ceballos, *Arte real*

[55] Roa Dávila, *De Regnorum Iustitia*, pp. 44–87.
[56] Mariana, *Del rey y de la institución real*, BAE, XXXI, pp. 478–87.

para el bien govierno de los reyes, príncipes, y de sus vasallos (1623), Diego Saavedra Fajardo, *Idea de un príncipe político cristiano representada en cien empresas* (1640), Joseph Laynez, *El privado christiano* (1641) and Juan de Larrea's *Allegationum fiscalium* (1645). Economic treatises where questions of taxation are debated include such *arbitrista* classics as Manuel González de Cellorigo's *Memorial de la política necessaria y útil restauración a la república de España* (1600), Sancho de Moncada's *Restauración política de España* (1619) and Francisco Martínez de Mata's *Memorial* (ca. 1650).[57] These seventeenth-century writers are very different from their sixteenth-century counterparts. They were less consciously academic and, by writing in the vernacular, intended their works for a wider reading audience. They were also very European and borrowed extensively from contemporary European theorists, most notably Jean Bodin, Giovanni Botero, and Justus Lipsius.[58] Nevertheless, as university educated men taught by Spanish scholastics, it is not surprising that their thought reflects the ideas of the School of Salamanca as well as the polarities within it.[59]

Evidence of this intellectual inheritance can be seen by comparing the views of Fray Juan Márquez and Fray Joseph Laynez. Márquez began his treatment of taxation in *El governador christiano* (1612) by submitting traditional Spanish scholastic fiscal theory to critical examination.[60] What he examines in particular is the assertion, attributed to 'men of good letters', that 'the prince cannot impose even necessary taxes without the consent of the kingdom, because they say that, not being (as he is not) the lord of their [his subjects'] possessions, he cannot help himself to them without the agreement of those who have to pay them. And in this custom are ... the kingdoms of Castile.' Márquez rejects this assertion, which he considers to be extreme, preferring instead to examine the matter objectively from the perspectives of divine, natural and human law. On the basis of divine and

---

[57] For the works of Martínez de Mata see *Memoriales y discursos de Francisco Martínez de Mata*, ed. Gonzalo Anes (Madrid, 1971). Other *arbitristas* also wrote on taxation. See, for example, José L. Sureda Carrión, 'Las doctrinas fiscales de Jacinto Alcaçar y Francisco Centani', *Anales de economía*, 6 (1945), 379–401.

[58] José Antonio Maravall, *Teoría española del estado en el siglo XVII* (Madrid, 1944) and *Estado moderno*, and J. A. Fernández-Santamaría, *Reason of state*.

[59] Luciano Pereña, 'Perspectiva histórica', in Francisco Suárez, *De Iuramento Fidelitatis. Conciencia y política* (Madrid, 1979), pp. 127–91; Franciso Murillo Ferrol, *Saavedra Fajardo y la política del barroco* (Madrid, 1989), p. 231. For the influence of the School of Salamanca on the early Spanish economists see Marjorie Grice Hutchinson, *Early economic thought in Spain, 1177–1740* (London, 1978), p. 122, and Jean Vilar Berrogain, *Literatura y economía. La figura satírica del arbitrista en el Siglo de Oro* (Madrid, 1973), p. 212.

[60] Fray Joan Márquez, *El governador christiano. Deducido de las vidas de Moysén y Iosue, príncipes del pueblo de Dios* (Salamanca, 1612), pp. 86–94.

natural law, he finds agreement in all of the 'ancient scholastics' that the king can impose taxes unilaterally as long as he possesses legitimate authority, can show sufficient cause, and ensure equity. Indeed, he argues that divine and natural law impose obligations on subjects to sustain their kings through taxes 'in conformity with the quality and greatness of the state'. He equates the right of kings to tax with their right to legislate, arguing that 'after the people elected them, and gave them supreme power absolutely, all jurisdiction resided with the Princes, and the people retained no liberty to refuse their orders, unless manifestly unjust ... and this we find in their right to tax'. And within this context he specifically rejects the claim that kings have no right to take the possessions of their subjects without their consent – an argument he considers to be 'extremely weak'. To impose just taxes, he asserts, it is not necessary for the king to be master of his subjects' properties, just as it is not necessary for the parliamentary proctors or the city aldermen to have dominion over them in order to approve taxes. 'The justification for taxes', he argues, 'does not depend on the dominion which he who concedes or imposes them has over the properties from which they are to be paid, but on the power to make law and on the cause for making it'.

By equating taxation with legislation Márquez makes it a matter of justice in a manner consistent with the basic principles of Thomistic theology. But he also understands that there is a political dimension to taxation and that the power of the king to tax also has to be viewed within the context of human law. Therefore he argues that, notwithstanding the conclusions to be drawn from the examination of divine and natural law, there exist kingdoms where 'by contract or by prescription based on immemorial custom' the subjects have established the principle that kings are not permitted to tax without their consent. This he considers to be the case in Castile. Such 'contracts', he argues, 'ought to be held inviolable, especially if sworn by oath'.

Reasons of political prudence also persuade Márquez to uphold the principle of consent. He is of the opinion that kings invite rebellion if they fail to seek consent for new taxes, especially in kingdoms which have acquired the right by contract or custom. By consulting their subjects, listening to their complaints and exercising moderation in the imposition of taxes, a king, he argues, would present himself more as a father than as a lord and win the hearts of his people. By seeking his subjects' consent, a king can also ensure that new taxes meet the requirements of distributive justice. Although a king may know best what level of taxation is needed, Márquez claims, the Cortes and cities (*reino*) know best what types of taxes, on which commodities, would be least harmful. Thus, he concludes, 'it is good to listen to their opinion so that the prince will not err in the choice of taxes nor in the justification for their distribution'.

In summary, while Márquez rejects the more extreme democratic opinions associated with the School of Salamanca, he ends up advocating the principle of parliamentary consent for taxation on different grounds. Princes, he asserts, should be counselled 'that in no manner should they impose new taxes on their states without the consent and agreement of the Cortes'. To seek consent 'will justify their resolutions, excuse many dangers of taxing their people unjustly, and make them more lovable in their eyes'.

Laynez in *El privado christiano* was also intellectually indebted to the School of Salamanca, but he drew on a different strain of thought from Márquez.[61] He begins his treatment of taxation with the radical proposition that 'possessions and persons alike belong to the king'. Then, sketching out a situation in which the kingdom is asked to 'serve with a quantity of some millions paid over the number of years, in the form, and with the conditions that are usual', he argues that no alderman could doubt his obligation to comply with the request even 'if necessary with the blood of his veins ... because always, if necessary, one has to drain the jug, empty the river and run the well dry'. Laynez cites several 'doctors' in support of his opinion, but he declares himself to be unsympathetic to the philosophers 'because in these centuries, and in my judgement, theirs is not erudition but idleness and vanity'. Nevertheless he follows their model by treating taxation primarily as a matter of justice. Using Castile as his obvious example, he likens the role of the aldermen whose responsibility it is to approve new taxes to that of judges whose duty it is to determine 'the justice of the new subsidy'. The aldermen, he maintains, occupy

offices as judges between the contributors on the one part and the public good on the other, judging between the merits of the King's cause ... and the excuses put forward by his vassals in order to free themselves from the tax. Putting these things into a balance they have to consider which is the greater danger to the public good ... having an obligation to decide in favour of the lesser harm, and consequently the greater common utility.

The aldermen, as Laynez sees them, have a moral obligation to make the correct choice. Whether by unjustly denying a subsidy, or by unjustly conceding it, they run a 'danger of committing a mortal sin, with an obligation to make restitution'. This danger is compounded by the fact that it is impossible to be mathematically precise in weighing the arguments; therefore to overcome their scruples they ultimately have to decide on a

[61] Joseph Laynez, *El privado christiano* (Madrid, 1641), pp. 211-20.

balance of probabilities. For Laynez, the benefit of a doubtful conscience should always go to the king in recognition of his 'great and urgent need for money, his inability to find other remedies, the obligation of the kingdom to provide for him in accordance with his quality and greatness, and to give to him what is necessary to conserve justice and peace and defend them in just wars'. The king's 'necessity, once stated', he argues, 'admits of no dispute'. And this was so, he continues, even when the king is prodigal, misspends the money previously provided, or imposes the types of taxes considered by certain 'Doctors to be by their very nature unjust'. In these cases, he contends, the only recourse available to the aldermen is not to deny the tax, 'but to insist on administering it themselves'.

Like their sixteenth-century predecessors, the political and economic writers of the seventeenth century questioned neither the right of kings to tax nor the obligation of subjects to pay. They shared the belief expressed by Baltasar Alamos de Barrientos that 'Taxes and royal impositions are necessary for the conservation of the kingdom, for maintaining obedience and royal authority, and for the costs of war and conservation of peace. To remove them entirely would cause the disintegration of the Empire.'[62] Nevertheless there were sharp differences among them, far greater than the polarities evident within the thought of the School of Salamanca and far more vigorously debated. These differences are nowhere more evident than in the contradictory doctrines articulated in the 1620s by Mateo Lisón y Biedma and Jerónimo de Ceballos.

Mateo Lisón y Biedma was an alderman in the city of Granada, a proctor in the Cortes of 1623, and an advocate of a strengthened parliamentary régime.[63] In his writings he decries the wretched state of Castile which he attributes entirely to excessive taxation. Following in the footsteps of Juan de Mariana, he adopts an extreme constitutionalist position, arguing 'that no law can be promulgated nor any contribution introduced into the kingdom without the consultative vote of the proctors in the Cortes and the decisive concession on the part of the cities'.[64] And like Mariana he denounces the efforts of the crown to subvert this process either by threatening or by bribing the proctors and aldermen for the purpose of gaining their consent – practices which both writers consider to constitute evidence of rampant tyranny. In Lisón's opinion, when the proctors and aldermen 'are

[62] Baltasar Alamos de Barrientos, *Tácito español* (Madrid, 1614), p. 421.
[63] Jean Vilar, 'Formes et tendances de l'opposition sous Olivares. Lisón y Viedma, *Defensor de la Patria*', *Mélanges de la Casa de Velázquez*, 7 (1971), 263–94.
[64] BL, Add. 9935, fos. 120–9, 'Papel de D Matheo de Lisón y Biedma. . . contra las premáticas sobre la fundación de los herarios. . .' (1627).

denied the liberty to vote what they feel in their consciences is most convenient and beneficial to the republic, any tax imposed will be unjust because in the liberty to concede and approve consists the justification to contribute and to pay tax'.[65]

Jerónimo de Ceballos was also an alderman, in the city of Toledo, but rather than being radicalized into opposition to the Olivares' régime as was Lisón, he became one of its leading apologists.[66] In his book, *Arte real para el bien govierno*, Ceballos included a chapter on taxation suggestively entitled: 'In which it is treated if kings, who recognize no superior in temporal matters, can demand loans and subsidies from their subjects for public causes even though the cities and their proctors in the Cortes refuse'.[67] In this chapter Ceballos upholds the absolute sovereignty of kings. Therefore, like the pro-absolutist scholastics whose writings Juan de Mariana had condemned, he finds it unthinkable that royal authority could possibly be exceeded in any matter by that of the Cortes and cities. He regards the principle of consent for taxation to be based strictly on human, not natural or divine law, and he asserts that the power possessed by parliaments is strictly to advise kings, not to overrule them. He writes:

the law of the realm requiring the convocation of the Cortes for the imposition of new taxes is a positive law. It allows His Majesty to explain to the proctors the public need ... and allows them to advise on the distribution of the subsidy in order to avoid damaging the realm and to ensure the greatest equity for all. In the case of necessity, the realm provides neither a grant nor a donation; rather it pays a debt owed by the subject to his king for the administration of justice and the conservation of peace.

In the case of Castile Ceballos argues that, since the vote of the Cortes is only consultative, with that of the cities being decisive, the Cortes should be dispensed with entirely, thereby excusing 'these convocations and the expenses incurred in them'. Furthermore, he asserts that consultations with either the Cortes or cities are not absolutely necessary, but only politically expedient. He states:

all kings and princes, who recognize no superior on earth, can impose new taxes and subsidies on their vassals even though contradicted by the kingdom. But to avoid scandal, and to give the subjects satisfaction as to the cause, the kings are accustomed to giving an account of their need to the proctors in the Cortes in order that they might know the just causes and act in accordance with reason. For the people

---

[65] *Desengaños de rey*, fos. 48–9.   [66] Elliott, *The count-duke of Olivares*, pp. 121–2.
[67] Lic. Gerónimo de Zevallos, *Arte real para el bien govierno de los reyes, principes, y de sus vasallos* (Toledo, 1623), pp. 110–15.

are a ferocious and untamable horse that has to be treated with art, as the lancer rides the horse, sometimes giving him loose rein, and sometimes tight.

In advancing these opinions, Ceballos does not consider himself to be abandoning the basic principles of Spanish scholasticism. He notes that 'all of this doctrine is based on the idea that kings and princes are not the absolute lords either of royal properties or of those belonging to their vassals, but prudent administrators for public causes'. Therefore taxation, in his view, rests ultimately 'on the public needs of the realm', not on the 'absolute will of the prince'.

The ideological divide separating Juan Márquez and Joseph Laynez on the one hand and Mateo Lisón y Biedma and Jerónimo de Ceballos on the other runs throughout the seventeenth-century literature on taxation. Those authors whose political orientation was pro-absolutist display a positive disposition toward royal taxation, emphasizing its benefits. Martin González de Cellorigo, for example, sees taxation as a potential instrument of government-sponsored social and economic reform. He takes issue with those who, following the 'voice of the vulgar', maintain 'that the Kingdom would only be restored if taxes were removed and royal exactions reduced'.[68] The more common opinion was that taxation serves the public good by providing the means to preserve the power and dignity of the king and, consequently, of the realm. In the words of Pedro Fernández Navarrete:

Since the saintly kings of Spain live in vigilance to maintain the good of their vassals and to avoid occasions for tears, it is just that, recognizing the benefits of peace and tranquillity ... [their subjects] understand that the grave illnesses afflicting kingdoms require copious bleedings and that there can be no peace without arms, no arms without wages, and no wages without taxes.[69]

Few of these pro-absolutist writers deny outright the principle of public consent or directly challenge the role of the Cortes and cities in the approval of taxation in Castile. But those who unquestionably accept this process, like Cerdán de Tallada, tend to emphasize the obligation of the proctors and alderman to approve the taxes proposed by the crown. For example, Cerdán de Tallada cites 'the common opinion of the Doctors' that subjects are 'so obliged to come to the aid of their King' that 'if they do not do so, or if

---

[68] Martín González de Cellorigo, *Memorial de la política necessaria, y útil restauración a la república de España, y estados de ella, y del desempeño universal de estos reynos* (Valladolid, 1600), fo. 29b.

[69] Pedro Fernández Navarrete, *Conservación de monarquias y discursos políticos* (Madrid, 1805), p. 111.

anyone impedes them in the payment [of taxes] he would incur a sin in addition to the punishment imposed by the King'.[70] A number of writers share Jerónimo de Ceballos' impatience with the long, elaborate, costly and uncertain procedures involved in the granting of consent and actively debate the circumstances in which the king could override a negative vote of the Cortes or bypass, in whole or in part, the established constitutional order of parliamentary and urban consent. For them the crucial concept is necessity. Fernández Navarrete argues that because subjects have an immediate obligation to serve their king with taxes, in times of desperate need a king has no reason to await 'the tardy resolutions of the Cortes'. He explains, by way of analogy, that 'when a pilot sails in fair weather he does not throw overboard the merchandise ... in his care; but when storms oblige him to lighten his ship, he does not await the consent of the owners to eject even the most precious luxuries'.[71] The leading political theorist of the reign of Philip IV, Diego de Saavedra Fajardo, also accepts the proposition that in times of necessity kings can impose taxes unilaterally, arguing that their right to tax belongs to them by virtue of their 'supreme dominion' and that when taxes 'are just and necessary, the consent of the subjects is not required'.[72] Nevertheless he considers it to be prudent for the king to seek parliamentary consent 'because everything that can be executed with absolute authority need not be'. This doctrine of necessity was very much in vogue at Philip IV's court where few would have contradicted Pedro Barbosa Homen's dictum that 'need renders licit what would otherwise be illicit'.[73]

Those writers who were constitutionalist in political orientation or generally hostile to taxation raise a very different set of issues for discussion. They underline the unpopularity of taxes among the members of the general public and warn of the potential for taxes to provoke revolt. Like Eugenio Narbona, they note that 'tributes and taxes' are 'the most abhorrent thing to the people' and advise kings to be cautious when imposing them.[74] Vicente Mut is blunt on this point. He writes:

The people greatly resent the imposition, because wealth is the security they love the most... They look at danger from afar, money from close-up ... They consider the

---

[70] Thomás Cerdán de Tallada, *Veroliquium in reglas de estado, según derecho divino, natural, canónico y civil, y leyes de Castilla* (Valencia, 1604), p. 97.

[71] Fernández Navarrete, *Conservación de monarquías*, pp. 111–12.

[72] Saavedra Fajardo, *Idea de un príncipe político cristiano representado en cien empresas*, ed. Vicente García Diego (Madrid, 1927), III, pp. 179–82.

[73] Pedro Barbosa Homen, *Discursos de la jurídica y verdadera razón de estado* (Coimbra, 1629), p. 211.

[74] Eugenio Narbona, *Doctrina política civil* (Madrid, 1621), p. 86.

war maintained at their cost to be unjust [and] counsel peace because the vulgar have no interest in reputation, nor in justice tinged with self-interest and, ordinarily, love money more than life.

Mut concludes: the king's subjects 'are more obedient when less taxed'.[75]

These writers tend to emphasize the importance of moderation in taxation. Taxes, they argue, should never be excessive and every effort should be made to ensure that the wealth of the kingdom is preserved. They argue that the true wealth of the kingdom is determined less by the size of the king's coffers than by the prosperity of its citizens. As Andrés Mendo states: 'The treasure of the kings is not the Fisc but having well-off subjects', to which he adds: 'Rarely does the Fisc grow without danger to the Republic'.[76] Mendo argues that taxation is 'a right' of kings tied to their 'dominion ... without which they could not maintain the state nor defend themselves against their enemies'. Nevertheless he urges kings to tax only when absolutely necessary, 'to adjust taxes to the strength of each person', and 'never to impoverish the kingdom'. Suárez de Figueroa makes the same point more graphically when he writes of the obligation that kings have 'to avoid occasions for bleedings' and to foster 'the blood and the substance of the body of which they are the head'.[77] Typically, these oppositional writers condemn the high costs of government, attack avaricious officials and tax collectors, and lament the depleted condition of the realm. Typically they also uphold the principle of consent and the right of subjects to reject government tax proposals. Andrés Mendo claims, more by way of injunction than as fact, that 'never' have Spain's 'Catholic Princes' agreed to impose heavy taxes, even 'those considered to be inexcusable, except with the consent of the Realm'.[78] In the same vein, Fray Juan de Madariaga reminds the proctors and aldermen whose responsibility it is to approve taxes that 'where just causes for the imposition of taxes are lacking, or more is conceded than can be afforded by the Kingdom, not only those who ask, but the Proctors of the Cortes who concede them, commit a sin and are obliged to make restitution to the Realm'.[79]

The opinions of all of these writers, whether pro-absolutist or constitutionalist, echo a debate that also consumed the political community in

---

[75] Vicente Mut, *El principe en la guerra y en la paz* (Madrid, 1640), p. 104.

[76] Andrés Mendo, *Principe perfecto y ministros avisados. Documentos politicos y morales* (León, 1662), pp. 39–40.

[77] Christoval Suárez de Figueroa, *Varias noticias importantes a la humana comunicación* (Madrid, 1621), p. 109.

[78] Mendo, *Principe perfecto*, p. 40.

[79] Fray Juan de Madariaga, *Del senado y de su principe* (Valencia, 1617), fo. 474.

seventeenth-century Spain. Indeed the intellectuals of the period were well-attuned to current political discussions.[80] Many of those who wrote on taxation, even some of the most academic, wrote within the context of actual subsidy debates. In his *De regnorum iustitia*, for example, Roa Dávila raises issues directly pertinent to the debate over the *millones* of 1588–90. Likewise Mariana's *De rege* and Alamos de Barrientos' *Discurso político* reflect debates over Philip II's proposed permanent subsidy in the late 1590s, just as Lisón y Biedma's *Apuntamientos* and Ceballos' *Arte real* reflect the debates provoked by Olivares' attempted fiscal reforms in the 1620s. On the reverse side of the coin, the debates that occurred within the royal councils, the Cortes, and the municipal councils 'reveal an extensive local awareness of theological and *ius commune* principles and of history and legislation', providing thereby strong evidence that 'the great neo-Scholastic and civil law theorists of the sixteenth century were not . . . of merely academic importance'.[81] The familiarity of royal councillors, proctors and aldermen with these ideas is not entirely surprising in that we might safely assume that most senior officials of the crown and many urban officials were university trained and had imbibed the wisdom of the School of Salamanca first hand.[82]

The debates that took place in the Cortes and the cities turned largely on two key issues: the reciprocal obligations of king and kingdom, and the appropriate balance between the king's financial needs and the capacity of the realm to pay. Those proctors who opposed the renewal of the *millones* in the late 1590s, for example, rested their case on the poverty of the kingdom. 'This kingdom', declared Gerónimo de Salamanca from Burgos, 'cannot provide any aid without notable damage . . . and if it does so it will not be doing His Majesty a service but a great disservice.'[83] Likewise at the Cortes of 1623 the dissidents argued that 'conserving the strength and wealth of His Majesty's vassals is judged to be the best service we can make to him', to

---

[80] Pereña, 'Perspectiva histórica', pp. 174–9.

[81] I. A. A. Thompson, 'Castile', in John Miller, ed., *Absolutism in seventeenth-century Europe* (London, 1990), pp. 74–5.

[82] On the education of the Habsburg bureaucracy see Richard L. Kagan, *Students and society in early modern Spain* (Baltimore, 1974); Janine Fayard, *Los miembros del consejo de Castilla (1621–1746)* (Madrid, 1974); and Jean-Marc Pelorson, *Les letrados. Juristes castillans sous Philippe III* (Poitiers, 1980). Prosopographical studies of Castile's urban élite are in their infancy and there is little knowledge yet of the educational backgrounds of the *regidores*. For pioneering studies in this area see I. A. A. Thompson, 'Cortes y ciudades: tipología de los Procuradores (extracción social, representatividad)', in *Las cortes de Castilla y León en la edad moderna* (Valladolid, 1989), pp. 221–38, and Adriano Gutiérrez Alonso, *Estudio sobre la decadencia de Castilla. La ciudad de Valladolid en el siglo XVII* (Valladolid, 1989), pp. 297–328.

[83] *ACC*, XII, pp. 444–5.

which argument Olivares' countered that 'as there is no kingdom without a king, nor king without a kingdom, it is essential that we give to each its due ... not seeking our own conservation but that of our king'.[84]

The intellectual indebtedness of the politicians to the political theorists is attested to by the academic tone and substance of these debates. In the Cortes of 1592–99, the proctor from Seville, don Rodrigo Sánchez Doria, set out as preamble to his arguments against Philip II's proposed subsidy the following analysis. 'I understand', he stated,

that the need of his Majesty and that of the kingdom are not two things, but one, and that it is almost impossible to separate them, as the harm or success experienced by the kingdom pertains to His Majesty, without these being two parts but one, and so much one that it is almost impossible, in the state of the kingdom today, to remedy the one [need] without very great damage to the other.[85]

At the opening of the Cortes of 1599 the president of the council of Castile countered this analysis in an equally academic fashion by stating that:

one cannot divide his Majesty and the Kingdom, as they are one thing, and if the head aches, which is his Majesty, all parts of the body ache, and if the body aches, the head aches, and [the King] being at present in such pain, the Kingdom, which is the body, has an obligation to attempt to relieve him, although it feels weak and burdened, in order to ensure that the pain does not become greater and the sickness incurable.[86]

Another link between political theory and political practice is revealed by the apparent acceptance by the proctors and aldermen of what Laynez described as the judicial nature of their function in the approval of taxation. For example, in 1594, Miguel de Salamanca, the proctor from Burgos, referred to the Cortes as the kingdom's 'proper tribunal'.[87] An anonymous letter dating from the 1640s presents the analogy in greater detail. The author argues that when voting for new taxes the proctors:

proceed. . .as judges to determine if the hardship in which his Majesty finds himself, and the Republic, is such that a new tribute is warranted ... because new taxes cause grief to the Realm. Thus they run an equal risk of committing a mortal sin by conceding His Majesty a greater quantity than what he needs ... taking account of the state of the Republic ... or, on the contrary, by denying the Prince what he needs for our defence ...[88]

---

[84] *ACC*, XXX, pp. 10–12. [85] *ACC*, XIV, p. 565. [86] *ACC*, XVIII, pp. 426–31.
[87] *ACC*, XIII, pp. 407–8.
[88] BL, Add. 9936, fos. 221–23. The allusion to the war with Portugal and to the proposal that the cities approve the tax on *juros* suggests that this anonymous letter was written in the 1640s.

When weighing the balance of probabilities between the king's needs and the kingdom's means, the proponents of taxation employed arguments identical to those of the pro-absolutist writers. At the Cortes of 1623 the crown advised the proctors that it is 'certain that when these two considerations are in competition, the first is to be given primacy'.[89] But the counter-argument as advanced by the constitutionalist writers was also well-established in political circles. For example, the solicitor to the city of Cordoba advised the aldermen there that in balancing king's needs with the kingdom's means 'the office of Your Excellencies in general and in particular, and what you have sworn to, is to see to the well-being of the republic and its villages'.[90]

Politicians, particularly the senior ministers of the crown, also joined with political theorists in openly and vigorously debating whether or not parliamentary and urban consent for taxation was constitutionally required. This was the principal topic for discussion at the meeting of the council of state on 22 September 1634.[91] The specific issue was whether the prospect of open war with France justified the introduction of new taxes without the approval of the Cortes. The arguments presented by the councillors reflect the divisions of opinion among contemporary political theorists. Francisco Antonio de Alarcón affirms categorically the right of the Cortes to approve new taxes, basing his case on the standard claim that, as the persons best informed of the state of their provinces, the proctors were most capable of balancing the subsidies with the strength of the contributors. 'On this', he argues, 'depends the justice of what is imposed.' José González and Antonio Contreras adopt the extreme opposite position, arguing that the defence of the realm supersedes all other considerations including the right of consent. 'Your Majesty does not have to negotiate with the proctors of the Cortes', they contend, 'because whether the vassals of these Kingdoms serve Your Majesty does not depend on their will.' Luis Gudiel y Peralta adopts a more moderate position. He agrees that the king can circumvent the approval of the Cortes, seeking the consent of the cities instead, but he considers the wisest course of action to be to follow tradition and make no change. In their contributions to this debate, the count of Castrillo and the count-duke of Olivares address the main point only indirectly. However, by condemning the parliamentary proctors and urban aldermen for their lack of cooperation and alleged peculation, they make their attitude toward the constitutionalist forces in Castile abundantly clear.

[89] *ACC*, XXXIX, pp. 140–3.
[90] AM Cordoba, Libros Capitulares, 1600, fos. 369–72, 30 August 1600.
[91] AHN, Est. lib. 853, fos. 1–68.

We can presume that it was within the context of these debates at the king's court during the mid-1630s that the written exchange between the count of Castrillo and his confessor took place. As we know, it was not unusual for senior government officials to seek theological counsel. And as we also know, in giving counsel Castrillo's confessor had an extensive body of scholarly opinion upon which to draw. In the document Castrillo's confessor agrees that just wars justify increased taxation. Therefore he is of the opinion that the consciences of those proctors voting in favour of additional taxation need not be troubled. But he qualifies this opinion by noting that: 'if the gravity of the taxes will harm and oppress the realm more than the actual hostilities ... they cannot be demanded or imposed in conscience because, however binding are the obligations of subjects and vassals to serve and defend their lord, they are never obliged to exceed what is possible'. In his view, the task of the proctors in these circumstances is to weigh carefully the cost of the tax to the realm against the potential costs associated with the actual dangers facing it, and to choose the lesser. Each proctor has to make this decision on his own, guided by his own, individual conscience. 'Although it is legitimate for a prince to use his authority to persuade him', he maintains, 'if the proctor reaches a contrary opinion he will sin if he fails to follow it.' As for seeking the advice of theologians and jurists, the confessor advises that each proctor should be prepared to follow his own mind 'because God gave men liberty and variation in their feelings and opinions and from this variety what is right will emerge'. If in doubt, however, he should accept the guidance of 'learned, grave and prudent men of approved life and Christianity', in which case the shared opinions of two or three eminent theologians could be accepted 'as probable'.

The political leanings of Castrillo's anonymous confessor were obviously 'republican' or constitutionalist – more compatible with the political doctrines espoused by Juan de Mariana and Mateo Lisón y Biedma than with those of Roa Dávila and Jerónimo de Ceballos. This conclusion leads one to suspect that this documented consultation might well be spurious. Despite its compelling verisimilitude, it is not impossible that it is yet another example of the genre of fictionalized dialogues that figured so prominently in the oppositional literature to royal taxation at the time. Yet, whether fictional or not, the manuscript helps us to gain insight into the political culture of Olivares' Castile.

To say that Castile's political culture was of a confessional nature may be an overstatement, but it contains more than an element of truth. Those directly involved in the making of complex political decisions on such issues as taxation were buffeted by competing pressures and divergent opinions.

That they sought certainty by seeking out expert opinion, or that they sought assurances that they were acting in good conscience, is hardly surprising. Their agonizing over political choices is abundantly evident, and nowhere more so than in Philip IV's correspondence with Sor María de Agreda. When their discussion turned to taxation Philip candidly admits to Sor María his dilemma as to how he might relieve his subjects from a crushing burden of taxation while meeting his obligations as king. He confesses to her in July 1656 that 'the necessitous state in which my vassals find themselves afflicts me greatly, and my suffering is increased by my not being able to remedy the situation as much as I would like since it results from the taxes required to provide for the defence of religion and the Monarchy'.[92] For her part Sor María stresses Philip's moral responsibility for the well-being of his subjects. 'For the love of God', she exclaims in November, 1661, 'would that taxes could be moderated for the poor . . . I am told that some villages are abandoned, that people are sustaining themselves on barley bread and hay, and that many are in despair.'[93]

When kings and statesmen, like Philip IV and the count of Castrillo, or indeed when parliamentary proctors and urban aldermen, faced politico-ethical dilemmas of this type, they had an extensive body of theological and political doctrine on which to draw. Their concern, therefore, was not simply to act in good conscience, but to make decisions based on a fully informed conscience. They achieved this purpose through the agency of their confessors who acted as the mediators between political theory and political practice. By drawing our attention to this intriguing aspect of seventeenth-century Spanish political culture, the written exchange between the count of Castrillo and his confessor, whether spurious or not, serves to enhance our understanding of the context of politics in Olivares' Castile.

[92] Silvela, *Cartas*, II, p. 452.   [93] Ibid., II, pp. 670–1.

3

Clio and the crown: writing history in
Habsburg Spain

RICHARD L. KAGAN

Veo con mucha simpatía este amor que sientes por Córdoba, tu patria
chica, que tanto se refleja en tu última carta.

I am very sympathetic to the love that you feel for Cordoba, your
home town, which is expressed so well in your last letter.

Juan Ginés de Sepúlveda to Francisco de Argote (1552)[1]

Writing in 1789, León de Arroyal, one of the lesser-known figures of the
Spanish Enlightenment, offered a somewhat unusual vision of his country at
a moment when the centralizing policies of Spain's Bourbon monarchy were
in full force: 'We ought to consider Spain', he wrote, 'as a country composed
of various confederated republics united under the government and protection of its monarchs. We should imagine each town as a miniature
kingdom, and the kingdom itself as a large town.'[2]

Help in the preparation of this essay was generously provided by Antonio Feros, Orest Ranum,
Geoffrey Parker, Marianna S. Simpson, Gabrielle Spiegel and the members of my 1993–94
Graduate Seminar in Habsburg Spain – Benjamin Ehlers, Alice Harris, Jeri McIntosh,
Cristina Sbarra and David Wood. I am grateful to them all. I am equally indebted to David W.
Cohen: his work on the 'production of history' (cf. David W. Cohen, *The combing of history*
(Chicago, 1993)) underlies my understanding of Habsburg historiography.
[1] *Epistolario de Juan Ginés de Sepúlveda*, ed. Angel Losada (Madrid, 1979), p. 197.
[2] León de Arroyal, *Cartas político-económicas al conde de Lerena*, ed. Antonio Elorza (Madrid,
1968), p. 205, letter dated San Clemente, 13 July 1789. The original reads: 'La España
debemos considerarla compuesta por varias repúblicas confederadas, bajo el gobierno y

For all its boldness, Arroyal's idea of a confederate Spain, a union of independent city-states or republics, actually belongs to a deep current in Spanish cultural and political life that John Elliott has conceived in terms of the vital and sometimes conflicting tensions between centre and periphery.[3] Other essays in this volume examine the extent to which this enduring theme in Spanish history manifested itself both culturally and politically. This essay addresses the question of centre versus periphery from a historiographical perspective and aims to compare the history produced by the monarchy's official chroniclers – the *cronistas del rey* – with that written for individual cities and towns. For heuristic purposes, I will refer to the former as royal history, and the latter, works of local history, as chorography.

On one level these two modes of historical production had similar aims. Methodologically, both paid lip service to humanist scholarship and sought to make history into a discipline based on documentary evidence and dedicated to accuracy and narrative truth. Yet the royal historians' unitary vision of Spain's past – and presumably its future – had little in common with that of the chorographers, many of whom, at least implicitly, shared Arroyal's vision of Spain as a union of independent republics.

I Royal history

Although royal history, generally in the form of court chronicles, had existed in Castile since the days of Alfonso X (1252–1284), the office of *coronista* or *cronista del rey* only dated to around 1450.[4] It was then that Juan de Mena, Latin secretary of King John II, was referred to as the *coronista del rey*. The circumstances surrounding the creation of this office are as yet unclear. The institutionalization of state-sponsored or 'official history' did not begin anywhere in Europe much before the middle years of the fifteenth

---

protección de nuestros reyes. Cada villa la hemos de mirar como un pequeño reino, y todo el reino como una villa grande.'
[3] See John H. Elliott, 'England and Europe: a common malady', in *Origins of the English Civil War*, ed. Conrad Russell (London, 1973), pp. 246–57, and especially his *Revolt of the Catalans* (Cambridge, 1963).
[4] Surprising as it may seem, the study of royal history during the Habsburg era has yet to attract serious scholarly attention. There is not even a definitive list of the scholars who occupied the important post of royal chronicler. In comparison, the creation and evolution of the office of Cronista Mayor de las Indias is examined in Romulo D. Carbia, *La cronica ofical de las Indias occidentales* (La Plata, 1934) and, more generally, Francsco Esteve Barba, *La historiografía indiana* (Madrid, 1964), pp. 112–36. For the *Cronista del Reino de Aragón*, see Conde de Viñaza, *Los cronistas de Aragón* (Madrid, 1904), and for those of Valencia, Vicente Castañeda y Alcocer, *Los cronistas de Valencia* (Valencia, 1920).

century.[5] In the case of Castile, Brian Tate hypothesizes that the *cronista del rey*'s appearance should be linked to the growing popularity of history itself and specifically to the monarchy's (ultimately unsuccessful) attempt to reassert its traditional monopoly over historical writing. In Tate's view, the factional conflicts of the era fostered the production of history, but history of a kind that the monarchy did not necessarily approve. When confronted with the prospect that history might do something other than offer a laudatory portrait of his achievements, John II offered Mena an extra salary (or *ración*) in exchange for an 'official' history of his reign. Mena's appointment, however, did not put an end to historical writing inimical to the monarchy's interests. Later in the century, for example, Lorenzo Galíndez de Carvajal, one of the Catholic Monarchs' chief advisers, still complained that 'everybody sets out to write what he pleases, praising only a few and prejudicing the many'.[6]

The desire to have a history that served the crown's interests also explains why Ferdinand and Isabel, shortly after their accession to the throne in 1474, dismissed the chroniclers appointed by their predecessors and replaced them with scholars of their own choosing. In addition, the monarchs endowed the office of royal chronicler with new prestige, partly by granting its incumbents a regular salary of 40,000 *maravedís* per annum (later doubled by Charles V). For their part, the royal chroniclers were expected 'to write, declare, and collect all the material pertinent to the royal chronicle', to emulate the style of Livy and other ancient historians and, finally, 'to embellish their chronicles with judgements based on philosophy and sound doctrine'.[7]

This, of course, was a tall order, although one which demonstrates that the Renaissance, historiographically at least, had reached Castile. It also speaks to the importance the Catholic Monarchs attached to the writing of history: royal history was to be a hedge against those individuals who, according to another royal chronicler, Gonzalo Fernández de Oviedo, wrote about the monarchy 'without any feeling ... with bad intentions...[and] simply to criticize'. For Oviedo, only a royal chronicler such as himself, paid out of the royal purse, could be trusted to write about royalty 'with the truth

---

[5] Bernard Guenée, *Histoire et culture historique dans l'occident médiéval* (Paris, 1980). See also François Fossier, 'La charge d'historiographe du seizième au dix-neuvième siècle', *Revue historique*, 258 (1977), 73–92.

[6] Robert B. Tate, 'Mythology in Spanish historiography of the Middle Ages and Renaissance', *Hispanic Review*, 22 (1954), 1–16. See also his 'El cronista real castellano durante el siglo quince', in *Homenaje a Pedro Sainz Rodríguez* (Madrid, 1986), III, pp. 659–68, and José Luis Bermejo Cabrero, 'Orígenes del oficio de cronista real', *Hispania*, 40 (1980), 395–409.

[7] Bermejo Cabrero, 'Orígenes del oficio de cronista real', p. 408.

and clarity that is required'. He even likened the office of *cronista del rey* to that of an 'evangelist' charged with the responsibility of memorializing for eternity glories and honours that would otherwise fade with time.[8] Official history, in short, was more objective and truthful history simply because it was produced by an officer of the crown.

The royal chronicler was therefore a court official first and a historian second. On the one hand, he was to write good, that is, truthful history – 'my job', wrote one seventeenth-century chronicler, 'is to tell the truth' – as well as to offer the moral instruction and advice that history, as a humanistic discipline, was expected to convey.[9] But royal chroniclers also had to write histories that embellished the honour and reputation of the monarchy itself. Pedro de Navarra underscored the complex relationship between 'truthful' history and history that served political ends in a treatise on royal chroniclers that he dedicated to Philip II in 1565. Navarra admitted that a royal chronicler required 'neutrality' if his writing was ever to gain authority and respect, but he also recognized that the chronicler had to offer 'a more perfect notice of the [prince's] good deeds and to put them in perpetual memory'. This balancing act was delicate, certainly one not easily learnt. For this reason Navarra suggested that princes looking for chroniclers should scrupulously avoid those 'who are ignorant of learning, crude in style, low in judgement, lacking in memory, quick in believing, slow in understanding, vile in blood, obscure of life and strangers to virtue and grace'.[10]

Few of the chroniclers who served the Habsburgs were as talented as those Navarra envisaged, but most understood the complex and sometimes contradictory nature of their responsibilities. But what kind of history were these chroniclers expected to write? Their first obligation was to craft a vernacular chronicle of contemporary events, a kind of *apologia* favourable both to the interests of the monarchy and the personal image of the monarch himself. Self-advertisement of this sort had been the task of the chroniclers who had served Spain's medieval monarchs, and this is exactly what Ferdinand and Isabel expected of Hernando de Pulgar, Galíndez de Carvajal and the other individuals they appointed to the newly regularized office of *cronista del rey*. After 1492, however, partly in keeping with the momentous events of that triumphal year, the monarchs developed an interest in history

[8] Gonzalo Fernández de Oviedo, *Libro de la cámara real del príncipe don Juan* (Madrid, 1880), p. 174.
[9] BNM, ms. 5732, fo. 49. Letter of Tomás Tamayo de Vargas, 18 August 1639.
[10] Pedro de Navarra, 'Diálogos qual debe ser el chronista del príncipe', in *Diálogos de la eternidad del ánima* (Tolosa, 1565). Pedro de Navarra is the *nom de plume* of Pierre d'Albret, bishop of Commenges.

with a more universalist bent, a kind of *De laude Hispaniae*, that would demonstrate the antiquity and grandeur of both Spain and its monarchy to a European audience. They entrusted this particular task to Antonio de Nebrija (officially appointed *cronista del rey* in 1509) and the transplanted Italian scholar, Lucio Marineo Siculo. Ideally, these humanist scholars would be able not only to describe the monarchy's achievements in glowing, Ciceronian Latin but also to document that the *imperium* of their Catholic Majesties was second to none. Aiding the two chroniclers in this enterprise was the creative mind of Annius of Viterbo, an Italian Dominican who, writing under the pen name of Berossus, a Chaldean historian of the third century BC, invented a royal genealogy 'proving' that the Catholic Monarchs were the direct descendants of Tubal, grandson of Noah and the legendary first ruler of Spain.[11]

Charles V did little to change this twofold division of the chroniclers' tasks, although the emperor's initial concern was a general history of Spain itself. Starting in 1523, the Cortes of Castile urged Charles to sponsor an authoritative, printed edition or *recopilación* of such older chronicles as Alfonso X's *crónica general*. 'It is right', the Cortes stated, 'that the truth about past things be known; this is not possible in other, private books [manuscripts?] that are being read.'[12] The emperor toyed with this project until 1539, when, following a direct appeal by the Cortes to the memory of his ancestors, he finally named Florián de Ocampo, one of Nebrija's pupils, to the office of *cronista del rey*, specifically assigning him the task of revising and publishing the *crónica general*. The methodical Ocampo, a scholar much criticized for his lack of critical judgement (and for 'dullness' by Washington Irving) may not have been the ideal choice, but by the time of his death in 1558 he had at least succeeded in publishing a narrative which began with Tubal and continued to the end of the Second Punic War (208 BC).[13]

Ocampo's successor on the project was Juan Paéz de Castro, a scholar quick to advise the emperor about the importance of writing history but one who did nothing to advance the *crónica general*.[14] Just the opposite was true

---

11 Annius' list of mythical Spanish monarchs was included in his *Commentaria super opera auctorum diversorum de antiquitatibus loquentium* (Rome, 1498). See Tate, 'Mythology in Spanish historiography', pp. 11–13.

12 *Cortes de los antiguos reinos de Castilla y León*, ed. Real Academia de Historia (Madrid, 1882), IV, p. 382. The Cortes presented similar petitions to Charles in 1525, 1528 and 1538.

13 Ocampo's work appeared as *Los cinco libros primeros de la crónica general de España* (Medina del Campo, 1553).

14 Paéz de Castro's 'De las cosas necesarias para escribir historia', which refers to his plans to write a history of Charles, is printed in *Ciudad de Dios*, 28 (1892), 601–10, and 29 (1892), 27–37.

of his replacement, Ambrosio de Morales (1513–1591). This Cordoban humanist evidently regarded the *crónica* as a matter of national pride, and in fact claimed to have become a historian after hearing an Italian ambassador criticize 'the Spaniards for not having written a history of their antiquities and deeds'.[15] The incident may be apocryphal, but the glowing and some-what uncritical compendium of Spain's Roman antiquities that Morales published in 1575 as *Antigüedades de las ciudades de España* does read as if it were written with this Italian ambassador in mind. So too do his additions to the crónica general, which brought the story forward to the eleventh century. Morales' history, however, was by no means comprehensive. He ignored, for example, the internal history of Al-Andalus, focusing instead on the Reconquest, the Spaniards' centuries-old determination to turn back the tide of Islam. In this sense Morales, who started work on these sections of the *crónica* around 1572, was evidently hoping to give his Italian acquaintance some perspective as to why Spain had successfully led the Holy League to victory against the Turks at Lepanto in 1571.[16]

Yet despite his patriotism, Morales left the *crónica* unfinished at his death in 1591. At this point a royal official upset by 'the annoyances and never finishing of the historians' advised Philip II to entrust the project to a *junta* composed of two or three scholars and one soldier. Such a *junta*, the monarch learned, could complete the *crónica* 'quickly and cheaply'.[17] But Philip – an early sceptic of collaborative history – rejected this cumbersome arrangement in favour of Esteban de Garibay (1533–1599), an energetic Basque historian who had already published a survey of Spanish history that began with the Creation and ended with King Pelayo in the eighth century.[18] But Garibay too proved a disappointment: during his five years as chronicler – an office he apparently exploited as a means of lending additional authority to his previous publications – he did little, if anything, to advance the *crónica general*.[19] Philip III (1598–1621) had better luck with

---

[15] Cited in Ambrosio de Morales, *Viaje santo .... por orden del rey Phelipe II a los reynos de León, de Galicia y Principado de Asturias* (Madrid, 1765), p. x.

[16] Morales' contributions to the *crónica* (libros 6–17) were published as *La coronica general de España* (Alcalá de Henares, 1574); *Los otros dos libros de la coronica general de España* (Alcalá de Henares, 1577); and *Los cinco libros postreros de la coronica general de España* (Cordoba, 1586).

[17] ABZ, carpeta 159, fo. 107. Juan López de Velasco, royal chronicler of the Indies, to Philip II. The original reads: 'en muy breve tiempo y no a mucha costa a S.M.'

[18] Esteban de Garibay, *Los xl libros d'el compendio historial de las chrónicas de España* (Antwerp, 1571).

[19] On 30 January 1592 Garibay petitioned for the office of *cronista* 'without salary'. However, one counsellor warned Philip that 'solo lo pretendo para sacar con mas authoridad a luz sus obras'. See ABZ, carpeta 160, fo. 54.

Fray Prudencio de Sandoval (1551–1620). Appointed royal chronicler in 1600, this Benedictine scholar proved exceptionally productive. In addition to a history of Charles V and other works, Sandoval published two books on the early kings of Castile and León that brought the *crónica general* forward into the twelfth century.[20] Even so, at his death in 1620, the *recopilación* of Spanish history envisioned by Charles V still had a long way to go.

At this juncture, Philip III abandoned this project for good, largely because Juan de Mariana's *General history of Spain*, published originally in Latin (1592) and then in Castilian (1601), provided what several generations of royal chroniclers could not: a comprehensive, albeit castilianized vision of Spanish history that emphasized the formative role of the monarchy in the creation of a unitary – and catholic – Spanish state. Mariana's history may not have been exactly what the Habsburgs wanted – Antonio de Herrera y Tordesillas (1549–1626), another of Philip III's chroniclers, described parts of the book as 'pure conjecture' and additionally faulted Mariana for having failed to do the archival research necessary 'to extract the whole truth, which is the soul of history'.[21] On the other hand, Herrera considered it 'the best history we have', and in 1622 probably helped to persuade Spain's new monarch, Philip IV, to respond favourably to Mariana's request for a subsidy to publish a revised and expanded edition of his great work.[22] When this appeared the following year, Mariana's history effectively became Spain's official history, a status it maintained for almost two centuries. Reprinted (in Castilian) in eighteen editions before 1800, the 'incomparable Mariana', as one eighteenth-century observer called him, offered a history with which 'even educated ladies of the provinces were familiar'.[23]

With the problem of the *crónica general* resolved, royal chroniclers in the seventeenth century turned to other subjects, mostly of a somewhat more monographic, and generally more contemporary nature. Specialization of

---

[20] These included *Chrónica del emperador de España Alonso VII* (Madrid, 1600), much criticized for its glorification of the Sandoval clan, the duke of Lerma in particular, and the *Historia de los reyes de Castilla y León* (Madrid, 1615). Sandoval's *Vida y hechos del Emperador Carlos V* was first published in 1604. For his biography, see Vicente Castañeda, *El cronista Prudencio de Sandoval* (Madrid, 1919).

[21] The original reads 'sacar en limpio la verdad, alma de la historia'. BNM, ms. 5781, fo. 130. For the reception of Mariana's history, see Georges Cirot, *Mariana historien* (Bordeaux, 1904) and Alan Soons, *Juan de Mariana* (Boston, 1982), pp. 23–46.

[22] For this decision, see BNM, ms. 18662, consulta de Cámara, 29 August 1622. The Cámara, recognizing that this 'eminent historian has done a great service for the Monarchy', recommended that Mariana be awarded 1,000 ducats.

[23] Antonio Valladares cited in Richard Herr, *Eighteenth-century revolution in Spain* (Princeton, 1958), p. 340.

this sort had in fact begun under Charles V,[24] but by the early seventeenth century the *cronistas del rey* were expected to concentrate on the 'history of these times'.[25] A consulta, drafted by the council of Castile in 1603, defined their responsibilities in no uncertain terms:

what the chroniclers have to do is not only write about the lives of kings and about the wars, treaties, victories and good and bad things that happen to them, along with the deeds and achievements they do and undertake; they must also observe and write a narrative about many other and varied things and events taking place in these kingdoms, including those that directly concern the monarchs and princes as well as their subjects and vassals.[26]

The council's tilt towards contemporary history was partly occasioned by the publication of Mariana's *Historia general*. More directly, it reflected the historical philosophy of Herrera y Tordesillas, the most influential and certainly most prolific and widely read royal chronicler of the early seventeenth century.[27] Herrera was much influenced by the great sixteenth-century Florentine historian, Francesco Guicciardini, especially by his belief that historians ought to write about contemporary events so that 'from a knowledge of such occurrences, so varied and so grave, everyone may derive many precedents, salutary both for himself and for the public weal'.[28] Herrera understood this to mean that history should be a 'guide for action', an argument developed in his *Discurso y tratado de la historia* which he dedicated to Philip IV. Here he expressed the idea that history's ultimate goal was to explain why things happened as they did, as well as the advice that historians could accomplish this goal best when they, following his example, focused on contemporary history. Herrera continued by claiming that historians' knowledge of contemporary events gave them a special

---

[24] For the emperor's *cronistas*, ten in all, see Albert Morel-Fatio, *L'historiographie de Charles Quint* (Paris, 1913), and Agustin Redondo, *Antonio de Guevara (1480?–1545) et l'Espagne de son temps* (Geneva, 1976), pp. 303–49.

[25] The phrase, 'historia de nuestros tiempos' may be found in ABZ, carpeta 160, fo. 54, consulta of 30 January 1592 advising on the appointment of Garibay as *cronista*.

[26] BNM, ms. 1753, fo. 49. This council prepared this consulta in response to a petition for the office of *cronista* from the Leonese historian, Antonio Llobera, who had expressed an interest in continuing the *historia general* in order to perpetuate the memory of the 'the great and glorious deeds of the Spanish nation'. The petition was rejected.

[27] Herrera has not received the scholarly attention he deserves. For a brief biography, see the introduction to his *Historia general de los hechos de castellanos en las islas e tierra firme del mar oceano*, ed. Mariano Cuesta Domingo (Madrid, 1991). Some of his political involvements are discussed in C. Pérez Bustamante, *El cronista Antonio de Herrera y la historia de Alejandro Farnese* (Madrid, 1933).

[28] Francesco Guicciardini, *History of Italy*, ed. and trans. Sidney Alexander (New York, 1969), p. 3.

obligation to offer monarchs sound judgement and advice. 'Simple narration', he wrote, 'is not enough ... Historians have an obligation to offer precepts and judgements.'[29]

Clio, in short, was to serve the crown, a concept which Philip IV (who, it might be noted, personally completed a translation of Guicciardini's *History of Italy* in 1633) embraced as his own. So, too, did Philip's chroniclers, virtually all of whom wrote books, propaganda tracts and other treatises that addressed contemporary issues and were principally designed to augment Philip's authority and reputation.[30] Herrera y Tordesillas did exactly this. So did Tomás Tamayo de Vargas, the Toledan antiquarian who, soon after his appointment as royal chronicler in 1626, was asked to write a pamphlet publicizing the Spanish recapture of Bahía from the Dutch. Francisco de Rioja was even more of an official apologist. Appointed royal chronicler in 1621 by virtue of his friendship with Philip's favourite, the count-duke of Olivares, Rioja never wrote much history. He served instead as the count-duke's publicist, drafting various treatises in which he defended both his patron and his policies from attack. For his part, Olivares placed great stock in the use of history as an instrument of state. 'Truly our faults are many', he once advised the king, 'but one that is particularly grievous is the little attention given to history. It would be wise if Your Majesty specifically ordered it to be written by one of your historians or someone else capable of doing it.'[31]

In keeping with their role as the king's servants, the *cronistas del rey* – the adjective *mayor* was added in the 1630s – were also expected to serve as censors, watchdogs on the lookout for any work of history that might prove embarrassing to the crown. An early instance of this occurred in 1599 when Herrera y Tordesillas, who had been recently appointed Cronista Mayor de las Indias, recommended to the council of State that Lope de Vega's poem, *La Dragontea*, which dealt with the exploits of Sir Francis Drake, be withdrawn from circulation because it 'contains many things about the Indies that are false and in prejudice of many individuals who have served there well'.[32] Thirteen years later state security was also at stake when this

---

[29] Antonio de Herrera y Tordesillas, 'Discurso y tratado de la historia', BNM, ms. 3011, fo. 151. This treatise was published in his *Discursos morales, políticos e históricos*, ed. Juan Antonio de Zamacola (Madrid, 1804).

[30] The translation is discussed by R. A. Stradling, *Philip IV and the government of Spain, 1621–1665* (Cambridge, 1988), pp. 310–11.

[31] Quoted in John H. Elliott and Francisco de la Peña, *Memoriales y cartas del Conde Duque de Olivares* (Madrid, 1978), I, p. 53.

[32] For this and the following incidents of historical censorship, see Antonio Domínguez Ortiz, 'La censura de obras históricas en el siglo xvii español', *Chrónica nova*, 19 (1991), 113–21.

same council learned that 'secret papers' belonging to Juan Fernández de Velasco, constable of Castile and a former president of the council of Italy, were being used to write histories containing material of potential embarrassment to the crown. The council responded by requiring all ambassadors and viceroys to deposit their papers in the royal archives at Simancas and also by recommending that 'no one except for the royal chroniclers should write history'.

Although this particular measure came to naught, Philip IV remained keenly aware that his future reputation rested on historians' interpretations of his reign. As Guicciardini's translator and something of an amateur historian himself, Philip might have understood that historical truth was a relative concept, yet he held to the idea that all history should be royal history, a reflection of the monarchy's particular vision of past events. This helps to explain why, towards the end of his reign, Philip commissioned one final 'official' history of his accomplishments after complaining that 'writers of foreign and ill-disposed nations constantly publish accounts of my kingdoms and policies which are set far apart from the truth of events'.[33]

For similar reasons, Philip took issue with and repeatedly sought to suppress histories which put purely local or regional interests ahead of those of the monarchy. Particularly bothersome in this respect were 'regional' histories of the kind being written and published in the kingdom of Aragon. Castilians had been critical of the way Aragonese scholars wrote history ever since the Middle Ages, but friction increased after the appearance of Lucio Marineo Siculo's *De rebus hispaniae memorabilibus* (Alcalá de Henares, 1533), a book which many Castilian scholars believed accorded unnecessary prominence to Aragon. The situation worsened after 1548 when Aragonese officials, interested in promoting a particularly Aragonese version of Spain's past, created the office of Cronista del Reino de Aragón, initially awarding the position to Gerónimo de Zurita. Since books published in Aragon did not require the permission of the council of Castile, histories receiving Aragonese approval frequently met with disapproval in Castile. Such an incident occurred in 1578 when Zurita sought royal permission to have the second volume of his history of Aragon published and distributed in Castile.[34]

---

[33] Philip to Juan de Oyenguren, 9 May 1661, quoted in Stradling, *Philip IV*, p. 32. To counter these 'false' histories, Philip commissioned the royal councillor Francisco Ramos de Manzano to write the official version of the history of his reign. Ramos de Manzano does not figure among the list of Philip's *cronistas* nor is there any evidence that he ever completed the history in question.

[34] Paéz de Castro temporarily blocked the book's publication, pointing to its factual errors together with what he described as unjust criticism of the kings of Castile. Zurita eventually

Aragonese–Castilian differences over the interpretation of history surfaced again in the early seventeenth century, a moment when various partisan interpretations of the Aragonese uprising of 1590–91 were circulating simultaneously in manuscript. Although none of these histories, including the virulently anti-Aragonese account of the incident by Luis Cabrera de Córdoba, ever got into print, in 1622 the Aragonese authorities unilaterally gave their approval to the publication of Gonzalo de Céspedes y Meneses' *Historia apologética de los sucesos de Aragón* (Saragossa, 1622). The book criticized the way Philip II had handled the uprising and led the council of State to order its immediate confiscation on the grounds of sedition.[35] However, the underlying issue – the ability of Aragonese authorities to sanction the publication of histories independently of the crown – did not go away and eventually led to more stringent measures. In 1637, for example, Philip IV, suspicious of Aragonese intentions in the war against France, ordered the council of Aragon not to approve publication of any 'book of history' without express royal consent and in 1645 he strengthened this law by stipulating that such approval could only come from a 'minister of state'. The identity of the minister who would oversee such matters was left unspecified, but presumably most of the work would have fallen to one of the royal chroniclers.[36]

These somewhat clumsy attempts at historical censorship never amounted to very much, but they reflected Philip IV's deep-seated determination to make certain that history served the monarchy's particular interests and concerns. Towards this end Olivares in 1639 even proposed the appointment of a *historiador de España* whose job, presumably, would be to write the kind of centralist history that Philip desired.[37] The office of 'Spanish historian' was never to be, but the count-duke almost got what he wanted when, in 1640, Philip appointed the Cronista Mayor del Reino de Castilla, José Pellicer de Tovar, to the new office of Cronista Mayor de Aragón, a position whose incumbent was supposed to write Aragonese history with a monarchical slant. Pellicer's *Idea del principado de Catalunya* (Madrid, 1642), which supported the monarchy's position during the Catalan revolt, was clearly the kind of 'Spanish' history envisioned by Olivares and Philip IV.

Pellicer was not the last royal chronicler to write history designed to serve

obtained the permission he needed with help from Ambrosio de Morales. For the controversy, see Ambrosio de Morales, *Apologia de una información al consejo del rey en defensa de los anales de Gerónimo de Zurita* (Madrid, 1610).
[35] The controversy, which lasted until 1648, is summarized in AHN, Inquisición, *leg.* 447/40.
[36] Cited in Domínguez Ortiz, 'La censura de obras históricas'.
[37] BNM, ms. 8369, fo. 170, Tamayo de Vargas to Uztarroz.

what the monarchy perceived as Spain's national interest. Juan Andrés de Uztarroz, Gil González de Avila and Luis de Salazar y Castro and other late seventeenth-century chroniclers wrote (prolifically) in a similar vein, seemingly attempting to appropriate Spain's history as if it were the crown's to make and to interpret as it saw fit. But this attempt to force Spain's historical memory through a single, centralist mould ran counter to other historiographical traditions which offered a distinctly less unitary vision of the Spanish past. One of these traditions, briefly mentioned above, was regional history, exemplified not only by the historians of Aragon but by other seventeenth-century scholars who published histories honouring the memory of Catalonia, Valencia, Navarre and so on.[38] Another, and even more vital, was chorography, a genre whose authors served the particular historical interests of individual cities and whose outlook on the past was distinctly local. It follows that chorography's interpretation of Spanish history was far less integrated, and far less monarchical, than that written by the historians who worked for the king.

II Chorography

Rarely used today, chorography (derived from the Greek word for the study or science of places) was a Renaissance commonplace, a term widely employed by geographers and historians alike. Ptolemy had defined it in opposition to geography: the latter, he wrote, 'is concerned only with regions and their general characteristics' while chorography, which was meant to study details, is concerned with 'the smallest places conceivable'.[39] Peter Apianus, one of Charles V's geography teachers, offered a similar definition: 'The aim of chorography is to depict a particular place, just as an artist paints an ear or an eye or other parts of a man's head.'[40] So understood, chorography is very close to what the seventeenth-century Spanish lexicographer, Sebastián de Covarrubias, wrote about *topografía* ('a description of a place') as well as *describir*, which he defines as 'the act of

---

[38] These 'regional' histories include Jeroni Pujades, *Coronica universal del principat de Cathalunya* (Barcelona, 1609); Gaspar Escolano, *Décadas de la insigne y coronada ciudad y reinado de Valencia* [1610] (facsimile edition, Valencia, 1972); Lope Martínez de Isasti, *Compendio historial...de Guipuzcoa* [1625] (Bilbao, 1972); Juan Dameto, *Historia general del reyno baleárico* (Mallorca, 1632); José de Moret, *Anales del reyno de Navarra* (Pamplona, 1684–1715); and Luis Alfonso de Carvallo, *Antigüedades y cosas memorables del principado de Asturias* (Madrid, 1695). In 1620 the marqués de Auñón completed, but never published, a *Historia general de la Corona de Castilla*. See *ACC*, xxxv (Madrid, 1912), p. 256.

[39] Claudius Ptolemy, *Geography*, trans. Edward L. Stevenson (New York, 1932), book I, chapter 1.

[40] Petrus Apianus, *Libro de cosmographia* (Antwerp, 1548), chapter 4.

narrating or indicating with a pen some place or past event so realistically that it appears as if it were drawn'. 'Description', he writes, is 'narration, written or drawn, like the description of a province or a map.'[41]

In its narrowest sense, therefore, chorography constitutes a detailed description of a particular place. This could take the form of a map or a city view similar to those published in Braun and Hogenburg's *Civitates Orbis Terrarum*. As a literary genre, however, chorography is inseparable from local history of the kind written in the sixteenth and seventeenth centuries. These written descriptions were frequently the work of antiquarians interested primarily in archaeology and a city's place in antiquity.[42] But chorography was not necessarily restricted to the long distant past; it could just as easily examine contemporary events, as was the case of Gaspar Roig i Jalpi whose histories of Girona and Manresa included chapters on the Catalan revolt of 1640.[43] It is wrong therefore to equate chorography with antiquarianism, as some scholars have done. Rather, in keeping with the terminology of Renaissance historiography, chorography is best conceived of as 'particular history', which focuses on a specific time or place, as opposed to the broader, more expansive concerns of a 'general history' such as Mariana's.

No matter how it is defined, chorography in various guises enjoyed unprecedented popularity throughout early modern Europe. In England it appeared in county histories and topographical maps by such authors as William Lambarde and John Speed; in Germany in the many books modelled on Konrad Celtis' 1502 history and description of Nuremberg; and in France in the form of various local histories highlighting the uniqueness of individual cities and towns.[44] In Spain, chorography was several

---

[41] Sebastián de Covarrubias, *Tesoro de la lengua castellana* [1611] (Madrid, 1979), pp. 457, 967.

[42] Two such books are Luis Pons de Ycart, *Libro de las grandezas y cosas memorables de la metropolitana, insigne y famosa ciudad de Tarragona* (Lérida, 1572), and Rodrigo Caro, *Antigüedades, y principado de la ilustríssima ciudad de Sevilla y chorographía de su convento jurídico, o antigua chancillería* (Seville, 1634).

[43] Roig i Jalpi takes pride that neither city participated in this revolt. See his *Resumen historial de las grandezas y antigüedades de la ciudad de Gerona, y cosas memorables suyas eclesiásticas y seculares, assi de nuestros tiempos, como de los pasados* (Barcelona, 1678) and *Epitome histórico de la muy ilustre ciudad de Manresa* (Barcelona, 1693).

[44] For British local history, Stan Mendyk, *Speculum Britannae: regional study, antiquarianism, and science in Britain to 1700* (Toronto, 1989) and his 'Early British chorography', *Sixteenth-Century Journal* 17 (1986), 459–81. For France, Claire Dolan, 'L'identité urbaine et les histoires locales publiées du xvie au xviiie siècle en France', *Canadian Journal of History*, 27 (1990), 278–298, and Edwin G. Ehmke, 'The writing of town and provincial history in sixteenth-century France: developing a myth of local identity', PhD thesis, University of Southern California, 1979. For Germany, see Gerald Strauss, *Sixteenth-century Germany and its topography and topographers* (Madison, 1959).

things at once. In the hands of cosmographers and geographers, it quickly took the form of large compendia attempting to provide a detailed look at the Habsburgs' rapidly growing empire. Fernando Colón never completed his ambitious topographical dictionary of Spain, but the manuscript, housed in the Biblioteca Colombina in Seville, served as starting point for such works as Marineo Siculo's *De rebus hispaniae*, as well as for Pedro de Medina's *Libro de las grandezas o cosas memorables de España* (Seville, 1548), which incorporated detailed descriptions of several hundred Iberian cities and towns. Chorography also served as the inspiration for many of the great geo-historical projects launched by Philip II, including the *Relaciones geográficas*; Morales' compendium of Spanish antiquities; and the topographical views of Spanish cities that Philip II commissioned from the Flemish painter, Anton van den Wyngaerde. For a moment, therefore, chorography entered the monarchy's service, joining a team, already comprised of architecture, cartography, painting and history, whose task was to demonstrate the grandeur of the Habsburg domain.

As a discipline, however, chorography was ill-suited for the role that Philip II had asked it to play. By definition, it was oriented to detail, to particularities, to highlighting minuscule details of small, even insignificant towns. In contrast, the monarchy, with its imperial pretensions, sought glory on a wider, almost universal scale. The later Habsburgs, lacking Philip II's topographical concerns, displayed little interest in continuing the *Relaciones geográficas* or even in publishing the *General corografía e historia de España*, a work Philip II had commissioned from the cosmographer Andrés García de Céspedes. These monarchs instead preferred history, a discipline which could not only assist directly with the serious business of state, but also offer them a large field in which to demonstrate their grandeur and importance. Even so, the seventeenth century for Spanish chorography represented something of a Golden Age owing to the patronage provided by municipalities who conceived of it as an ideal means of expressing their own, somewhat particularized vision of the Spanish past. In essence, therefore, chorography served as the counterpoint to royal history, offering the cities a role in Spanish history denied them by the *cronistas del rey*.

Although traces of what Adeline Rucquoi has called an 'urban imagination' can be found in a variety of early medieval texts, Spanish chorography was essentially a fifteenth-century creation, the byproduct of attempts by various municipal governments to acquire some of the trappings already enjoyed by the nobility, among them, lands, jurisdictions, genealogies and titles.[45] Starting around 1400, for example, Seville staged an annual Christmas pageant featuring minstrels singing the praises of that city's singular marvels, both past and present, and for Mérida there exist fragments of a text, probably written about mid-century, offering a description (in Castilian) of that city's walls and other noteworthy monuments.[46] By the century's end other cities had their own panegyrics, although by this time these tended to be written in Latin and modelled on such Italian treatises as Flavio Biondo's *Roma instaurata*, and its companion piece, *Roma triumphans*. The first of these encomia, which were generally more descriptive than historical, was *Descriptio cordobae*, the work of an anonymous (and possibly Italian-trained) author ca. 1485. Others include Jeroni Pau's *Barcino* (1491) – a glowing account of Barcelona; Alonso de Proaza's *Oratio luculenta de laudibus valentiae* (Valencia, 1505); and, an anonymous *laudatio* (ca. 1512) in honour of Burgos.[47] Despite this effort to highlight each city's uniqueness, these encomia were essentially alike, portraying each as a composite of the ideal city outlined by Aristotle, Augustine and Alberti: populous, self-sufficient and prosperous; healthy and clean; pious; well-governed; filled with magnificent buildings of noble design; and inhabited exclusively by noble, industrious and virtuous folk.

Despite these pretensions, the popularity of these Latin encomia was relatively short lived. Starting around 1520, possibly in connection with the nationalistic fervour associated with the revolt of the *comuneros* in Castile and its Valencian counterpart, the *Germanías*, Spanish chorography became distinctly more 'Spanish'. To begin with, it replaced the Latin of the humanists with the vernacular. Secondly, it became much more historical, essentially combining what had been two distinct genres – the *laudatio* and the urban chronicle – into one.[48]

The first chorography to combine all of these elements was Gonzalo

---

[45] See Adeline Rucquoi, 'Des villes nobles pour le roi', in *Realidad e imágenes del poder. España a fines de la edad media*, ed. Adeline Rucquoi (Madrid, 1988), pp. 195–214.

[46] The poems praising Seville, the work of Alfonso Alvares de Villasandino, are published in the *Cancionero de Juan Alfonso de Baena*, ed. José María Azaceta (Madrid, 1966), pp. 66–75. For Mérida, see BNM, ms. 4235, 'Fragmento de la descripción de Mérida', fo. 184–5.

[47] For the Cordoba text, see Manuel Nieto Cumplido, *Córdoba en el siglo xv* (Cordoba, 1973), pp. 57–71. The most recent edition (and translation) of *Barcino* is *Barcino de Jeroni Pau*, ed. Josep Maria Casas Homs (Barcelona, 1957). For Burgos see BNM, ms. 18,729/19, 'In Burgensis civitatis laudem Joanni de Velasco Castellae Comitistable dicata'.

[48] Urban chronicles in Spain have not received the scholarly attention they deserve. Two medieval examples include Joan Francesc Bosca, *Memorial historic*, ed. Jaume Sobreques i Callico (Barcelona, 1977), and 'Los anales de Garci Sanchez, jurado de Sevilla', ed. Juan de M. Carriazo, *Anales de la Universidad Hispalense*, 14 (1953), 3–363.

Ayora de Córdoba's *Epílogo de algunas cosas dignas de memorias pertene-cientes a la ilustre y muy magnífica i muy noble i muy leal ciudad de Avila* (Salamanca, 1519). Ayora, one of King Ferdinand's chroniclers, intended this book to serve as a reminder of Avila's many contributions to the glory of the monarchy, hence the subtitle: 'Avila del Rey'. By writing in Castilian, Ayora pointedly hoped to reach a wide audience. He also established a precedent: virtually every other work of Spanish chorography published in the sixteenth and seventeenth centuries would also be written in Castilian, including those written for cities where the population customarily spoke Catalan or Valencian. Ayora's approach to the history of Spain's Middle Ages established another precedent. Whereas royal history focused on princely *gestae*, Ayora concentrated on the city itself, first by presenting a catalogue of the many services which the nobles of Avila, as loyal vassals, rendered to the monarchy during the Reconquest, and then by listing the many royal gifts and privileges the city had received in return. Ayora thus presents Castilian history as a reciprocal, almost contractual relationship between city and crown that worked to the mutual advantage of both. Furthermore, by alluding to the privileges (*fueros*) by which Castile's cities traditionally defended their prerogatives against the monarchy, Ayora anticipated many of the arguments utilized by the *comuneros* in their revolt against Charles V. Ayora, moreover, practised what he preached, becoming a prominent rebel, who, even after years of exile, remained unrepentant for his role in the *comunero* revolt.[49]

Following the *Epílogo's* publication, histories for other cities soon began to appear. Anton Beuter used the occasion of the three-hundredth anniversary of Valencia's conquest from the Moors to write his *Historia de Valencia* (1538), published first in Catalan and then in Castilian translation.[50] Meanwhile, Luis de Pereza, an obscure Sevillian clergyman, completed a ponderous, two-volume history of Seville that exalted not only the city's antiquity but also its imperial heritage by crediting Julius Caesar with the city's reconstruction and restoration in the first century BC.[51] And sometime before 1541, the Toledan author, Pedro de Alcocer, began his *Historia o descripción de la ciudad imperial de Toledo* (Toledo, 1554) in an effort to give that city its rightful place in Spanish history. Alcocer's book is

---

[49] See E. Cat, *Essai sur la vie et les ouvrages du chroniquer Gonzalo de Ayora* (Paris, 1890).

[50] Pedro Antonio Beuter, *Primera part d' la historia de Valencia q tracta de las antiguedades de Spahnya y fundacio de Valencia* [1538] (facsimile edition, Valencia, 1982). The Castilian version appeared in 1548. Part II of this history was published (only in Castilian) in 1550.

[51] Luis de Pereza, *Historia de Sevilla*, ed. Francisco Morales Padrón (Seville, 1979) publishes extracts from the original manuscript, 'Antiquíssimo origen de la ciudad de Sevilla'.

of especial interest here because it became a paradigmatic text, establishing what might be called a chorographic convention scrupulously followed by other authors seeking to put their particular city on the map.

In essence, this convention offered authors a means of demonstrating the glories of any city or town within the broader context of Spanish history. It included a geographical description of the city that recounted, generally in glowing, hyperbolical language, the benefits of its physical location, the fertility of its surrounding countryside, and the abundance of its commerce. Consequently, each city appeared as if were a terrestrial paradise, another Eden, where there was never hunger, sickness or want. The convention also prompted authors to include an account of the city's foundation – an act generally attributed either to Tubal, Hercules, or one of the mythical monarchs invented by Annius of Viterbo – together with an etymological discussion of its name. It was also necessary to demonstrate the importance and privileges of the city in Roman times as well as to provide information about the city's 'Christian antiquity', notably its conversion to catholicism, an act which authors, in keeping with the legend of St James' visit to the peninsula, wanted to link with the Apostle himself.[52] The lack of sources made this a somewhat difficult task until the end of the sixteenth century when the Toledan Jesuit, Gerónimo Román de la Higuera (1538–1614), composed his famous *cronicones*, attributing them to such authors as Flavius Dextrus, Maximus and Luitprando.[53] Although widely denounced by some scholars as the forgeries they were, the *cronicones* proved an immediate success as they provided the historical documentation chorographers needed to prove not only the arrival of Santiago in their city but also the names of their first bishops, martyrs and saints.[54]

Concern with their city's Christian heritage also led most chorographers either to ignore Spain's Muslim centuries or to write about this era in terms of resistance against Islam. As in the case of royal history, therefore, the Middle Ages were generally reduced to little more than an account of the Reconquest, or, as in the case of Ayora's book, a catalogue of the city's contributions to this crusade. Convention also required chorographers to

---

[52] On the legend, T. D. Kendrick, *St James in Spain* (London, 1960) and, more recently, Ofelia Rey Castellao, *La historiografía del voto del Santiago* (Santiago de Compostela, 1985).

[53] The standard account of these forgeries is José Godoy Alcántara, *Historia crítica de los falsos cronicones* [1868] (facsimile edition, Madrid, 1981).

[54] Julio Caro Baroja, *Las falsificaciones de la historia* (Barcelona, 1991) overstates the extent to which single individuals like Higuera are responsible for the 'falsification' of Spanish history. Village *éruditos* and royal chroniclers had a common interest in documenting Spain's 'Christian antiquity', often at the expense of historical truth. However, the influence of known 'forgers' such as Higuera merits detailed study.

portray their city's perpetual loyalty to the monarchy. For the same reason it was necessary to skip over or even to ignore those historical moments that contradicted the image of the city as the ever-faithful vassal. Alcocer thus ended his narrative with the Catholic Monarchs, which allowed him to avoid mention of Toledo's active participation in the *comuneros* revolt.

Finally, Alcocer's convention included both the Aristotelian image of the city as a just, well-governed republic and the Augustinian image of the city as a *civitas cristiana*, a 'holy community' rooted in religion and faith. This community is also presented as if it were a *cuerpo místico*, a mystical body, or as a 'soul': eternal, unchanging, impervious to the vagaries of time. The city is therefore *always* faithful, *always* noble and *always* loyal to its lord, regardless of the misdeeds of some individuals, generally described as members of the popular classes (*canalla* or *vulgo*), who, by definition, do not form part of the community. Language such as this enabled Diego de Colmenares, historian of Segovia, to excuse his city for its involvement in the *comuneros*.[55]

This idealized image of the city as *civitas* further enabled chorographers to argue that population had nothing to do with a city's importance. Grandeur in their eyes was a function of the quality, not the quantity of a city's inhabitants, a position that enabled Dr Vicente Mares, in *La Fenix Troyana* (Valencia, 1681), a history of the Levantine village of Chelva, to argue that his *patria* was 'noble' despite a declining population of no more than 600 households. For similar reasons, chorographers rarely made reference to the presence of Jews or Moors in their cities, emphasizing instead the number and importance of the local nobility, generally by including genealogies of the city's most prominent families. Nobility was also reflected in the magnificence of a city's public buildings as opposed to the houses of its ordinary citizens. This explains the absence in Spanish chorography of a book similar to John Stow's *Survey of London* (1600), which offered a detailed account, borough by borough, of that city's urban development.

Despite these and other historiographical limitations, the convention outlined above lasted with only minimal changes until the end of the eighteenth century. Titles vary – *Descripción de* ..., *Excelencias de* ..., *Discursos históricos de* ..., *Resumen histórico de* ..., *Compendio* or *Reseña histórica de* ..., *Tratado de las antigüedades y grandezas de* ..., *Trofeos de* ..., *Anales* or *Crónicas de* ..., as well as *Historia de* ..., a term utilized only by

---

[55] Colmenares attributed the revolt to the 'impetu furioso del vulgo', 'la canalla'. On the other hand, 'no haberse hallado en el alboroto, no solo persona noble, pero ni aun ciudadano de mediano porte'. Diego de Colmenares, *Historia de la insigne ciudad de Segovia y compendio de las historias de Castilla* [1636] (facsimile edition, Segovia, 1975), II, pp. 182–3.

authors attempting to use their work for purposes of moral instruction.[56] But whatever the exact title – in reality, the differences between such older historical subgenres as history, annals, chronicle and decades were becoming more and more tenuous – the importance of these books is reflected in the demand on the part of individual municipalities, each of which sought to have a chorography of its own.

Burgos is a case in point. Eager to have a history comparable to the one Alcocer wrote for Toledo, in 1581 the municipal government (or *ayuntamiento*) eagerly accepted the offer of Fray Gerónimo Román, a scholar already known for his chronicle of the Augustinian Order, to write

a history of the many great services this city has rendered to past monarchs of glorious memory as well as the distinguished persons who have come from this republic, including kings, nobles and grandees, men distinguished in arms and in letters and in public office. [He is] also to describe the antiquity and nobility of the city itself.

The city subsequently signed a contract with Román which outlined, chapter by chapter, the contents of the proposed book. In exchange, the city agreed to pay Román the handsome sum of 1,300 ducats. In the end, despite what appears to have been good faith on the part of both parties, the book was never written, mainly because Burgos failed to obtain the royal permission necessary to take out the loan it needed to pay Román for his services.[57]

This anecdote illustrates the importance accorded to works of local history by the oligarchies who dominated most of Spain's *ayuntamientos*. If the latter did not directly commission these books, they were generally prepared to offer would-be authors subventions of various sorts. The city of Huesca did this in 1619 by offering to pay for the publication of a history of the city that Francisco Diego de Aynsa had recently completed.[58] In comparison, the municipal governors of Murcia took a much more active role in the composition of Francisco de Cascales' *Discursos históricos de la ciudad de Murcia y su reino*, first published in 1621. As early as 1608 the city

---

[56] Juan Pablo Martyr Rizo pointedly used his *Historia de la muy noble y leal ciudad de Cuenca* [1629] (facsimile edition, Barcelona, 1979) to offer advice about the proper role of the *privado* in government.

[57] Burgos: Archivo del Ayuntamiento: Libros de Actas, 13 April, 1581, fo. 113. The original reads: 'un libro de la ystoria della y de los muchos y gran servicios que esta ciudad a hecho a los reyes pasados de gloriosa memoria y las personas senaladas que an salido desta republica ansi de reyes grandes y senores y caballeros y personas generales en letras y en armas y cargos publicos y de la demas antiguedad y nobleza desta ciudad.'

[58] See Francisco Diego de Aynsa, *Fundación, excelencias, grandezas, y cosas memorables de la antiquíssima ciudad de Huesca* [1619] (facsimile edition, 1987), Introduction.

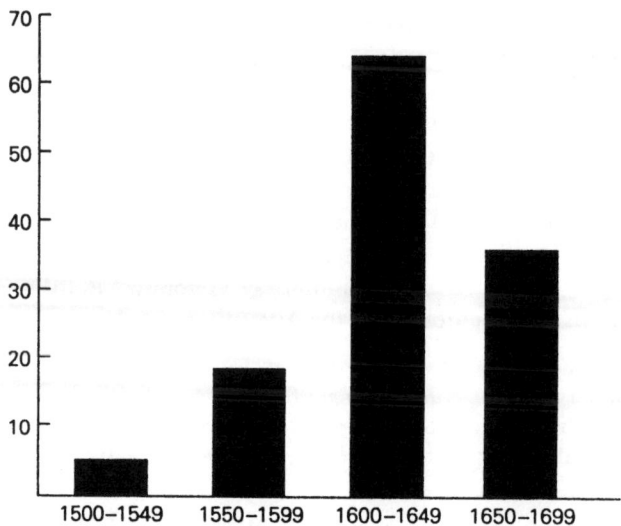

Figure I   Chorography in Habsburg Spain: published works and manuscripts

councillors established a special commission charged with the oversight of this work. In addition, they facilitated Cascales' research in the municipal archives and provided him with a list of the noblemen whose genealogies he was to include in the book – a list, not surprisingly, that included most of the families represented on the council itself. Finally, once the manuscript was complete, the council subsidized the book's publication with a special tax and ultimately rewarded Cascales with the title of city chronicler (*cronista de la ciudad*).[59]

Few *ayuntamientos* were as intimately involved in the production of history as Murcia's, but municipal governments everywhere encouraged the writing of local history. By the seventeenth century these books had in fact become a kind of talisman that helped to strengthen local identities and to fend off completing claims to greatness by other cities. As a result, publication of these histories soared, reaching a peak in the first half of the seventeenth century (Figure I). The rhythm of publication dropped thereafter, but by 1700 there was only a handful of cities that did not have a published history of its own. (Burgos was one, although it did have several in manuscript.) Even more surprising is the number of small towns with histories proclaiming their *antigüedades y grandezas*. Barco de Avila was

[59] The relevant documents are summarized in Juan Torres Fontes, 'Notas y documentos sobre el Licenciado Cascales', *Murgetana* 23 (1964), 61–76.

little more than a village, but owing to the efforts of Luis Alvarez, a local scribe, its *Grandeza, antigüedad y nobleza de Barco de Avila*, was published in 1652.[60] Alcántara, Bujalance, Elche and Vélez Málaga were other small municipalities which had similar histories; but perhaps the most unusual publication was *Verdadera relación y manifiesto apologético de la antigüedad de las Batuecas* (1693), which examined the history of La Alberca, an isolated village located in the mountains south of Salamanca.[61]

Who wrote these books? The authors were primarily local scholars who, as they themselves admitted, either wrote out of local pride (*obligación del amor del patria*) or 'to preserve the memory' of significant local personages or events. Others wrote for personal and often purely political ends. This certainly applies to a history of Calatayud whose author, Miguel Martínez de Villar, a local cleric, claims to have written the book in the hope of demonstrating that his city merited a bishopric.[62] Fernando Albia de Castro, a lawyer from Logroño, intended his history of that city (1633) to serve as means of justifying why that city deserved a vote in the Castilian Cortes.[63] There were also clergymen who only wanted to represent their city or town as a *civitas cristiana*. Consequently, some of these histories did little more than to describe local sanctuaries and to outline the biographies of local martyrs, saints, bishops, etc.[64]

Whatever the specific rationale behind each individual work, these chorographies shared some common characteristics. Despite an avowed acceptance of the necessity of writing history that conformed with truth, for example, few local historians hesitated to substitute fiction for fact in order to defend their city's honour or to assure it a distinguished role in Spain's history. Diego Murillo, Saragossa's historian, openly admitted that he used his pen not 'as a writing instrument but as a lance and a shield to defend against attacks and to fight', by which he meant to defend his city's reputation against Castilian scholars such as Cabrera de Córdoba who had

---

[60] Alvarez originally wrote the work ca. 1620.

[61] The book is the work of Tomás González de Manuel, 'presbitero y vecino del lugar de La Alberca'. I have utilized the second edition (Salamanca, 1717).

[62] Miguel Martínez del Villar, *Tratado del patronado, antigüedades, gobierno, y varones illustres de la ciudad y comunidad de Calatayud y su arcedeanado* (Saragossa, 1598).

[63] Fernando Albia de Castro, *Memorial y discurso político por la muy noble y muy leal ciudad de Logroño* ... (Lisbon, 1633).

[64] A typical example is Fernando Lorenzo Vera y Rosales, *Discurso histórico del origen, ocultación, hallazgo, y culto de la milagrosissima, y antiquissima imagen de la N.S. de la Iniesta, sita en la iglesia parrochial de San Julián de Sevilla y las grandezas y excelencias de la misma muy noble, y muy leal ciudad* (Seville, 1688).

accused it of sedition for its role in the Aragonese uprising of 1590–91.[65] In a similar vein, Diego de Colmenares informed the municipal commission appointed to review his history of Segovia that he wrote for 'the glory of our ancestors, the example of our descendants'. He added that 'When all of the cities of Spain, and even some towns, have histories, it is wrong that a city whose antiquity, lustre and nobility is equal to or even greater than that of most cities does not have a history of its own.'[66] To defend, to glorify, to honour, to protect – chorographies were rarely objective or disinterested accounts of a city's past. Rather they were a species of polemical, patriotic works meant to underscore, via history and description, the unique characteristics of a particular place.

This tendency to magnify the importance of one's own *patria*, usually at the expense of a nearby or rival town, did not go unnoticed. Bartolomé Leonardo de Argensola, the Aragonese historian and poet, criticized local chroniclers for what he described as their 'excessive' local pride. Boosterism of this sort also led to what other prominent scholars referred to as *disparates*, or abject nonsense, a glaring example of which was Martín de Roa's attempt to prove that Isidore of Seville was actually from Cordoba. 'Roa was so attached to Cordoba', wrote one critic, 'that he practically ignored the grandeurs of other cities along with the saints and distinguished people who came from them.'[67] Despite such criticisms, Roa – who was surely among the 'antiquarians' denounced by Baltasar Gracián as 'material and mechanical, lacking in judgement and short on genius' – was an author in demand.[68] After publishing his history of Cordoba, he wrote similar books for Ecija, Málaga and Jérez de la Frontera.[69]

The popularity of chorography in seventeenth-century Spain can be interpreted in several ways. The importance these works accorded to the genealogies of the local nobility suggests that the genre, in part at least, represented the voice, the means of expression of Spain's urban oligarchies, many

---

[65] See Fray Diego Murillo, *Fundación milagrosa de la capilla angélica y apostólica de la Madre de Dios del Pilar y Excelencias de la imperial ciudad de Zaragoza* (Barcelona, 1616).

[66] See Colmenares, *Historia de Segovia*, I, p. 62. Recognizing the importance of this history, the Segovian *ayuntamiento* rewarded Colmenares with a grant of 600 ducats.

[67] See BNM, ms. 8389, fo. 195, Lic. Rodrigo Caro to Juan Andres de Uztarroz.

[68] Baltasar Gracián, *El Criticón*, ed. M. Rovara-Navarro (Philadelphia, 1939), Lib. II, crisi 4, p. 151.

[69] Martín de Roa, *De cordobe in Hispania betica* (Lugduni, 1617), trans. *Antiguo principado de la España ulterior o Andaluz* (Cordoba, 1636). By the same author, *Santos Honorio, Estichio, Esteban. Patronos de Xerez de la Frontera: Nombre, sitio, antigüedades de la ciudad* (Seville, 1617); *Málaga y su fundación, su antigüedad eclesiástica y seglar. Sus santos* (Malaga, 1622); *Ecija. Sus santos, su antigüedad eclesiástica y seglar* (Seville, 1629).

of which were busily consolidating their powers and privileges. For these nobles, histories lauding the achievements of their ancestors served as proof positive of why they themselves merited privileged positions within the town halls. In some cases, moreover, the genealogies in the histories offered families of New Christian lineage an escape from this particular taint. Cascales, for example, did his best to 'clean up' the genealogies of those Murcian town councillors whose families were widely known to be of *converso* descent.

It is also possible to consider the rise of Spanish chorography as a political as opposed to a purely social phenomenon. It defended and, in a way, helped both to create and sustain the forces of localism by arguing for the historical importance of the kingdom's municipalities at a time when municipal councils everywhere believed that the monarchy was threatening to impose new taxes and to deprive their cities of their hard-won traditional privileges and rights. This particular concern is reflected in chorography's emphasis on local *fueros* together with the laws and institutions which accorded each city a separate and distinctive legal identity. It is also possible to conceive of the genre in purely literary terms, that is, as an 'intertextual' response to royal history in which the cities (that is, the kingdom) played secondary and very limited roles as compared to those accorded to the monarchy. But whatever the precise causes for the popularity of this genre – and there are undoubtedly others not summarized here – chorography inverted the focus of Spanish history, altering what was in principle an account of princely *gestae* into one which privileged the cities and, above all, the nobles inhabiting them. Chorography offered municipal leaders, and the cities they embodied, a historical 'space' denied them by the historians employed by the crown.

Despite the tendency of chorography to challenge royal historiography on this basic point, the language employed in these works is not one of resistance or even one of opposition between the interests of the 'country' against those of the 'court'. Rather, the chorographies, in order to defend and support municipal liberties, underlined the importance of a mutually beneficial, reciprocal or contractual relationship between the monarchy and the municipalities.

Yet, and as Richard Helgerson reminds us in his study of sixteenth-century English chorography, 'At the root of all representation is differentiation.'[70] From this perspective, the multitude of chorographies that appeared in the seventeenth century offered a vision of the kingdom quite

---

[70] Richard Helgerson, *Forms of nationhood: the Elizabethan writing of England* (Chicago, 1992), p. 135.

distinct from that of royal history. The latter gravitated towards a unitary, almost homogeneous view of Spain, in which the kingdom was little more than a theatre for the demonstration of monarchical grandeur. In comparison, the kingdom outlined in the chorographies is much more transparent, largely because each of these histories treats its particular municipality as a microcosm, a *patria* totally distinct from – and of course, better than – neighbouring cities and towns. Interestingly, most of these chorographies scarcely take note of the existence of other cities, let alone the relationships, commercial or otherwise, between cities. Everything is concentrated on the one, as if it were an independent, quasi-autarkical republic. Furthermore, and the point is worth emphasizing, chorography, simply by relegating the monarchy to the background of the historical stage, did relatively little to promote the idea of a unitary state. In fact, it probably did the opposite, reinforcing the sentiments of those who, like Cristóbal Sanz, author of a history of the Levantine town of Elche (1621), distinguished between the obligation to *patria* (homeland) as opposed to that owed to the *ley* (law) and to the *rey* (king).[71] This manifesto, which so favoured local as opposed to national attachments is precisely the idea Spanish chorography attempted to convey. For this reason, it would be interesting to know whether León de Arroyal had read any of these works before developing his notion of Spain as a collection of confederated republics.

The question of how these chorographies were interpreted leads to a final set of questions: who read these works? And, equally importantly, *how* were they read? The history of the book in early modern Spain remains relatively unknown. Without detailed studies of libraries, reading habits and the size and distribution of individual editions, these and other questions pertaining to the market for and reception of individual books are difficult to resolve.[72] Nevertheless, it appears that chorography had various markets, some far removed from the communities they were intended to serve. First of all there was the king. Many local histories included a dedication to the king, and some were clearly meant to be presented as a gift to the monarch. In fact, copies of many, although by no means all of these municipal histories are listed in a 1637 inventory of the library of the royal palace in Madrid.[73]

---

[71] Cristóbal Sanz, *Excelencias de la villa de Elche* (Elche, 1954). The original manuscript dates from 1621.

[72] For an introduction to the history of the book in Habsburg Spain, see Fernando Bouza Alvarez, *Del escribano a biblioteca* (Madrid, 1993). See also Keith Whinnon, 'The problem of the best-seller in Spanish Golden Age literature', *Bulletin of Hispanic Studies*, 57 (1988), 189–98.

[73] BNM, ms. 18791, 'Indice de los libros que tiene Su Magestad en la torre alta desta alcázar de Madrid, año de 1637'.

Whether Philip IV ever read these books is unknown; but they were almost certainly read by his chroniclers, an audience quick to fault them both for their scholarship – generally regarded as inadequate – and, as Tamayo de Vargas once wrote in reference to a manuscript history of Segovia, their failure to contribute to 'the credit of the nation'.[74]

On the other hand, most chorographies travelled little if at all. Many remained in manuscript, and those that were published normally appeared only in single editions and in print runs limited to five hundred copies or less. Geographical distribution was also circumscribed except in a few instances when an individual municipality underwrote the costs of distributing multiple copies to a wider audience.[75] Chorographies in this sense had publishing histories akin to books currently published by Spain's banks, city governments and other public agencies, few of which are ever marketed commercially and circulated much beyond a local or regional readership. Sixteenth- and seventeenth-century chorographies had similar markets. *Zaragozanos*, it seems, read only Saragossan histories; *sevillanos*, only books pertaining to Seville, establishing a tradition of local reading that continues even today.

The circulation of chorographies within these localized markets is difficult to reconstruct, but what happened to Albia de Castro's *Memorial y discurso político de Logroño* (Lisbon, 1636) may be instructive. In this instance, the author, long resident in Lisbon, published the book privately and subsequently presented a copy to Logroño's municipal council. The latter immediately established a committee to examine the work and to congratulate Albia de Castro for his efforts on behalf of his native town. Its next step was to deposit a copy of the book in the municipal archive and to arrange to have additional copies 'distributed among the nobles, aldermen, clerics and illustrious persons of the city'.[76]

If the circulation history of this book is at all representative, it suggests

---

[74] AHN, Cons. 7155, n.f.; petition of Lic. Pedro Suarez de Castro Orejón, a lawyer from Segovia, asking for a licence to print his manuscript, 'Del origen de los apellidos de Tapia y Arevalo y la antigüedad de la villa de Pedraça y mucho de la de Segovia y su puente y otras cosas curiosas'. Tamayo de Vargas, a royal chronicler, wrote that it did not matter if the book ever appeared 'porque no contiene doctrinas que deba saberse ni hay en él cosa que aumente el crédito de la nación'. He was also upset by the author's reference to Madrid as an 'aldea de Segovia, cosa sin ningún género de fundamento'.

[75] In 1690, for example, the *ayuntamiento* of Cadiz sent fifty copies of Fray Jerónimo de la Concepción, *Emporio del orbe. Cádiz* (Amsterdam, 1690) to various ministers in Madrid as part of its effort to end Seville's monopoly of trade with the Indies. The *ayuntamiento* had previously subsidized Fray Jerónimo's research and paid for the book's publication in a luxurious folio edition, printed in Amsterdam.

[76] Albia de Castro, *Memorial y discurso político* (Lisbon, 1636), prólogo.

that chorography, faithful to its intellectual goals, did not seek a broad, anonymous clientele. Rather it aimed to cultivate, and to instruct, readers who could easily identify with the *civitas* being described. In the first instance, these readers were members of the urban élite: churchmen, local notables and other individuals anxious to read about the deeds of their ancestors, the history of the institutions to which they belonged, and the antiquity of their city or town. Yet chorography also found an audience among city-dwellers of humbler rank. Workers and artisans did not necessarily read these works, but one did not need to be literate in order to learn about their message. In Zamora, for example, local holidays offered occasions for preachers to instruct church-goers in 'histories' pertaining to the city's past. For example, a diarist reported that when, on 2 January 1674, a preacher in the cathedral 'began the sermon with praise for Numancia, the city of Zamora, its nobility, citizens and officials...[and] everyone was delighted'.[77] Other instances exist where sermons served similar purposes and if these did not reach a broad enough audience, town councils frequently utilized commemorative festivals as a way of teaching the local populace about the myths and historical moments that made their city unique. Little is known about the procession which the city of Granada staged annually on 6 January to celebrate its day of deliverance from the Muslims in 1492, but in Valencia, which organized an immense festival every one hundred years in order to commemorate its reconquest in 1238, a series of elaborately painted canvases, triumphal arches, street altars and theatrical representations brought to the public the same patriotic messages that a reader could find in the pages of Beuter, Escolano and other historians of the city.[78]

As for the question of how these books were read, chorographies seem to have been compared with and interpreted in conjunction with Mariana's general history or one of the other 'regional' histories published in the course of the seventeenth century. Joseph Conchillos' history of Tudela, for example, published in 1666 with the impressive title of *Historical and juridical fortress, literary and titulary wall* ('Propugnáculo histórico y jurídico, muro literario y titular'), began as a series of sermons delivered in

---

[77] *Diario de Antonio Moreno de la Torre 1673–79*, ed. Francisco Javier Lorenzo Pinar and Luis Vasallo Toranio (Zamora, 1990), p. 74. Entry for 2 January 1674: 'Entró el sermón con alabanças a Numancia, ciudad de Zamora, nobleça, ciudadanos, maiordomos, ponpa de la grandeça de la fiesta. Dió gran gusto.' In the seventeenth century scholars in both Soria and Zamora claimed that their city was originally Numancia.

[78] The festivals of 1638 are recorded in Marco Antonio Orti, *Siglo cuarto de la conquista de Valencia* [1640] (facsimile edition, Valencia, 1988). See also, in this volume, James Casey, 'Patriotism in early modern Valencia', pp. 196–7.

response to José de Moret's *Investigaciones históricas de las antigüedades del reyno de Navarra* (1665), a book which had challenged the idea that Tubal founded Tudela.[79] Conchillos' purpose was to defend his city's honour, and in doing so, instruct his listeners (and later, his readers) in the traditions and glories of their native town.

Chorography in this sense served as a teacher, albeit one with a very specific task: to instruct the inhabitants of a particular place how to think about the community in which they lived. It also provided these same individuals with a language they might use to locate themselves in the world, to distinguish themselves from the inhabitants of other nearby, often rival, cities and towns. Finally, it sought to convert these inhabitants into citizens, members of a community sharing a common past. Chorography thus offered Spain's city dwellers a history with which they might identify and claim as their own. This history, of course, was meant to be *their* history, not the history sponsored by the monarchy and composed by the chroniclers employed by the king. In this way, to gloss Arroyal, each town could imagine itself as a kingdom, a place which encapsulated the entire history of Spain. But this history, however particularistic, was not incompatible with the history articulated on behalf of the crown. It is difficult to say which of these histories – the royal or the chorographic – had greater purchase, especially at the local level. It does seem, however, that royal history, which extolled Spain and its monarchy, could not be read without reference to works celebrating, and indeed magnifying, the importance of the home town.

---

[79] Joseph Conchillos, *Propugnáculo histórico y jurídico, muro literario y titular. Tudela ilustrada y defendida* (Saragossa, 1666). Conchillos writes that Moret wanted to give Pamplona, rather than Tudela, the honour of being the oldest Navarrese city because, 'como hijo de Pamplona y tan afecto a su patria quisiera darla mas antigüedad' (p. 37).

Part II

*The pattern of society:
community and identity in Habsburg Spain*

4

✳

Toledanos and the kingdom of Granada,
1492 to the 1560s

LINDA MARTZ

The centre–periphery balance within the Iberian peninsula was one of shifting fortune and power, but few would deny that during the reign of the Catholic Monarchs the balance shifted toward the centre. The territorial expansion of the crown of Castile in these years was dramatic: the conquest of the Canary Islands, the reconquest of kingdom of Granada, and the discovery of the New World. In this same period an internal expansion began that lasted until the later years of Philip II's reign: by the 1560s many Castilian cities had doubled in size, and the local economies prospered.[1]

This is certainly the case for Toledo, the most important city of the central region and, with a population of some 55,000 souls in 1561, also the largest.[2] Despite setbacks – the arrival of the Inquisition and the onus of fighting on the losing side in the *comunero* revolt – the city successfully exploited the opportunities offered in the new territories and met the challenges posed by an increasing population. Part of the credit for this positive response belongs to the city's active middle class citizens. They provided the money, expertise and energy to build up the local cloth industries, and they supplied the skills necessary to satisfy the ever increas-

---

Translations are by the author unless otherwise attributed.

[1] Carla Rahn Phillips, 'Time and duration: a model for the economy of early modern Spain', *American Historical Review*, 92 (1987), 531–62, for a stimulating and wide-ranging discussion that includes population, as well as an extensive bibliography; for the boom years of the sixteenth century, see 536–41.

[2] Linda Martz, *Poverty and welfare in Habsburg Spain: the example of Toledo*, (Cambridge, 1983) pp. 94–100 for the population of Toledo from 1528 to the 1620s.

ing demand for men trained to keep records and accounts, to read, analyse and write reports and to administer finances, whether on the local level or in distant outposts. If by 1600 the *arbitrista* González de Cellorigo lamented the absence of productive, hard working men of 'the middling sort',[3] in 1500 they were numerous and active in the city of Toledo.

Many men of the middling sort who resided in Toledo were of *converso* origin, descendants of Jews who converted to Christianity. It has been estimated that in 1486 *conversos* accounted for 16–20 per cent of the city's population, so they were a sizeable minority.[4] In general terms, the social structure of this minority reflected that of the majority Old Christian society of the period, insofar as those at the bottom outnumbered those at the top. Of the 513 *conversos* whose occupations and status are known in 1495–97, some 299 (58.28 per cent) were artisans and labourers.[5] But *conversos* formed a strong contingent at the middle level, primarily in occupations having to do with business, money and the keeping of records. The combination of the seventy-nine merchants and thirty-four money managers (tax-farmers, money changers) counted in 1495–97 comprised the second largest group after the artisans and labourers, with 22 per cent of the total.[6] As for record-keeping, of the thirty-three public notaries in Toledo at this time, twenty were *conversos*.[7] Unfortunately, the total number of Toledo merchants and financiers in this period is unknown, but it is likely that *conversos* accounted for the majority.

Men of the *converso* middle class represented a dynamic element in Castilian society, with values and mores that at times clashed with those of the Old Christian majority. *Conversos* did not attain fame and fortune by wielding a sword on the battlefield but rather by wielding a pen, and possibly an abacus, in the secretariat or the counting house. In the fifteenth century they gained positions in the church and the governing councils of

---

[3] John H. Elliott, *Imperial Spain, 1469–1716* [1963] (reprinted edition, London and New York, 1990), p. 310.

[4] Linda Martz, 'Converso families in fifteenth- and sixteenth-century Toledo: the significance of lineage', *Sefarad*, 48 (1988), 118–19, for the sources and the many qualifications for this estimate.

[5] Francisco Cantera Burgos and Pilar León Tello, *Judaizantes del arzobispado de Toledo habilitados en 1492 y 1497* (Madrid, 1969), for a list of the 1,640 conversos who participated in the general pardon of 1495–97; no occupation is recorded for the majority of the entries.

[6] Ibid. The small shopkeepers are not included in the tally for merchants, but the fifteen *traperos* are, as is one *factor de mercader*. The money managers include fifteen *arrendadores*, twelve *cambiadores*, two *contadores de cuentas*, one *recaudador*, one *negociador en corte* and three *corredores*.

[7] Francisco de Borja San Román, *Los protocolos de los antiguos escribanos de la ciudad imperial* (Madrid, 1934), p. 14, for the number of public notaries.

Toledo as *regidores* (city councillors) or *jurados*, members of a non-voting, advisory council that included a fair number of merchants, financiers and notaries.[8] Others earned distinction on a still higher level, as royal servants and bishops of realm. This success in attaining royal, municipal and church offices, combined with their predilection for business activities and the dubious Christianity of many, contributed to the prejudice and hostility directed against them. In 1449 and 1467, Toledo experienced anti-*converso* uprisings that included street battles between *conversos* and Old Christians, as well as rulings which attempted to exclude *conversos* from holding public offices or church benefices on the basis of their Jewish origin: the 'pure blood' statutes.[9] The most brutal blow directed against *conversos* in the fifteenth century was the Inquisition, installed in Toledo in 1485. Few Toledo *conversos* escaped some form of punishment by the Inquisition.

Despite the unhappy experiences of the fifteenth century, many *converso* families exhibited a remarkable resilience in recovering or maintaining their prestige. Some retained their municipal offices in Toledo despite the arrival of the Inquisition, and others bought an office in the sixteenth century. Some reached even higher by buying a village and adding the lustre of lordship (*señor de*) to the family name. Many who rose to prominence in the sixteenth century made their fortune through wool or silk, although the large wholesale merchants often dealt in a surprising diversity of products. Tax-farming was another lucrative, if risky, activity. While some families specialized in tax farming, the lines between merchants and tax-farmers were fluid and porous. Of the many men whose careers might illustrate these generalizations, those who appear here are men who achieved some renown in the kingdom of Granada, the last great frontier of the Iberian peninsula, finally reconquered from the Moors in 1492 by the Catholic Monarchs.[10]

[8] Francisco Márquez Villanueva, 'Conversos y cargos concejiles en el siglo XV', *Revista de archivos, bibliotecas y museos*, 63 (1957), 503–40, for converso office-holders in the fifteenth century. Antonio Domínguez Ortiz, *Los Judeoconversos en España y América* (Madrid, 1971), pp. 24–8. Jean-Pierre Molénat, 'L'oligarchie municipale de Tolède au XVe siècle', in *Tolède et l'expansion urbaine en Espagne (1450–1650)* (Madrid, 1991). For the Toledo council of *jurados*, Francisco José Aranda Pérez, *Poder municipal y cabildo de jurados en la edad moderna* (Toledo, 1992), which has limited material for the fifteenth century but the seventeenth century is well covered. In the Toledo Inquisition records of 1495–97, *conversos* account for eight *jurados* and one *regidor*.

[9] Eloy Benito Ruano, *Toledo en el siglo XV. Vida política* (Madrid, 1961), provides the most detailed coverage for fifteenth-century Toledo. Albert A. Sicroff, *Los estatutos de limpieza de sangre. Controversias entre los siglos XV y XVII*, trans. Mauro Armiño, (Madrid, 1979).

[10] Miguel Angel Ladero Quesada, whom I would like to thank for bibliographical material, has made the kingdom of Granada in this period a specialty. See his *Castilla y la conquista del reino de Granada* (2nd edition, Granada, 1993); *Granada después de la conquista: repobladores y mudéjares* (2nd edition, Granada, 1993), and his edited collection, *La incorporación de*

One of the earliest *toledanos* to gain recognition in the kingdom of Granada was the royal secretary, Fernán Alvarez de Toledo-Zapata.[11] One of six royal secretaries in 1493, Fernán Alvarez was described by the Jesuit chronicler, Jerónimo Román de la Higuera, as 'so acceptable to the Catholic Monarchs that few were more favoured by them than he'.[12] The secretary accompanied Queen Isabel during the Granada conquest and was rewarded in 1492 for this and many other services with the office of Chief Notary of the kingdom of Granada, a title that Higuera concludes 'made him a grandee'.[13] While the chronicler's assessment of the social prestige conferred by this appointment is exaggerated, Fernán Alvarez did purchase a village that gave his heirs claims to a title. In 1487, he paid a million *maravedís* to the second count of Fuensalida, Pedro López de Ayala, for the village of Cedillo.[14] In an entail the secretary created for his eldest son in 1495, Antonio Alvarez de Toledo-Zapata inherited this village and was to enjoy the title of count of Cedillo after his father's death, but for unexplained reasons the family did not use the title of count until 1624.

Despite his new office in the kingdom of Granada, the secretary and most of his large family – nine siblings and twelve children – continued to live in Toledo. In an era when many families were of substantial size, and promoting one's relatives was considered an obligation, the success of one family member ensured that others soon became visible and prosperous. The Toledo-Zapata family was most visible in the parish of San Salvador, where the secretary founded a large burial chapel in the parish church; his brother, Diego López de Toledo, founded what would become a Franciscan nunnery known as San Miguel de los Angeles; and at least three brothers lived in large, adjacent residences. They were also a force to be reckoned with in the city's governing council, where five brothers enjoyed an office of *regidor*: the royal secretary, Luis Alvarez Zapata, Pedro Zapata, Diego López de Toledo and the illegitimate Juan Alvarez Zapata. In addition to the secretary, two brothers were involved in the royal finances: Diego López

Granada a la corona de Castilla. Actas del symposium conmemorativo del Quinto Centenario (Granada, 1993).

[11] Material about the secretary and his family is based upon RAH, CSC, cod. 9/229, Jerónimo Román de la Higuera, 'Familias de Toledo', fos. 193–234; Francisco Márquez Villanueva, *Investigaciónes sobre Juan Alvarez Gato. Contribución al conocimiento de la literatura castellana del siglo XV*, (Madrid, 1974); Maria del Pilar Rábade Obradó, *Una elite de poder en la corte de los Reyes Católicos. Los Judeoconversos*, (Madrid, 1993), chapter 2.

[12] RAH, CSC, 9/229, Higuera, fo. 222.   [13] Ibid., fo. 223.

[14] Jean-Pierre Molénat, 'Tolède et ses finages au temps des Rois Catholiques. Contribution à l'histoire sociale et économique de la cité avant la révolte des Comunidades', *Mélanges de la Casa de Velázquez*, 8 (1972), 348–50, 370, 374.

was a royal *contador* and Pedro Zapata assisted a royal treasurer.[15] Nor did the church escape the family's purview. Yet another brother, Francisco Alvarez de Toledo, was *maestrescuela* of the Toledo cathedral, a dignity the family monopolized until the 1550s. The attainments of the secretary and his family might serve as a model for those hoping to establish their claims to social distinction in this period.

The wealth and power of the secretary allowed him to marry two of his daughters to men of minor nobility. Catalina de Toledo married a native of Cordoba, Martín Alonso de Montemayor, lord of Montemayor, of the house of the counts of Alcaudete, and Constanza de Toledo married Pedro de Ayala, the lord of Pero Moro and San Andrés, a bastard son of the second count of Fuensalida. With all these achievements and connections, it might be thought the family would escape the Inquisition, but at least two brothers were punished. Friar García Zapata, a Jeronomite in the Toledo monastery of La Sisla, was burned at the stake some time between 1486 and 1492, and the *maestrescuela* was imprisoned in 1505 on a bevy of charges that would have sent a lesser man to stake, but he was eventually exonerated.

Although the secretary and many of his brothers preferred life in Toledo despite the presence of the Inquisition, no family worth its salt would allow the opportunities available in the newly conquered kingdom of Granada to escape its grasp. The most active family member who settled in Granada was the secretary's illegitimate brother, Juan Alvarez Zapata, a *regidor* in Toledo as well as in Granada, where city councillors were known as *veinticuatros*. He served the crown in such financial posts as paymaster of the infantry and the fleet of Granada and was also a tax-farmer.[16] But he must have made a considerable sum of money from other endeavours, as he bought a property called Guajaras, which seems to have included what are now three separate villages: Guajar Fondón, Guajar Alto and Guajar-Faraguit.[17] Since the paymaster and his wife had no children of their own, they adopted two boys, both of whom inherited an entail and were married to women of the prestigious Mendoza family. The eldest boy, Juan Alvarez Zapata III, became lord of Guarajas and wed Francisca de Mendoza, a daughter of the *adelantado* Diego Hurtado de Mendoza. The younger son, Hernando Alvarez Zapata, became lord of Guajar Fondón, and married

[15] María Jesús Urquijo, *Archivo General de Simancas: Registro General del Sello*, xv (Madrid, 1989), no. 2142: 3 September 1498; no. 2995: 16 December 1498. Pedro Zapata assisted the royal treasurer, Alfonso Gutiérrez de Madrid, in collecting the rents of the Hermandad.

[16] Rábade, *Elite*, pp. 43–6 for the posts of Juan Alvarez Zapata.

[17] RAH, CSC, cod. 9/300, Tablas Genealógicas, fo. 46v, for the village, titles, marriages and lineage. Luis de Salazar y Castro calls the property bought by Juan Alvarez Zapata 'Guajaras'.

María de Mendoza, the daughter of the count of Monteagudo.[18] While the secretary had formed impressive marriage alliances for two of his daughters and his eldest son married into the Ponce de León family of Andalusia, none of these spouses boasted so resonant a surname as Mendoza. Clearly, Juan Alvarez Zapata benefited enormously from the opportunities in the kingdom of Granada.

Aside from serving as a place where men might obtain a title and marry their children well, the kingdom of Granada produced the best silk of the Iberian peninsula. Silk linked the cities of Toledo and Granada for many years, with the old Moorish kingdom supplying the raw material that was woven and finished in Toledo. By 1590, and probably much earlier, Toledo was the second largest producer of silk cloth in the crown of Castile, surpassed only by Granada.[19] No doubt many factors contributed to the enthusiasm of Toledo merchants for silk. One was the weight of the product, light enough to be transported in sizeable quantities by mule over the forbidding terrain that stretches between Granada and Toledo. Another incentive was the high return garnered from the expensive, luxury items made from silk. But perhaps the most significant consideration was the 1492 reconquest and the subsequent opportunities available for Castilians in Granada. Ambitious *toledanos* moved into the peripheral kingdom early on, establishing a network of buyers and tax-farmers who played an important role in Granada silk.

Documents are scarce for the years before the sixteenth century, but two *toledanos*, Rodrigo de San Pedro and Alonso de León, a *jurado*, appear as

---

[18] AGS, CJH, *leg.* 24, fo. 543: 'Hernán Alvarez Zapata, veinticuatro de Granada, sobre alcabalas y tercias de Guajar Alfondo [Guajar Fondón] en el reino de Granada'.

[19] Juan Ignacio Fortea Pérez, *Córdoba en el siglo XVI. Las bases demográficas y económicas de una expansión urbana* (Cordoba, 1981), p. 316. Michael Weisser, 'The decline of Castile revisited: the case of Toledo', *Journal of European Economic History*, 2 (1973), 614–40, mentions the importance of silk (618–19), although silk is excluded from the information presented to demonstrate Toledo's industrial output on page 632. David R. Ringrose, 'The impact of a new capital city: Madrid, Toledo, and New Castile, 1560–1660', *Journal of Economic History*, 33 (1973), 761–91, fails even to mention silk; only taxes on wool and linen (769–70) are used to support the conclusions about the city's industrial production (784–7). David R. Ringrose, *Madrid and the Spanish economy, 1560–1850* (Berkeley and Los Angeles, 1983), explains in footnote 39, p. 271, that in Toledo silk was more valuable than either wool or linen, but no taxes were collected on silk 'until after the city's decline was well under way'; presumably this accounts for the omission of silk in the discussion of Toledo's industrial sector in this work as well. It is worth wondering if the conclusions about the city's industrial output and its decline offered in these three works might be altered if silk were included.

tax-farmers for the silk rent in the city of Málaga from 1492–94.[20] It has been suggested that an undated document bearing only the meagre heading,'The people that I, Alfonso de la Torre, and Juan de la Torre my brother, give as collateral for the Asiento de la Tabla', refers to the Granada silk rent.[21] The total collateral raised by the Torre brothers was a substantial 25,000,000 *maravedís*, given by seventy prosperous *toledanos*, including the royal secretary Fernán Alvarez de Toledo-Zapata. His contribution offers a clue to dating the document, as the secretary died in 1504, so the money must have been raised before then. But even if the approximate date is established, there is no way of knowing whether this Asiento de Tabla has anything to do with Granada silk.

The crown had an interest in Granada silk in the form of a sales tax levied on the product, and in 1505 this complicated tax and the means of collecting it were reformed.[22] Who would collect the royal rents or taxes was usually determined by auction, with the highest bidder carrying the day, but bids had to be backed by adequate collateral or surety. The Asiento de la Tabla is an example of communal surety, with the risk spread among many, but the surety offered by some bidders came from much smaller groups, often consisting largely of relatives.[23] Obviously, both bids and surety varied according to the estimated yield of the rent, and the Granada silk rent involved more money and required a higher bid than, for example, one of the salt mines of the realm.[24] As the sixteenth century progressed, the crown annuities known as *juros* became a more common means of guaranteeing the bids of tax-farmers, although real estate continued as a prominent security. From 1505 to 1564, nearly sixty years, *toledanos* won the bid to farm the Granada silk rent, with the exception of one seven-year interval from 1553–60 (see Table 1).[25] *Toledanos* dominated the position of chief tax-

[20] Francisco Bejarano, *La industria de la seda en Málaga durante el siglo XVI* (Madrid, 1951), pp. 25, 27.

[21] The document, from AGS, CC, Personas, letra T, has been published in Antonio Blanco Sánchez, *Entre Fray Luis y Quevedo. En busca de Francisco de la Torre* (Salamanca, 1982), pp. 221–3, who states that the document is related to the Granada silk rent.

[22] Ramón Carande, *La hacienda real de Castilla. II: Carlos V y sus banqueros* (Madrid, 1949), pp. 314–18. K. Garrad, 'La industria sedera granadina en el siglo XVI y su conexión con el levantamiento de las Alpujarras (1568–1571)', *Miscelánea de estudios árabes y hebraicos* (Granada, 1956), pp. 83–5.

[23] AGS, CJH, *leg.* 44, fo. 105 for Diego García, tax-farmer of the salt mines of Espartinas, who was backed in large part by the San Pedro family of Toledo.

[24] For the salt mines of Atienza in the 1550s, the tax-farmer owed the crown some 8.5 million *maravedís* annually. See AGS, CJH, *leg.* 25, fo. 131, and Modesto Ulloa, *La Hacienda real de Castilla en el reinado de Felipe II* (Madrid, 1977), p. 381.

[25] The information about the chief tax-farmers, the years in which they served in this post, and the amount they paid annually to the crown is taken from Carande, *La hacienda real,* chapter

Table 1. *Tax farmers of Granada silk, 1505–69*

Years	Amount paid annually (*maravedís*)	Tax-farmers
1505–07	7,950,713	Juan de la Fuente and Fernando Hurtado (from Toledo)
1508–10	7,950,713	Juan de la Fuente
1511–16	7,427,000	Juan and Diego de la Fuente, brothers
1517–24	11,003,120	Juan de la Torre and Alonso de Toledo (from Toledo
1525–31	12,687,000	Juan de la Torre
1532–38	13,947,000	Juan de la Torre
1539–46	19,250,000	Juan de la Torre
1547–52	20,313,000	Juan de Alcocer, vecino of Toledo (from Toledo)
1553–60	25,938,000	Díaz Sánchez de Avila
1561–63	42,617,634	Juan de Alcocer and Alonso de la Torre
1564–68	53,106,597	Diego Núñez, from Segura de León and Gerónimo de Salamanca, householder of Antwerp
1569–73	64,129,212	Hernán Díaz de Alcocer, Antonio Alvarez de Alcocer, regidor of Toledo, and Manual Caldera

farmer almost until the second Revolt of the Alpujarras, a *morisco* uprising of 1568–70 that virtually destroyed the Granada silk trade.

The first Toledo family to appear as chief tax-farmers for the Granada silk rent is the Fuente. Members of this family attained distinction in the mid-fifteenth century when they used the surname of Jarada, but in 1505, one family member, Rodrigo de la Fuente, was condemned by the Inquisition and burned at the stake.[26] In this same year, a son of Rodrigo named

---

7 and pp. 599–602; Garrad, 'Industria sedera granadina', pp. 73–98; and for the later years, Ulloa, *Felipe II*, chapter 11.

26 José Carlos Gómez Menor, *Cristianos nuevos y mercaderes de Toledo* (Toledo, 1970), pp. 79–94, for the Fuente family. Martz, 'Families', 130–2 and chart 2 for Rodrigo de la Fuente and his ten children, based on AGS, CR, *leg.* 98–3, which includes the will of Rodrigo de la Fuente. The most distinguished family member of the fifteenth century was *alcalde* Diego González Jarada, who lost his municipal office in 1449.

Juan de la Fuente became chief tax-farmer, a post he retained until 1516. At times Juan was assisted by others who acted as joint tax-farmers; his brother Diego de la Fuente from 1511–16, and in earlier years, Fernando Hurtado. It is likely that Fernando Hurtado was also a relative, as Diego de la Fuente's wife, Guiomar Hurtado, had a brother named Fernando Hurtado. What is true of many commercial companies of this period appears to be true of the large-scale tax farms: the majority of the partners or associates were related either through blood or through marriage. Members of the Fuente family and their relatives probably abounded in the numerous lesser positions of the Granada tax-farm.

Succeeding Juan de la Fuente in the post of chief tax-farmer of the Granada silk rent was a man named Juan de la Torre. He came from a long line of Torre males, some of whom achieved fame and notoriety in fifteenth-century Toledo. In 1452, a man named Alfonso González de la Torre was a *regidor*, probably a member of the citizen's bench rather than the more prestigious noble's (*caballeros*) bench.[27] The Torre name appears again in 1467, during the rebellion of the Magdalena, when two brothers, Fernando and Alvaro de la Torre, apparently both *regidores*, entered the Toledo cathedral with arms to wage battle for the *converso* cause against the Old Christians; both met their end by hanging.[28] Then in 1485, as the Inquisition was setting up a tribunal in Toledo, a Bachelor de la Torre was accused of being the ringleader in a plot to murder the inquisitors during the Corpus Christi celebrations and he too was hanged.[29]

While the Torre family contributed its share of rebels and heretics, it also produced some successful merchants and financiers who dealt in expensive cloth and large sums of money. In 1496, Alonso de la Torre, together with Diego de la Fuente, provided luxury cloth to the household of Prince John and ladies of the royal household, and in later years they supplied the royal household with imported cloth from Florence and London.[30] For the crown, Alonso de la Torre signed a letter of exchange worth 750,000 *maravedís* for three galleons that served in Naples, and a man of the same

[27] RAH, CSC, 9/229, Higuera, fo. 198v. Pedro de Alcocer, *Historia, o descripción de la imperial ciudad de Toledo* [1554] (facsimile edition, Toledo, 1973), fo. 78v.

[28] Benito Ruano, *Toledo*, pp. 94–102. The author is not consistent about what office Fernando de la Torre occupied; on p. 95 he appears as a *jurado*, but on pp. 97, 101, and 109 note 83 he is called a *regidor*. It is possible that he held both offices at one time or another.

[29] For a contemporary narrative of the early years of the Inquisition in Toledo, see Fidel Fita, 'La inquisición toledana', *Boletín de la real academia de la historia*, 11 (1887), 289–322. RAH, CSC, 9/229, Higuera, fo. 235v, reports that Bachelor de la Torre was married to Costanza del Marmol, a descendent of the physician Dr Alfonso Chirino.

[30] Betsabé Caunedo del Potro, 'Un importante papel de los mercaderes de Toledo a finales del siglo XV. Abastecedores de la casa real', *Anales toledanos*, 16 (1983), 141–6.

name appears as a tax-farmer of the Bulls of Crusade in archbishopric of Toledo in 1494. In 1488 the merchant Alonso de la Torre was paid 609,792 *maravedís* from the royal treasury, and in 1498 he was one of five merchants who were collectively owed 10,000,000 *maravedís* by the crown.[31] It is impossible to say if the Alonso de la Torre involved in all these undertakings is the same individual, but if more than one man is involved, they probably formed part of the same family.

The pernicious and widespread custom of giving the same name to numerous contemporaries and to men of several generations gives ample reason for caution in identifying specific individuals. The name Juan de la Torre serves as one example of the profusion of homonyms, as between 1480 and 1530 at least four men shared this name. One was known as El Gordo (the fat man), and he lived in the parish of San Ginés with his wife, Elvira Ortiz, who had been imprisoned by the Inquisition.[32] Another homonym, given the nickname of El Viejo (the elder), married María de la Fuente, a daughter of the Rodrigo de la Fuente executed by the Inquisition in 1505. Still another, known as El Mozo (the younger), lost his father to the Inquisition and by 1528 had become a *jurado* of the city (see Figure 2).[33] In 1495–97 El Mozo lived in the parish of San Vicente, but his wife, Francisca de la Fuente, ended her days in the city of Granada with her Torre in-laws. Finally there is the tax-farmer, Juan de la Torre, the eldest son of Alfonso González de la Torre.[34] In official documents, Juan de la Torre never mentioned the name of his mother, an omission that suggests she suffered some sort of unfortunate contact with the Inquisition. These many Juan de la Torre obviously formed part of a family group, but it is difficult to establish the exact relationship.

The Juan de la Torre who became chief tax-farmer in 1517 had experience in silk before this date. He and two brothers, *jurado* Alonso Alvarez Husillo and Diego López Husillo, operated a commercial company that

---

[31] Ladero Quesada, *La hacienda real de Castilla en el siglo XV* (Laguna, 1973), pp. 293, 313.

[32] Martz, 'Families', charts 3 and 7 for Elvira Ortiz, a daughter of the Jarada-Fuente and the Martínez Cabal families.

[33] Cantera Burgos and León Tello, *Judaizantes*, p. 7, for Juan de la Torre, El Mozo, who lived in the parish of San Vicente and paid 10,000 *maravedís* for himself and his children, 'nietos de un condenado'. According to Aranda Pérez, *Poder municipal*, p. 188, Juan de la Torre, El Mozo, was a *jurado* for the parish of San Ginés from 1528–40.

[34] Gómez Menor, 'Sobre la familia toledana de la Palma', *Anales toledanos*, 11 (1976), 213, note 13, from AHPT, prot. 1225, fo. 285, 2 June 1512, for the children of Alfonso González de la Torre. Since the name of Juan de la Torre appears first, it is likely he was the eldest son. For reasons of chronology, the father of Juan de la Torre must be a younger homonym of the Alfonso González de la Torre who was a *regidor* in 1452.

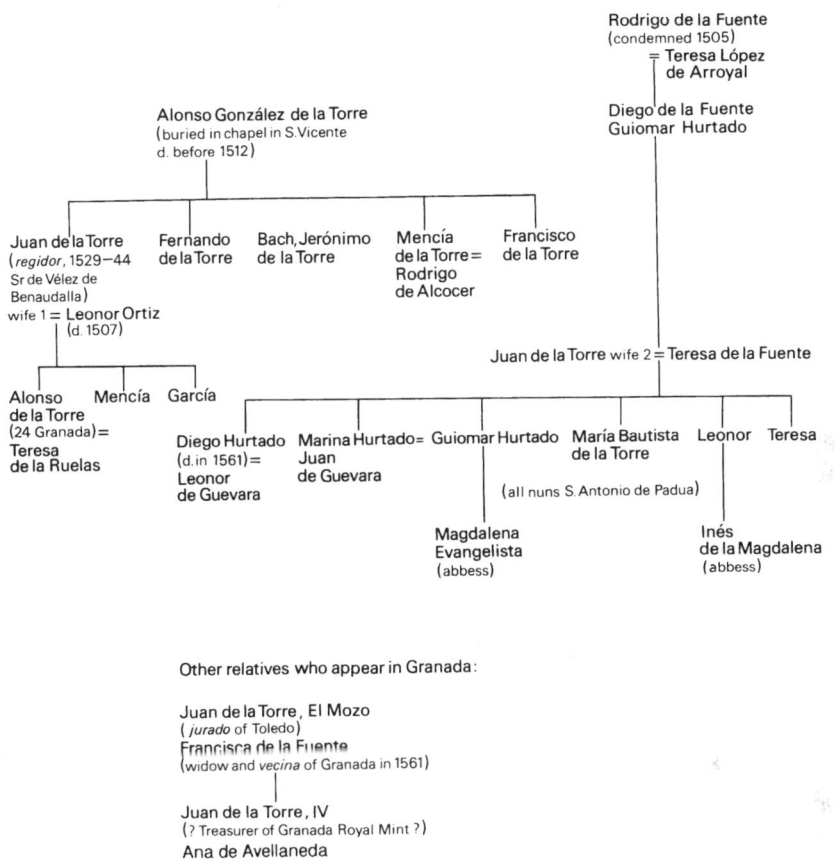

Figure 2   *Regidor* Juan de la Torre

dealt in silk in the cities of Granada and Valencia.[35] This company preceded and endured through Juan de la Torre's first tax-farming contract of 1517–24, as in 1525 the tax-farmer and his Husillo partners gave testimony about the abilities of a young relative who had been orphaned and was brought up and trained by his uncles in the silk business. As for the Husillos, some of whom adopted the surname of Cisneros in the sixteenth century,[36] they continued in the silk business and prospered. In the 1560s, Juan Sánchez de Cisneros paid 2,500 ducats to the crown for the purchase of

[35] AGS, CC, *leg.* 173–34. Emancipation of Francisco de Santo Domingo, 1525.

[36] Gómez Menor, 'La progenie hebrea del padre Pedro de Ribadeneira, S.I.', *Sefarad,* 36 (1976), 307–32. Martz, 'Families', 134–5, 150.

an office known as Receiver-General (*Depositario-General*) of the city of Toledo, a post the family retained into the seventeenth century.[37]

Juan de la Torre may have been related to the Husillo through his first wife, Leonor Ortiz, whose origins are unknown. She died in 1507 leaving behind three young children (see Figure 2).[38] Given that Juan de la Torre was married and had three children in 1507, he must have been born in the 1480s, since within the merchant community males usually established their households at about 25 years of age. As a widower with young children, Juan de la Torre soon remarried. In choosing his second wife, Teresa de la Fuente, it might be said that he married the Granada silk rent, for she was a daughter of Guiomar Hurtado and the Diego de la Fuente who acted as joint tax-farmer with his brother Juan from 1511 to 1516.

In an era when most commercial undertakings were conceived and operated as extensions of the family, care was required in choosing one's in-laws. The need to acquire reliable business associates may have contributed to the endogamy practised by many middle class *conversos* of Toledo. In marrying a daughter to a local *converso* of equal social status, one got a known quantity, a son-in-law of similar background and values, trained in business and finance, bound to loyalty and fidelity not just by a dowry and a marriage contract but by long-term bonds and attachments. Given their common heritage and vocations, it is likely that the Fuente, the Torre and the Husillo families had been intermarrying for many years, both before and after conversion. But events of the fifteenth and sixteenth century – conflict and persecution in the form of the Inquisition and the pure blood statutes – may have led to a heightened ethnic definition that reinforced marriage within the community.[39] Whatever the causes, ethnic, social and occupational endogamy appears to be far more frequent for the majority of the Toledo *converso* community than the more spectacular cases of exogamy, such as the marriages already noted for offspring of the royal secretary and his illegitimate brother in the kingdom of Granada.

In Juan de la Torre's first contract from 1517 to 1524, he shared the Granada silk tax farm with an unidentified Alonso de Toledo, but from 1524 until 1546, he was on his own. The Granada silk rent involved large sums of

---

[37] AGS, Dirección General de Tesoro, Inventario 24, *leg.* 322, no foliation (n.f.); AM Toledo, 'Libro de la razón de los corregidores, dignidades y regidores...', n.f. (hereafter 'Libro de regidores').

[38] AHPT, prot. 1268, fos. 239v-40, 12 (?) July 1507: *poder de testar* of Leonor Ortiz. That Leonor's spouse is the future tax-collector is confirmed by her statement that he was a son of Alfonso González de la Torre.

[39] This topic is explored further in Martz, 'Pure blood statutes in sixteenth-century Toledo: implementation as opposed to adoption', *Sefarad*, 54 (1994), 83–107.

money, and in keeping with the general rise of prices in sixteenth-century Castile, the sums of money became ever larger as the century progressed. In the early years when the Fuente family controlled the tax farm, the amount paid annually to the crown was between 7.4 and 7.9 million *maravedís*. Juan de la Torre started out in 1517 paying 11 million *maravedís* a year, and by 1539–46 it was close to 20 million *maravedís*. But this pales beside the rise of 1561–64, when Juan de la Torre's son, Alonso de la Torre, took over the tax farm with a bid of more than 42 million, a 60 per cent increase over the nearly 26 million paid in 1553–60. The hefty sum of 1561–64 reflects the fiscal needs of the crown, which had pawned all its income from the silk rent, and nearly all other rents, in the interests of making Europe safe for catholicism. Garrad argues persuasively that the enormous increase in taxation was one of the causes leading to the decadence of the Granada silk industry and an important factor in precipitating the *morisco* uprising of 1568.[40]

Before the collapse of the 1570s, the Granada silk rent appears to have been lucrative, and the tax-farmers attempted to make it even more so. Prized for its quality by Castilians and foreigners alike, Granada silk was often in short supply. To satisfy the demand and increase the money collected in taxes, the tax-farmers illegally imported lesser quality silk from Murcia and Valencia, mixed it with Granada silk and charged the same amount of money for the inferior mixture. As early as 1525 the city councillors of Granada gained an order (*cédula*) from the emperor banning the entry of Murcian and Valencian silk into Granada.[41] This seems to have inspired little compliance, since in the Castilian Cortes of 1537 the deputies from the city of Granada complained that Juan de la Torre was continuing the same practice.[42]

Aside from tampering with the quality of the silk, the chief tax-farmer possessed unlimited opportunities to buy silk for himself and his friends at favourable prices, notwithstanding royal regulations to the contrary. In 1501 the Catholic Monarchs forbade the tax-farmers from buying any silk outside the *alcaicería*, the place where all the raw silk was collected, assessed, bought and sold and taxed, which meant they had to pay the same taxes as everyone else. But in the 1540s, Juan de la Torre got permission to buy privately 2,000 lb of silk a year. According to a 1543 report of the Granada *corregidor*, he took advantage of this concession to buy 30,000 lb of silk, a quantity estimated as a third of the total exported from Granada,

---

[40] Garrad, 'Industria sedera granadina', pp. 93–6.   [41] Ibid., p. 82.
[42] Ibid., p. 82, from M. Colmeiro, *Cortes de los antiguos reinos de León y de Castilla* (Madrid, 1861–1902), IV. Cortes of 1537, pet. 123, p. 680.

making him 'the largest exporter of the kingdom of Granada'.[43] That a royal ruling of 1552 prohibited the chief tax-farmer and his assistants from buying any silk for resale implies that later tax-farmers continued the practices of their predecessors.[44] In defence of the tax-farmers, collecting the money owing on Granada silk was a complicated business. In 1561 it was described as 'a rent of great risk and danger',[45] a truism that applies to any commodity affected by the vagaries of weather and the health and productive capacity of living organisms like silkworms and mulberry trees.[46]

But profit appears to have outweighed risk during the years when Juan de la Torre was chief tax-farmer. The first outward sign of increased prosperity occurred in 1529 when Juan de la Torre bought an office of *regidor* in his native city of Toledo from don Alvaro de Ayala, the father of the fourth count of Fuensalida.[47] The list of merits submitted by Juan de la Torre to qualify for this office include no genealogy other than the name of his father, and statements to the effect that he was a man of property and wealth who owned impressive houses in Toledo and, probably of greatest importance at this time, that he had supported Charles V in the *comunero* rebellion. Another sign of success is Juan de la Torre's appearance as a deputy (*procurador*) for the city of Toledo in the Castilian Cortes of 1538, which was held in the imperial city. He and the other Toledo deputy had the honour of sitting together on a special bench in front of the monarch, a far better seating arrangement than that given to the deputies from other cities. Possibly this token of esteem played a part in convincing Juan de la Torre to support the emperor's request for an enormous subsidy, and to persuade other Toledo *regidores* to do the same.[48]

Following in the wake of the successful tax-farmer were his relatives. From the 1520s to the 1540s, the Torre family boasted an ever larger contingent in the local governing councils of Toledo. Four Torre men appeared in the council of *jurados* – Juan, El Mozo; Rodrigo; Alonso; and

[43] Garrad, 'Industria sedera granadina', p. 87.
[44] Manuel Garzón Pareja, *La industria sedera en España. El arte de la seda de Granada* (Granada, 1972), p. 424.
[45] AGS, CJH, *leg.* 41, fo. 33.
[46] James Casey, *The kingdom of Valencia in the seventeenth century* (Cambridge, 1979), p. 86 for the effect of floods on the mulberry trees and silk production in Valencia.
[47] AGS, CC, *leg.* 198, fo. 28: hearing for *reguría* of Juan de la Torre, May 1529, organized by *jurado* Juan de la Torre, El Mozo. The tax-farmer sat on the citizens' bench; don Alvaro de Ayala was a *caballero* of Calatrava and chief huntsman of Charles V.
[48] Colmeiro, *Cortes*, v, p. 36 for the seating arrangements of Juan de la Torre and the *jurado* and *licenciado*, Garcia de León; pp. 96–7 for a 'Carta de creencia de Carlos V a Juan de la Torre y el Licenciado León. . .para tratar con la ciudad sobre un servicio extraordinario de 200 o 150 cuentos', 28 January 1539, from AMT, Cajón 8, *leg.* 1, no. 56.

Gonzalo de la Torre. As of 1539, Alonso de la Torre, possibly the same man who had been a *jurado*, became a *regidor*, retaining his seat until 1545.[49] The sudden spurt of Torre men in local politics reflected the family's increasing prosperity and reputation. Even if the Torre family did not boast as many *regidores* as the Toledo-Zapata family in earlier years, they were a force in local governing circles. Aside from the benefits of prestige and the opportunity to influence local policy, the purchase of either of these offices provided the owners with exemption from direct taxes, from billeting troops, from being jailed for debts, and the privilege of having any legal cases decided by a special judge.[50]

That Juan de la Torre was a householder, or *vecino*, in both Toledo and Granada indicates he had ties and loyalties in each city. In Granada his duties as chief tax-farmer required a residence and a substantial family presence, while Toledo was his native city, the place where his ancestors and those of his two wives were born and buried. Juan de la Torre remained active in Toledo until the 1540s. He established a chantry in the family chapel in the parish church of San Vicente in 1536, naming his eldest son, Alonso de la Torre, as patron.[51] Four of his and Teresa de la Fuente's daughters were placed in the Toledo nunnery of San Antonio de Padua.[52] Two of these daughters inherited their father's talent for administration: María Baptista served as abbess of San Antonio for nine years, and Guiomar Hurtado governed with such success that she was transferred to another convent to serve as abbess. However, in 1544 Juan de la Torre renounced his office of *regidor* in Toledo, probably indicating that he was transferring his main residence to the city of Granada.[53]

The tax-farmer had good reason to abandon Toledo for the periphery, as he and his family enjoyed substantial prestige and property in the

---

[49] AMT, 'Libro de regidores', n.f. Alonso sat in the fourth old seat on the left side.

[50] Aranda Pérez, *Poder municipal*, p. 68, for the list of privileges granted to the *jurados*. The privilege of not being imprisoned for debts does not seem to have applied to *jurado* Rodrigo de Alcocer, who was jailed in 1559 for not paying what he owed on his contract for the salt mines of Atienza. See Ulloa, *Felipe II*, p. 381.

[51] AGS, CM, *leg*. 64, fo. 38. I believe Alonso de la Torre to be a son of Juan de la Torre's first wife, Leonor Ortiz, as a son of this name is mentioned in her *poder de testar*, but it is possible that this son died and Juan de la Torre had another son named Alonso with his second wife. The founder of the chapel in the parish church of San Vicente was Alfonso González de la Torre.

[52] Antolín Abad Pérez, *Soledad Sonora. Monasterio de San Antonio* (Toledo, 1980) for the history of the convent, pp. 5, 104–6, for Juan de la Torre's daughters and their deeds. Gómez-Menor, *Cristianos*, doc. 285, from AHPT, prot. 1282, fo. 234, 9 June 1532.

[53] AMT, 'Libro de regidores'. Juan de la Torre occupied the twelfth old seat on the right side and he renounced his seat to Diego de Ayala.

kingdom of Granada. Elites of the realm sought his opinion about silk. In 1545, the marquis of Ceñete asked him for a comparative assessment of the colour, price and quality of the silk cloth manufactured in Toledo and Granada.[54] And in 1546, he was one of six men who served on a committee dedicated to reforming the royal taxes imposed on Granada silk.[55] Headed by the archbishop of Granada and the president of the royal chancellery court, Juan Niño de Guevara, yet another *toledano*, the results of the committee's efforts were codified in royal legislation.[56] But the most impressive sign of material success occurred some time before 1553, when Juan de la Torre became the lord of Vélez de Benaudalla, a town about twenty-five miles south of the city of Granada.[57] As is true of the royal secretary Fernán Alvarez de Toledo-Zapata, Juan de la Torre left to his eldest son an entail that included the title of lordship over a village. Other family members also advanced their social status in the southern kingdom. The eldest son, Alonso de la Torre, became a city councillor of Granada, and Juan de la Torre IV, whose precise linkage within the family is uncertain, became treasurer of the Granada Royal Mint.[58]

Juan de la Torre's name appeared as chief tax-farmer of the Granada silk rent for the last time in 1546. By then he was getting on in years – he must have been in his sixties – and possibly weary of collecting the tax on Granada silk. From 1546 to 1552, Juan de Alcocer, a native and a *jurado* of Toledo but a householder of Granada, took over the post. It could be that Juan de Alcocer outbid Torre for the silk rent, but certain facts suggest this was a friendly take over. Marital links existed between the two families, as one of Juan de la Torre's sisters, Mencía, was married to a Rodrigo de Alcocer. In 1547 Juan de Alcocer advanced 25,000 ducats to the crown in

[54] Miguel Lasso de la Vega y López de Tejada, Marqués del Saltillo, *Doña Mencía de Mendoza, marquesa del Ceñete (1508–1554)* (Madrid, 1942) p. 50. 'Me haréis placer de avisarme si los colores de las felpas que ahí se hacen son mejores que las que se hacen en Toledo, y si son más ligeras, cubiertas, y el precio que cobran cada vara'.

[55] AGS, CMC, época 2, *leg.* 851: 'Seda del reyno de Granada. Pareceres que dieron el arzobispo de Granada y otros partes particulares . . .' April 1546.

[56] *Nueva recopilación de las leyes de estos reynos* (Madrid, 1772), Lib. 9, Titulo 30: 'Nuevo arancel de los derechos de la seda de Granada . . .'

[57] AGS, CJH, *leg.* 24, fo. 543, regarding the need to contact Juan de la Torre in 1553 about the *alcabalas* and *tercias* of Vélez Benaudalla; and *leg.* 41, fo. 39 for Teresa de la Fuente, widow of Juan de la Torre, señor de Vélez de Benaudalla.

[58] Francisca de la Fuente, a *vecina* of Granada in 1556 and a widow of Juan de la Torre, El Mozo, had a son named Juan de la Torre, also a *vecino* of Granada in 1556, whom I believe to be the treasurer of the royal mint. Juan de la Torre IV was treasurer in 1562 (AGS, CJH, *leg.* 43, fo. 106) and had given up his office by the 1580s, according to the dates given by Garzón Pareja, *La real casa de la moneda de Granada* (Granada, 1970), pp. 8–11.

the name of Juan de la Torre.[59] And in later years Juan de Alcocer acted as joint tax-farmer with Juan de la Torre's son, Alonso de la Torre.

The chief tax-farmer from 1553 to 1559, Díaz Sánchez de Avila, a city councillor of Granada and the lord of Casulas, was a rival and not a *toledano*.[60] Juan de la Torre's death in about 1553 may have enabled Díaz Sánchez to wrest control from the Toledo contingent and win the bid to farm Granada silk from 1553 to 1560. But Díaz Sánchez de Avila died in 1557, and in this year Alonso de la Torre joined with Juan de Alcocer to bid for the silk rent from 1561 to 1568. To raise the surety needed to secure their bid, Alonso offered his own possessions and persuaded members of his large family and others to do the same.[61] His step-mother, Teresa de la Fuente, contributed some 12,000,000 *maravedís* on the property that she and Alonso had inherited in a entail founded for them by Juan de la Torre. Alonso renounced his rights to all the entailed items he inherited from his father, even including the persons and possessions of some forty *moriscos* in his village of Vélez de Benaudalla, whose appraised value was 6,225,000 *maravedís*. The treasurer of the Granada Royal Mint volunteered his office, worth 4,000,000 *maravedís*. Alonso de la Torre's wife offered 1,760,000 *maravedís*, and his step-sister Marina Hurtado and her spouse provided 2,000,000 *maravedís*. According to Alonso de la Torre's estimate, the surety he offered amounted to more than 38,000,000 *maravedís*, a figure that gives some idea of the wealth assembled by his father.

In 1561, just as their first contract was beginning, Torre and Alcocer asked for and were granted a four-year extension on their contract, which now ran from 1561 to 1572.[62] In addition, Alonso reminded Philip II of an unpaid debt of 12,000,000 *maravedís* the emperor owed to his deceased father. In 1561, Philip agreed to pay Alonso 8,000,000 *maravedís* of this debt on condition that both he and his family cease all efforts to collect anything more from him. Finally, Alonso asked that some of his backers be freed from their obligations of collateral, including the *morisco* villagers of Vélez de Benaudalla, the treasurer of the Granada Mint, his step-mother, and the father-in-law of Juan de Alcocer, Juan Núñez de Madrid, who had volunteered a *juro* of 12,000,000 *maravedís*. The new collateral consisted of a large number of *juros*, many issued to cover the 1558 crown appropriation of the gold and silver coming from the Indies for various merchants, that belonged

---

[59] Carande, *La hacienda real*, p. 329.
[60] Ibid., p. 325. Ulloa, *Felipe II*, p. 363, for his title of señor de Casulas. According to Alfonso María Guilarte, *El régimen señorial en el siglo XVI* (Madrid, 1962), doc. 23, Díaz Sánchez bought Casulas from Rodrigo de Ulloa.
[61] AGS, CJH, *leg.* 41, fos. 39 and 43. [62] AGS, CJH, *leg.* 41, fo. 33.

to Juan de Curiel de la Torre, whose name suggests that he too formed part of the extensive Torre family.[63]

After all these modifications, the tax-farm of Torre and Alcocer lasted only until 1564.[64] Juan de Alcocer ceded his part of the contract to Alonso de la Torre in 1563, and soon afterwards a rival group, headed by Diego Núñez, a householder of Segura de León in Extremadura, backed by Gerónimo de Salamanca, who resided in Antwerp, outbid Torre by offering more than 53 million *maravedís* a year. In 1568, Salamanca sought and received the backing of the ever-present Genoese, but this contract was voided because of the *morisco* uprising. The next year, *toledanos* again appear as tax-farmers in the form of Hernán Díaz de Alcocer, the Toledo *regidor* Antonio Alvarez de Alcocer, and Manual Caldera. Not surprisingly, they too failed to meet their bid and soon sought backing from the Genoese. The Granada silk rent limped along until the end of the century, rarely paying the amount bid by the chief tax-farmers, even though the bids diminished to 33-35 million in the late 1580s and 1590s.

Much of the silk cloth woven in Granada was exported abroad, to Italy, Portugal, Flanders and the Indies, but much of the raw silk was exported to the industrial cities of Castile.[65] That the early tax-farmers were natives of Toledo must surely have contributed to the impressive development of silk manufacture in the central city. Having a *toledano* serve in this post gave Toledo merchants an inside track on the supply of the raw material, leaving other cities to find their silk where they could. Cordoba, for example, was forced to rely upon inferior Murcian silk as early as 1538.[66] A common point of origin and ethnicity did not always lead to cooperation, but it is likely that the Toledo silk merchants recognized a valuable monopoly when they saw one, prompting them to put aside the inevitable quarrels, rivalries and skirmishes in the interests of gaining wealth for themselves and their city, much as they had done in earlier years when they underwrote the mysterious Asiento de la Tabla.

If Juan de la Torre and many of Toledo's silk merchants clearly profited from Granada silk, so too did the artisans of Toledo who found employment in the manufacture of silk. In 1562 the master silk weavers of Toledo, who formed a guild, El Arte de la Seda, under the advocation of Our Lady of the

---

[63] AGS, CJH, *leg.* 41, fos. 36 and 37; Juan de Curiel de la Torre was treasurer of the *mesas maestrales* of the three military orders in 1561. Ulloa, *Felipe II*, pp. 770–1, for the *juros* given to Curiel de la Torre in 1561 to repay him for others he held in the Casa de la Contratación.

[64] Ulloa, *Felipe II*, pp. 363–9 for details of tax-farmers up to 1599.

[65] Garrad, 'Industria sedera granadina', p. 90.

[66] Fortea Pérez, *Córdoba*, pp. 321–3.

Rosary, numbered 423.[67] By the standards of the time, this is an impressive number. In 1561, the city of Toledo counted 11,254 households, so the 423 master silk weavers account for 3.75 per cent of the total, which probably made them the largest guild of the city.[68] Cordoba, thought to be third behind Granada and Toledo in the manufacture of silk cloth, had only 295 master silk weavers in 1594–97.[69]

The figures for the master weavers do not tell the whole story of the number of people employed in the weaving of silk. Each master weaver might own anywhere from one to eight looms, and the number owned by the Toledo masters is unknown. But in the 1590s, the 284 master silk weavers of Cordoba owned a total of 632 looms, an average of 2.2 looms per master.[70] If this average is applied to the 423 Toledo masters, they had about 930 looms. As for the people who worked each loom, five has been suggested as the maximum number.[71] Erring on the conservative side and using an average of two, as many as 1,860 people may have been involved in the weaving of silk cloth in Toledo in 1562. This is 16.52 per cent of the 1,561 house-holders, but only 3.3 per cent of the estimated 56,270 inhabitants. However, weavers were not the only people involved in the manufacture of silk. The dyers, spinners and twisters are excluded, to mention but a few of the many people involved in the labour-intensive process of manufacturing silk cloth and other products. Adding to this the merchants who dealt in silk, it is clear that silk was a big business indeed.

Not only were the master silk weavers of Toledo numerous, at least some of them were relatively prosperous. In the late 1550s the guild became embroiled in three costly legal cases aired in the Royal Council. By 1562, when a fourth case was added, 84,000 *maravedís* had been spent in legal fees, although 30,000 *maravedís* were still owing to the lawyers. In addition, the guild kept a Poor Chest (*Arca de los Pobres*) funded by money from fines and the charges for examinations of apprentices. According to the man who kept the accounts of the Poor Chest, obviously not a disinterested witness, from the late 1550s until 1562 the guild had paid out annually 64,000 *maravedís* to

---

[67] AGS, CR, *leg.* 240, fo. 5: 'Luis de Santa Ursula y consortes, maestros del arte de la seda, vecinos de Toledo, y Yuste Berdugo y consortes, vecinos de la dicha cibdad'. My thanks to José Luis Rodríguez de Diego of the Archive of Simancas for help with this document.

[68] For the 1561 census in its entirety, see Linda Martz and Julio Porres, *Toledo y los toledanos en 1561* (Toledo, 1974). Unfortunately, few occupations are given in the census, and only 192 silk weavers, 3 silk spinners and 2 silk dyers are mentioned.

[69] Fortea Pérez, *Córdoba*, pp. 315–16 gives the number of masters as 295; however on p. 363, cuadro 54, based on the same document, the number of masters is given as 284.

[70] Ibid., p. 363 for the number of looms per master, which ranged from one to eight.

[71] Domínguez Ortiz, *Orto y ocaso de Sevilla* (3rd edition, Seville, 1981), p. 47.

those in need, excluding burials for the poor. He also testified that the money paid to the needy represented only a third of the money in the Poor Chest, so the total collected annually by the guild was about 192,000 *maravedís*.

Three of the cases being litigated by the guild were against the men who imported the raw silk, supplied the credit, and distributed and sold the finished product, or the municipal corporations to which these men belonged. One dispute was with the *regidores*, who wanted some say in the appointment of guild inspectors (*veedores*) and examiners, a pretension resisted by the silk weavers who claimed they had appointed both of the officials 'from time immemorial' and that this prerogative, included in their regulations, had been approved by the emperor. With the council of *jurados* the guild members argued the right to have their own house or meeting place in the city, a claim resisted by the *jurados* on grounds that this would lead to the creation of a league or monopoly. The third squabble was with the silk merchants of the city over the way in which silk cloth was made.

If these three disputes prompt thoughts of the familiar antagonism between capitalists and labourers, the fourth case does not. It was among the guild members themselves, split between the wealthier members, ten to fifteen of whom controlled the offices of the guild, and the less wealthy, who resented their monopoly. In the end, however, the two factions united in a common cause, voting in 1562 to continue the three legal cases still pending and to divide the estimated cost of past and future litigation (112,500 *maravedís*) among the membership. Compared with the vast sums relating to the Granada silk rent, those of the guild seem paltry, but on the scale of the working man they are substantial.

On all levels of society, silk played a vital role in the economy of Toledo. Granada was not the only place in the periphery that provided silk for the looms of the central city, as Toledo merchants were also active in the peripheral kingdoms of Valencia and Murcia. Within these two kingdoms, the export of raw silk to Toledo and other areas was at times criticized as detrimental to the local economy.[72] In Murcia, for example, in 1504 and again in 1570, concerned citizens bemoaned the lack of silk cloth manufactured in the city, pointing out that if more silk were worked there, the jobs created would benefit both rich and poor residents.[73] In a region rich in raw silk, Murcians who wanted finished products were forced to pay high prices to merchants from Toledo and other places. The connection between silk

---

[72] Casey, *Valencia*, p. 87, for the complaints of Valencia, but these occurred in 1621, when the local silk industry was in decline.

[73] Francisco Chacón Jiménez, *Murcia en la centuria del quinientos* (Murcia, 1979), pp. 343–6.

manufacture, job creation and increased income for the citizenry had obviously been understood and acted upon by the Toledo mercantile contingent as far back as 1505, when Juan de la Fuente became the chief tax-farmer of the Granada silk rent. What Murcia lacked, an enterprising bourgeoisie,[74] Toledo had in abundance. Thanks to their energy, the raw material from the periphery enriched those who lived in the centre of the realm, from the wealthy tax-farmers down to the humble silk spinners.

Those most visibly enriched were the merchants and the tax-farmers. Watching these men as they sought to move up the social scale, the first step on the ladder for many was securing a municipal office, whether in Toledo or Granada. In Toledo, merchants and financiers abounded as *jurados* and as citizen *regidores*, many of whom played an active role in city council business, particularly in organizing the unending deficit-financing schemes of the period. For those interested in silk, these offices enabled them to exercise some influence in the city's policy towards the silk trade and over the guild of master silk weavers. And some, like Juan de la Torre, represented the interests of their city in the Cortes. Those who rose the highest might buy a village, but the cost of this precluded most, and some may not have been attracted by becoming a dynastic landowner, preferring to reinvest their money in trade, urban real estate or more liquid instruments. However they chose to invest their earnings, it is fairly clear that some Toledo *conversos* enjoyed upward mobility and a fair degree of political and economic power.

Perhaps they enjoyed too much power, for in 1566 the crown imposed a pure blood statute on the citizen's bench of the Toledo city council, emulating an earlier statute enacted in the Toledo cathedral chapter in 1548.[75] In contrast with the fifteenth-century statutes, those of the sixteenth century contained no accusation of judaizing against those being excluded, a charge the fervent anti-*converso* Juan Martínez de Silíceo, cardinal-archbishop of Toledo and the driving force behind the 1548 cathedral statute, would surely have mentioned had it been applicable. This omission implies that these men had become sincere practitioners of Christianity and that the original mission of the Inquisition had been achieved. But instead of commending *conversos* for their progress in attaining religious conformity, the sixteenth-century statutes held them responsible for the sins of their ancestors who had been punished by the Inquisition. Not only did they inherit this stigma, but also a long list of undesirable features – personality

[74] Ibid., p. 346.
[75] Sicroff, *Estatutos*, Cap. 3, for the cathedral statute; Martz, 'Pure blood' for the city council statute.

traits, occupations and values – seen to characterize their ethnic group. The later statutes rekindled all the old animosities between the so-called two lineages: the pure Old Christians versus the impure *conversos*.

The statute imposed upon the mercantile-minded citizen's bench in 1566 did more than threaten some with the loss of their office on the basis of genes and ancestors. In theory, the Toledo city council was evenly divided between citizen and noble *regidores*, with twelve men sitting on each bench. The new royal decree upset this balance by reducing the number of citizen *regidores* to eight and increasing the nobles to sixteen, a clear indication of which estate was favoured and which was expendable. The 1566 statute carried a fairly strong message that the contribution and values of the citizen *regidores* were of little worth. If an increasing preference for aristocratic values is evident in many areas of Europe, the pure blood ethos was unique to Spain, and it placed a double onus upon the most productive and dynamic minority of Castilian society. That Toledo seems to have been the only city council that suffered the imposition of a pure blood statute in the sixteenth century suggests that some of the city's *converso* community had been too successful and too resilient, evoking fear and jealousy among those who watched their activities and upward progress.

5

✳

Castile, Spain and the monarchy: the political community from *patria natural* to *patria nacional*

I. A. A. THOMPSON

Significant historical periods are characterized by the frontiers within which a man extends his affections.[1] Multiple monarchies, modern state, nation-state: each involves different patterns of community consciousness; the transformation from one state to the other has at its heart the creation of a new consciousness of community. The capability of a particular perception of community in any given area to stretch to embrace territorial and dynastic expansion and to overcome competing loyalties is an essential key to the development and subsequent cohesion of the state as nation. The consciousness of community is not, of course, singular. Communities coexist, in concentric layers, or in adjacent sectors, imposing different loyalties which are not necessarily mutually exclusive, although they may ultimately be so.[2] The hierarchalization and the rehierarchalization of community loyalties is what the political process, at bottom, is all about. The affective is perhaps the determining dimension in the building of nations in contradistinction to the construction of states. Put another way, political history is contingent on the meaning of *patria*.

This essay is an elaboration of a paper presented at the II Seminario de Historia Moderna de España, 'Del Renacimiento al Barroco. Cambio y Continuidad en la España Moderna (1450–1650)', conducted by John Elliott for the Fundación Duques de Soria in July 1992.
Translations are by the author unless otherwise attributed.
[1] Kohn as quoted by J. A. Maravall, *Estado moderno y mentalidad social (siglos XV a XVII)* (Madrid, 1972), I, p. 473.
[2] See Peter Sahlins, *Boundaries: the making of France and Spain in the Pyrenees* (Berkeley, 1989), p. 7.

John Elliott's abiding interest in the themes of *patria*, national sentiment and community has been apparent throughout his long catalogue of distinguished contributions to Spanish and early modern European history.[3] This essay takes up one aspect of the role of nationalism in the configuration of the early modern state to which he drew attention in his examination of the early seventeenth-century Spanish reform movement, but which has hardly been pursued by historians since. Though coming to the problem of the relationship between centre and periphery, Madrid and the provinces, Castile and Aragon, from the perspective of Catalonia, Elliott recognized that there was also a distinct Castilian perception of empire and that the attempts of ministers to restructure the monarchy and the acute heightening of Catalan national sensitivity that followed were themselves in part responses to a revived Castilian nationalism which was both a reaction to the way the monarchy had failed to develop as a political community in the past and a determining element in the way it was to develop in the future.[4]

Surprisingly, however, the concept of castilianism and the nature of a specifically Castilian (as opposed to Spanish) perception of the monarchy has remained almost entirely unexplored. It has generally been deemed sufficient to portray Castile as the imperial power, hi-jacking the mantle of Spain, and hence for no distinction between Spain and Castile to seem to be needed. Castile and Spain have become conflated, used interchangeably and apparently indiscriminately by even the most careful of historians. No serious consideration has been given to why one term was used to stand for, or rather than, the other. Studies of the language apart, there is virtually no literature on castilianism in the early modern period to compare with the attention that has been paid to Catalan or Basque national sentiment, for example. Even Maravall's wide-ranging and authoritative discussion of the historical development of such concepts as *reino*, *patria* and *nación* has nothing to say about castilianism, and indeed does not recognize the application of these concepts to Castile *per se* as a distinct problem.[5]

As a result the complexities of Castilian consciousness and thus the Castilian response to the monarchy have been simplified and misunderstood; so too, inevitably, has the dynamic of state formation in post-reconquest Spain. The belief in the castilianization of Spain as one of the

---

[3] Notably in *The revolt of the Catalans* (1963), 'Revolution and continuity in Early Modern Europe' (1969), 'Self-perception and decline in early seventeenth-century Spain' (1977), 'Spain and its empire in the sixteenth and seventeenth centuries' (1982) and, most recently, 'A Europe of composite monarchies', *Past and Present* 137 (1992), 48–71.

[4] John H. Elliott, *Spain and its world 1500–1700* (New Haven and London, 1989), p. 236.

[5] Maravall, *Estado moderno*, I, p. 457ff.

principal driving forces in both the formation and the deformation of the monarchy has become a convention not only of historiography but of history, and hence of politics. The subordination of a liberal, constitutionalist periphery to an authoritarian and dogmatic core has come to be seen as *the* historic problem of modern Spain. Without denying the political convenience of portraying a 'continentalist' Castilian centralism as the evil genie of modern Spanish history,[6] it might be suggested that there is an alternative history of castilianism which was not represented by the ideology of imperialism and which involved not so much the 'castilianization of Spain', as the 'hispanization and dehispanization of Castile'. That history could (to suggest a common victimhood) be summarized as the 'peripheralization' of Castile.[7] If it is true that 'a nation's history is the history of that nation's idea of itself as a nation',[8] this omission has had its effect on the history of Spain no less than on that of Castile.

I Community, kingdom and monarchy

The concept of Spain and Castile not merely as territories but also as peoples and heritages was well established in popular and court literature by the later Middle Ages.[9] Yet despite the fusion of *reino* and *tierra*, kingdom and land, *tierra* and *patria*, land and country, and both *tierra* and *patria* with Castile by the fifteenth century, the extension of the sentiment of *patria* to the entirety of Spain that Maravall argues for did not supersede either provincial, local or civic patriotism. Indeed, the idea of community as a national entity remained underdeveloped not only with respect to the union of the crowns, but also in regard to the component kingdoms of the crown of Castile itself.

For the great bulk of writers, following the Aristotelian tradition, the community found its expression first of all in the city, the aggregation of the natural community of the family in its most perfect, that is, complete and self-sufficient, form. From García de Castrojeriz in the fourteenth century to Saavedra Fajardo in the seventeenth, the city was the quintessential embodiment of community, and the first *patria* to which the citizen owed duty and loyalty. But the broader geography of the community, the

---

[6] See, for example, J. Beneyto, *España, meseta y litoral* (Madrid, 1983).

[7] M. González Herrero, *Memorial de Castilla* (Segovia, 1978), p. 120, 'Castilla ha sido la primera víctima, y una de las más sacrificadas del Estado español.'

[8] Sestán, quoted by Maravall, *Estado moderno*, I, p. 517, n. 121.

[9] See G. Davis, 'The development of a national theme in medieval Castilian literature', *Hispanic Review*, 3 (1935), 149–61.

ship of the city to a greater political community, was something that, given the structure of the monarchy, received remarkably little attention.

The common view that kingdoms were established either by conquest and annexation or by a union *aeque principaliter* did not lead to the acceptance of the kingdom, the monarchy, or the empire as a natural community obliging the same loyalty and sacrifice as its component parts. Such a view could better follow from the classic alternative account of the kingdom as the organic growth of the family. This is the position expounded in the early seventeenth century by Juan Pablo Mártir Rizo, representing perhaps a greater recognition of the recent historical expansion of the political community: 'There are four sorts of community: that of the household; that of the neighbourhood; that of the city; and that of the kingdom. And just as a household is composed of many people together, in the same way many households make up a neighbourhood, many neighbourhoods a city, and many cities a kingdom.'[10] But if, for Mártir Rizo, the kingdom was a true political community, it was a community not of citizens, but of cities. The city thus remained the basic unit of political organization, even within the kingdom.

The concepts of community current in Renaissance Spain therefore reinforced the sense of belonging and obligation towards the locality formed by the common bonds of family, place, language, laws and customs, but contributed little to a theory of association between the city, or the locality and the kingdom, and *a fortiori* between one kingdom and another, diverse in government, culture and history. Without such a theory, there was no bond between the kingdoms but a common ruler, a common faith and the contingency of common interests. Neither the subordination of kingdoms by conquest nor their association *aeque principaliter*, with each retaining its own laws, privileges and justice, by itself provided the basis for mutual obligation. For Las Casas (*De Regia Potestate*, written by 1566), 'man belongs by birth to his city, or *patria*, as the member of a species; but to the kingdom or the province only generically';[11] there was no obligation, there-

---

[10] Juan Pablo Mártir Rizo, *Norte de príncipes y vida de Rómulo*, ed. J. A. Maravall (Madrid, 1988), p. 17: 'Las comunidades son cuatro: la de la casa, del barrio, de la ciudad, la del reino; y como de muchas personas juntas se compone una casa, así de muchas casas se hace un barrio, de muchos barrios una ciudad y de muchas ciudades un reino; y como las personas son partes de la casa, así las casas son parte del barrio, de la ciudad y del reino, mas son partes del barrio por sí, y de la ciudad por razón del barrio, y del reino por razón de la ciudad.'

[11] 'El hombre pertenece por nacimiento a su ciudad o patria, como miembro de una especie, pero al reino o a la provincia sólo genéricamente', Bartolomé de las Casas, *De Regia Potestate, o derecho de autodeterminación*, ed. L. Pereña *et al.* (Madrid, 1969), p. 41.

fore, on either the citizen or the city, even when part of a kingdom, to sacrifice themselves to aid another city, or another part of the kingdom, or the kingdom as a whole (*regnum non est patria civitatis*). Vitoria (1486–1546) and Suárez (1548–1617), who were the most prominent political thinkers to broach the problem, both held that the common subjection of different kingdoms, such as Castile or Aragon, to a single ruler was irrelevant to their functioning as 'perfect communities'. Indeed, Suárez, though writing sixty years later, went further than Vitoria in this respect, and distinguished between 'lesser communities' (cities, provinces and small kingdoms dominated by one capital city) and 'extensive communities', like the monarchy of Spain, created either by the *accidental* inheritance of separate kingdoms, 'which have no point of union other than the person of a common king', or by the permanent union of different provinces into a single kingdom with a common law and polity, thus forming a 'moral community' (such as Castile). But even in the latter case, each individual province might, depending on its usages and customs, traditional constitution and collective consciousness, still be considered to be a distinct community.[12]

The expansion of the monarchy between 1474 and 1519 and the multiplication of kingdoms, with the union of the crowns, the acquisition of Granada, Sicily, Naples, Navarre and the connection with Flanders and the empire, called for a reconfiguration of the bonds of political association that went beyond late-fifteenth century concepts of community that were rooted ultimately in the self-sufficient, social harmony of the city.

There was, of course, always more than one possible model of the structure and purpose of the monarchy, and more than one Castilian response to it; as Juan Alfonso de Lancina noted in the late seventeenth century, diversity could be considered a good or a bad thing: 'All these provinces are different in law, constitution, customs and usages, and while some think this is a reason for discord, others regard such variety as a force for stability.'[13] A unitarist 'Castilian imperialism', or 'Leonese castilianism' as it might be termed, undoubtedly existed,[14] though rather more at street level and in the minds of non-Castilians or non-imperialist Castilians than is

---

[12] Francisco de Vitoria, *Political Writings*, ed. Anthony Pagden and Jeremy Lawrance (Cambridge, 1991), pp. 301–2; Francisco Suárez, *De Legibus V (III 1–16) De Civili Potestate*, ed. L. Pereña and V. Abril (Madrid, 1975), p. 250.

[13] 'Todas estas provincias son diferentes en leyes políticas, usos y costumbres, y lo que algunos les parece que sea causa de discordia, otros juzgan que con esta contraposición sean más estables,' J. A. de Lancina, *Comentarios políticos*, as cited in S. Magariños, *Alabanza de España* (Madrid, 1950), p. 115.

[14] See P. Corominas, 'La guerra nacionalista de las comunidades de Castilla' in *El sentimiento de la riqueza en Castilla. Por Castilla adentro* (Madrid, 1951), p. 324.

to be found either in serious comment or in the practices of government. Much more pervasive was a sort of confederal 'Castilian hispanism', advocated by a long line of humanists, intellectuals and administrators (Fernán Pérez de Guzmán, Diego de Valera and Alfonso de Palencia at the end of the fifteenth century; Juan de Mariana, González de Cellorigo, Suárez de Figueroa, Saavedra Fajardo and others, in the first half of the seventeenth), which envisaged the integration of the various kingdoms in a political association in which both benefits and burdens were shared in just proportion but in which the individuality of the laws, customs and historic personality of each was retained. But alongside these there was also a Castilian *anti*-hispanism, a kind of 'Castilian separatism', for which the accident of common lordship implied no common obligation beyond a natural charity and solidarity. In the long shifting dialogue between these views, it is arguable that the unheard, silent voice has been this powerful undertone of Castilian opinion which looked neither to a unitary monarchy, conjoined for whatever end; nor to a confederal monarchy in which the individual members cooperated for a common divine or imperial purpose on a reciprocal and equitable basis; but to a simple coexistence of self-supporting, independent kingdoms each acting in its own best interests.

The medieval conception of Spain as a geographical and moral entity fragmented into culturally diverse, self-sufficient political communities which should be governed in their own individual interests, in accordance with their own laws and customs conformable to their own situation, climate, history and temperament, and in which natives should be preferred in office and foreigners excluded from its benefits, and whose resources should be devoted to their own well-being, was a Castilian no less than an Aragonese position that can be found repeated continuously in the petitions of the fifteenth-century Cortes and reiterated in a series of writings from the last testament of Isabella the Catholic herself, through Cisneros, Alonso de Castrillo, Soto, Vitoria, Las Casas, Alamos de Barrientos, Fernández Navarrete, Quevedo, Solórzano Pereyra, and Saavedra Fajardo, to Cardinal Portocarrero on the eve of the Bourbon Succession.[15]

Equally consistent was the belief, enunciated in a particularly unambiguous manner by a royal councillor of Castile early in the reign of Philip IV, restating what the Comuneros and the Cortes had asserted a hundred years before, that 'the taxes that are imposed should be for the defence of the province that pays them, and for its own ends, and not to subsidize other

---

[15] Exemplary is petition 6 of the Cortes of 1506, 'cada probincia abunda en su seso, y por esto las leyes e hordenanças quieren ser conformes a las probincias, y no pueden ser yguales ni disponer de una forma por todas las tierras', *CLC*, IV, p. 225.

princes, or even for other associated kingdoms even if they belong to the same king'.[16]

The paradox that Castile in the sixteenth and seventeenth centuries sent so much of its wealth to support Habsburg forces in Italy, Flanders and Germany was sustained by associating Castile with the preservation of the faith, the common good of Christendom, the service and reputation of its prince, and primacy in the monarchy of which it was the 'chief', the 'heart and the head', but most of all by the strategic (and self-interested) argument for conducting its defence in its neighbour's house.

Of course all arguments were used, often simultaneously – the defence of the faith, duty to the king, self-interest, the obligations of privilege – though the claim of the king to justify taxation with reference to 'the support of our estate' was resorted to noticeably less as the reign of Charles V progressed. By the reign of Philip II if the king stressed 'the common cause of Christendom for which I have such responsibility', or the 'service of Our Lord and the defence and conservation of these kingdoms', the case most readily accepted by those who were voting the monies was the 'defence of these kingdoms'. The obligation of the subject in law and custom to support the greatness of the king's estate was not by itself sufficient to be binding at the international level without being buttressed by more immediate considerations.[17] It is not coincidental that the motto 'as loyal as a Castilian' should have been coined to express the very essence of castilianism.

II *The sense of Castile*

Castile's hostility to involvement in the empire to which it was to be harnessed with the accession of Charles V hardly needs labouring.[18]

---

[16] Garci Pérez de Araciel, 'Discurso en que se trata si los reyes de Castilla pueden imponer nuevos tributos sin concesión de las ciudades que tienen voto en Cortes', BL, Egerton ms. 347, fo. 621v: 'los tributos que se imponen sean para la defensa de la misma provincia que los paga, y para los mismos fines, y no para socorros de otros príncipes, ni aun para el de otros reynos agregados, aunque sean del mismo rey'.

[17] Presidente de Castilla in Cortes 29 December 1598, 'La obligación que tienen estos reynos por derecho natural y positivo de sustentar al Rey en la grandeza de su real estado, y acudir con todo lo necesario para los poder defender de sus enemigos, que lo son juntamente ... e nuestra santa fé católica, cuya defensa por nuestros pecados se ha reducido casi a sola esta corona', together with the costs of defence of the other kingdoms and states, so that 'gozando éstos solos de paz y tranquilidad, a quien como cabeza de todos los demás y donde su magestad tiene su asiento y principal afición los incumbe acudir al remedio', *ACC*, XVIII, pp. 33–4.

[18] H. Pietschmann, 'El problema del "nacionalismo" en España en la edad moderna. La resistencia de Castilla contra el Emperador Carlos V', *Hispania*, 180 (1992), 83–106.

Virtually ignored, though more profound, is the parallel resistance to the integration of Castile into a peninsular union which is apparent from the time the marriage of Isabella of Castile and Ferdinand of Aragon looked like bringing about the conjunction of the two crowns. If the reaction to the Habsburg yoke expressed 'a sort of national sentiment which, though still diffuse, was beginning to take shape in the years 1518–20', as Joseph Perez writes, that sentiment was in reality only a prolongation and an accentuation of something that had been developing in the face of a rather different threat for forty years or more.

The difficulty of integrating the Spanish monarchy into a single community is usually perceived as a problem of the 'national constitutionalism' (in Elliott's terminology) of the kingdoms of the crown of Aragon. By contrast, the association of Castile with the monarchy has been taken for granted. The monarchy is thought of as an almost exclusively Castilian empire, an instrument of centralization, authoritarianism and castilianization, a vehicle for the advancement of Castilian interests and for the imposition of Castilian law, government and policy on a subordinate periphery. The *fueros* (or constitutions) of Aragon are, however, only half the story. Equally resistant to such integration was a sort of Castilian *foralismo*, a deep-rooted separatism and a persistent tendency within Castile to deny commitment not only to the wider monarchy but, even more remarkably, to the idea of Spain itself.

Alongside the unrestrained enthusiasm for peninsular unity expressed in certain political and cultural quarters in the later fifteenth century, there was an equally pronounced sense of Castilian territoriality, in which the Aragonese were regarded as no less foreign than Gascons and Navarrese.[19] The pious hope of the Catholic Monarchs, when abolishing the customs barriers between Castile and Léon and Aragon in 1480, that, 'since by the grace of God our kingdoms of Castile and Aragon have been united and we hope from now onwards by His goodness they will remain united and continue within our royal crown, it is right that all natives of those kingdoms should trade and do business with each other',[20] was to receive short shrift from the Castilians. On that specific issue of trade, future Cortes in the sixteenth century were to continue to petition for export

---

[19] *CLC*, III, p. 19 (1419, cap. 15): 'que non estasen en los dichos mis regnos [merchants] gascones nin navarros nin aragoneses nin otros estranjeros'.

[20] 'Pues por la gracia de Dios los nuestros reinos de Castilla e de León e de Aragón son unidos, e tenemos esperanza que por su piedad de aqui adelante estarán en union e permaneceran en nuestra corona real, que ansi es razon que todos los naturales dellos se traten e comuniquen en sus tratos e fazimientos', *CLC*, IV, p. 185.

restrictions 'for the kingdoms of Valencia, Aragon, Navarre and Portugal', as they had in the fifteenth.[21] The attempt by Ferdinand and Isabella to create a feeling for 'the common good of all our kingdoms' clearly did not work. The opposition in Castile to the regencies of Ferdinand the Catholic was more than just the obviously personal and factional. Juan Maldonado, writing between 1523 and 1526, says most people believed on the death of Isabella that Ferdinand would not be obeyed by the Castilians, 'because the Castilians had suffered long enough being ordered about by the Aragonese'.[22] Antipathy between Castilians and Aragonese, as indeed the common antipathy among all the nations and provinces of Spain, was something frequently commented upon by native and foreign observers as emblematic of the absence of that mutual affection that was the very essence of community.[23]

Anti-Aragonese sentiment in Castile (as reflected in the Cortes) was the expression of a pre-nationalist counter-identity defined in the fifteenth century mostly in terms of the territory of the king's jurisdiction – 'these realms', 'our realms', 'my native people'. However, the union of the crowns of Castile and Aragon, while on the one hand generating an intense, if frequently propagandist, euphoria for Spain, also had quite the contrary effect of accelerating the emergence of a much more positive proto-national sense of *Castilian* consciousness. With the conjunction of the two crowns, the neutral, generic distinction between 'these [kingdoms]' and 'those', normal in the language of the Cortes throughout the fifteenth century, was made more specific, more sharply defined and more self-consciously national by the more frequent use of 'Castile' and 'Castilian' that can be noticed first of all in the petitions of the 1473 Cortes, and then again in 1515, 1518, 1520 and the other Cortes of the 1520s. Castile was being castilian-ized.

---

[21] *CLC*, IV, p. 415, Cortes of 1525, petition 21.

[22] J. Maldonado, *La revolución comunera*, ed. V. Fernández Vargas (Madrid, 1975), p. 41 – 'pues bastante tiempo habian sufrido los castellanos estar mandados por los aragoneses'; and according to Sandoval, Ferdinand himself felt bitter at what he regarded as 'the ingratitude of some Castilians', P. de Sandoval, *Historia de la vida y hechos del emperador Carlos V*, I (Biblioteca de Autores Españoles, 80, Madrid, 1955), p. 30.

[23] 'Among themselves the Spaniards are at daggers drawn', wrote the Frenchman Bartélemy Joly, travelling in Spain in 1603–4, 'each extolling his own province over that of his companions and out of an exaggerated desire for singularity creating far greater differences between their nationalities than we have in France. The Aragonese, the Valencians, the Catalans, the Basques, the Galicians, the Portuguese bait each other, throwing in each others' faces the vices and failings of their provinces; but should a Castilian appear among them, then see how at one they are in launching themselves upon him all together, as bulldogs upon a wolf'. *Viajes de extranjeros por España y Portugal* (Madrid, 1959), ed. J. García Mercadal, II, p. 125. See also A. Castro, *Aspectos del vivir hispánico* (Madrid,

The *comunero* movement continued this legacy. It was not just anti-Flemish and anti-imperialist; it was also anti-Spanish, castilianist and separatist.[24] The contrast in the public pronouncements in the Cortes of 1518 and 1520 between the Crown's use of 'Spain' and the cities' use of 'Castile' is marked and revealing.[25] The *comunero* cities were concerned only with their own relationship with Charles V and I as king of Castile; they were indifferent to the simultaneous disturbances in Valencia, and did not even properly include Andalusia within their orbit. Cardinal Adrian reported to Charles V in July 1520, 'They are saying expressly that the revenues of Castile should be spent for the benefit of Castile and not of Germany, Aragon, Naples, etc., and that Your Majesty should govern each country with the money you get from it.'[26] The same sentiment was repeated in the 1523 and subsequent Cortes in demands that the revenues of Castile should be spent in Castile and that the other kingdoms should pay their own defence costs themselves.[27] Castilian unhappiness at involvement with the Crown of Aragon and particularly with an Italo-Aragonese foreign policy which brought it into confrontation with France, lasted throughout the reign of Charles V, if not beyond,[28] and the persistent determination to maintain their separateness from Aragon was expressed in numerous petitions of the Castilian Cortes. Exemplary, and extraordinary only in its explicitness, is petition 42 of 1532, asking the emperor to enforce the laws restricting the holding of ecclesiastical benefices in Castile to 'natives born and bred of father and mother in these kingdoms', particularly 'as regards the Aragonese and Navarrese, which are kingdoms in themselves, distinct and separate, with their *fueros* and their own Cortes'.[29]

1970), p. 37, quoting Gonzalo Fernández de Oviedo; J. Sánchez Montes, *Franceses, protestantes, turcos. Los españoles ante la política internacional de Carlos V* (Pamplona, 1951), p. 28.

[24] A cleric, preaching to the *regidores* of Toledo in the spring of 1520, insisted that 'la subjeción destos reynos' was not inherited from their ancestors and urged them to follow 'doctrina de muchos notables varones castellanos, cuya memoria es inmortal en las tierras, por que ganaron libertad para sy e para sus reynos, los quales ovieron gloria en ser libres', J. Perez, 'Tradición e innovación en las Comunidades de Castilla' in *V simposio Toledo renacentista (Toledo, 24–26 Abril 1975)* (Madrid, 1980), II, 2, p. 49.

[25] M. Fernández Alvarez, 'La política exterior', *Las Cortes de Castilla y León en la edad moderna* (Valladolid, 1989), p. 354.

[26] 'Dizen expresamente que las pecunias de Castilla se deven gastar al provecho de Castilla y no de Alemania, Aragón, Napoles etc y que VM ha de governar cada una tierra con el dinero que della recibe', Perez, 'Tradición e innovación en las Comunidades de Castilla', p. 43.

[27] Petitions 44 of 1523 Cortes, 4 of 1528, 118 of 1539.

[28] J. M. Jover, *Carlos V y los españoles* (Madrid, 1963), p. 197.

[29] '... con los Aragoneses y Navarros, pues son reynos por si, y distintos y apartados y tienen sus fueros y se juntan a Cortes por sy'. They continued to be regarded as foreigners, even in the seventeenth century, Juan de Solórzano Pereyra, *Política indiana* (Biblioteca de Autores

It is the strength of this specifically Castilian (as opposed to – and often in opposition to – Spanish) sentiment that is so marked at the end of the fifteenth and the early sixteenth centuries.[30] A manuscript account of the 1521 siege of Logroño, used by Fernando Albia de Castro in his *Memorial por Logroño* [1633], describes an unnamed orator exhorting the citizens to 'defend your country [*patria*], and die gloriously for it, for the service of your king, and for Castile . . . we oppose ourselves willingly to the fury of the French not only for ourselves, but for the protection and defence of Castile': there was no place for Spain in the hierarchy of his loyalties.[31] Pulgar's *Claros varones de Castilla* was written in the mid-1480s as a conscious castilianization of Fernán Pérez de Guzmán's 'Loores de los claros varones de España'. The Colegio Mayor de Santa Cruz, in Valladolid, was founded in 1484 as an all-Castilian institution, its foundation charter insisting that students were to come from as many parts of the crown of Castile as possible. Though not excluded, students from the crown of Aragon were to be treated no differently from the French or the Portuguese.[32] This castilianism is expressed in a variety of ways, but most demonstrably in the more universal use of 'Castilla' rather than, or instead of, 'España'. The Italian interlocutor in Juan Maldonado's *De motu Hispaniae* comments, 'How surprised I am to hear Spaniards commonly called Castilians and Spain Castile'.[33] A generation later the situation would be just the reverse.

This explicit, proto-national, 'greater' Castilian identity was, however, a recent, unset and relatively weak sentiment, largely reactive to a perceived threat to the independent future of the country, as in 1473 and 1518. It was

Españoles, vol. 254, Madrid, 1972), p. 299, 'y parece que los [Navarrese and Aragonese] debemos contar en la clase de estrangeros, como a los portugueses, italianos, flamencos y otros, cuyas provincias no están unidas a los dichos reynos de Castilla y León, y las Indias accesoriamente, sino con igual principado, y conservando sus leyes y fueros con que se governaban antes de su unión y agregación.'

30 See Davis' examples in *Hispanic Review*, 3 (1935); O. H. Green, *Spain and the Western tradition* (Madison, Wis. 1965), III, p. 84.

31 '. . . defender su patria, morir gloriosamente por ella, y por el servicio de su rei y de Castilla', 'voluntariamente nos oponemos a la furia francesa no solo por nuestro particular, sino por el amparo y defensa de Castilla'. Fernando Albía de Castro, *Memorial y discurso político por la muy noble y muy leal ciudad de Logroño*, ed. J. Simón Díaz (Logroño, 1953), pp. 152, 156.

32 For Fernando del Pulgar, *Claros varones de Castilla*, ed. R. B. Tate (Oxford, 1971), p. 5; M. Sobaler, *Los colegiales mayores de Santa Cruz (1484–1670): una élite de poder* (Salamanca, 1987), p. 103.

33 'Cuanto me estraña al oir llamar vulgarmente castellanos a los españoles y a la España Castilla', Maldonado, *Revolución comunera*, p. 37. Despuig's *Los col·loquis de Tortosa* (written before 1557) makes a similar point, 'almost all Castilian historians fall into the same error of writing Castile when they mean all Spain'; cited in John H. Elliott, *The revolt of the Catalans* (Cambridge, 1963), p. 53.

also less well supported by legal and institutional buttresses than the national identity of its Aragonese neighbours.

Castile was itself a composite kingdom within a monarchy that was an aggregate of monarchies. Castile was both a core kingdom and an empire brought together during the course of the Reconquest by the aggregation of conquered lands with defined territoriality but with indistinct political, legal, cultural and historical personalities which had been largely obliterated by the process of conquest and resettlement, and it may be that the open-ended nature of the Reconquista, the protracted indefiniteness of the extent and the limits of the territory of the crown of Castile, compared with the kingdoms of the crown of Aragon, the accretion of successive layers of space external to the core kingdom but themselves emotionally void of political personality, ruptured the territorial coincidence between community loyalty and political obedience. A clear vision of castilianism was therefore blurred by this parallax between a core and an extended Castile. Eight kingdoms continued to be individually represented in the Castilian Cortes (Castile, Leon, Toledo, Murcia, Cordoba, Jaén, Seville, Granada) and even in the early sixteenth century it was common to refer pluralistically to 'the crown of the kingdoms of Castile, and of Leon, and of Granada'. Although that formulation did not last long before it was superseded by the singular 'Castile', it continued to be usual to refer to the territories contained within the crown of Castile in the plural as *estos reinos*. The crown propagated a jurisdictional not territorial sense of political association. In this respect Pulgar's complaint that service to lesser lords tended to be put before obedience to the king is revealing.[34]

The 'national constitution' of Castile also lacked the mythic historicity of the Aragonese Laws of Sobrarbe or the *Constitucions* of Catalonia; a common body of law for Castile that was in the process of codification was not fully to materialize until the publication of the *Nueva recopilación* in 1567. The very size of Castile militated in practice against the judicial unity imposed by a single *audiencia* in Saragossa, Barcelona or Valencia, and the high-court system tended to replicate the 'provincial' structure of the kingdom (Valladolid, Ciudad-Real/Granada, Seville, Galicia, Asturias). Ecclesiastical divisions also failed to respect 'national' circumscriptions, not only internally – most notably with the historic rivalry between the archbishoprics of Toledo and Santiago – but also across frontiers; for example, the Spanish province of the Dominican order (also called 'de Castilla')

---

[34] J. M. Nieto Soria, *Fundamentos ideológicos del poder real en Castilla (siglos XIII–XVI)* (Madrid, 1988), p. 131.

included the Basque region and Navarre, but not Aragon or Andalusia, which were separate provinces. The repeated petitions of the Cortes for a codification of the laws, for the imposition of a common set of weights and measures, and, on a different plane, for the compilation of a general history of Castile, such as Galíndez de Carvajal was preparing,[35] were at the same time the expression of a more active castilianist sentiment in the early sixteenth century and the reflection of its past weakness.

Castile was, of course, also defined institutionally by its representative assembly, the Cortes. However, the peculiarities of representation in the Cortes, limited to the proctors of eighteen provincial capitals who were mandated to refer back to their cities for instructions on all matters of importance, tended to reinforce a particularist rather than a universalist vision of Castile. The prevalent sense of community in Castile was civic rather than national; Castile was a community of substantial, semi-independent cities and towns, not (at least until the eighteenth century) dominated, as Catalonia, Valencia and Aragon, by a single mega-capital city. That structure as a community of cities was embodied in the composition of the Cortes. The defeat of the *comuneros* checked the potential for the development of the Cortes as an institution representative of the realm as a whole, and in Castile after 1521 the political community was forced back to urbanism in resistance to the pressures of a central power seeking to employ national institutions in its own interests. Throughout the period of the active existence of the Cortes until 1664, the crown promoted a Cortes representative of the community of the kingdom as a whole; the cities, on the other hand, insisted on a Cortes representative of the civic communities of which the kingdom was composed, and the reality was that the Cortes represented the cities that represented Castile, not Castile itself. Thus, whereas in the non-Castilian foral kingdoms association with a monarchy perceived as Castilian reinforced provincial nationalism, institutions and constitutional myths,[36] the demands of that same monarchy inhibited such a consciousness within Castile itself by reinforcing the concept of Castile as a community of cities, rather than as a single community of the realm.

III   The hispanization of Castile

This relative weakness of a Castilian sense of identity standing between local patriotism and its immersion in a broader Spanish national sentiment,

[35] See, for example, petitions 35 of 1518, 57 and 95 of 1523, 47 of 1532, 90 and 113 of 1538, 71 of 1542, 66 of 1548, 124 of 1551, 39 of 1558.

[36] I. Sánchez Bella, *Génesis del estado moderno en España* (Madrid, 1956), p. 20.

immeasurably facilitated the transition of Castile from opposition to acceptance of an imperial role which is sometimes seen as the crucial development in the history of the monarchy. By the mid-sixteenth century Castile had become hispanized. By the second half of the century the semantic castilianization of Spain remarked upon by Maldonado and Despuig has not only gone, it has been reversed. Now the Castilians do not speak of Castile when they mean Spain; they speak of Spain when they mean Castile. 'Castilla' as an expression of community identity seems almost to disappear from the political lexicon. Indicative is the total absence of histories of Castile, compared with the great wave of Spanish histories and chronicles produced by Florian de Ocampo, Pedro de Medina, Garibay, Ambrosio de Morales and Mariana, among others, between the 1540s and the 1580s.[37] The vocabulary of community description is 'Spain', even where there can be no doubt that Spain meant Castile, and where Spain made no sense in geographical, linguistic, political or juridical terms. In Luis de Zapata's *Miscelánea*, for instance, the section listing what was exceptional about Spain includes the Indies 'annexed to the royal crown of Spain'; 'Castilla' scarcely figures. Martín González de Cellorigo's *Memorial* abounds in references to 'our Spain'; Castile is mentioned twice.[38] How is this semantic shift to be read? The appropriation of Spain by Castile, as non-Castilians and their historians were wont to complain? Or the absorption of Castile by Spain? – the 'immersion of the Castilian into the Spanish', as Represa puts it? This is an area in which impression is hardly an adequate methodology, but over the long term there is a good deal of truth in Represa's observation, 'It certainly seems, therefore, that Castilian consciousness was slowly being diluted during the course of the sixteenth, seventeenth and eighteenth centuries' – although the process was not uninterrupted.[39]

There is, of course, nothing new about a consciousness of Spain in the mid-sixteenth century. The question is whether what we have here is a real extension of identification with Spain or, as Koenigsberger suggests, 'a Castilian imperialism', produced by the alliance of the Castilian ruling

---

[37] See, in particular, B. Sánchez Alonso, *Historia de la historiografía española* (Madrid 1947–50); G. Cirot, *Les histoires générales d'Espagne entre Alphonse X et Philippe II (1284–1556)* (Paris, 1905); F. Pierce, *La poesía épica del Siglo de Oro* (Madrid, 1961); A. Soons, *Juan de Mariana* (Boston, 1982).

[38] See Maravall, *Estado moderno*, I, pp. 484, 519, n. 192, 521, n. 229 for other examples of the indiscriminate use of 'Spain' for 'Castile', especially when referring to the language.

[39] 'Parece, por tanto, seguro que la conciencia de castellanidad fue diluyéndose lentamente a lo largo de los siglos XVI, XVII y XVIII', Armando Represa, *El pendón real de Castilla* (Valladolid, 1983), p. 64.

classes with the dynastic and religious ambitions of the Habsburgs, 'that can only very marginally be identified with Spanish nationalism'.[40]

However, this notion of a *Castilian* imperialism is very much the view from the edge. Whatever the Aragonese, or the Neapolitans and Sicilians may have thought about the domineering arrogance of Castile and the monopolization of posts by Castilians, Castilians themselves seem to have felt short-changed by the monarchy.[41] To them it appeared that Castilian rents were open to all, Castilian benefices were open to all, power and office in Castile were open to all; but ordinary Castilians in all other parts of the monarchy were excluded from the very benefits that were so readily available in Castile to others. Castile, open to all, was excluded by all. 'No Castilian in other kingdoms gets any reward or opportunity at all, because what is available in each of them is for their own natives, and it is only those of Castile who are disadvantaged in this way.'[42] There is still a great deal more that we need to know about administrative structures, practices and appointments policies, but, although the operational perspectives of the central government in Madrid could perhaps be described as Spanish, or peninsular, or even integrationist, they were certainly not castilianist. The conciliar system itself was on one level an image of a monarchy of equals, enshrining the separate juridical personalities of Castile, Aragon, Navarre, Italy, Portugal and Flanders, and with them a bureaucracy that preserved prescriptive rights for the Aragonese, for example, though not for the Castilians. At the same time, the traditional distinction between business councils and regional councils was also a distinction between different perceptions of the monarchy propagated through different patronage and career circuits. The contrast between the keen awareness of *naturaleza* in the *consultas* of the council of Aragon and the near indifference to national

---

[40] H. G. Koenigsberger, 'Spain', in *National consciousness, history, and political culture in early-modern Europe*, ed. O. Ranum (Baltimore and London, 1975), p. 171.

[41] Alonso Gutiérrez, 23 October 1577, 'siendo los estados de Flandes patrimonio de VM que razón ay en el mundo para que alla no seamos rescividos en la forma que los son en España los de aquellas provincias', BNM, ms. 1749, fos. 61–70; Consejo de la Cámara, 4 March 1590, opposing the grant of naturalization to a Valencian, 'pues allá han cerrado la puerta a los de Castilla como se sabe', AHN, Cons. *leg.* 4412, n. 32; *ACC*, xvi, 639–40, petition 27 of the 1592–98 Cortes asking for the Burgundian style of the royal household to be castilianized; Cristóval Suárez de Figueroa, *El Pasajero*, ed. F. Rodriguez Marín (Madrid, 1943), p. 7; Diego de Saavedra Fajardo, *Locuras de Europa* (Madrid, 1944), p. 100, complaining that the Portuguese maintained a monopoly of their own offices, but enjoyed those of Castile and the rest of the monarchy.

[42] Consejo de la Cámara 23 January 1639, AHN, Consejos, leg. 4427, n. 119; Cortes 1559, petition 24, 'como es notorio en los otros estados patrimoniales de Vuestra Magestad no las dan [naturalization papers] ni conceden a ningunos naturales destos reynos, aunque en aquellos estados hayan hecho muchos y muy señalados servicios'.

origins in those of the council of War is clamant. Councils, like that of War, without regional affiliation, and most of the central secretariats, acted as agents of administrative and bureaucratic unification. Within certain broad rules – the preference for Castilians in supervisory posts, the preference to natives in non-military offices, the exclusion of non-Spaniards from places in the Spanish infantry – the council of War was positively non-nationalistic, recommending an Aragonese for promotion in the Armada del Mar Océano in 1607, for example, because it considered it 'appropriate to employ and occupy persons from that kingdom', and nominating to posts without reference to nationality.[43] There were a number of known non-Castilians in the secretariats of war from the end of the sixteenth century, for instance, and no doubt a good many more who are not known.[44]

At the same time there was a good deal of sensitivity, informal as well as formal, to national expectation in appointments outside Castile, the count of Barajas advising in 1588 that, although there was no legal obligation for the governors of the Military Order of Calatrava in Aragon and Valencia to be natives, 'it would be as well if they were in order to be in good stead with the natives'.[45] It was the king, however, who held most rigidly to the principle of the separateness of his individual kingdoms. Not only Philip II, but Philip III and Philip IV as well, intervened to prevent appointments and administrative actions which violated the formal or customary requirements of the kingdom concerned, and thus to check the development of a greater uniformity in government or the formation of a single bureaucratic hierarchy that could have given a sense of administrative unity to the monarchy as a whole.[46]

Castilians were, therefore, understandably sensitive within the monarchy to their own lack of political personality as embodied in exclusive rights, privileges and exemptions. Castile's status as the 'chief', the 'head and the heart', by which the régime had endeavoured to cajole Castile into the monarchy, was the only ground upon which to appeal for a share in the advantages of empire; it seemed by comparison both an empty and a burdensome honour. 'The greater the power of princes', wrote Saavedra

[43] AGS, GA 669, Council of War, 20 November 1607.
[44] For example, Tomás Fermat, in the war secretariat 1596–1610/21, was a Valencian; Francisco Lobo Castrillo, in the secretariats of war and state under Philip III, was probably Aragonese, and certainly Navarrese on his mother's side; Sarassa, Gil Tomey, Coloma, Bolea, officials in the secretariat of war under Philip IV, were probably also non-Castilians.
[45] BL, Add. 28365, fo. 57.
[46] For example, AGS, Est. 167, fo. 4, Philip II on consulta of Cámara de Castilla, 7 October 1590, re Navarre; R. A. Stradling, *Philip IV and the government of Spain 1621–1665* (Cambridge, 1988), p. 282, re Portugal.

Fajardo in his *Locuras de Europa,* 'the less the liberty of the dominant nation and the greater its outlay in sustaining his conquests.'[47]

IV The crisis of 'Spain'

Not surprisingly, therefore, with the economic and military reverses of the last decades of the century, there was a widespread disenchantment, an acute awareness that the monarchy as a whole was at odds with itself, that the body lacked cohesion and the parts were alienated from the head, and a growing concern as to whether the monarchy could survive in its existing form, or whether it was not too diffuse and too diverse to be viable.

There was an increased feeling of distrust for non-Castilians, or perhaps just an increased sensitivity to the disaffection of the Portuguese, the Aragonese and the Catalans, highlighted by the seditious activities of Portuguese separatists like Sor María de la Visitación, Fray Miguel de los Santos and Gabriel de Espinosa, the pastry cook of Madrigal who purported to be the real king of Portugal, and by the uprising in Saragossa and its aftermath at the Tarazona Cortes in 1591 and 1592.[48] Nobody could be relied upon but the Castilians. Alamos de Barrientos is the paradigm: 'In Flanders, the rebels are enemies openly and the rest, have no doubt, are secretly. The Italians and Portuguese are also secret enemies. The Aragonese are disaffected. And so the only friends of this crown without reservation are the Indies and the kingdoms of Castile as a bloc.'[49]

This in turn generated in Castile a real resentment of the burdens of empire and a growing perception of the contradictions between local interests and the politics of the monarchy. The complaints, common in the 1590s

---

[47] Saavedra Fajardo, *Locuras de Europa,* p. 108, 'cuanto mayor es la potencia de los príncipes, es menor la libertad de la nación dominante, y mayores sus gastos para sustentar las conquistas.'

[48] See the remarks of the Conde de Luna on Castilian hostility to Aragon and Madrid's delight at the suppression of the disturbances in Aragon in 1591–92, 'pareciendo que se habia conquistado un reyno de enemigos', Lupercio Leonardo de Argensola, *Información de los sucesos del reino de Aragón en los años de 1590 y 1591,* ed. X. Gil Pujol (Saragossa, 1991), pp. xiii, xlv; Elliott, *Revolt of the Catalans,* pp. 12–15; in his despatch of 22 October 1588, the Venetian ambassador, Lippomano, reported on the disaffection in Aragon, Catalonia and Portugal, 'the whole is held together by the authority and wisdom of the king, and if he were to die everything would fall into confusion and danger', *CSP Venetian,* VIII, p. 407; Alonso Gutiérrez, in a 'Relación de arbitrios propuestos para la defensa de la monarquía de España' of 1 May 1602, also commented on the discontent of the Portuguese and their 'deseo de tener rey propio, qualquier que sea, y desasirse de la corona de Castilla', BNM, ms. 2347, fo. 19.

[49] Baltasar Alamos de Barrientos, *Discurso político al rey Felipe III al comienzo de su reinado,* ed. M. Santos (Barcelona, 1990), p. 31.

and at the accession of Philip III, burst out again around 1618 with the renewal of the *millones* tax and the certainty of involvement in the European war.[50] The sense of an empire parasitic on Castile is overwhelming, and comes as much from within government as from outside it.[51] Whereas in the high sixteenth century, Castile's position as head and heart of the monarchy had been invoked in aid of its participation in the benefits of the monarchy, in the seventeenth century it was employed in order to plead for its conservation from its burdens.[52]

Such criticisms did not, of course, necessarily imply a repudiation of the monarchy, but they exposed serious cracks in the two pillars that upheld it, loyalty to the prince and the cause of the faith. They raised the issue of a separation of the interests of Philip II from those of the king of Spain/ Castile, and they brought into question the obligations of Castile to the community of Christendom as a whole,[53] a sentiment expressed in lapidary

[50] Elliott, *Revolt of the Catalans*, pp. 183–92.

[51] Obeso Pizarro, 16 February 1599, *ACC*, XVIII, p. 523; don Baltasar de Góngora (Córdoba) 14 October 1617, 'siendo ansi que este solo reino de Castilla...acude siempre a la defensa y guarda de los demás reinos de su monarquía, justo sera que S. M., como tan buen rey, por materia prudente de su estado, mire por su conservación', *ACC*, XXX, p. 65; don Baltasar de Barahona in vote in *ayuntamiento* of Granada, 25 October 1622, on the provision of 30,000 soldiers, 'el repartimiento que se ubiere de hacer sea en todos los reynos desta corona y en el de Aragón, Navarra, Cataluña, Portugal y todos los demás', because all benefit, AGS, PR 91, fo. 42; Council of Finance, 2 December 1618, AGS, CJH 402; Council of Castile, 1 February 1619, A. González Palencia, ed., *La junta de reformación 1618–25*, Archivo Histórico Español, V (Valladolid, 1932), p. 12; and Quevedo's notable lines: 'En Navarra y Aragón no hay quien tribute un real, Cataluña y Portugal son de la misma opinión. Sólo Castilla y León y el noble reino andaluz llevan a cuestas la cruz'.

[52] President of Finance in Junta del Refuerzo de la Armada y Galeras, 23 October 1620, 'No se puede valer Vuestra Majestad ni se vale sino de solo el reino de Castilla, porque Aragón, Valencia, Cataluña y Nabarra no ayudan a cosa destas, ni de los estados que Vuestra Majestad tiene en Italia se aprovecha para estas necesidades ... Y no le parece que puede ser buena materia de estado consumir y acabar la substancia destos reinos de Castilla que son la rayz y corazon desta monarquía,' AGS, GA 1305.

[53] These two issues were at the core of the arguments of two papers of the 1590s, dealing with a projected tax on flour, which revealed a growing alienation (or an increased readiness to express that alienation) from extra-peninsular involvements, whether in the defence of the 'private patrimony' of the king in the Netherlands or in support of catholicism everywhere. The first was one of the themes of Gonzalo de Valcárcel's *Discurso relativo al tributo de la harina* (probably of 1595): 'El modo natural de distribuir las cargas y tributos a los reinos es que a cada uno se reparta lo que toca a su propia conservación y defensa; de aquí es que siendo los estados de Flandes patrimonio de su Majestad y no miembro del reino de Castilla, parece que están más cerca los bienes libres y muebles que tiene su Majestad para proseguir aquella guerra, pues este reino está obligado a sus propias necesidades y no a empeñar sus hijos para rescatar los extraños, poniéndose en estado que no pueda defender sus propias tierras y vasallos ... ningún reyno está obligado de ponerse en tanta necesidad como quedaría Castilla con este tributo para socorrer otras provincias', BL, Add. 9933, fo. 77v and cited in C. Gómez Centurión, *La Invencible y la empresa de Inglaterra* (Madrid, 1988),

form by Francisco de Monzón (*procurador* for Madrid) in 1593: 'since they want to be damned, let them be damned'.

But Monzón went further than that, continuing, 'All the funds needed for the defence, good government, peace and stability of the kingdom of Portugal should be got from that same kingdom, and the same should apply to the kingdoms of the crown of Aragon ... without its being necessary to take anything at all from these kingdoms of Castile.'[54] Monzón's call for the complete disassociation of Castile from concern with the monarchy was echoed by a number of others over the years. The response of Don Antonio Fernández de Llanos y Ribera, in the *ayuntamiento* of Zamora on 28 December 1622, to the suggestion that Castile undertake the financing of 30,000 soldiers 'for the defence of the kingdom' is particularly expressive: 'But since this concerns most directly Navarre, Vizcaya and the kingdoms of Aragon and Valencia, because it is there, and in Portugal, where the frontiers lie across which our enemies come to attack us, and as it seems this defence touches them more immediately and they are more relieved and less overburdened with taxes, they should raise and pay for these soldiers among themselves. Perhaps afterwards, following *their* example, Castile could give what help it can.'[55] Such attitudes are a salutary counter to the mass of providentialist, 'anti-Machiavellian' propaganda for the 'divine monarchy'

p. 131; a similar position was taken by Pedro de Ribadeneira a little earlier, T. Egido, ed., *Satiras politicas de la España moderna* (Madrid, 1973), p. 19. The second issue was addressed both by Valcárcel, 'La religion católica y la causa y defensa de ella es comun a toda la cristiandad, y si estas guerras importan para esto, no toca a los reynos de Castilla llebar toda la carga, estándose los demas reynos, príncipes y repúblicas a la mira' (BL, Add. 9933, fo. 6v), and in another paper on the same subject in the Cortes in 1596, which argued that the defence of the faith 'es causa comun al Papa y a todos los príncipes christianos y a todos obliga, y por la parte que toca al rey Nuestro Señor toca a todos sus estados de Portugal, Aragón, Navarra, Sicilia, Napoles, Milan, Indias, etta., y Castilla por su parte ha contribuido gran suma por esta causa y estando tan consumida y miserable haver ya cumplido con esta,' 'Cortes del año del 1596', BNM, ms. 1750, fos. 293–5v.

54 'Para la defensa y buen gobierno y paz y quietud del reyno de Portugal, todo el caudal que para esto sea necesario se saque del mismo reyno, y lo mismo para los reynos de la corona de Aragón...sin que sea necesario que destos reynos de Castilla se haya de sacar cosa ninguna', *ACC*, XII, pp. 473, 475 (19 May 1593). And on a later occasion, Antonio de Salamanca and nine others, in the *ayuntamiento* of Zamora, 28 December 1622: the Infanta should defend Flanders with its own taxes and revenues.

55 'Pero pues esto toca mas ynmediatamente a Nabarra, Bizcaya, Reynos de Aragon y Valenzia por caer en estas partes y en la de Portugal las fronteras y de donde salen a ynquietarnos los enemigos, parece que pues a ellos les toca mas zerca esta defensa y estan mas descansados y menos cargados de tributos, que entre ellos se paguen y repartan estos soldados, y que despues a exemplo suyo ayude Castilla con lo que pudiere' – note the ironic reference to the official line that, once established in Castile, the measure would be an example for the others to follow.

or the 'missionary state' pumped out by predominantly clerical fundamentalists.[56]

What is patently clear, if only from the increasing frequency with which once again the term 'Castilla' is used, is that this crisis of monarchy, the perception of the hostility of its associates and of its excessive fiscal burdens, helped to bring about a revived sense of Castile as an entity distinct both from the monarchy and from Spain in the early years of the seventeenth century. It is the 'restoration of Castile' that is the aim of Fernández Navarrete's *Conservación de monarquías*, for example, and the political satire of the period also contributed to a specifically castilianist perspective on the problems of government and society.[57] At the same time a new interest in the Castilian past is manifested in Philip III's reign. Antonio de Herrera's *Historia general de los hechos de los castellanos*, Sandoval's *Historia de los reyes de Castilla y de León*, commissioned by Philip III, and the *Historia general de la corona de Castilla* that the marquis of Auñón wanted to dedicate to the Cortes in 1620, are among the first histories of Castile written for the better part of a hundred years. Indeed, it was the explicit purpose of Fray Juan de Arévalo to make his *Crónica de los antiguos condes y primeros reies de Castilla* of 1615 a history worthy of Castile's position in the monarchy.[58]

But a profounder expression of this castilianist revival is the still somewhat strange matter of the *patronato* of Santa Teresa. In October 1617, the proctor general of the Discalced Carmelites petitioned the Cortes of Castile to adopt Teresa as patron of Spain in view of the great devotion to her in 'all these kingdoms of Spain, and especially in those of the Crown of Castile, where the saint was born and died and her uncorrupted body rests'. With only one vote against, the Cortes agreed, setting out in their reasons for approving that, in addition to her obvious merits, 'this realm in particular is mindful of the favours Our Lord has done it in having placed in these kingdoms such a holy and marvellous woman, who was raised in Castile and

---

[56] Not without reason – given the unreliability of other instruments – did Fray Juan de Salazar insist that 'el principal instrumento del imperio es la lengua': 'Con este escuadrón de letrados, que son por la mayor parte religiosos o eclesiásticos seglares ... fortifican su imperio y monarquía, no menos que con los presidios y tercios de soldados', *Política española* [1619], ed. M. Herrero García (Madrid, 1945), p. 152.

[57] See M. Etreros, *La sátira política en el siglo XVII* (Madrid, 1983) and Egido, *Sátiras políticas*; though 'Castile' was still vastly outnumbered by 'Spain' in the titles of these satires.

[58] Included in Herrera's *Historia general del mundo*, Maravall, *Estado moderno*, I, p. 521, n. 242; *ACC*, xxxv, pp. 255–6; and in T. Egido, 'Las Cortes y la cultura', *Las Cortes de Castilla y León en la edad moderna* (Valladolid, 1989), p. 455, n. 147; Sánchez Alonso, *Historiografía española*, II, p. 195.

who has so honoured this nation'.[59] The move was certainly seen by the supporters of the patronage of Santiago as castilianist in inspiration, and their opposition was in part a Spanish response, refuting the suggestion that 'Santiago remains as patron of the Spains, and Saint Teresa be patron only of the two Castiles' (Quevedo in *Memorial por el patronato de Santiago* 1627), and denying the authority of a merely Castilian Cortes to determine the *patronato* of Spain – 'the Cortes of Madrid do not comprise the totality of the kingdoms of Spain', whereas 'his patronage extends throughout all the lands and domains of the king of Spain and the whole of his monarchy' (Pedro Losado de Quiroga, 1628).[60] Victory went ultimately to Santiago, but the polemic and the rancour generated by the issue and the depth of feeling on both sides point to an acute crisis of the national psyche, and to a dangerous fault-line running not only between Castile and Spain, but also between different integrationist and separatist visions of Castile.[61]

V War and the new 'Spain'

In this climate of disenchantment, there was a common recognition of the need to restore unity or cooperation, and perhaps even more important of the need to reconcile Castile to the monarchy. Unity is the central theme in Cellorigo, Suárez de Figueroa, Saavedra Fajardo, as well as outsiders like Campanella.[62] The question was how to do it.

---

[59] 'Este reino en particular está reconocido de las mercedes que Nuestro Señor le ha hecho por haberle dado en estos reinos esta santa y prodigiosa muger y criada en Castilla, que tanto ha honrado esta nación', *ACC*, XXX, pp. 507–9, 24 October 1617; XXXI, pp. 52, 349, 16 November 1617, 3 March 1618.

[60] Quevedo, *Su espada por Santiago* (1628), 'Santiago general patrón se queda de España pues que puede y la que hoy se pregona en Avila o en Alba sea patrona', in *Obras completas de Don Francisco de Quevedo Villegas*, ed. L. Astrana Marín (Madrid, 1941), pp. 822–67.

[61] Elliott comments on the issue, particularly in 'Self-perception and decline in early seventeenth-century Spain', *Spain and its world*, pp. 260–1, though not in this specific context, and there is much more to be got out of the incident.

[62] Martín González de Cellorigo, *Memorial de la política necesaria y útil restauración a la república de España*, ed. J. L. Pérez de Ayala (Madrid, 1991), p. 156, 'para todo cualquier buen efecto es muy necesario que el príncipe haga sola una ciudad a su reino, y le juzgue por tal y le trate, conserve y comunique de la misma manera que si fuese una pequeña aldea'; ibid., p. 192, crucial is the establishment of 'una unión tan indivisible ... concertando sus súbditos los unos con los otros y todos juntos, en si mismo establece una república apacible, firme, estable, armoniosa ...' ; Suárez de Figueroa, *El Pasajero*, pp. 24, 25, 'De algunas historias colijo ser importantísima para el aumento de valor la mezcla de naciones'; and Saavedra Fajardo's view that a monarchy composed of juridical equals was a necessity for effective defence, 'y esto no puede ser si las coronas no se reducen a una', *Locuras de Europa*, pp. 101, 100, 104. For Campanella's more vigorous 'Leonese' line, A. Pagden, *Spanish imperialism and the political imagination* (New Haven and London, 1990), p. 41.

One approach, given the lack of a positive basis for natural unity deriving from a common identity, was to reinforce the providentialist, even apocalyptic role of the monarchy. As Fray Juan de Salazar explained in his *Política española* (1619), 'With this aim, the kings of Spain put all their efforts into the unity of the Catholic religion so that their peoples, realms and estates should love each other, not allowing to live amongst them Jew, Moor or any heretic who might impede or contribute to the undoing of this bond and union.'[63] This is in a direct line with the dévot critique of Philip II's monarchy by the unionists of the Espelunça circle of Miguel de Piedrola, Dr Alonso de Mendoza, Lucas de Allende, Guillen de Casaus and subsequently Lucrecia de León.[64]

On the other hand, the 'castilianist' solution tended to be exclusively fiscal, a redistribution of the costs of the monarchy, and with it a more precise separation of functions within the monarchy – as Fernández Navarrete put it:

It seems fair that, dividing the costs proportionately, Castile should bear the charge for maintaining the royal household, guarding its coasts and the Indies run, and that Portugal should pay for its own garrisons and for the East India fleets, as it did before it was incorporated into Castile, and that Aragon and Italy should defend their own coasts and maintain the ships and militia needed for that. It does not seem reasonable that the head should wither and grow weak whilst the other members, which are very rich and populous, admire the burdens it carries. It is more just that the provinces that abut enemy borders contribute more for their own defence.[65]

Given the general governmental principle that associated funding and administration, such a distribution of costs would inevitably have implied a corresponding distribution of offices. It is in this context of a disturbing mood in Castile of disillusion with the monarchy that Olivares' attempt to establish a new framework of Iberian cooperation or confederation in the 1620s takes its place.

The exact nature of the political community Olivares was promoting has been much debated – castilianization or hispanization? Union, federation, or mere cooperation?

Jover Zamora has contrasted the approaches to union of Olivares and his near contemporary, the Aragonese prelate and political writer, Don Juan de Palafox, as characterized by an insistence on uniformity (whether castilianizing or hispanizing) on the one side, as against cooperation and respect for

---

[63] Salazar, *Política española*, p. 151.
[64] R. L. Kagan, *Lucrecia's Dreams* (Berkeley, 1990), pp. 96–7.
[65] Pedro Fernández Navarrete, *Conservación de monarquías*, Discurso XXIII, Biblioteca de Autores Españoles, 25 (Madrid, 1926), p. 496.

national differences on the other;[66] but it may be that in reality there was less difference than Jover suggests. It is worth looking at the arguments Olivares used to justify 'union', or *correspondencia* in the Catalan version of the Union of Arms. Olivares did not present union as a natural development, rooted in common character, customs, or characteristics. On the contrary, he recognized the difficulty of even a mere union of arms which did not involve any alteration of laws or government, given that 'the kingdoms are many and their humours different' and given 'the coolness and the distance they have felt between them thus far' (*la sequedad y separación de corazones que hasta ahora ha habido*). The contrast between this and the kind of union Sir Thomas Craig was advocating between Scotland and England is striking. What made union possible was not any common nature or feeling, indeed 'today the common people regard the other nationals little differently from foreigners', but the simple fact that they had been ruled for so long by a single prince and that they should have common interests of defence and religion: 'at one in mutual affection, in obedience to their prince, in their zeal for their religion, and in the aim of maintaining the whole body of this monarchy and the common cause of Christendom'.[67]

It is worth noting the practical, utilitarian nature of this appeal. The proposal to reduce the kingdoms to the laws and customs of Castile was limited to what was needed to facilitate the working of government and the freedom of action of the king. The purpose of the Union of Arms was to provide a framework for a working alliance of confederates, not to create a new nation.[68] The political community envisaged in the Union of Arms was very much in line with what Castilian unionist reformers like Cellorigo and Suárez de Figueroa were advocating and a lot more like Palafox's than Jover argues; that is to say, Olivares' policy of union remained within the bounds of prevailing perceptions of community.

In any event, the Union of Arms was almost immediately abandoned in 1626 for a series of demands for a more or less straightforward monetary contribution.[69] How seriously the full programme was ever intended to be

---

[66] J. M. Jover Zamora, 'Sobre los conceptos de monarquía y nación en el pensamiento político español del XVII', *Cuadernos de historia de España*, 13 (1950), 101–50.

[67] John H. Elliott and F. de la Peña, *Memoriales y cartas del conde duque de Olivares* (Madrid, 1978), I, p. 183 note, *et seq.*

[68] Or as Olivares himself put it, 'no soy yo nacional, que es cosa de muchachos', *Memoriales y cartas*, I, p. 43; see the argument in 'The government of Spain in the reign of Philip IV' in I. A. A. Thompson, *Crown and Cortes: government, institutions and representation in early-modern Castile* (Aldershot, 1993), chapter 4, pp. 12–13.

[69] For F. Bronner, 'La unión de armas en el Perú. Aspectos político-legales', *Anuario de estudios americanos*, 23 (1967), 1133–76, at pp. 1166, 1134, the project was transformed immediately into a simple increase in taxes, the council of the Indies recognizing that any

more than a pretext for such an outcome is an open question, but what is clear is that the military proposals of the Union would have expanded provincial institutions, not diminished them, and therefore institutionalized provincialism, not eroded it.[70]

Olivares' more radical vision of the new political community, aiming to 'familiarize' and to make the separate kingdoms 'brothers' ('*hermanarlos a todos*') through intermarriage, mutual access to office and reciprocity, in the hope of diluting separatist sentiment, has left no comparable programmatic expression to the Union of Arms.[71] The extent to which this policy was effective has not been fully investigated, but there does not seem to have been much serious effort to put it into practice for well over a decade. There was some limited legislation in response to the petitions of the 1626 Cortes to earmark posts for Aragonese in the council and the *audiencias* of the Indies, though on a much more limited scale than had been requested. This was not, of course, the legitimation of access for Aragonese to posts in Castile and the Indies, which in both law and practice already existed in the sixteenth century, but a quota system, a form of positive discrimination.[72] The motive (if we are to believe what Olivares told Castilian councillors) was not only to introduce Aragonese into Castilian institutions, but also to persuade the Aragonese to allow Castilians into theirs, so meeting a perennial Castilian grievance.[73] Yet there were no Aragonese appointed to the council of Castile throughout the reigns of Philip IV and Charles II, and

'socorro recíproco' was an impossibility; for M. A. Echevarría Bacigalupe it was 'inviable', 'Estado moderno e integración político-económica: la unión de armas en Flandes' in *Estado y fiscalidad en el antiguo régimen*, ed. C. Cremades Griñán (Murcia, 1989), p. 391.

[70] In Peru, it was recognized that its consequence would be to increase the independence of the Indies, Bronner, 'La Unión de las Armas en el Perú', p. 1156; in Flanders, it led in July 1628 to the creation of two *tercios* of natives and twelve companies of native horse, the localization of fund management, and increased local power, Echevarría Bacigalupe, 'La unión de armas en Flandes', 387, 389, 391; see also my 'Aspects of Spanish military and naval organization during the ministry of Olivares' in I. A. A. Thompson, *War and society in Habsburg Spain* (Variorum, Aldershot, 1992), chapter 4, pp. 15–17.

[71] Elliott and Peña, *Memoriales y cartas*, I, p. 97. Cellorigo and Suárez de Figueroa, among others, had argued along similar lines.

[72] From 1515 in the case of the Navarrese, from 1585 in that of the Aragonese according to I. Sánchez Bella, 'Reserva a aragoneses de plazas de justicia y gobierno en Indias (siglo XVII)', *Actas IV symposium historia administración* (Madrid, 1983), pp. 683–701; but even before this the Aragonese were never in practice acted against, Solórzano Pereyra, *Política indiana*, III, pp. 299–301. Solórzano says that whilst his book was at press (1647) Philip IV had granted the Aragonese 'que aun en todos sus consejos, audiencias y tribunales de Castilla y de las Indias, haya de haver precisamente por lo menos un ministro que sea natural de aquel reyno, y así se ha puesto en execución', *op. cit.*, p. 301.

[73] Consulta 20 October 1626, AHN, Est. libro 741, fo. 352, 'empeçando a introducir a los tribunales de acá aragoneses, sería fácil el disponer que allá se admittiesen castellanos'.

during the former reign only 230 of 4,964 habits of the Military Orders went to natives of the crown of Aragon, as opposed to 435 to Italian vassals, and 25 to Portuguese.[74]

It was the war with France in 1635 and the revolts in Catalonia and Portugal in 1640 that really brought non-Castilians into office in numbers. It was only after the Evora riots that the *junta* was set up 'to see that the Portuguese be regarded as natives in Castile, and the Castilians in Portugal', and over half the Catalans awarded habits received them in the years around 1640. The ideal of a non-national monarchy was never nearer to reality than in the middle decades of the seventeenth century, though in fact as much, if not more, was done to *hermanar* all Spaniards, in the ways Olivares had proposed, after his fall than during his own ministry.[75] The return of 'hot war' to the peninsula after 1636 internationalized war and government as well as finance. The armies and the armadas were multinational conglomerates. Spaniards, and especially Castilians, were no longer the dominant elements. The levy of 'foreign' troops from Flanders and Italy (and elsewhere) was a deliberate policy to relieve Castile of the continuous drain of manpower which it was incapable of sustaining. What was true of the troops, went *a fortiori* for the commanders. As generals, viceroys and councillors foreigners had a place in mid-seventeenth-century Spain not paralleled since the reign of Charles V. In the council of War between 1635 and 1665 30 per cent of the members were foreigners (mainly Italians and Portuguese). All this was the consequence not of a deliberate policy of union, but of the pressing need for financial and military expertise, to reward political loyalty and to enhance the authority of military leaders. It was the counterpart to the unprecedented contributions the rest of the monarchy was making to its survival.

For Castilians the arrival of these 'foreigners' in high office was a colonization such as they had not experienced since 1517. Their response was, as on the earlier occasion, a bitter resentment of the foreigners' political and

---

[74] E. Postigo Castellanos, *Honor y privilegio en la corona de Castilla* (Soria, 1988), pp. 205–6. J. Fayard, *Les membres du conseil de Castille à l'époque moderne (1621–1746)* (Geneva and Paris, 1979), p. 230; the governor of the council from 1630 to 1634, Miguel Santos de San Pedro, sometimes said to be Aragonese, is listed by Fayard as from the province of Palencia, p. 239.

[75] Not until 1635 was any significant number of non-Spaniards appointed to the council of War, and there were probably nearly as many between 1644 and 1665 as in the years immediately before. In 1646 the earmarking of offices for Aragonese in the imperial administration was extended to Naples, Milan, Sicily, the Indies and the Council of Castile, and by 1660 Aragonese were serving the presidency of Nueva Granada and four *plazas* in the *audiencias*, as well as two governorships in the Indies, Sánchez Bella, 'Reserva a aragoneses', p. 695.

military prominence in the government of Spain. That prominence was a very visible sign that the balance of the monarchy had been profoundly, and perhaps permanently, altered. The sense of a displacement of Castile must have been deeply disturbing. However, the targets of Castilian resentment in the 1630s and 1640s were not the Catalans, nor the loyal Aragonese, Valencians, Navarrese and Basques who had contributed to the war against the French, but the Italians and the Portuguese, the latter not least, or perhaps above all, because they were suspect in religion.[76] Paradoxically, the separatist revolts of 1640 may have done more to forge a common feeling between Castilians and Aragonese than the propaganda of decades. War made it necessary to maximize human resources, to secure the services of all parts of the monarchy and then to reward loyalty. The grants of corporate naturalization made by the Cortes of Castile to Ceuta, Tortosa, Tarragona and Gerona for their heroic resistance were a concrete recognition of that fact. Jover may be right, therefore, that the threat to the integrity of the monarchy presented by the separation of Portugal generated a heightened sense of *Spain*, as the succession question did again at the end of the century. Ironically a crown now largely divorced from its open-ended commitment to the defence of Christendom seems in the second half of the seventeenth century to have found a greater willingness in its subjects to accept a common obligation to the monarchy as a whole than ever before.[77] What is also a marked feature of these years is the increasing propensity to apply the spirit of *patria* not simply to the land of one's birth but also to the greater political collectivity to which one belonged.[78] The nationalization and the politicization of *patria* was for the new Spain a secularized version of what the 'divine monarchy' had been for the old. However, this revival of

---

[76] Indicative of popular opinion is the case, reported by the Jesuit letter writers on 19 August 1638, of the Portuguese lawyer who was sent by the Royal Council to Antequera to investigate a dispute between civil and ecclesiastical jurisdictions only to have a *sanbenito* nailed to his door, *Memorial histórico español*, xv, pp. 1–5.

[77] For one illustration, the town of Verin (Orense) congratulated the king on success in Catalonia, giving thanks to God 'que fue servido de permitirlo para que Vuestra Magestad desta gloria y triunfo contra los enemigos de la Corona alcance la union de toda la monarquia', AGS, CJH 1109, 7 November 1652.

[78] For Pedro González Salcedo, in 1671, *patria* was not only the corner where one was born, but the people who made up the kingdom, J. A. Maravall, *La philosophie politique espagnole au XVIIe siècle* (Paris, 1955), p. 96; an anonymous treatise on the succession after Carlos II by 'un buen compatriota Español', in Haus-, Hof- und Staats-Archiv, Vienna, Spanien Varia fasz. 80, 'de los grandes apenas se reconoze un buen patriota'; the 'alianza y unión' of 15 December 1676, signed by the grandees to remove the Queen Mother and Valenzuela, declared it would regard any opponents 'como enemigos privados del rey y de la patria', Juan Cortés Osorio, *Invectiva política contra D. Juan José de Austria*, ed. M. Etreros (Madrid, 1984), p. 257.

'Spain' was a process that must be related to two other quite contrary developments: the devaluation of the civic *patria* and the appearance of a new kind of regional localism.

VI   *Provincialization*

One response of the Cortes cities to Olivares' decision in 1632 to remove from them the right of veto, their *voto decisivo*, and thus to transform the Cortes from a meeting of agents of the cities into an assembly of the realm, was the promotion of a new politico-administrative space based on the province. This was a step that had profound importance for the development of Castilian local administration and for the articulation of central power in the localities. In the later sixteenth century the sense of province does not seem to have been particularly strong – several places surveyed in the *Relaciones topográficas* of the 1570s did not know which city represented them in the Cortes; Iniesta did not know whether it was in Castile or in Aragon. In the middle of the seventeenth century, however, the individual Cortes cities were emphasizing their role as representatives of their provinces in order to defend their civic autonomy against the Cortes. In Burgos, Juan de Cañas spoke of 'the authority this city has had since time immemorial from its people, province and kingdom'. One of the points made by Valladolid to argue that the *procuradores* of the city should be elected by the *ayuntamiento*, and not by its 'noble lineages' (*casas de los linajes*) was that it had 'as its province, Olmedo, Medina del Campo, Medina de Rioseco, Tordesillas and many other places for whom Valladolid as provincial capital now speaks in the Cortes, which the city's noble families could not represent.[79] Our first obligation, declared Don Gerónimo de Carvajal in Salamanca, is the defence of 'our province' (*nuestra provincia*).[80]

There was a palpable widening of the political process in Castile from the middle decades of the century from city to province. In 1660, for example, Valladolid conformed with a request of the *Procurador del Común* that, whenever the *ayuntamiento* discussed the letter of summons to the Cortes and met to issue instructions for its proctors, 'he too should be summoned as the matter concerns the province and the commonality of the city'.[81] In Orense, the aldermen, who on 10 July 1673 were discussing the prorogation of the *millones* and various other taxes heard and approved a petition 'asking the city that...it publicly order the districts of the province to send

[79] Don Sebastián Montero, in *ayuntamiento* of Valladolid, 29 January 1655.
[80] *Ayuntamiento* of Salamanca, 13 November 1648.
[81] *Ayuntamiento* of Valladolid, 16 June 1660.

one person each with full powers to authorize the city to approve and ratify everything negotiated and agreed with His Majesty on the said matter'. The petition was carried despite its being totally without precedent.[82]

The demand by the 'provinces' for equal precedence with the 'kingdoms' in the public ceremonies of the Cortes, made in the Cortes of 1655 by provincial capitals (cabezas de provincia) which had not been capital cities during the Middle Ages (cabezas de reino), was in its way a repudiation of the pre-eminence of the ancient territoriality of the Reconquest and an assertion of the new administrative province as an authentic territorial community.[83] It points to the emergence of a new political cartography that enabled the Cortes cities both to re-affirm their authority as provincial capitals, particularly in fiscal and military administration, as against the district capitals, juridically independent towns (villas exentas) and their other challengers, and to make it impossible for an independent Cortes to operate effectively without their administrative cooperation.

What is of crucial importance is that the elaboration of the concept of the province by the cities was paralleled by the development of a new provincial administration by the state, part of a major, and still to be properly investigated, reform and re-organization of fiscal and military administration in the later part of the reign of Philip IV and in that of Charles II. This was itself a response to the success of the cities, and was to lead via a series of fiscal reforms to the establishment of the province as a coherent administrative unit under the intendant in the eighteenth century. The province provided the cabezas de provincia with a new basis for local dominance, but one that now was shadowed, or was part of, or was being superseded by the provincial administrative agents of the state. It is perhaps within this new, modern, uniform political geography in which the cities were articulations of a centralized system radiating from a common centre in Madrid, that we should see the role of the Cortes cities following the last meeting of this assembly in 1664.

The growth of provincialism, both within Castile and within Spain, was also related to developments in military organization and the course of military events in the seventeenth century which tended to enhance provincialism and to create new institutional forms for the expression of provincial sentiment, rather than to advance the integration of the monarchy as a whole. This was most apparent in naval organization. In the reign of Philip III, the Catalan galley squadron, the Denia galleys in Valencia, and the contracts signed for the maintenance of provincial squadrons in the Armada

---

[82] Archivo Histórico Provincial de Orense, Actas 34, fos. 43–6.
[83] ACC, LIX, part 1, p. 305ff.

del Mar Océano with the provinces of Guipuzcoa, Vizcaya and the Cuatro Villas (Cantabria) in 1617–18 set the pattern. It was to be continued with the formation of the Galicia Squadron in 1624. The squadrons, paid and fitted out by the provinces, were to sail under the province's name, be commanded by native generals, admirals and captains, manned by native seamen, winter in their own province, and, in the Galician case at least, serve provincial interests (*para la guarda y defensa de la costa del reyno de Galicia*). The net effect, it was recognized, by shaking natives out into their own provincial squadrons, was to provincialize the entire Armada and to weaken the specifically royal component in the fleet.

Similarly, territorial defence and the problems of military recruitment were leading towards a similar sort of provincialization. That was clear enough in the crown of Aragon, in for example the projected militia of Valencia of 1643, which the viceroy promised 'not to move outside the limits and boundaries of this kingdom either in whole or in part, in any event or unforeseen circumstance, because this batallion of militia is to serve solely for the defence of this kingdom and within its boundaries, and in no other manner'. But it was also apparent within Castile. From the late 1630s the *tercio provincial*, taking its name from its place of origin, raised, officered, manned and reinforced by natives, played an increasingly prominent part in proposals for the reform of the recruiting system and the militias.[84]

Moreover, the very experience of war, especially of front-line provinces like Galicia, Extremadura and Andalusia, sharpened their sense of separateness from parts of the kingdom less burdened and less ravaged. Army structure tended to reinforce this separateness by taking on provincial forms and imposing a further institutional definition on the sense of region.[85] Significantly, it was as provinces that Galicia and Extremadura, by their financial contributions to the war effort, acquired their votes in the Cortes, the purchase and the cooperation both a definition of regionality and an expression of regional solidarity.[86] But everywhere the intolerable burdens of war forced localities to think first of themselves and of what was best for themselves and their regions, rather than of the generality. The contemplation of breaking away from Castile altogether was the ultimate response.

---

[84] See my 'Aspects of Spanish military and naval organization during the ministry of Olivares', pp. 15–17.

[85] The attempt by the marquis of Leganés, as captain-general of the army of Extremadura, to convoke an assembly of Extremaduran towns in 1645, followed, two years later, by another proposal, this time by the city of Cáceres, to set up a *junta* of the province, is a vivid illustration of this symbiosis.

[86] F. Lorenzana de la Puente, 'Extremadura, siglos XVII–XVIII. La frontera como condicionante político', *Revista de Extremadura*, 7 (1992), 49–70.

Andalusia was the most notorious case, but there were worries about the loyalty of Extremadura and Galicia also; and Vizcaya, which even late in Philip II's reign seems still to have been associated with the Cortes of Castile within the province of Burgos, had separated itself by the time of Philip IV, and was rejecting the authority of Castile altogether, refusing either to use stamped paper or to plead in the *chancilleria* of Valladolid.[87] Even the obsession of the citizens of Logroño with Cantabria and the province of Rioja can be understood in the context of that city's unhappiness at being regarded as part of the province of Burgos.

There is the sense of a new perception of space in seventeenth-century Spain, a narrowing of mental horizons, evidence for which is provided by the decadence of general histories and the corresponding growth of historical writing in the provinces, not only in the crown of Aragon, but about Galicia, Cantabria, Vizcaya and La Rioja, characterized, as Sánchez Alonso notes, by 'a certain sharpening of regionalist fervour which gives the works a political tone'.[88] The revival of 'Castile' was itself a form of provincialization. In reality it was as much, if not more, the revival not of the greater Castile that stretched from the Atlantic to the Mediterranean, but of the little Castile of the heartland of the meseta. It is much more common in the seventeenth century than in the sixteenth to find the kingdom divided into Old Castile, New Castile and Andalusia, and for a 'little' Castile (*esta pobre de Castilla la Vieja y la Nueva*) to be spoken of as apart from some of the component parts of a 'greater' Castile, such as Asturias and Galicia.[89] Domínguez Ortiz talks of an 'Andalusian front' in the Cortes in the seventeenth century; but equally there are indications of a Castilian front, and the hostility of Old Castile to Andalusia in the Cortes is apparent.

It is tempting to see in all this not only the retreat of 'Castile', fragmented by its own internal particularisms, the abandonment of the Cortes being perhaps the clearest symptom of that fragmentation, but also, from the way the province of Rioja was being spoken of in the same breath as 'the four

---

[87] *ACC*, XII, p. 302, 16 January 1593; A. Rodríguez Villa, ed., *La corte y monarquía de España en los años de 1636 y 1637* (Madrid, 1886), pp. 249–50, 16 January 1638.

[88] Sánchez Alonso notes the increasing number of histories of the ancient kingdoms in the early seventeenth century characterized by 'un cierto exacerbamiento del celo regionalista que da tono político a las obras', *Historiografía española*, II, p. 162. Lupercio Leonardo de Argensola's expressed aim was to separate the history of Aragon from that of Castile or Spain 'sobre todo en estos tiempos en que apenas se distinguen los reinos de España', Gil Pujol (ed.), *Información de los sucesos del reino de Aragón*, p. xxxv.

[89] For example, Atilano de Obeso, *procurador de Cortes* for Zamora 11 December 1599, *ACC*, XVIII, p. 523; AGS, GA 913, council of War, 14 June 1625, ordering levies from Portugal, Aragon, Galicia and Asturias 'sin tocar en ninguna parte de los de Castilla'.

provinces of the *señorío* of Vizcaya, Alava, Navarre and Aragon',[90] for example, or Asturias was matched with 'the kingdoms of León and Castilla la Vieja, señorío of Vizcaya, kingdoms and provinces of Andalusia, Extremadura, Aragon, Valencia, Catalonia and Navarre', the elevation of the province to a par with the historic kingdoms. The moral community of the kingdom was being broken down into a set of administrative and emotional equivalences. As an early eighteenth-century Asturian asked rhetorically, 'Is not the king the common father of the state, favouring every village, city and province without discrimination?'[91]

VII   *The* patria natural *: city and metropolis*

In the first decades of the seventeenth century the city *república* was still at the core of the sense of community. Although *patria* could have national connotations even in the middle ages, and Maravall has documented numerous instances of its use in such a sense, it remained into the seventeenth century first of all a designation of the city. The emotive power of the city is reflected in the wave of municipal histories and panegyrics published from the 1590s to the 1650s, or so. In 1633, the royal purveyor in Lisbon, Don Fernando Alvía de Castro, dedicated his *Memorial por Logroño* to the city itself: 'as a son of Your Lordship and as an obligation that each of us has (as Plato says) to serve his *patria*, being born for that more than for one's own personal good' – he had been away from Logroño (*mi cara Patria Logroño*) for twenty-six years.

Despite the administrative, legislative and fiscal penetration of the state, the city had not lost all sense of being a semi-autonomous political community. The oaths of the *regidores* and *procuradores*, for example, placed the obligations of municipal office firmly in a municipal framework, with little or no reference to the broader national community. The continuing political, economic and social importance of the city is reflected in the movement of prices for municipal office, which increased substantially between 1580–1600 and leapt to a peak in the early 1630s at a level often two or three times as high as at the beginning of the century.

What generated these obvious manifestations of civic commitment in the fifty or so years from about 1590? The outburst of local community

---

[90] *ACC*, LX, part 1, p. 5, 8 March 1656.
[91] 'No es el rey padre común de la república para beneficiar sin distinción a cada pueblo, ciudad y provincia?', Don Domingo Uriarte Arguelles 1724, cited in F. Tuero Bertrand, *La creación de la real audiencia en las Asturias de su tiempo (siglos XVII–XVIII)* (Oviedo, 1979), p. 373.

consciousness was not unique to Spain, and it might reasonably be seen as a defensive movement against, or at least as the obverse of, the exaltation of royal and state power. The authority of the cities and their *ayuntamientos* was under attack not only from the centre but also from the localities by the sale of offices and by the granting of judicial exemptions to their subject villages, and from within by the liturgical challenge of the post-Tridentine parish. The rupturing of the community of the city by the entry of outsiders and pluralists into its councils is reflected in a series of complaints in the Cortes in the last two decades of the century. One reason for the fabrication of civic pride may simply have been the need to forge a new alliance between the commons and their ruling oligarchies.

In these circumstances, a critical new factor in the trajectory of the political community was the rise of the metropolitanism of Madrid. From the restoration of the court in 1606, Madrid rapidly developed into a sort of *patria común*. 'Es Madrid, patria de todos' as Calderón put it. Francisco Santos, the author of *El no importa de España* (1667), was born, he tells us, 'in the great homeland (*patria*) of the world, in the mother of the living, in the oratory of Heaven, in the cloak of the poor, there with the empire of the globe, in the seat of the greatest monarchs on earth, in Madrid'.[92]

The shift in the centre of gravity of political and economic opportunity from the city to the court, which though present in the sixteenth century became irresistible after 1598 as a result of the increased exploitation of local office for national political ends, the decline of the urban economies and the collapse of municipal finances, increased the relative importance of crown and grandee patronage and drew a corresponding proportion of the ruling élites away from the cities. The ruling oligarchies were thus split by a new political divide between residents and absentees, between *república* and *corte*, which was to lead in some cities to attempts from the 1640s onwards to restore traditional community solidarities by allying the *regimiento* with the broader body of *caballeros* within the city against the outsiders.

Madrid was the great honey-pot of the seventeenth century. By its domination of the economic life of the Spanish interior, Madrid acted as a powerful magnet on regional society. The balance between the localities and the centre was completely upturned by the disproportionate growth of economic and social opportunities in the capital. It was Madrid that had become the great engine of personal wealth and social promotion. Opportunity had become centralized. The central bureaucracy was by its very

---

[92] See also Gonzalo de Céspedes y Meneses, quoted in Green, *Spain and the Western tradition*, III, p. 82.

nature destructive of local patriotism and contributed greatly to the social dominance of Madrid and the 'national' role of the capital.[93] Whilst the processes of modernization became concentrated in Madrid, the provinces became parochialized, by-passed by the flow of economic and social benefits of that modernization. There was little in the localities which could offer much resistance to the attraction of the career opportunities and the spectacular rewards held out by the capital. The local community, constrained liturgically by the post-Tridentine attack on the profane, the secular and the heterogeneous, its public communal festivals turned in to the enclosed parochial devotions of the seventeenth century, was losing some of its most important forms of ceremonial expression.[94] The drying up of the production of municipal histories coincides with a permanent fall in the value of municipal offices in the 1640s and the abandonment of the *ayuntamientos*. The absenteeism of the *regidores*, declining attendance, the reduction in the number of meetings seem to have been general in the cities from the later seventeenth century. The cities were being abandoned by the rich. Only two of the nineteen leading land owners of Salamanca listed in the Ensenada Catastro of the 1750s were resident in the city; thirteen were living in Madrid.[95]

VIII Towards the new patria

As Madrid in its progression from court to capital sucked in the élites from the cities, it centralized, intellectualized and repoliticized their 'patriotism'. Local patriotism – 'this pestilence of localism', in the words of the early eighteenth-century reformist intellectual, Feijóo – was left to be plebeianized, despised and condemned as petty, divisive, dangerous and pernicious.[96] The new secular, state patriotism of the eighteenth century,

---

[93] See 'War and institutionalization: the military-administrative bureaucracy of Spain in the sixteenth and seventeenth centuries' in Thompson, *Crown and Cortes*, chapter 2. Whereas in the reign of Philip IV half of Fayard's councillors of Castile wanted to be buried in their native province, in the reign of Charles II only 15 per cent did, and in Philip V's only 6 per cent, *Les membres du Conseil de Castille*, p. 524.

[94] M. Flynn, *Sacred Charity. Confraternities and Social Welfare in Spain 1400–1700* (Ithaca, N.Y., 1989), pp. 122, 124.

[95] J. Infante Miguel-Motta, *El municipio de Salamanca a finales del antiguo régimen* (Salamanca, 1984), p. 60.

[96] 'El pensar ventajosamente de la región donde hemos nacido sobre todas las demás del mundo es error entre los comunes comunisimo', Feijóo, *Teatro crítico* (1726–40), as cited in Magariños, *Alabanza de España*, p. 325. Don Lunes de Valdés, a proponent in 1726 of an *audiencia* for Asturias, deriding his opponent Don Domingo Uriarte Arguelles, 'habla como paysano, o Patriense', Tuero Bertrand, *Creación de la real audiencia en las Asturias*, p. 452.

though not discontinuous from the late medieval national *patria* that was in increasingly generalized use during the reign of Charles II, is of an entirely different intellectual, political and even emotional order from that combination of 'nationalist fervour, unquestioned daughter of vanity and envy', and vassalatic fidelity, which characterizes the Spanish patriotism of the Baroque. 'The *patria*...which we ought to value above our own private interests,' declared Feijóo, 'is that body politic in which, under a civil government, we are united beneath the yoke of the same laws. Thus Spain is the object of the love of the Spaniard.'[97]

The transformation of the meaning of *patria* is the key to the shift in the location of community loyalty. It was, of course, a long, uneven and ambiguous process, but by the time Miguel Antonio de la Gándara wrote his *Apuntes sobre el bien y el mal de España* in 1759 it surely had been completed: 'I have no other country, no other county, no other home, no other flesh nor blood than Spain, Spain, Spain.' The *patria particular* of the province, the diocese, the city, the district, was crushed between the prolonged decadence of the city as an economic, social and political force, and the correlative centralization of wealth, status and power in Madrid. It is not surprising that with the gradual recovery of the Spanish economy from the 1680s or so and in the relative buoyancy of much of the first two-thirds of the eighteenth century adherence to the state should have been strong. Pierre Chaunu pointed many years ago to the broad positive synchrony between the general state of the economy and the cohesiveness of the monarchy. It is a perception whose value deserves to be worked out at all levels of community consciousness.

It is the breaking down of primary loyalties into fragments which had no autonomy except as part of a greater political whole that largely freed Spain from the competition of a Castilian national loyalty that could have hampered the hispanization of the state under the Bourbons. Castilianism seems, however, to have been a relatively weak sentiment; clearly, except at moments of especial stress, much weaker than the sense of national commu-

---

[97] 'La patria...quien debemos estimar sobre nuestros particulares intereses,' declared Feijóo, 'es aquel cuerpo de estado donde, debajo de un gobierno civil, estamos unidos bajo la coyunda de las mismas leyes. Así España es el objeto del amor del español', Feijóo, *Teatro crítico* (1726–40), as cited in Magariños, *Alabanza de España*, p. 325. See also the definition of 'patria' in the *Redactor General* of 1810: 'Patria no es precisamente este *pueblo, provincia o estado* que nos ha visto nacer sino aquella *sociedad*, aquella *nación* donde, al abrigo de leyes justas, moderadas y reconocidas, hemos gozado de los placeres de la vida, el fruto de nuestros sudores, las ventajas de nuestra industria y la *inalterable* posesión de nuestros derechos *imprescriptibles*', P. Vilar, 'Estado, nación y patria en las conciencias españolas: historia y actualidad', in his *Hidalgos, amotinados y guerrilleros. Pueblo y poderes en la historia de España* (Barcelona, 1982), p. 270.

nity that existed in Catalonia, Aragon, etc. There was lacking in castilianism that affective dimension that always seems to have been a characteristic of Spanishness. The expression *nuestra España* ('our Spain'), the prevalence of which Pierre Vilar regards as the touchstone of national sentiment,[98] is extremely common from at least the later fifteenth century onwards; there is no equivalent feeling attached to Castile. The instances of *nuestra Castilla* are so rare that the contrast cannot be accidental.[99] The vicissitudes of castilianism under the Habsburgs were a comment on the fortunes of a Spanish state the character of which had still to be determined. Indeed, it may well be that the nationalization of the *patria* in the later seventeenth century and the victory of a Spanish nationalism over what was politically its most important rival was a vital emotional precursor of Bourbon constitutional reformism, which of course not only suppressed much of the institutional distinctiveness of the foral kingdoms but also decastilianized those fundamental symbols of Castilian separateness, the Cortes and the council of Castile. The establishment of a Spanish patriotism in the eighteenth century and its attendant concept of citizenship depended in no small measure on the inherent weakness and subsequent etiolation of castilianism.

[98] Vilar, 'Patria y nación en el vocabulario de la guerra de la independencia española' in *Hidalgos, amotinados y guerrilleros*, p. 223.

[99] Without any claim to comprehensiveness, or even to thoroughness, I have one record of 'nuestra buena Castilla' (Olivares, 1639), in G. Marañón, *El Conde-Duque de Olivares* (Madrid, 1952), p. 447, and one of 'nuestros Castellanos' (Don Melchor Alfonso Mogrovejo, BL, Egerton ms. 331, fo. 241v); Alonso de Castrillo (1521) writes of 'nuestra lengua castellana'. There are personifications of Castile, notably in verses and satires – 'la venerable dueña de Castilla, aquella gran matrona ... la señora Castilla' – but they are usually plaintive or admonitory; seventeenth-century Castile was, it would seem, more to be pitied than worshipped.

6

Aragonese constitutionalism and Habsburg rule:
the varying meanings of liberty

XAVIER GIL

On 30 January 1576 a tense meeting took place in London between William
Cecil, Lord Burghley, and Antonio de Guaras, a Spanish merchant who
served as a vital means of communication between London and Madrid
since the two governments had broken diplomatic relations in 1569. The
reason for the meeting was the offer that Queen Elizabeth had received to
put herself at the head of the States General of the Low Countries, a
possibility which naturally concerned the Spanish authorities. Guaras
argued that Elizabeth should not become involved in these affairs, but
rather concern herself with France and Scotland, her traditional enemies.
Once order was re-established in the Low Countries, Guaras said, England
would have nothing to fear. Further, Guaras protested that the Spaniards
were being called foreign intruders with regard to the Low Countries, a
manifest error since, as he reminded his interlocutor, these were patrimonial
states of the Spanish crown.

Burghley imparted a new tone to the conversation by referring to the
harshness of Spanish dominion and affirming that Holland and Zeeland
would cling doggedly to their privileges, like Aragon. They would succeed,
he said, with the assistance of neighbouring countries, since one of these
privileges was that if the king violated the constitution another prince would
be elected. Guaras retorted that, regarding Aragon, it was necessary to view

Translated from the Spanish by Bruce Taylor.

the case on its merits: Aragon was originally a free dominion, where the king was elected by the people on the condition of defending their privileges. In remembrance of this, the Cortes continually re-enacted the ceremony of election to demonstrate that the prince received his authority by this procedure, and not by inheritance or conquest. As a result, Aragon had been able to preserve its privileges intact and today the king was more loved and feared there than in any other of his dominions. Further, the Aragonese were more disposed to die in the king's service than many of his other subjects and among them there was not so much as a thought of religious dissent. On the other hand, Guaras continued, the Low Countries were not elective but patrimonial, they were over-run with heretics and had taken up arms against the king, which was like doing so against God himself. Burghley replied reminding him of the iniquities of the Alba régime and saying that Elizabeth had offered to mediate in the Dutch conflict. In passing, he added that the queen was angry at the imprisonment of Englishmen by the Inquisition. Sensing that the meeting was becoming serious, Guaras ended it, given that his instructions were only to listen and inform. The conclusion he drew from it was that Elizabeth would assist the rebels, and this he relayed to Madrid.[1]

Gauras' opinion about the relations between the king and his Aragonese subjects exemplified much contemporary thinking about this particular subject. Throughout Europe, scholars and diplomats alike conceived of the Aragonese monarch as an elective ruler whose authority over his subjects was limited by an oath in which he swore to uphold their traditional laws and privileges. 'Saragossa [the capital] lies under royal authority, but enjoys infinite privileges', observed Francesco Guicciardini in 1511, 'for which reason Queen Isabella, when irritated at so many privileges and liberties, was wont to declare: "'Aragon is not ours; it is necessary that we conquer her once again'".[2] A similar view of Aragonese privileges – and liberties – can be found in the reports of Venetian ambassadors, as well as in the works of political writers such as Fadrique Furió Ceriol, François Hotman and Juan de Mariana. Whether to applaud it, censure it or simply to remark upon it, the fact is that Aragon in the sixteenth century frequently appeared

---

[1] *Calendar of State Papers, Spanish, 1568–1579* (London, 1894), pp. 519–21, letter of Antonio de Guaras to Zayas, 1 February 1576. On Guaras as agent in absence of an ambassador resident, see Wallace T. MacCaffrey, *Queen Elizabeth and the making of policy, 1572–1588* (Princeton, 1981), pp. 166, 191–4, 313.

[2] Francesco Guicciardini, *Viaje a España* (Madrid, 1952), p. 46; he repeats it in p. 66. Successive ambassadors were to reproduce the statement attributed to Isabella.

as a kingdom protected by its privileges from the authoritarian tendencies of monarchy.[3]

As time passed, however, Aragon's reputation for liberty largely disappeared. In the second half of the seventeenth century, above all in England, writers of revolutionary or liberal persuasion held that the foundations of medieval liberty once common to much of Europe had receded before the royal despotism of the continent. The oath by the crown to uphold the laws of Aragon appeared in their treatises as a notable example on the list of victims of that lamentable historical tendency.[4]

To many, therefore, Aragon had seemingly suffered serious reverses. The Habsburgs had neutralized, if not suppressed, the most salient characteristics of Aragonese legal particularism and established their dominion over the kingdom. It would be simplistic, however, to accept at face value this assessment of a historical process lasting nearly two centuries. Changes in opinion did not always reflect changes in reality, and in any case the history of Aragonese liberties is not so well defined as to preclude other interpretations.

In 1969, in his wide-ranging discussion of revolution and stability in early modern Europe, John Elliott underscored the need to consider the relationship between *patria*, or nationhood and corporative constitutionalism, drawing particular attention to the various intellectual influences that contributed to the concept of community as a legal and historical entity. More recently, he has discussed the composite nature of early modern monarchies, and its importance for understanding both the development of royal authoritarianism and the resistance to centralized authority by regional élites.[5] An analysis of Aragonese constitutionalism under these premises, within the political framework of relations between the centre and

[3] Eugenio Albèri, *Le relazioni degli ambasciatori veneti al Senato durante el secolo decimosesto*, series I, V (Florence, 1861), pp. 25–6, 84–5, 152, 241, 291, 391–3; VI (Florence, 1862), p. 363. Fadrique Furió Ceriol, *El concejo y consejeros del príncipe* [1559], ed. D. Sevilla Andrés (Valencia, 1952), pp. 131–2; Juan de Mariana, *Historia general de España* (Latin edition, 1592); and *Del rey y de la institución real* (Latin edition, 1599), both in Biblioteca de Autores Españoles, XXX and XXXI (Madrid, 1950), pp. 5 and 485, 487, respectively; François Hotman, *Francogallia* (1573), ed. R. Giesey and J. H. M. Salmon (Cambridge, 1972), pp. 308–15.

[4] James Harrington, *The Commonwealth of Oceana*, in his *Political works*, ed. J. G. A. Pocock (Cambridge, 1977), p. 264. William Pryne, *Soveraigne power of parliament and kingdoms* [1643]; Henry Neville, *Plato redivivus* [1681]; Algernon Sydney, *Discourses concerning Government* [1698], all three quoted by R. E. Giesey and J. H. M. Salmon, 'Introduction', to Hotman, *Francogallia*, pp. 116, 121–2.

[5] John H. Elliott, 'Revolution and continuity in early modern Europe', *Past and Present*, 42 (1969), 35–56 (now in his *Spain and its world, 1500–1700* (New Haven and London, 1989), chapter 5, esp. pp. 103–8); 'A Europe of composite monarchies', *Past and Present*, 137 (1992), 48–71.

the periphery of the Spanish monarchy, therefore seems an appropriate contribution to the present volume.

In his widely read treatise *Govierno del ciudadano* of 1578, the Aragonese rhetorician and legal scholar Juan Costa (1549–1595) discussed his ideas on the public behaviour of the citizen. Much influenced by Italian humanist writings on the *vita civilis*, Costa's *ciudadano* was a *pater familias*, endowed with civic virtues and deeply committed to the service of the republic. Following Cicero, Costa considered obligations to the *patria* to be the first of the temporal order, immediately behind obligation towards God. One of these civic duties was the responsible discharge of public office. This was a delicate task, but for Costa the recipe for success was simple, although hardly original: to align oneself unfailingly with the dictates of the laws and statutes of the province, 'because law is the heart of civic government ... for while many cities live without walls, none may live without laws'.[6]

Costa's ideal citizen lived in an abstract republic, but at the time similar recipes for civic success were invoked by numerous Aragonese politicians and jurists in express reference to their own kingdom and its relations with the Spanish monarchy. For these writers, the central issue was the preservation and observance of the *fori, privilegia, libertates, consuetudines regni Aragonum*. In the Middle Ages the pattern of Aragonese law had registered tendencies both in favour and against royal authority, but by the mid-sixteenth century its localist, popular and customary features had come to the fore. Crucial among these were various restrictions limiting the exercise of royal authority within the kingdom together with a cluster of privileges, originally embodied in the *Privilegio General* of 1283, which established a contractual basis for Aragonese government.[7]

The centrepiece of this contractual system was the Cortes, which, even in the sixteenth century, remained the supreme legislative body in Aragon. The contrast with Castile was manifest. There, starting in the late Middle Ages, the Cortes had lost its legislative powers and the monarchy was able to pass laws without the assembly's participation or consent. In Aragon, on the other hand, not only did the king and kingdom together in the Cortes remain the legislative body *par excellence*, but the capacity of the king or his

---

[6] Juan Costa, *Govierno del ciudadano. Trata de cómo se ha de regir a sí, su casa y república* (2nd edition, much enlarged, Saragossa, 1584), pp. 624–6, 714–19. First edition, entitled *El regidor o ciudadano* (Salamanca, 1578). Costa was a lecturer in rhetoric at the University of Salamanca and then of law at the universities of Saragossa, Huesca and Barcelona. He was also politically active as a city official in his native Saragossa.

[7] The best overview is Jesús Lalinde Abadia, *Los fueros de Aragón* (Saragossa, 1979).

viceroy to dictate statutes was subordinated to the superior laws passed by the Cortes. At the same time it was expressly decreed that both the king and his officers were subject to the law, 'with neither fraud nor machination', as Ibando de Bardaxi made clear in one of the best treatises on Aragonese *fueros*.[8] The rule of law, born of the common accord between crown and estates and binding on all, was a basic principle of government and remained at the core of Aragon's political culture.

The rule of law was something which Aragon shared with other European states, but Aragon possessed something distinctive in the office of the *Justicia*, which represented an unusual *iux medium* between king and kingdom. This office can be traced back to the late twelfth century, but it was in the fifteenth century that the *Justicia* emerged as the supreme judge of the Cortes and the official interpreter of Aragonese *fueros*. Moreover, the court of the *Justicia* served as the protector of the four *procesos forales*, or court procedures which guaranteed individual rights in a way similar to the later English *habeas corpus*.[9]

Accompanying the emergence of the *Justicia* as the linchpin of Aragon's foral régime was the development of the legend of the laws of the ancient Pyrenean kingdom of Sobrarbe, and with it an account of the origins of Aragon itself. The so-called 'laws of Sobrarbe'[10] were partial fabrications, but they nevertheless served to transmit the basic premises of the Aragonese political system, among them the following account of the emergence of the office of *Justicia* itself:

The office of *Justicia* of Aragon (according to our ancestors) was established in the following manner. Certain peoples conquered from the Moors a certain part of the kingdom in the mountains of Sobrarbe, and since these were communities with neither governor nor alderman, and given that there were many disputes and debates among them, it was determined that, to avoid such problems and so that they might live in peace, they should elect a king to reign over them ... but that there should be a Judge between them and the king, who would hold the title of *Justicia* of Aragon. It is held by some that the *Justicia* was elected before the king, and that the king was elected under such conditions. Since then there has always been a *Justicia* of Aragon in the kingdom, cognisant of all procedures regarding the king, as much in petitioning as in defence.[11]

[8] Ibando de Bardaxi, *Comentarii in quatuor aragonensium fororum libros* (Saragossa, 1592), fos. 23v, 47v.

[9] The four procedures are known as *manifestación, aprehensión, firma* and *inventario*. See Víctor Fairén Guillén, *Antecedentes aragoneses de los juicios de amparo* (Mexico, 1971).

[10] The best study of these laws is Ralph E. Giesey, *If not, not: the oath of the Aragonese and the legendary Laws of Sobrarbe* (Princeton, 1968).

[11] From Juan Ximénez Cerdán, *Letra intimada*, printed in *Fueros y observancias de Aragón* (Saragossa, 1624), fos. 44–50, at fo. 44v.

Successive generations of chroniclers and jurists polished and refined these ideas which, expanded as necessary, became the ideological basis of Aragonese politics throughout the sixteenth and seventeenth centuries.

The publication of the Aragonese *fueros* in 1552 marked yet another important element in the emergence of the Aragonese patria. This volume, which had been commissioned by the Aragonese Cortes, included a 'preface' that reconstructed the history of the kingdom according to the legend of Sobrarbe. It boldly affirmed that: 'In Aragon kings were preceded by laws which the people continued to observe, even after the king had been elected among them, and which were added to as the king and kingdom saw fit.'[12] In addition, by outlining the fundamental components of Aragonese government – elective and limited monarchy, the contractual nature of legislation, etc. – this legal compendium symbolized the Aragonese *patria* itself.

Following the publication of these *fueros*, Aragonese political writers elaborated upon the uniqueness of Aragonese laws and institutions. The most prominent of these thinkers was Jerónimo de Blancas (d. 1590), a lawyer who, as chronicler of the kingdom, was the successor of the great Aragonese historian, Jerónimo Zurita (1512–1580). Blancas wrote a number of notable works on the celebration of the Cortes and the coronation of the Aragonese kings, as well as the *Aragonensium rerum comentarii* (1588), his most influential treatise. This work, composed in a beautiful and impassioned style which allowed Blancas to dodge frequent historical inaccuracies, offered the most complete account yet of the supposed history of the *Justicia* and the kingdom and presented, in six lapidary *fueros de Sobrarbe*, the conditions that the king was obliged to accept in order to be recognized. A detailed account of the conditions agreed upon in the *fueros* of Sobrarbe constitute the treatise's core:

These conditions are above all the compendium of all our laws and liberties; in accordance with these a mediating judge is established between the king and the people (two powers which together tend to be so conflictive and each the opponent of the other), as a bond of union between two extremes ... With these laws and statutes our forefathers buttressed the edifice of the kingdom they were restoring. The principal support of liberty was therefore enshrined in the prefecture of the mediating judge. Thus, power is conferred on the king, and on the mediating judge the moderation of that power, rendering our government both temperate and harmonious.[13]

---

[12] Quoted according to the edition of the *fueros* mentioned in the previous note.

[13] Jerónimo de Blancas, *Comentarios de las cosas de Aragón*, trans. M. Hernández (Saragossa, 1878), pp. 267, 38.

Yet the idea of the equivalence of the laws of Sobrarbe and the Aragonese *patria* was not confined to the pages of political treatises. It was central to Aragonese culture itself and could be found, for example, in the kingdom's heraldic shield, which prominently displayed in one of its quarters the famous tree of Sobrarbe. The Sobrarbe legend, moreover, became history, accepted not only by Aragonese historians such as Bartolomé Leonardo de Argensola,[14] but also by the authors of general histories of Spain and those of its individual kingdoms.[15] In addition, Aragonese lawyers presented the legend as evidence in a series of tumultuous cases brought before the tribunals of Saragossa during the 1580s to determine the extent of the monarchy's powers to alter certain Aragonese institutions. The most important of these cases, the so-called 'dispute over the foreign viceroy', originated in Philip II's attempt to appoint a non-Aragonese to the office of viceroy in the hope that freedom from family ties with the local aristocracy would afford this official greater success in quelling the rampant banditry and rural unrest. The lawyers opposed to this policy regularly had recourse to the account of the foundation of the kingdom and the office of *Justicia* in an effort to justify their claims that the royal authority in Aragon was limited by law.[16]

Although historians have generally overlooked the contributions of this Aragonese *foralista* school to the development of European constitutionalist thought, but as the meeting between Lord Burghley and Guaras seems to suggest, contemporaries were not unaware of the basic arguments that rendered Aragonese laws and institutions unique.[17]

Aragonese writers also took pride themselves in the uniqueness of their

---

[14] Argensola affirmed that the *fueros* of Sobrarbe 'united those once irreconcilable qualities, monarchy and liberty, and for this reason the *fueros* of vassalage in Aragon are called liberties'. See Bartolomé Leonardo de Argensola, 'Alteraciones populares de Zaragoza. Año 1591' (1625), BNM, ms. 12985, fo. 5v.

[15] Ambrosio de Morales (Philip II's official chronicler), *Corónica general de España*, IV (Cordoba, 1584), book 13, chapter 2; Gaspar Escolano, *Década primera de la historia de la insigne y coronada ciudad y reino de Valencia* [1610–11], enlarged edition by J. B. Perales (Valencia, 1878–1880), book 2, chapter 16 and book 5, chapter 26 (I, pp. 196, 550); Pedro Salazar de Mendoza, *Monarquía de España* [1601], II (Madrid, 1771), book 3, chapters 2 and 3.

[16] ADZ, ms. 164, a volume for this contention containing several abstracts on the history of Spain, which includes the Sobrarbe story (fos. 138off.). By the late seventeenth century, don Juan Luis López, marqués del Risco, produced a thick volume by compiling excerpts of historical texts and arguments used by a dozen lawyers around 1590: Biblioteca del Real Seminario de San Carlos, Saragossa, 'El fuero de Sobrarbe con historia y notas'.

[17] With the exception of Ralph Giesey in *If not, not*, and in his introduction with J. H. M. Salmon to Hotman's *Francogallia*, Blancas and the other Aragonese authors go unmentioned in the studies dealing with these issues.

political organization. Although it was common among contemporary authors to underline the political originality of their respective countries, in Aragon this feeling was especially strong, and not without reason. This is apparent in the warning with which Miguel de Molino opened his widely read *Repetorium fororum* of 1513:

The practice of lawsuits and cases in this kingdom of Aragon is more convoluted than in any other province, since a large part of common law is complicated and corrected by the *fueros* and *observancias*, and even the terms and words used in these laws are quite unknown by those foreign to the practice, however qualified and learned they may be when they arrive.

Other commentators insisted likewise: 'The task of explaining [the Aragonese judicial system] to foreign nations and kingdoms would be endless, since the terms which we use are only intelligible and comprehensible to native Aragonese.'[18]

Aragonese awareness of their unique juridical status was heightened by the kingdom's subordinate position in the Spanish monarchy created after the marriage of Isabel of Castile and Ferdinand of Aragon in 1469. Some seventeenth-century Aragonese writers looked back upon this union with a critical eye, convinced that it had opened the door to the erosion of Aragonese liberties, possibly even the end of the Aragonese *patria* itself. Thus Vicencio Blasco de Lanuza in 1622 interpreted the death of King Ferdinand and his succession by the Habsburg monarch, Charles V, as nothing short of disastrous for the future of Aragon.

They [the Aragonese] could well see that his [i.e. Ferdinand's] successor was of such calibre as to inflate the world with the fame of his deeds and exploits, as all hoped would be the case and which indeed came to pass. However, it seemed to them that the successors of the Catholic King would not be kings of Aragon, as he and his predecessors were, and that their heroic deeds would not be attributed to them, but would glorify and be numbered under the name and lordship of Castile, where the attributes of royal majesty and dignity would be exercised. This prospect and the strength of affection that they held for him caused them to grieve and lament his death more than that of any prince before him.[19]

---

[18] Michele de Molino, *Repertorium fororum et observantiarum regni Aragonum* [1513] (3rd edition, Saragossa, 1585), second prologue, n.p.; Francisco de Gurrea y Aragón, conde de Luna, *Comentarios de los sucesos de Aragón en los años 1591 y 1592* [ca. 1600] (Madrid, 1888), p. 61.

[19] Vicencio Blasco de Lanuza, *Historias ecclesiásticas y seculares de Aragón* (Saragossa, 1622), I, p. 89.

Lupercio Leonardo de Argensola (1559–1613), poet, writer and official chronicler, expressed similar concerns:

Recently [he was writing ca. 1610] I resolved to continue the study of our history from the point where Gerónimo Zurita finished [the reign of Ferdinand the Catholic]. Since the crowns of Aragon and Castile became inseparately united at that moment, a great deal of care and no little artifice will be needed to write the History of the Emperor Charles V so that it might also keep the name of History of Aragon...particularly now that the kingdoms of Spain are barely distinguished from each other, and so many are ignorant of the fact that Naples and Sicily belong to this Crown [of Aragon].[20]

Aragonese fears of absorption into the monarchy were by no means unfounded, and indeed contributed to considerable speculation about the meaning of the term liberty itself.

'What is liberty?', asked Juan Costa in his treatise on the *ars historica* (1591). 'It is the power to live as one wants. Who lives as he wants? He who behaves uprightly and submits himself to the laws of reason, is a model of cautious and thoughtful living.'[21] Costa offered further considerations on liberty in his work on the citizen, where he declared to be false the opinion of those who 'hold it as servitude that men should live observant of the law and obedient of their kings'. This error, he wrote, derived from a mistaken view of what constituted servitude, which was in fact a condition peculiar to beasts and those unable to control their passions, who 'follow their appetite, without subjecting it to reason, neither recognizing a sovereign nor acknowledging a law under which they might be governed. There is no liberty so agreeable as that enjoyed when a king is good and pious.'[22]

Yet Costa did no more than expound recognized theories regarding the *homo politicus*. More precise in his definitions was Juan López Galván, a lawyer clearly in favour of full royal authority, who distinguished two types of liberty: natural liberty and 'that of the *fueros* and *observancias* of this kingdom, achieved by the preservation and conservation of the laws and

---

[20] Lupercio y Bartolomé Leonardo de Argensola, *Obras sueltas*, ed. conde de la Viñaza (Madrid, 1889) I, pp. 371, 365. It is interesting to compare Argensola's fears with those of individuals opposed to the dynastic union between England and Scotland. See *The Jacobean Union. Six Tracts of 1604*, ed. Bruce Galloway and Brian P. Levack (Edinburgh, 1985), pp. 72–3, 'A treatise'. Its anonymous author, who favoured the union, rejected this reasoning by pointing out that the fame of two such powerful kingdoms would last and that the new name of 'Britain' would not cause the oblivion of the names of England and Scotland, in the like manner that Athens, Thebes and Sparta kept theirs under that of Greece.

[21] Ioannes Costa, *De conscribenda rerum historia* (Saragossa, 1591), p. 78.

[22] Costa, *Govierno del ciudadano*, pp. 606–7.

fueros of this kingdom'.[23] 'Liberties', therefore, distinguished the Aragonese political régime. It follows that the historian Gerónimo Zurita explained that the reason why the monarchy in 1515 incorporated the recently conquered kingdom of Navarre into Castile rather than Aragon was 'not to allow the Navarrese...to wish for more privileges and liberties'.[24]

Yet the question of what liberties and a free political régime consisted was one that many contemporary writers found difficult to answer. Machiavelli, for example, contrasted a 'civil and free life' with one that was 'absolute and tyrannical', a 'free state' with a 'regal state'.[25] The Aragonese political régime was unusual for the immunities and exemptions enjoyed by its subjects, but at the same time the 'regal' element was not only prominent, but completely unquestioned. However, this regal principle was limited, as most sixteenth-century Aragonese authors took care to underline every now and again. The reason for this, according to the narrative of Sobrarbe as expounded by Blancas, was the following: the early Aragonese debated the advantages of having a king, but, 'intoxicated with the sweetness of liberty, the thought of submitting themselves to the authority of an individual made them tremble: this, in their view, was like forging the fetters of their own slavery'. However, after consultation and further debate, they agreed to elect a king, a *primus inter pares*, Iñigo Arista, who was placed under the scrutiny of the *Justicia* and accorded few powers.[26] It is therefore revealing that Miguel de Molino, when turning to discuss the figure of the king in his *Repertorium*, began by declaring that in Aragon the crown did not enjoy such wide jurisdiction as it did in other kingdoms, and that he would next set out all that was forbidden to the king by the *fueros*.[27]

By contrast, the term 'Libertates Regni' is among those discussed most extensively in this same work. Molino declares that the origin of these liberties lay in the election of Iñigo Arista at Sobrarbe, and that they were to be observed by all under oath, from the king down to the lowest royal official. These liberties, he further explained, consisted of 'many things': freedom from torture; the need to have the consensus of the Cortes to

---

23 Biblioteca del Colegio de Abogados de Zaragoza, A 8-4-2: Juan López Galván, *Alegaciones sobre el virrey extranjero*, included in a volume of allegations by several authors (Saragossa, 1591), fos. 201v–2.

24 Gerónimo Zurita, *Los cinco libros postreros de la historia del rey Don Hernando el Católico. De las empresas y ligas de Italia*, VI (Saragossa, 1580), fo. 378v. See also fo. 301.

25 Niccolò Machiavelli, *Discorsi sopra la prima deca di Tito Livio*, book I, chapter 9; book III, chapter 3, ed. Sergio Bertelli, together with *Il Principe* (6th reprint, Milan, 1979), pp. 154, 386–7.

26 Blancas, *Comentarios*, p. 36.

27 Molino, *Repertorium*, entry 'Rex Aragonum', fos. 291v–6v.

establish laws and impose taxes; the requirement that only Aragonese natives could hold public office; restrictions on the king's power to require his Aragonese subjects to fight in wars outside the kingdom, etc. Blancas also devoted attention to the liberties, compressing these into twelve basic elements along the lines followed by Molino. Furthermore, he indicated that the best defence of these against the abuses of royal officials were the foral procedures of the court of the *Justicia*.[28]

Thus, there was no clear distinction between the corpus of liberties and the means of ensuring their preservation. Such liberties embraced and affected questions of public and private rights. The need for the estates to concur with the crown in the making of laws was for Blancas 'the strongest bond...the foundation of liberty'; and with good reason, since, in the opinion of another author, 'imposed laws smell of servitude'.[29] On the other hand, in the sphere of private law 'liberties' were increasingly associated with the shelter offered by the four foral procedures. Outstanding among these was the *manifestación*, a procedure that permitted an Aragonese accused under royal justice to place himself in the custody of the *Justicia* while his case was under review. It is worth noting that Antonio Pérez took advantage of this particular privilege – 'one of the most powerful liberties in the kingdom', according to Ibando de Bardaxí – when he fled from Castile to Aragon in 1590.[30]

Together, the liberties consisted of regulations which, directly or indirectly, placed specific limitations on royal authority, particularly in the field of penal law. They represented the cornerstone of the Aragonese contractual régime and embodied the peculiar legal character of the kingdom. Confronted by the authoritarian tendency of the crown, individual rights fell into greater relief along with a heightened concern for their preservation. For this reason, the call to govern according to the rule of law became a call to defend liberties considered to be under threat.[31] Out of the two means of limiting authority that were conceived in this period – first, a natural constitutional order (where the king was subject to the dictates imposed by natural law); and, secondly, the specific political régime (a

---

[28] Molino, *Repertorium*, fos. 207–9v; Blancas, *Comentarios*, pp. 324–33.
[29] Blancas, *Comentarios*, p. 344; Diego Jerónimo Galván y Alayeto [1644], quoted by Manuel Danvila, *Examen histórico-foral de la constitución aragonesa* (Madrid, 1868), I, p. lxiv.
[30] Bardaxí, *Comentarii*, fo. 396v.
[31] Jesús Lalinde Abadía, 'El pactismo en los reinos de Aragón y Valencia', in Juan Vallet de Goytisolo *et al.*, *El pactismo en la historia de España* (Madrid, 1980); by the same, 'Los derechos individuales en el Privilegio General de Aragón', *Anuario de historia del derecho español*, 50 (1980), 55–68.

product of the exercise of human will)[32] – in sixteenth-century Aragon writers vehemently asserted that limitations on royal authority were not only natural, but above all the fruit of the will of a group of far-sighted men, the signatories to the original agreements at Sobrarbe.

These juridical liberties were, however, based on an even deeper historical conviction that Aragon had always been essentially free. For Blancas, Aragon was a kingdom 'that had been conquered from the Moors by the valour of kings with the assistance and favour of their subjects, and was in consequence free'.[33] This original freedom imparted a special character for, as Zurita made clear when discussing the concession of the *Privilegio General* of 1283, natives 'harboured the conviction that Aragon neither amounted to nor was epitomized by the strength of the kingdom, but by liberty, being the will of all that when liberty was overthrown, so the kingdom would end also'. This idea was also enshrined in a provision of the Cortes of 1451, later copied by Blancas: 'It has always been said, and experience has proved, that given the great barrenness of this land and the poverty of the kingdom, if it were not for her liberties the people should leave and take up residence in other more fertile lands and kingdoms.'[34]

According to Blancas, moreover, Aragonese liberty was free of licence and passion. Zurita had earlier made a similar point but, more cautious, he warned of the need to 'strike a very fair and just balance, because, just as the ancients taught us that there is nothing sweeter than liberty, so we must also be mindful of the fall of very great republics through having used their liberties licentiously and without moderation'.[35] Here precisely lay the fulcrum. And there was no shortage of writers who argued that the balance had shifted seriously to the detriment of royal authority. Such was the case with Peter Martyr of Anglería, the notable Italian humanist at the court of the Catholic Monarchs. Noting the difficulties encountered by Ferdinand and Charles V at their respective Cortes of 1510 and 1518, he censured the

---

[32] António M. Hespanha, 'Qu'est-ce que la "constitution" dans les monarchies ibériques de l'époque moderne', unpublished paper. I thank the author for having provided me with a copy of the typescript.

[33] Jerónimo de Blancas, *Coronaciones de los serenísimos reyes de Aragón* [1585], published by J. F. Andrés de Uztarroz (Saragossa, 1641), p. 9.

[34] Gerónimo Zurita, *Anales de la Corona de Aragón* [1562], 1st part, book IV, chapter 38, ed. Angel Canellas (7 vols., Saragossa, 1967–1977), II, p. 141. Zurita states in the same page that the grant of this General Privilege was rather a confirmation of old privileges and customs than a new grant, and that this 'is the main one of the liberties that we today have'. Blancas, *Comentarios*, p. 325.

[35] Blancas, *Comentarios*, p. 5; Zurita, *Anales*, 2nd part, book 17, chapter 30 (Canellas edn., VII, p. 376). Zurita makes this comment when dealing with the Cortes of 1461, held in a context of wars.

'subterfuges of those who, freed by their national *fueros*, refuse to reconcile themselves to the king's government ... To this disobedience of the king they give the name of liberty, a state where right cannot be exercised, even though justice is asked.' Similarly, in 1586 a Venetian ambassador pointed out that the laws of Aragon 'tend more to disordered licence than liberty in moderation'.[36]

To combine such terms as liberty, order and authority in a harmonious fashion was – and remained – a difficult task for political theorists and government officials alike, both inside and outside Aragon. Just at that time Jean Bodin explained in the preface to the *Six Books of the Republic* that he wanted to refute certain ideas which he considered disastrous for a society, among them those which 'under the pretext of exemption from burdens and popular liberty, arouse subjects against their natural princes, opening the door to a licentious anarchy, which is worse than the harshest tyranny in the world'.[37] Bodin had the ravages of the French Wars of Religion very much in mind in composing his work. Political realities, and in particular the many confrontations of those years, played a decisive role in imparting new expressions or adding new interpretations to key words of contemporary political language. In late sixteenth-century France the term *politique* began to be used of those who advocated compromise on religious issues in order to secure peace, being employed as much in a pejorative as in a complimentary sense. Similarly, in the Low Countries, theories of resistance towards the government of Philip II, based on the constitutional defence of local privileges, acquired a new meaning, favouring the practice of reformed religion. Thus, the defence of traditional liberties and immunities also implied the demand for religious freedom, a major new development.[38]

It would not be long before a situation of extreme conflict developed in Aragon: the uprisings of 1591, whose effects were similarly reflected in political language. During the course of these events the word 'liberty' would acquire a wide range of sometimes contradictory meanings. 'The whole republic remains in such an uproar that it will risk anything in defence of liberty', Philip II was informed by the committee of ministers

---

[36] Anglería, quoted by José Antonio Armillas, 'Aragón visto por un humanista: Pedro Mártir de Anglería', *Estudios (Zaragoza)*, 3 (1974), 32, 37; the ambassador, Vicenzo Gradenigo, in Albèri, *Relazioni*, first series, v, p. 392.

[37] Jean Bodin, *Les six livres de la République* [Latin edition, 1576], ed. Ch. Frémont, M.-D. Couzinet and H. Rochais (Paris, 1986), p. 14.

[38] Nicolai Rubinstein, 'The history of the word *politicus* in early-modern Europe', in Anthony Pagden, ed., *The languages of political theory in early-modern Europe* (Cambridge, 1990), pp. 55–6; Martin van Gelderen, *The political thought of the Dutch Revolt, 1555–1590* (Cambridge, 1992), chapter 6.

established to resolve the crisis. The committee added that the rebels demanded that officials of the Holy Office be Aragonese, 'since the Castilians betray them and break down their liberties'.[39] Ironically, the meaning the committee attached to 'liberty' was precisely that given by radical Aragonese. In effect, it was cries of 'Liberty! Liberty!' in the streets of Saragossa that ignited the disturbances of May and September of that year. In government circles, on the other hand, where the increasing radicalism of the conflict was attributed to the work of groups of activists who had terrorized a large part of the city, the meaning of the word was very different. So much is apparent in the well-known letters that Philip II sent to a nobleman and to the cities and towns of the kingdom to explain the real reason behind his sending of an army to Saragossa to put down the rebellion: 'That the respect for the Inquisition be restored, as is right in such dangerous times, and the use and exercise of your *fueros* be free, so that our Lord be served thereby and so as you may live in that security which I would have you enjoy.' A little later he repeated a similar idea in his instructions to the marquis of Lombay, the personal envoy he sent on a peaceful mission to complement the military intervention. The objectives that he entrusted him were, he said, to ensure that

the exercise of the *fueros* of the kingdom be restored and freed so that no similar oppression may be suffered either now or in the future ... I am sending you to muster and direct the good so that they may enjoy liberty and tranquility ... You are going there to procure the liberty of the good and principally that of the Diputados [the highest officials of the kingdom] and of the *Justicia* of Aragon and the rest.[40]

It is possible that the king's letters deliberately used the key word 'liberty', already so widely employed by the Aragonese nationalists, so as not to concede the radicals either exclusive use or defence of the term. Whatever the case may be, that autumn the term acquired its two opposing and antithetical meanings, an opposition that was already implicit, but which now came to the fore. Although there are few indications of the significance of this dilemma for the members of the Aragonese ruling class during those difficult months, it was no doubt an issue which perplexed them greatly.

---

[39] ABZ, *carpeta* 186, doc. 6, *junta* to king, 11 June 1591.
[40] The letters to the nobleman, the count of Morata, and to the towns, dated 15 October 1591, are to be found respectively in *Colección de documentos inéditos para la historia de España* (CODOIN), XII (Madrid, 1848), pp. 460–1; and in Gonzalo de Céspedes y Meneses, *Historia apologética de los sucessos del Reyno de Aragón y su ciudad de Çaragoça, años de 91 y 92* [1622] (facsimile edition, Seville, 1978), pp. 162–3. The instruction to Lombay, of 5 November 1591, in CODOIN, XII, pp. 491–9. For a good summary of those events, see John H. Elliott, *Imperial Spain, 1469–1716* (Harmondsworth, 1970), pp. 277–83.

In the context of the time, however, 'liberties' did not only refer to the complementary or antagonistic element of kingship, although this has been the most publicized meaning as much in contemporaneous political writing as in the bulk of later historiography. Political life did not reduce itself to the relationship between king and kingdom. Aragonese society contained well-known conflicts of interest between social groups, interests that tended to be represented under the title of 'liberties'. The most obvious case was that of the nobility. According to the legend of Sobrarbe, the electors who signed the agreement were twelve *seniores*, or lords, with whom the king was required to partition any conquests they achieved against the Muslims. From them, so it was held, descended the *ricos hombres* and their feudal dominion, the so-called 'absolute power', one of the most onerous seigneurial régimes of Western Europe.[41] This fact imparted a baronial element to much of the foral system until its abolition in 1711, and has been the cause of continual historiographic debate as to its most liberal or oppressive features. In fact, the Aragonese case is an excellent example of the ambiguities of the aristocratic or corporative constitutionalism so characteristic of early modern Europe.[42]

A similar issue involved the traditional immunities of the Aragonese church, all of which were jealously defended by the clergy in numerous conflicts of jurisdiction with lay authority. An especially serious conflict over these immunities erupted during the Cortes of 1646. 'Ecclesiastical liberty is. . .little respected', angrily protested the spokesmen of the clerical estate, who openly criticized the *Justicia*'s court and its foral procedures. They continued by announcing that the clergy 'does not desire the abrogation of the *fueros* nor any diminution in the liberties of the kingdom, nevertheless such liberties do not lead them to forget the dignity of their estate'.[43]

---

[41] Blancas, *Comentarios*, pp. 36–7. The author who most explicitly developed such a genealogy as a legitimation of feudal rights was Juan Francisco Montemayor de Córdoba, *Sumaria investigación en el origen y privilegios de los ricoshombres o nobles, caballeros, infanzones o hijosdalgo y señores de vasallos de Aragón y del absoluto poder que sobre ellos tienen* (Mexico, 1664), esp. chapter 1. This very genealogy was also referred to in a more flexible way in order to justify other cases of social dominion, like that of the *próceres* (urban patriciate) of Calatayud: Miguel Martinez del Villar, *Tratado del patronato, antigüedades, govierno y varones ilustres de la ciudad y comunidad de Calatayud y su arcedianato* [1598] (facsimile edition, Saragossa, 1980), pp. 52–5.

[42] Michael Roberts, 'On aristocratic constitutionalism in Swedish history, 1520–1720', in his *Essays in Swedish History* (London, 1967), chapter 2; Elliott, 'Revolution and continuity', p. 105; Lalinde, *Fueros de Aragón*, pp. 74, 112.

[43] ADZ, ms. 722, fos. 409–10 and 666, texts from the Ecclesiastical Estate, 23 January and 4 May 1646.

Finally, a third and very strident indication of these conflicts over the meaning of the term liberty concerned the so-called Saragossan *Privilegio de los Veinte*, a special tribunal charged to defend the grazing rights of its citizens' livestock. The tribunal's origin lay in a medieval royal privilege, albeit one which was never ratified by the Cortes as a *fuero*. Many Aragonese communities complained about the tribunal's wide powers, and in one of the many lawsuits brought against it, the opposing party declared that the *Privilegio de los Veinte* 'expressly contravened the *fueros* and laws of this kingdom' and bound it over not to employ 'absolute power'. In reply the defence made clear that the *Privilegio* did not belong to Aragonese common right, but was rather 'extraordinary and particular and a counter-liberty', an 'extravagant and particular concession' that was also 'liberty'. It stated, in sum, that the *Privilegio* 'is liberty against the subjection to the observance of the *fueros* ... thus permitting the just and beneficial enjoyment of that liberty'.[44]

What these examples make clear is that Aragonese thinking over the meaning of the *fueros* was never totally united. Opinions differed, as did administrative and juridical practices, and to disregard these divisions is seriously to impair our understanding of the place of the *fueros* in early modern Aragon. Complicating matters even further was a debate over what it meant to defend Aragonese liberties. For many, the defence of the *fueros* was simply a matter of protecting them against the intrusions, real or imagined, of the crown. But who was responsible for the *fueros*' defence? To begin with, the king. Traditional ideas regarding the development of royal authoritarianism has led most historians to dismiss the possibility that kings, and much less Philip II, should act in this way. However, this cannot be ruled out, since the kings had sworn to protect the *fueros* in good faith. In this context it should be noted that Philip II had an admirable understanding of Aragonese law and on occasion even refused to sign certain decrees since, as he made clear in a note to his secretary 'there is a problem because those [decrees] for the three kingdoms of Aragon, and in particular that for Aragon itself, will not be obeyed and are against the *fueros*'. For this reason Philip ordered the decrees to be redrafted.[45]

Apart from the king, the Cortes also served as the guarantor of *fueros* and

[44] ADZ, book 775, no. 11: Dr José Ozcáriz Vélez, *Discurso iuridico y foral*, 1671 (quotes, in pp. 24–5); ibid., no. 9. Francisco Lucas Lamata, *Discurso apologético sobre el uso y inteligencia del Privilegio de Veinte*, undated (quotes, in pp. 3, 19).

[45] BL, Add. 28263, fos. 7, 236, king to Vázquez, undated (belonging to the 1570s). For another example of Philip's concern for the *fueros*, see in the same volume his letter of 3 February 1581. I owe these references to the kindness of Geoffrey Parker. See also a third example on p. 252 below.

liberties. Traditionally, private individuals had recourse to the Cortes to resolve private grievances. Although such opportunities gradually receded as the Cortes of Aragon met at increasing intervals, the parliamentary channel was not necessarily the best means of protecting individual liberty. The historiographical tradition of many countries (somewhat Whiggishly) exaggerates the importance of parliaments in the defence of liberty. In Castile, however, both personal and communal liberties were better defended juridically in the law courts than politically in the Cortes.[46] A similar situation pertained in Aragon. Likewise, the council of Aragon, which so often acted zealously to safeguard royal prerogative, was also mindful of Aragonese customs, including the tradition of reserving offices for natives.[47] Finally, the Court of the *Justicia* (here thanks to its four foral procedures) helped to guarantee Aragonese liberties, both in individual cases and for the kingdom as a whole.

The effectiveness of these various channels for the defence of legality varied with time. Their origins can be traced to a *fuero* of 1300 authorizing resistance to any royal official who contravened a *fuero*.[48] Contemporary political writers also supported this particular right. 'Officials must not serve or obey mandates and letters against the *fueros* ordered by the lord king or by another', declared Ibando de Bardaxí in his gloss on the oath of the *fueros* by the king. Miguel de Molino was even more succinct: 'Liberties can be defended with impunity even against a prince because this is natural justice.'[49]

Herein lay the theory of foral resistance. Its ingredients were, first, of a legal nature, that is to say, the *fuero* of 1300 and those which regulated the oath of the king; and, secondly, of doctrinal nature and connected to the legend of Sobrarbe.[50] It is important to note, however, that this theory was not formulated using the term 'resistance', but as a defence of the *fueros* and liberties. In a phrase similar to that cited above, Molino asserted that the Aragonese could defend their liberties 'with impunity ... even against the

---

[46] I. A. A. Thompson, 'Castile: polity, fiscality and fiscal crisis'; and 'Castile: absolutism, constitutionalism and liberty', both in P. T. Hoffman and K. Norberg, eds., *Fiscal crises, liberty and representative government, 1450–1789* (Stanford, 1994), pp. 143–4, 148–50, 196, 217.

[47] Juan Luis Arrieta Alberdi, *El Consejo Supremo de la Corona de Aragón, 1474–1707*, forthcoming, 3rd part. I thank the author for having allowed me to read the unpublished typescript.

[48] *Fueros, observancias y actos de corte del reino de Aragón*, ed. P. Savall and S. Penén (Saragossa, 1866): 'De inmunitate ecclesiarum et monasteriorum', I, pp. 21–2.

[49] Bardaxi, *Comentarii*, fo. 47v; Molino, *Repertorium*, fo. 207v.

[50] Giesey provides details to this respect, including the later contribution by Antonio Pérez: *If not, not*, pp. 63, 150–1, 161, 222.

lord king, without being labelled resistors'. Blancas, who shared Molina's views on this particular issues, explained that defence of the *fueros* should be conducted 'without fear that through it our name would be tarnished, as would otherwise be the case, with some clumsy note of resistance'.[51]

Clearly, the term 'resistance' had negative connotations in Aragon, even for the most nationalist writers. Miguel de Molino and Pedro Molinos used it only to describe the resistance of vassals against seigneurial officials, behaviour which both found clearly reprehensible, although the former admitted that resistance was legitimate against appointed officials refusing to comply with foral requirements.[52] Yet even the staunchest defenders of the *fueros* were reluctant to link resistance with armed resistance against the king. Thus, Gerónimo Zurita referred to the decisive battle of Épila of 1348 between a union of nobles and Peter IV, as 'the last known occasion that the defence of the liberty of the kingdom was used as justification for the ancient practice of taking up arms against the kings'.[53]

What is interesting about Aragonese theories of resistance is their independence from both the Calvinist thesis of the obligation of lesser magistrates to resist the governor, which was so prevalent in France and the Low Countries, and Castilian neo-scholastic theories about tyrannicide. With respect to Calvinist influences, it should be pointed out that Zurita and Blancas compared the *Justicia* of Aragon with the ephors of Sparta, but this was little more than another example of the contemporary rhetorical taste for classical references. It was the French monarchomachs who attributed to the ephors a crucial revolutionary role, and François Hotman in particular who portrayed the Aragonese *Justicia* as nothing less than a new ephor.[54] As for Castilian neo-scholasticism, it seems only to have arrived during the 1620s, initially manifesting itself in a treatise by the count of Guimerá, who openly formulated the doctrine of tyrannicide. Previously, its influence was limited.[55]

Aragonese constitutionalism, in other words, was not imported. It had deep native roots, and fed off a legal community that regarded Habsburg

---

[51] Molino, *Repertorium*, fo. 207v; Blancas, *Comentarios*, p. 325.

[52] Molino, *Repertorium*, entry 'Resistentia', fos. 286–9; Pedro Molinos, *Práctica iudiciaria del reino de Aragón* [1575] (3rd edition, Saragossa, 1649), pp. 365–6.

[53] Zurita, *Anales*, book VIII, chapter 29 (Canellas edn., IV, pp. 145–6).

[54] Zurita, *Anales*, 1st part, book VIII, chapter 32 (Canellas edn., IV, p. 158); Blancas, *Comentarios*, p. 333; Hotman, *Francogallia* (ed. Giesey and Salmon), p. 313.

[55] Gaspar Galcerán de Castro y de Pinós, count of Guimerá, 'Sucesiones reales de Aragón' (BNM, ms. 2038), fos. 57–8v. This work, undated, might belong to the 1620s or 1630s. It seems that, as years went by, neo-scholastic ideas on popular sovereignty transferred to the king became more common in Aragon: see note 77.

ministers and tribunals as both foreign and opposed to the *fueros*. But whereas the lawyers were reluctant to transform the doctrine of protecting the *fueros* into one of armed resistance against the monarch, some of the rioters in the streets of Saragossa in 1591 embraced this more radical idea. One of their pasquinades read: 'The king who in unseemly fashion / tyrannizes liberties / should not be offended by the truth / when he is reputed a tyrant. / Let him not be surprised when peasants, / taking the *fueros* in their own hands, / defend them on their own / since they cannot trust the nobles.'[56]

Clearly, a radical understanding of liberty was in the air, but when in the midst of the riots, the *Justicia* Don Juan de Lanuza hoisted the Aragonese standard of St George he took his stand on the *fueros*, particularly the *De Generalibus Privilegiis Regni Aragonum* of 1461. This decree, originally designed to prevent the incursion into Aragonese territory of Catalans and Valencian militias, required the kingdom's authorities to confront foreign invaders.[57] From this perspective, the king's army was, in Aragonese eyes, a foreign army, and this explains why the *Justicia* raised the standard of St George – an action that caused the king summarily to condemn him to death as a traitor.

This harsh sentence illustrates the distance separating Saragossa from Madrid. Aragonese officials may have thought of the king's troops as foreign invaders, but officials at the royal court thought differently. Few cases in fact reveal more dramatically the difficulties of accommodating old laws and traditions to the new reality of composite monarchies. 'Now that we are all under one and the same king', an agent sent by Saragossa wrote back from Madrid, 'these troops cannot be declared to be foreign'. 'Foreign', another Aragonese envoy explained from Madrid, 'does not include His Majesty's other kingdoms, since this was the case only when Castile had her own king, and now that all kingdoms belong to one king and lord, these are not foreign.'[58]

The uprising of 1591, the punishments meted out by the king, and the Cortes of Tarazona the following year marked the beginning of a new period in the history of Aragon. In this new political climate, the old term 'liberties' acquired new meanings. The question was extremely delicate since 'to proclaim liberty' now appeared synonymous with promoting disturbance.

---

[56] AGS, Est. *leg.* 339, book 2, fos. 39, 46v.   [57] *Fueros de Aragón*, I, pp. 21–2.

[58] The agent from Saragossa, quoted by Encarna Jarque and José Antonio Salas, *Las alteraciones de Zaragoza de 1591* (Saragossa 1991), p. 129; the letter by the other envoy, from the city of Jaca, is to be found in AM Jaca, box 59, doc. 6, letter of 4 January 1592

This was admitted by the officers of the kingdom who advanced measures to punish those who 'had put up resistance or interfered with the discharge of their duties in the name of liberty or uproarious and mutinous disturbance, or incited the people to the same'.[59] A similar understanding of the term can be found in the Cortes' announcement that 'those who proclaimed liberty or promoted sedition or mutiny' were to be excluded from availing themselves of one of the favourable procedures of native law, while the proclamation of liberty 'without authority or right' was also penalized.[60]

This Cortes did not abolish the right of foral resistance in the literal sense. Its aim was rather to avoid irresponsible invocation of the liberties, given the popular emotions they whipped up during the uprisings, and to protect the integrity of the *fueros* and, simultaneously, the honour and reputation of the kingdom itself. At the same time, Aragonese politicians, writers and chroniclers attempted to restore the kingdom's good name. Branded as traitors by various Spanish and foreign writers, the Aragonese set about proclaiming their loyalty to the king and minimizing the importance of the uprisings of 1591. One of the main contributors to this task was Lupercio Leonardo de Argensola who wrote a brief report on the uprising in which he claimed that the significance of the shouts of liberty proclaimed in Saragossa's streets should not be misunderstood. Argensola explained that 'this was a cry repeated many times by the common folk this day and others, but which did not signify the abandonment of the jurisdiction of the king so much as "long live the *fueros* and laws which...are commonly known as *fueros* and liberties".' Argensola's brother Bartolomé made a similar argument in his response to the Castilian historian Luis Cabrera de Córdoba, who attributed the disturbances to the defence of Aragonese liberties. Argensola emphasized that 'the *fueros* of this kingdom are called liberties, and hence this author [Cabrera] should understand that when the people proclaimed liberty it was not their intention to deny the king their obedience, but to ensure that the order of their *fueros*, sworn by kings and subjects, be observed'.[61]

---

[59] BNM, ms. 9823, fos. 143v-5, *diputados* and town officials to marquis of Lombay, 10 December 1591.

[60] *Fueros de Aragón*, 'De la via privilegiada' and 'De la pena de los sediciosos', I, pp. 427-8, 441.

[61] Lupercio Leonardo de Argensola, *Información de los sucesos del reino de Aragón en los años de 1590 y 1591* [1604], introduction by X. Gil (Saragossa, 1991), pp. 90-1; Luis Cabrera de Cordoba, *Historia de Felipe II, rey de España* (ca. 1614) (Madrid, 1877), III, pp. 520 and 554, note 1, by Bartolomé. For a first approach to this collective enterprise to recover good fame for Aragon, see my introduction to Lupercio's *Información*, esp. pp. xii-xxi.

This attempt on the part of the Argensola brothers and other authors to restore Aragonese honour does mean that attachment to the *fueros* was diminishing. However, whereas emphasis had once been on Aragonese exemptions, it was now placed on the cooperation between king and kingdom and on the loyalty of the Aragonese.[62]

This new climate of opinion was partly the direct result of the monarchy's efforts to pacify Aragon following the crisis of 1591–92, but it also reflects the arrival in Aragon of the school of neo-stoic thought associated with Justus Lipsius. The great Flemish thinker corresponded with the Argensola brothers as well as with other Aragonese men of letters. In two of his letters Lipsius amicably disagreed with Lupercio when he complained of contemporary evils, reminding him of the great gift enjoyed by Spaniards – peace – as against the calamity of war suffered in Flanders.[63] Lipsius' authoritative remark cannot have fallen upon deaf ears, but must have confirmed the Aragonese leaders in their now manifest concern to maintain public order. The will to ensure social and political stability, an objective that depended to a considerable degree on consolidated royal authority, was therefore a significant factor in the relations between crown and kingdom.

Another new element in Aragonese political thought was *epickeia*, the art of interpreting the law benignly on the merits of each case.[64] However, the application of discretion to the Aragonese legal system, which was based on the idea of contract and took pride in the literal observance of its *fueros*, opened the unattractive prospect of undesirable styles of government. This was precisely the case of another contemporary novelty, 'reason of state',

---

[62] Both Argensolas, however, did make reference to the right of armed resistance. Lupercio Argensola, *Información*, p. 33: 'In Aragon it is believed that when the provisions of the Justicia of Aragon are not obeyed, right is placed in arms, and that everyone can defend them with no penalty', referring to recent disturbances in Teruel. Bartolomé Argensola in 'Alteraciones populares', fos. 8v-9 writes: 'Although it was not written in the *fuero* of Sobrarbe, it was never doubted that it had its origins in the very beginnings of this kingdom, and that [the right] to take up arms whenever the just defence of our liberty required it, was established in our law, as natural law.' He made this statement in reference to various aristocratic uprisings in the Middle Ages. Both works remained unpublished.

[63] Alejandro Ramírez, *Epistolario de Justo Lipsio y los españoles (1577–1606)* (Madrid, 1966), letters 80 and 87, pp. 327–9 and 368–71.

[64] Bartolomé Leonardo de Argensola dedicated a sonnet to don Fernando de Borja, viceroy of Aragon in the early 1620s, after having discussed this issue with him, as he himself informs us: *Rimas*, ed. J. M. Blecua (Madrid, 1974), II, p. 115. This aspect needs further study. On the *epickeia*, see Pier Giovanni Caron, *Aequitas romana, misericordia patristica ed epicheia aristotelica nella dottrina dell'aequitas canonica. Dalle origine al Rinascimento* (Milan, 1971), esp. pp. 51–3, 70–4, 98. I owe this reference to Julio Pardos.

which was specifically rejected by Bartolomé Leonardo de Argensola and the count of Guimerá as condoning arbitrary government.[65]

Thus in the seventeenth century several factors emanating from both inside and outside Aragon contributed to a partial modification of the kingdom's political climate. One of these was the intense fiscal and political pressure exerted by the régime of the count-duke of Olivares during the 1620s and 1630s. Another was the emergence of new opportunities for employment in imperial administration for Aragonese lawyers and bureaucrats.[66] Meanwhile, Aragonese legal scholarship lost most if its former ideological edge. Legal scholars adopted an increasingly historicist approach to the *fueros*, and in doing so fomented new interest in the history and literature of the kingdom's remote past.[67]

Of continuing interest for these scholars was the legend surrounding the laws of Sobrarbe and the foundation of Aragon. The legend had new detractors, among them the Franco-Basque writer Arnald Oihenart and especially Pierre de Marca, a French bishop who was later became the stern administrator of Catalonia under French dominion.[68] Both considered the legend little more than a myth, although their objective was less to elucidate historical truth than to favour French designs on the Basque Country, Spanish Navarre and Catalonia. Yet the legend had its supporters in the great polymath and historian Juan Francisco Andrés de Uztarroz, as well Antonio Lupián, and the count of Guimerá, all of whom accepted the veracity of the Sobrarbe narrative as set down by Blancas.[69] Another supporter was the Valencian jurist Lorenzo Matheu y Sanz, who based his exposition of the contractual character of the political régimes of Aragon, Catalonia and Valencia on the laws of Sobrarbe, declaring that 'although it is true that these once existed, the original was lost and today only a few

---

[65] Bartolomé Argensola, 'Alteraciones populares', fo. 104v; Guimerá, 'Sucesiones reales', fos. 18-09.

[66] For a general approach, see Xavier Gil, 'Olivares y Aragón', in *La España del conde duque de Olivares*, ed. John H. Elliott and Angel García Sanz (Valladolid, 1990), pp. 575-602.

[67] Lalinde, *Fueros de Aragón*, pp. 124-6, 134; Ricardo del Arco y Garay, *La erudición aragonesa en torno a Lastanosa* (Madrid, 1934); by the same author, *La erudición española en el siglo XVII y el cronista de Aragón Andrés de Uztarroz* (2 vols., Madrid, 1950).

[68] Arnald Oihenart, *Notitia utriusque Vasconiae, tum Ibericae, tum Aquitanicae* (Paris, 1638), book II, chapter 10; Pierre de Marca, *Histoire de Béarn* (Paris, 1640), book II, chapter 9.

[69] Juan Francisco Andrés de Uztarroz, 'Noticia', in J. Blancas, *Coronaciones de los serenissimos reyes de Aragón*, published by him together with two treatises on Cortes by J. Blancas and J. Martel (Saragossa, 1641), n.p.; Antonio Lupián Zapata, 'Reyes de Sobrarbe defendidos', [1661] (BNM, ms. 2054); Guimerá, 'Sucesiones reales', fos. 85v–86.

fragments remain ... collected by inquiring observers of antiquities'.[70] Pedro Abarca also rallied to the defence of Sobrarbe in his genealogical study of the kings of Aragon. Even so, he felt obliged to conclude his book with a lament: 'Oh, luckless kings [the first of Sobrarbe and Aragon], who although your reigns were made so glorious by their endeavours and conquests, are now barely worthy of more history than the doubts and interminable struggles that historians can muster.'[71]

Compared to these bookish struggles, however, the war waged during the 1640s against the French army occupying Catalonia posed a far greater threat to Aragonese liberty. The threat of a French invasion of the kingdom loomed large, and was viewed by most Aragonese as a genuine national emergency. Under these circumstances, and against the background of arguments in favour of elective monarchy put forward by the leaders of the Catalan and Portuguese revolts, the Aragonese reflected once more on the twin considerations of authority and liberty. What was now being discussed, however, was not the liberties of Sobrarbe, over which even some Aragonese scholars had their doubts, but an abstract liberty about which only strong convictions were aired. Alarmed by reports of revolution in various European countries and fearful that factions and civil discord would soon break out in Aragon, a plethora of writers inspired by neo-Tacitean ideas set out vigorous arguments in favour of order, hierarchy and stability. Faced by the double threat of foreign invasion and internal rebellion, royal authority appeared the best guarantee against the siren voices of misunderstood liberty to which the masses would fatally succumb.

'Rebels usually tend to claim magnificent terms of liberty and other just images to mask the evil of their souls', warned Antonio Fuertes Biota, who also made clear that

it is not the same to be without a lord and to be in liberty, since the latter is a worthy condition governed by laws, and the former uncertain and dissolute ... The name of liberty tends to be the best and greatest mask used to cover tyranny, because of its popularity among those masses whom they will later oppress by force of arms.

This idea was very similar to that held by Juan Costa, but instead of his civic confidence an intense concern at the hydra of popular rebellion prevailed. Fear and contempt towards the people combined in these writers who saw no solution other than strong authority. According to Luis de Mur, 'trouble-makers claim liberty, not because they lack it themselves, but

[70] Lorenzo Matheu y Sanz, *Tratado de la celebración de Cortes Generales del reino de Valencia* (Madrid, 1677) pp. 215–17, 220.
[71] Pedro Abarca, *Los reyes de Aragón en anales históricos* (Madrid, 1682) (quote, in fo. 52).

because they want others to lose it'. In effect, 'rebels ... aspire to liberty and ... impede liberty; this word is convincing to the masses and the fruit of their desire is slavery'. Under these assumptions the prevalence of general rebellion was, for Felipe Vitrián de Biamonte, a terrifying possibility: 'If all provinces rose up and conspired under the name of liberty and community, the situation would be hopeless.'[72]

The principle of authority espoused by these writers could only be delivered by the monarchy, which also explains their staunch defence of Habsburg legitimacy in the aftermath of the revolt of the Catalans and the Portuguese in 1640. However, these writers were not only Aragonese who sought the protection of the king; their opinions were shared by a broad spectrum of Aragonese who feared the threat of French invasion. There was no shortage of protest and dissent, but the need to defend the kingdom against foreign attack led to a collaboration between king and kingdom. Although its economy suffered, at least Aragon was not invaded and there were no major popular uprisings.[73] Thus, while the leaders and propagandists of the Catalan, Portuguese and other anti-Habsburg revolts brandished the word liberty as an escape from the despised Spanish dominion, in Aragon liberty was construed as a protection against French dominion.

It is not surprising that this approach coincided with that of those Catalans who remained loyal to Philip IV, many of them exiled in Saragossa and Madrid. Their feelings were summarized in the declaration by the nobleman Ramón Dalmau de Rocabertí, who presented a sombre picture of the Catalan situation, characterized by subjection, confiscation and opprobrium, products of the 'licentious and lustful liberty of the French'. More surprising is the similarity between these sentiments and those of helpless peasants living in hamlets near the battle front in northern Aragon: both declared themselves ready to sacrifice their lives and property for Philip IV.[74]

[72] Antonio Fuertes y Biota, *Alma o aforismos de Cornelio Tácito* (Antwerp, 1651), pp. 714, 437, 439; Luis de Mur, *Tiberio ilustrado con morales y politicos discursos* (Saragossa, 1645), pp. 26, 33; Felipe Vitrián de Biamonte y Manrique, *Fragmentos de lugares concernientes a los Estados de Flandes, de texto y glosa de la historia francesa de Argenton* (Saragossa, 1636), p. 32. Although Mur was not Aragonese, but Navarrese, it is not hazardous to assume that his work must have circulated among Saragossan circles.

[73] Xavier Gil, '"Conservación" y "defensa" como factores de estabilidad en época de crisis. Aragón y Valencia en la década de 1640', in John H. Elliott, R. Villari *et al.*, *1640. La monarquía hispánica en crisis* (Barcelona, 1992), pp. 44–101.

[74] Ramón Dalmao de Rocabertí, *Presagios fatales del mando francés en Cataluña* (Saragossa, 1646). He praised the temperament of loyal Catalans, ready to offer goods and offices 'en el holocausto grato, en el que entre mayores llamas quisieron primero morir a todo que faltar a

Religious orthodoxy also helped seal the collaboration between king and kingdom. On the strength of claims, baseless or not, that the French spread blasphemy and heresy, Vitrián de Biamonte pointed out in his work on Flanders that the iconoclastic fury of the Low Countries began with the evils of 'rebellion and freedom of conscience'.[75] In the light of this claim, the similarity between Aragon and the Low Countries suggested by Lord Burghley in 1576 seemed to have receded with the passage of time. However, this did not mean that in Aragon the *fueros* had ceased to be the focus of political life. On the contrary, despite the evident consolidation of royal power and the equally manifest novel practices of authoritarian government, political culture remained centred on the *fueros* and high politics continued to be determined by contractual ideas. So much was apparent at the Cortes of 1645–46, both in the extensive legislation carried out there and in the swearing of the oath of the *fueros* by Prince Baltasar Carlos, who once again renewed the ancestral bond that imposed limits on royal power. A discussion of the need to proceed by this oath by an anonymous author, who must have belonged to the circles of government, underlined 'how much more convenient this arrangement was in Aragon than in other kingdoms', saying that other examples drawn from the history of other kingdoms were of no use 'given the specialization and singularity of the *fueros* so tenaciously defended by the Aragonese'. As he prosaically put it: 'the people of this kingdom are so observant of their *fueros* and customs that even the opening of a door in a wall dividing the town hall of Saragossa (where the Cortes usually meets) and the archbishop's palace so that Queen Isabella could pass through required an act of court'.[76]

Years later, in 1676, the possibility that the sickly Charles II might travel to Saragossa to swear the *fueros* of Aragon was discussed. The kingdom's representatives attempted to convince the king that he was obliged to do this on the authority of the narrative of Sobrarbe: 'Before going on to elect the king our people desired to make laws through which he might later govern them, and thus they set down what we now call the *fueros* of Sobrarbe, being an acknowledged principle from that day forward that in Aragon laws existed before kings.' The *fueros*, they continued, were made by the Aragonese people in a state of liberty, and constituted and made public 'by the

su natural señor' (pp. 93–4; the previous quote, p. 85). The peasants wrote to the king asking for protection and an end to the billetings, and they declared that they preferred 'perder todos sus haciendas, aventurar las vidas, ver despedazados los hijos, llevar las mujeres y sobre todo morir tristemente, que conservarse ricos y poderosos aunque vasallos de otro rey': quoted by Gil, ' "Conservación" y "defensa" ', p. 93.
[75] Vitrián de Biamonte, *Fragmentos*, p. 34.
[76] BL, Add. 13997, fos. 109–28; quotes, at the title and fo. 119 and 126.

supreme power of the people, to whom by natural and divine law belonged the right of legislation'. In Aragon, kings 'do not possess more or greater political power than that which the people desire voluntarily to accord them ... Absolute power does not lie in His Majesty, but only in the Cortes where the king and kingdom come together and in whom, thus united, resides the power of legislation.'[77]

Charles II travelled to Saragossa, swore the *fueros* and celebrated the Cortes along the lines set down in these declarations. The Aragonese foral tradition had neither been halted nor diminished in strength, whether in the realm of proclamations or in that of the Cortes since, unlike Castile, Catalonia and Valencia, Aragon maintained a tenuous continuity of parliamentary activity during this reign.[78] However, if the foral tradition had not lost strength during the seventeenth century, it is no less true that since the end of the sixteenth century the meaning of this tradition had changed, both with respect to legal and juridical formalities and to political life in the broadest sense.[79] In the latter case, *fueros* and 'liberties' had ceased to carry an implicit sense of defence against the crown. Rather, they were now seen as perfectly compatible with royal authority and even, in the view of some authors, inconceivable without it.

It was, then, an evolution similar to that experienced by another time-honoured concept in the European constitutionalist tradition of the fifteenth and sixteenth centuries: *police*. From signifying limits to royal power in the classic formulation of Claude de Seyssel, *police* had come to mean civil organization, a regulation of the ordered community. This re-interpretation brought changes in notions of legality and the decline of traditions of resistance.[80] In Aragon the unambiguous foral proclamations did not question the pillars of royal authority, unlike in Catalonia, Portugal and Naples, whose revolts imparted a republican, secessionist and some-

---

[77] Diputados del Reino, *Discurso histórico-foral jurídico-político en orden al juramento que los supremos y soberanos Reyes de Aragón (salva su real clemencia) deben prestar en el nuevo ingresso de su govierno y antes que puedan ussar de alguna jurisdicción* (Saragossa, 1676), fos. 164, 167–8v (a copy is to be found at the Biblioteca del Colegio de Abogados de Zaragoza).

[78] On the strengths and weaknesses of parliamentary politics during the seventeenth century, see Xavier Gil, 'Crown and Cortes in early-modern Aragon: reassessing revisionisms', *Parliaments, estates and representation*, 13 (1993), 109–22.

[79] Thus warns Jesús Morales Arrizabalaga against the tendency to regard the *fueros* as fixed both in number and nature: 'Procedimientos para el ejercicio gubernativo y contencioso de la jurisdicción de la Real Audiencia de Aragón en el siglo XVIII', *Anuario de historia del derecho español*, 59 (1990), 534, 545.

[80] Gerhard Oestreich, *Neostoicism and the early-modern state* (Cambridge, 1982), chapter 9; R. J. W. Evans, *The making of the Habsburg monarchy, 1550–1700* (Oxford, 1979), pp. 100–1, 106–7.

times anti-aristocratic sense to their traditional contractualisms. Numerous writings of historians and antiquaries bolstered the enduring vigour of Aragonese national sentiment, now incorporated, but perfectly distinguishable, within the composite Spanish monarchy. These writers exercised a role similar to their Italian counterparts who, in the climate of the Catholic Reformation, made themselves champions of national pride in a conservative rather than seditious cast of mind.[81]

This attitude on the part of Aragonese theorists and politicians had unmistakably conservative effects. But in the realm of ideas it did not differ all that much from the innovative reflections on liberty taking place elsewhere in Europe. For example, Anthony Ascham, an English parliamentary politician, wrote a treatise on the political revolutions of those years under the influence of Hobbes, as he himself recognized. In it he commented that the original freedom to populate the world left men in a state of war. In this state of affairs a desire for security led to the promulgation of laws and a corresponding decline in liberty.[82]

In Aragon royal authoritarianism on the one hand and *fueros* and liberties on the other, were now seen as compatible, as together they provided the desired security. The contemporary opinions voiced by English Whig theorists regarding the decline of the liberties of Aragon and other continental nations were not incorrect but, generally speaking, theirs were not unbiased analyses of European politics, so much as partisan commentaries in the English political debate. Nevertheless, such opinions crystallized later in the Whig conception of political development. However, for many contemporaries the alternative to absolutism was not English parliamentarianism but popular rebellion, the military anarchy of the Thirty Years' War, or subjection to a foreign power.[83] The Aragonese ruling classes faced the reality of these alternatives dramatically throughout successive crises. In the long run, without forgetting the tensions and protests which took place, the majority inclined towards the loyalty to the crown, reticent immediately after 1591, increasingly open and active from the 1630s.

The Aragonese neo-Tacitean writers carried this political option to its furthest theoretical development, which permitted them to present new

---

[81] Felix Gilbert, 'Italy', in *National consciousness, history and political culture in early-modern Europe*, ed. Orest Ranum (Baltimore, 1975), pp. 21–42.

[82] Anthony Ascham, *Of the confusions and revolutions of governments* (2nd edition, London, 1649), p. 109.

[83] See John Miller, 'Introduction', in *Absolutism in seventeenth-century Europe*, ed. Miller (London, 1990), p. 19. In the same sense, J. H. Burns points out the need to recover the meaning that the term absolutism had before the liberal controversy: 'The idea of absolutism', ibid., p. 23.

interpretations of that most diverse concept, liberty, now harmoniously married to royal authority. 'Disloyalty', Luis de Mur admonishingly pointed out, 'provokes discord and breaks the bonds of peace giving birth to tyranny in sacrilegious spoliation of public authority and the liberty of citizens, to the detriment of the natural and political laws of the rights of peoples.' On his part, in a tract aiming to refute the arguments in favour of Portuguese rebellion and secession, Antonio Fuertes y Biota offered reasons that he no doubt considered equally applicable to Aragon and other kingdoms: 'The kings . . . of the House of Habsburg . . . have always undertaken to maintain the laws and privileges of each individual through having been Princes in nations where satisfaction has always been found in the just and legitimate pursuit of privileged liberty.'[84]

As these and other examples show, the political language and culture of early modern Aragon gave rise to varying meanings of the word liberty. For this and other reasons, they constitute a singularly interesting case within Europe as a whole during the early modern era.

---

[84] Mur, *Tiberio ilustrado*, p. 40; Antonio de Fuertes y Biota, *Anti-manifiesto o verdadera declaración del derecho de los Señores Reyes de Castilla a Portugal* (Bruges, 1643), p. 175.

7

Patriotism in early modern Valencia

JAMES CASEY

Early modern Europe was a mosaic of overlapping political units, of city states and lordships and multinational empires. Human geography dictated solidarities which might be vaster or smaller than the political boundaries, while ties of religion or caste or clientage constituted alternative focuses of loyalty to those of the emerging state.[1] The Spanish monarchy, with its multi-ethnic and multicultural character, constitutes an interesting example of the conflicting forces at work in this period. The revolts of the 1640s in Catalonia, Portugal, Sicily and Naples have provoked questions about the nature of the modern state, and its ability, or failure, to ground political allegiance on firmer social and cultural supports. A sense of pride in the local *patria* was certainly well developed. In that slow-moving, pre-industrial world men were more keenly aware than today of differences in house styles, dress, plants, vernacular tongues shading off into dialects – the whole complex of factors which might shape a national character, about which the sixteenth-century writers were not slow to speak.[2] On the other

---

Translations are by the author unless otherwise attributed.

[1] A stimulating sense of the rival claims of human geography and political allegiance emerges from two classic works on the early modern period of Fernand Braudel, *La Méditerranée et le monde méditerranéen à l'époque de Philippe II* (Paris, 1949), and Lucien Febvre, *Philippe II et la Franche-Comté* (Paris, 1912). See also Peter Sahlins, *Boundaries: the making of France and Spain in the Pyrenees* (Berkeley, 1989).

[2] M. Herrero García, *Ideas de los españoles en el siglo XVII* (Madrid, 1928). There is an interesting discussion of ideas of Catalonia in R. García Cárcel, *Historia de Cataluña: siglos XVI-XVII* (Barcelona, 1985), I, pp. 40-187.

hand, in an age in which cosmographies, those intriguing blends of history and geography, were the chief forms of presenting one people to another, the awareness of collective identity was grounded in a shared tradition of law, religion and historical memory. Good government, in order to maintain the tradition in its pristine form, was the essence of 'patriotism', as the early modern period understood the term. The guardians of the national memory were not the school-teachers of a later age but the lawyers and the king. It was when the issue of good and bad government became acute, as the cases of Catalonia and Portugal in 1640 seemed to demonstrate, that love of *patria* might be the spur to separatism.[3]

Valencian writers have long agonized over the apparent failure of their own homeland to develop a proper sense of collective identity. Mainly Catalan speaking, with the proto-democratic institutions typical of medieval Catalonia, Valencia seemed content, in the words of one witness of the revolutions of 1640, to be 'a kingdom in name alone'.[4] Certainly this was not that Valencians of the time lacked an awareness of themselves as a people, nor a sturdy belief in the virtues of patriotism. 'One's homeland is like another kind of God', said Vicente Mares in the book he dedicated in 1681 to his parish of Chelva. 'It is one's first and main family.'[5] The comparison with the family, taken from a classical source, would evoke an immediate response in his readers. Just as one knew a man by his ancestors and relations, so one could make a shrewd guess about his character from the environment – its proud or shameful history as well as its material poverty or abundance. But of what environment should one speak? Patriotism, unlike modern nationalism, was inclusive rather than exclusive. His readers, Mares assumed, would be interested first in the history of the world – for were they not all men, fashioned by the same creator? Then they would want to know about 'our Europe', 'our Spain', 'the kingdom of Valencia', then finally 'my homeland' (*mi patria*), the upland market town of Chelva.

The kingdom of Valencia might, indeed, seem almost as fanciful a concept, seen from Chelva, as Spain or Europe. The topography of the region is one of the most impenetrable in Spain – a mass of hills, tumbling down from the central tableland to the Mediterranean, enfolding narrow valleys and small coastal plains. 'Seven days long' from north to south,

---

[3] John H. Elliott, *The revolt of the Catalans: a study in the decline of Spain 1598–1640* (Cambridge, 1963); John H. Elliott *et al.*, *1640. La monarquía hispánica en crisis* (Barcelona, 1992).

[4] F. M. de Melo, *Historia de los movimientos y separación de Cataluña* [1645] (Barcelona, 1969), p. 98.

[5] Vicente Mares, *La Fenix Troyana* (Valencia, 1681), prologue.

according to the autobiography of James I of Aragon who conquered it from the Muslims in the thirteenth century, 'and there is no more delightful place under heaven than the city of Valencia and that whole kingdom.'[6] The political unity of the region had taken shape in the central Middle Ages as a set of small Muslim lordships or kingdoms, centred mainly on Dénia, Murcia and Valencia City itself. A series of campaigns between 1233 and 1245 brought most of these under the crown of Aragon, though the area to the south of the mountains of Xixona (that is, much of the province of Alicante) was only incorporated in 1304, and was claimed by the crown of Castile for longer than that. The Christian kingdom of Valencia was a composite society. Aragonese settlers, with their Castilian speech, populated much of the north-west, while Catalan speakers dominated the coastal plains and big towns. Above all, the conquest was achieved by a series of treaties which allowed the majority of local Muslims to stay on their lands but forced them to vacate the main strongholds. Down to the early seventeenth century nearly a third of the population was Muslim, conferring on the territory customs, dress, housing, speech and popular religion which were distinctive. This territory housed nearly 100,000 families on the eve of the expulsion of the *moriscos* in 1609. The backbone of its human geography was the network of towns ranging from the capital city, with its 12,000 households (one of the biggest urban populations in Spain) down through historic centres like Xàtiva (cradle of the Borgia popes) to market towns and seaports like Cullera, Vilajoiosa, Gandía, Dénia, settlements of only a few hundred families but authentic regional capitals through their protective walls, privileged fairs, collegiate churches or convents, historic families. Some of these towns had been alienated from the royal domain – Gandía, Dénia, Cocentaina, Segorbe – mostly in the fifteenth century through the service of families like the Sandoval or the Borgia to Alfonso the Magnanimous and Ferdinand the Catholic. Such a fragmentation of authority was a major source of political controversy. 'The vassals and subjects of the king can have no greater sense of hurt and sorrow', thought the chronicler Viciana, 'than when the king separates them from his patrimony and crown, for it is almost as if enemies were to conquer them.'[7] The history of medieval Valencia, and the political consciousness of the kingdom, had been formed by the struggle to make the Aragonese barons obey the general laws of the land, the *furs*, and to stop further grants of fiefs by the crown.

---

[6] Quoted in Manuel Sanchis Guarner, *La ciutat de Valencia* [1972] (5th edition, 1989), p. 72. The words were allegedly spoken by an Aragonese baron to the king.

[7] Martín de Viciana, *Crónica de la inclita y coronada ciudad de Valencia* [1563–6]; new edition by S. García Martínez (Valencia, 1972–83), III, fo. 150.

It was not that the Valencians did not appreciate nobility, for true nobility was virtue employed in the service of the commonwealth. The traditions and heroic deeds of great families constituted for the chroniclers of the early modern period one of the symbols of collective identity. Without a hierarchy of honour the commonwealth 'will not be without tyrants who will oppress it'.[8] And Viciana in 1563–6, like his successor Gaspar Escolano in 1610–11, pays great attention to the aristocratic lineages associated either with the conquest of the kingdom in the thirteenth century or with the expansion of the crown of Aragon in Italy in the later Middle Ages. But, essentially, the historical memory was of a Valencia organized as a series of royal towns within whose extensive townlands the knights had been rewarded for their valour with farms, not fiefs. Alfonso the Benign in 1329 had allowed such landlords, with three Muslim or fifteen Christian tenant families, to exercise civil and petty criminal jurisdiction over them. As these settlements grew in the later Middle Ages and early modern period they often acquired full autonomy by grant of the crown; but bitter rearguard actions were fought by the parent towns against such separations down to the seventeenth century. Conflicts of this kind seem to have played an important part in the great revolt of the towns in 1519–22, the *Germanias*.[9]

The tradition of the Muslims, inherited by them from the Romans, was of the city-state with its surrounding *villae*, rural settlements over which an urban patriciate exercised military and judicial authority. The Valencian nobility developed primarily as an urban élite, a mixture of knights and 'honoured citizens'. Claiming aristocratic status for the latter, one authority noted that at the time of the conquest the towns were like 'little republics with their own civil and military government', and those who ruled them were 'similar in some respect to those invested with military fiefs'.[10] By the time this was written, a clearer distinction had emerged between the estates – between those who held fiefs, and within towns between those of knightly lineage and those who were only citizens, however honourable. But such developments were still uncertain and contested in the early Habsburg period. Francisco March, one of the leading magistrates of Valencia city, who died in 1616, refers to himself in the civic annals which he edited, as a 'citizen', but he was also lord of the *morisco* village of Benamir and his son

---

[8] Viciana, II, fo. 20v. See also the work of the 'honoured citizen' Onofre Esquerdo, *Nobiliario valenciano* (ca. 1686), published by José Martínez Ortiz (Valencia, 1963), pp. 19–20.
[9] R. García Cárcel, *Las Germanías de València* (Barcelona, 1974), p. 163. For the long-standing tension between towns and barons, see Joan Reglà, *Aproximació a la història del país Valèncià* (Valencia, 1968).
[10] M. Madramany, *Tratado de la nobleza de Aragón y València* (Valencia, 1788), p. 410.

sat in the Valencian Corts in the estate of the nobility. His contemporary, the knight Bernardo Catalá de Valeriola, could complain to his diary in 1598 about the opposition of March and his fellow magistrates to the participation of the nobility in an embassy of condolences to Philip III on the death of his father – 'in truth, they are plebeians and men of the *Germanías*' but a few years earlier he had joined March and a few other citizens on a pilgrimage among friends to the Carthusians of Portaceli.[11] Since the knights were allocated a quota of city offices – two of the six posts of *jurat* or aldermen, annually renewable – their commitment to the urban society was total. Indeed, echoes of the more fundamental division between the towns and the great feudal lords who refused to obey the *furs* could still be heard in the complaint of the *jurats* in 1624 against their successors. Did not most of the fief-holders now enjoy the favour of the court? Were they not absentees on imperial service? Most of them 'live in other kingdoms and spend there the rents which they draw from here, depriving the natives and inhabitants of the benefit'.[12]

The self-image of Valencia was that of a proud city-state. Its maritime situation, noted the chronicler Escolano, had created wealth, cosmopolitanism and a certain 'sharpness of wit'.[13] Son of an honoured citizen and rector of one of the city parishes he manages to ally a respect for the chivalric tradition of the knights with a basic commitment to the urban community. Binding that community together was a certain democracy – not unqualified, but distinctive enough. 'Where there is much counsel there is much health', ran one of the *furs*, providing for the election of four deputies from each guild to constitute a general assembly which would advise the magistrates on the government of the city.[14] The elections were controlled by the magistrates, whose own election was in great measure subject to the approval of the king. Nevertheless it is surely true that there was a tradition of lively, public debate in Valencia which would be hard to find in Castilian towns of the period. Nor were the honoured citizens, who monopolized the magistracies along with the knights, as yet a narrow oligarchy. Joan Lluch Ivars, successor to March as keeper of the civic annals and one of the leading politicians in the Valencia of Philip IV, was described as a silk-weaver at the

11 S. Carreres Zacarés, ed., *Libre de memòries* (Valencia, 1935), I, pp. xxii–xxiii; Archivo de la Corona de Aragón, Cons. *leg.* 1357, consulta 16 April 1626 and *leg.* 1356, memorial of 19 January 1646, for information on the March family; S. Carres Zacarés, ed., *Autobiografia* (Valencia, 1929), p. 17, for Catalá.

12 AM Valencia, Cartas Misivas 59, *Jurats* to king, 27 February 1624.

13 Gaspar Escolano, *Década primera de la historia de Valencia* [1610–11], ed. S. Garcia Martinez (Valencia, 1972), IV, p. 848.

14 Pere Hieroni Taraçona, *Institucions dels furs* (Valencia, 1580), p. 165.

baptism of his first son in 1599, then as a merchant in 1602 and, finally, as a *ciutadà*, a 'citizen' in 1604.[15] Unlike Barcelona there was no cooptive club for this class; the transition into it depended on lifestyle (living off rents) and social acceptability. In 1633, it is true, arrangements similar to those of Barcelona were adopted, confining city office to a fixed list of life-tenured knights and citizens. But, until then, Valencians might be forgiven for thinking of their town as a place of 'much counsel'.

This 'Hanseatic city' referred to itself as 'the head and mother' (*cap e mare*) of the kingdom. It was the *jurats* who escorted each new king into the cathedral for the solemn swearing of its laws and privileges; and it was the city archive which housed the original of each new collection of *furs* conceded by the king in parliament. It was also the *jurats*, as noted earlier, who represented the kingdom at the formal expression of condolences on the death of the king. The splendid embassy dispatched to court in September 1598 comprised four city magistrates, each escorted by two lackeys and four pages, 'all dressed in mourning'. And Francisco March could not conceal his pleasure that 'all Madrid came out to see the *jurats* of Valencia enter'. So great was the crush along the streets of Atocha and San Jerónimo 'that they would not let us pass'. And on 11 November the formal visit to the palace was escorted by all the Valencian nobles who happened to be in Madrid at the time, accepting their subordinate role as attendants. A city-state, without doubt.[16]

Yet the increasing fiscal pressure from the crown had led to an alternative view of the kingdom as 'those who paid the taxes'. From the thirteenth century a parliament or Corts had been called together, representing the bishops, cathedral chapters, convents and military orders (the first estate), the nobility (several hundred families of knights, who could satisfy their fellows as to their pedigree) and representatives of the towns. The actual definition of nobility posed many problems. Honoured citizens were eligible for habits of the military orders if their families were known from the Middle Ages, but not eligible to sit in the second estate; personal nobility was attached to valour or learning, but the qualification for entry to the second estate was increasingly, by the seventeenth century, lineage. A joint petition from the three estates, if approved by the king, constituted a *fur*, a binding law for the kingdom as a whole. But many laws were particular to one of the estates – an *acte de cort*, and legislative activity hardly constituted a major focus of collective political identity.

---

[15] *Libre de memòries*, I, pp. xxiii–xxiv.
[16] Ibid., II, p. 1039. Cf. Joan Fuster, *Nosaltres els Valencians* (Barcelona, 1962), pp. 41–58.

Rather, it had been the need to raise taxes which had led to the development of the 'Generality' of the kingdom – the *Generalitat*. Traditionally
subsidies were apportioned as quotas – of a hundred parts, twelve to be
found by the first estate, forty-four by the second (and its vassals), and
forty-four by the third (of which the city of Valencia paid half). From about
1400 the growth of taxation led to the imposition of permanent export dues,
administered by a committee of the estates, the *Diputació*. Out of the
100,000 *lliures* or so a year which these brought in, the *Diputació* was
supposed to accumulate a reserve with which to pay occasional subsidies to
the crown, build up an arsenal for the defence of the kingdom and subsidize
embassies of protest to Madrid against infringements of the *furs*. The
diputats clearly acquired increasing importance during the Habsburg period
for reasons which are not entirely clear. The *Generalitat* building, one of the
great monuments of Renaissance Valencia, was begun in 1482 and sump-
tuously decorated at various stages in the sixteenth century, notably with
the superb murals of the estates in session by Joan de Sarinyena in 1593.[17]
Escolano records in 1610 how impressive the *diputats* looked in ceremonial
procession, preceded by their male bearers. But they never quite managed
to eradicate the image of the city-state. At the funeral services for dead
kings, they would enter the cathedral briefly to salute the viceroy and *jurats*,
then leave. At the bullfight held in October 1638 to commemorate the fourth
centenary of the capture of the city from the Muslims they went to their
seats overlooking the market square while the *jurats* escorted in the viceroy.

The rise of the *Generalitat* reflected a new fiscalism, which would lead in
the end to a new kind of state. A developing school of political economy was
paying greater attention to the material resources of a country. Typically,
much of Escolano's work of 1610–11 is taken up with refuting Giovanni
Botero, who in various books pioneering the new ideas between 1588 and
1591, argued that Spanish power was fragile because the economic infra-
structure was weak.[18] Awareness of natural resources was fundamental to
the great Valencian writers like Viciana and Escolano, but the scale
remained local and the focus traditional. For Vicente Mares his homeland of
Chelva was like a garden surrounded by mountains which kept out hot or
cold winds and whose cladding of thyme and juniper kept the plague at bay.
It was 'the high mountains, covered with rosemary and other herbs', which
Bernardo Catalá admired on his pilgrimage to Our Lady of the Fountain of

[17] Sanchis Guarner, *Valencia*, p. 194. Cf. Lorenzo Matheu y Sanz, *Tratado de la celebración de
cortes generales* (Madrid, 1677).
[18] Giovanni Botero, *The reason of state*, ed. D. P. Waley (London, 1956).

Health near Vinaroz.[19] And one feels that for Catalá, an inveterate traveller but often sick, the geography of the kingdom was marked out by the shrines with their healing waters and relics.

The little walled towns, whose justices had periodically to inspect the markers which circumscribed the limits of their jurisdiction, were other centres of security. Typically about fifteen to thirty miles apart, or a day's travel on horseback, they jealously safeguarded the territory within which their bees could swarm and their sheep roam. Above all, they defined that territory in terms of the jurisdiction which their magistrates could exercise: the inspection of village markets for fraud, the collection of taxes to maintain irrigation channels and the local castle where the territory's inhabitants could take refuge. The chroniclers Viciana and Escolano, like the proceedings of the Corts, are marvellous sources for the reconstruction of a lost topography. Beyond the municipal frontier was a wider world, marked out essentially by needs of supply. Through the pages of the diary kept between 1589 and 1629 by Joan Porcar, a priest of the city of Valencia, one can recapture some of the excitement with which the arrival of the great logs rolled down the river from Aragon and Castile was greeted every spring, and the greater anxiety, as in the hunger year of 1605, with which ships bearing wheat from Sicily were awaited. The mercantilism of the seventeenth century tended to impose constraints, fitting human geography on to a procrustean bed of state needs. Attempts to tax the grain from Sicily, to stop the import of linen from France during time of war, or to exclude English ships importing spices through Alicante (which breached the Portuguese monopoly), all provoked great hostility in Habsburg Valencia.[20] Valencians were certainly aware of a regulated market, but its boundaries were both narrower and wider than those envisaged by Madrid.

Influences of climate, history and religion had combined to create for the Valencians, thought Escolano, a well-defined character. The sign of Scorpio and a latitude where Venus and Mars held sway conferred on 'those of this nation a sweetness in their temperament and dealings, yet at the same time a mettlesome, quick temper'; while their trade had made them unusually open and intelligent.[21] For Escolano's generation the wealth of a people was its patrimony in a broad sense – its historical traditions as well as its physical

---

[19] *Autobiografía*, p. 3,941. Cf. V. M. Rosselló, 'El mapa del Regne de València de 1693', in *Homenatage al doctor Sebastià Garcia Martinez* (Valencia, 1988), II, pp. 177–99.

[20] J. Casey, *The kingdom of Valencia in the seventeenth century* (Cambridge, 1979), pp. 80–1; E. Salvador, 'Un memorial de Vicente Villaragut y Sanz', *Actes du Ier Colloque sur le pays valencien à l'époque moderne* (Pau, 1980), pp. 99–115.

[21] *Década primera*, I, pp. 187–91; IV, p. 848.

resources. The frontiers of the kingdom were marked out by the monuments of piety and ancestral virtue. As the Corts of 1604 put it, God had shown Valencia 'great and extraordinary favours' in raising on its soil, or attracting to it, so many holy people, 'who by their exemplary lives and saintly deaths have shed lustre on this kingdom'.[22] The city of Valencia had surrendered to the Christians on 28 September 1238, vigil of the feast of St Michael the Archangel, but it was on 9 October that the mosques were finally re-consecrated to Christian worship and this was the day that the Valencians commemorated as the anniversary of their nationhood. Into the celebration was woven tribute to St Denis the Areopagite, whose feast coincided with this date, to St Michael and to St George, the warrior saint who was alleged to have appeared to the Christians at the decisive battle of El Puig the year before Valencia fell. The figure of St George served as a rival, throughout Catalonia and Valencia, to St James, who was alleged to have appeared to the Castilians shortly before in 1212, at their decisive encounter with the Muslims of Andalusia. Though the legend of St James and Compostela was familiar to the Valencians, and taken seriously by Escolano, this smacked as much of traditional Catholic, European piety as of Spanish patriotism. It was St George who became the patron of the nobility of Valencia and co-patron, with Our Lady, of the chivalric order of Montesa, the enduring symbol of the crusading frontier in Valencia. But St George could not compete in popular acclaim with the two Vincents. St Vincent the Martyr, put to death around AD 305, represented the continuity of Valencian history, beyond the interval of the Muslim invasion, with a Roman, Visigothic and European past. Symbolizing the fact that 1238 had been a reconquest, not a conquest, King James I had placed his banner in the shrine of St Vincent, where it still hung in the seventeenth century. The other Vincent, St Vincent Ferrer, was the great fifteenth-century Dominican preacher, who had carried the Catalan tongue and the fame of Valencia beyond the Pyrenees into France, and local pride in his achievement surfaced in the request of the Corts of 1604 that his feast day be kept not just in his homeland but throughout Christendom.

One of the great forces binding Valencians together in an awareness of their collective identity was surely the periodic re-enactment of events from the country's past. Street theatre was important in all pre-industrial societies in building up a sense of belonging and counteracting the potentially divisive pull of family or caste or privileged corporation. At a critical time for relationships between the crown of Aragon and Castile, Valencia cele-

[22] E. Ciscar, ed., *Cortes del reinado de Felipe III* (Valencia, 1973), *fur* 250.

brated in the autumn of 1638 the fourth centenary of its birth as nation. For three nights, beginning on 8 October, the people were enjoined to place torches and lanterns on the façades of their houses – the prize went to one with no fewer than 500 lights. These *luminarias* were followed on St Denis's Day itself with a sermon in the cathedral, in Valencian, followed by a play about King James' father written by the great Calderón, who had won Valencian hearts with a visit to the city a few months earlier. On 10 October there was the elaborate procession of civic dignitaries and the guilds, with their banners and bands of musicians, to the shrine of St Vincent the Martyr, past houses hung with tapestries and roadside altars or tableaux, illustrating in paint and sculpture the devotion of the Valencians to the faith. On three successive days bullfights and tilting at the ring by the nobility were arranged in the market square.[23] The proceedings would surely merit further investigation of their symbolism. One notices the key role played by the *jurats* as organizers, and the importance of the market square as the focus of popular festivity. Along the processional route the convents seem to be the fixed stages, rather than the houses of the nobility who, indeed, play a rather subdued role in the whole affair. The roadside altars illustrate essentially the virtues of the Catholic faith; King James and his knights seem to fade into the background – and only the Jesuits bothered to represent the reigning dynasty, Philip IV and his family. Devotion to saints could be a useful neutral ground on which to meet political opponents, of course. The count of Oropesa, viceroy of Valencia, clashed with the city magistrates in 1646 over elections to office, but, stricken by the plague that autumn, he requested to have the image of Our Lady of the Forsaken, patron of the city, taken into his palace. And, in thanksgiving for his recovery, he helped to endow the new shrine which is one of the masterpieces of the Baroque in Valencia.[24]

If 1238 was Valencia's birthday, 1245 was surely its confirmation as a state, for it was then that it became apparent that it would not simply be incorporated piecemeal into Aragon or Catalonia but would receive its own code of laws, the famous *furs*. The latter are one of the great monuments to the thirteenth-century mind, reflecting that early renaissance of classical learning and Roman law which characterized Europe at the time. Less philosophical than the contemporary lawbook of Alfonso the Wise of Castile, the *Siete Partidas*, these decrees of King James and his clergy, barons and honoured citizens (as Escolano described the participants) were

[23] See the description in Marcos Antonio Ortí, *Siglo quarto de la conquista de Valencia* (Valencia, 1640).

[24] J. B. Perales, *Décadas de la historia de Valencia* (Valencia, 1878–80), III, p. 780.

a precocious attempt to apply rational principles rather than feudal custom to social relationships. They were 'laws made level by religion', as Escolano put it, using a term – *nivelar* – which may refer to the technical ingenuity required to keep the water flowing smoothly along Valencia's famous network of irrigation canals.[25] James I proclaimed a 'general peace' in the new kingdom, limiting feuding to the individuals who claimed injury and forbidding general vengeance against another's friends and supporters. His successor Peter II reinforced the message: 'for you are all brothers, born again from the same father, your creator and redeemer'. Such words cut little ice with the barons, who kept up a long struggle against this common-wealth spirit, and even as late as 1626 the Corts had to affirm all must obey the law of the kingdom. The irony is that Valencia long remained notorious in Spain for its feuds, even after Ferdinand the Catholic virtually forbade the individual duels allowed under the *furs*. The tension between the claims of law and honour probably reached its peak in the reigns of Philip II and Philip III, to judge by the protests of the Corts of 1585, 1604 and 1626 against what they regarded as high-handed action by the king's judges. The issue is a complex one. The *furs* had sketched out a wider notion of the commonwealth than the solidarities of lineage and clientage with which many Valencians were happier. The king's judges could claim that they were acting in the spirit of the law. The marquis of Tavara, a tough viceroy (1619–22), who clashed with the estates over the execution of a headstrong young noble, won some approval from the peaceable priest, Joan Porcar; but in 1616 Porcar betrayed a certain sympathy in his diary with the nobles, 'defenders of the liberty of the land' against judges who detained without trial.[26]

The role of the king had, of course, been fundamental in the birth and subsequent development of Valencia. One glimpses it in perhaps the most significant work of political theory to be published in Habsburg Valencia, Tomás Cerdán de Tallada's *Rules of State* of 1604.[27] Underlying his analysis is the perceived distinction between the commonwealth or *república* and the 'state', the king's estate or *estado real*. The first is the collectivity of individuals and communities whose rights and obligations are set out in the laws of Valencia. The second is the prerogative of the prince, designed to keep the natural harmony of the laws. If he lives up to his high calling, the

---

[25] *Década primera*, III, p. 491; Thomas Glick, *Irrigation and society in medieval Valencia* (Cambridge, Mass., 1970), p. 85.

[26] *Coses evengudes en la ciutat y regne de València 1589-1629*, ed. V. Castañeda Alcover (Madrid 1934), I, paragraph 1246. Cf. Taraçona, *Furs*, IV.15 and III.23.

[27] *Veriloquium en reglas de estado* (Valencia, 1604).

prince is 'like God on earth ... the image of the divine majesty which he represents'. Born around 1534 Cerdán had lived to see the gradual break-down of the *república* – the proliferation of lawsuits, the speculation by grain-hoarders with that most sacred trust of the poor, the ecclesiastical tithe, the disruption in families caused by greed as eldest sons inherited the estates and forgot their obligations, the absenteeism of feudal lords which caused distress to their vassals ... His attempt, as a royal judge, to invoke the state to redress the wrongs of the commonwealth, led to his suspension from office under viceroy Aytona (1580–1595), and house arrest (though now a very old man indeed) for 'impertinence' in 1613.[28]

Cerdán's aim, in his vigorous, impetuous prose, was to restore the equi-librium of the state and the commonwealth to that happy principle of self-regulation which he found in nature. The responsibilities of the state, he thought, were threefold: the maintenance of justice, general administration (including defence and revenue collection), and grace or favour to loyal ser-vants. Justice was best left in the hands of native ministers. They knew 'the secrets of a realm', the 'reputation and esteem of particular families', and could be relied upon to 'guide matters of government along the paths laid out by their ancestors'. Outsiders, bereft of such ties and eager to feather their own nests, were 'lovers of novelty' and liable to turn into tyrants. But general administration – the raising and spending of the king's revenue, not least – required more flexibility. Valencia was now part of a plural monarchy: 'wherever Your Majesty is, there is a common *patria* for all those who dwell in your kingdoms'.[29] Hence the king must take policy decisions at a supranational level and, for this purpose, he would need to include among his advisers Valencians as well as Castilians and others. This idea is a repe-tition of that expressed by the Valencian humanist Fadrique Furió Ceriol in his *Council and councillors of the prince,* published in 1559 and reworked in an English edition of 1570. Furió Ceriol was a noble who had taken part in the Valencian Corts before rising in the service of Charles V. Like Cerdán, his concern was that outsiders tended to rule tyrannically. As Valencia was now part of a federal monarchy, what could be more reassuring for its people than to have their representatives in positions of power at court?[30]

---

[28] Archivo de la Corona de Aragón, Cons. *leg.* 703, viceroy to king, 24 September 1613.

[29] *Veriloquium*, p. 60. The reference to native ministers actually applies in the text to Spaniards as against foreigners, but I have interpreted the sense as applying also to Valencians as against Castilians. A fuller study of Cerdán's complex and fascinating treatise would be desirable.

[30] *El consejo y los consejeros del príncipe* (Antwerp, 1559). An English edition was printed in 1570. Furió attended the Corts of 1585, cf. E. Salvador, ed., *Cortes valencianas del reinado de Felipe II* (Valencia, 1973), p. 159.

Cerdán and Furió both addressed the problem of the changing nature of the state more powerful now as a judicial instrument but also more remote from the Valencian homeland. The point of friction was liable to be the 'patrimony of the king', that fund which he would need in order to carry on government as government was then understood: to defend and reward his subjects. But which subjects, in the end, would benefit from Valencian money? Philip II, after the loss of the Armada in 1588, approached the Valencians, like all his other subjects, for help, inaugurating a policy which would mature in the Union of Arms proposed by Olivares in the 1620s, in which the various kingdoms of the monarchy would shoulder a common responsibility for defence.[31] Certainly there was in Valencia a loyalty to 'Spain' on which the monarchy could build. The chroniclers Viciana and Escolano set their homeland firmly in a shared Roman and Visigothic heritage. Viciana, though betraying a certain nostalgia for the 'invincible house of Aragon' and aware of the different history of those 'great, broad kingdoms' of Castile, was happy to record their joint triumphs. First had come the conquest of Granada in 1492, for which 'it was needful that the invincible crimson bars of Aragon should be put alongside the lions of Castile' on their common flag. Then had come the taking of Mexico and Peru, to which Viciana devotes several pages. And the victory over the 'ferocious Germans' at Mühlberg in 1547 was a triumph for 'Spanish' arms. 'Take for your battle cry', Charles V allegedly told his men, 'St James, St George, Spain, Empire'.[32]

Viciana, a notary who represented his town of Burriana in the Corts of Charles V, came from a knightly family down on its luck. His world was that of chivalry, of the loyalty of the Valencians to their natural lord, the king. His voice is echoed in that of the Corts, with its repeated, passionate protestations of devotion to the royal service. To an ageing Philip II in 1585 it expressed its appreciation of his 'many labours in so many heroic enterprises which have brought such renown', resolving to support his wars, for the Valencians and their ancestors 'in the service of Your Majesty and of the royal crown have distinguished themselves more than other nations'.[33] But the one thing on which the Corts always insisted was that its subsidies must be regarded as absolutely voluntary and not taken as a precedent. Normally from the time of Ferdinand the Catholic they amounted to 100,000 lliures payable over six years. Since Charles V called a Corts nearly every six years, he seems to have done quite well – not least since, as the Valencians kept

---

[31] On the Union of Arms see the classic study by John H. Elliott, *The count-duke of Olivares: the statesman in an age of decline* (New Haven, 1986).

[32] *Crónica*, III, fos. 120–120v.   [33] *Cortes del reinado de Felipe II*, p. 152.

protesting, their kingdom was 'utterly ruined' by the consequences of the war of the *Germanías* (1519–22). Under Philip II this reference began to wear thin and was quietly dropped, but the individual subsidies did not get bigger and the Corts got fewer (only two, in 1564 and 1585). Philip III's decision in 1604 to take 400,000 *lliures* over sixteen years was ominous, not because the actual sum was particularly great but because it implied that the Valencians would be making a standing contribution to the monarchy over a very long time. That was the real issue in 1626. The sum voted was just a little over twice that given to Philip III, payable over much the same period. But the terms of the debate made it clear that Valencia was now expected to pay 'Spanish' taxes as of right and not as of favour. The initial request of the crown anyway was for men, not money, to constitute a 'Spanish' army. As the Aragonese chronicler Dormer recalled, later in the century, 'The Valencians considered that asking the kingdom for troops was an attempt to force them to take part in the war, which they said was contrary to their liberty, and that by following this road one would have conscription, as in Castile, and the way would lie open to making all the kingdoms the same.'[34]

Even the fairly moderate subsidy voted in 1626 was too much for the diarist Joan Porcar. He had already been intensely annoyed by the subsidy given to Philip III in 1604, and was bitter against the deputies of 1626 – 'traitors to God, their patria and to the *furs* of this land', who had sacrificed the commonwealth 'in order to get rewards for themselves'.[35] The fiscal question was complicated by the fact that the existing dues of the *Generalitat* had to be doubled anyway in 1604 in order to strengthen the defences of the kingdom against the Muslims. Though Porcar, as a priest, was vaguely interested in the contribution of the monarchy to the victory of Catholic arms over 'the Lutherans' in Bohemia in 1620, he thought that the real enemies of Valencia were nearer home. Tax collection was a sea of corruption and harassment, whatever its nominal purpose – a proliferation of guards and inspectors and notaries, in the pay of the city, the *Generalitat* and the king, enforcing three different sets of excise dues. Those who had added to this burden on the poor included his own former superior don Francisco López de Mendoza, who had started climbing the ladder of promotion as rector of St Martin's parish in 1597, becoming president of the first estate in 1626 and (as Porcar tells us), leading the vote for a subsidy in return for a bishopric. Then there was the premier nobleman of the

---

[34] Diego José Dormer, 'Anales de la Corona de Aragón', ms. 9/490 of the Real Academia de Historia, fo. 228. Cf. Dámaso de Lario, *El comte-duc d'Olivares i el regne de València* (Valencia, 1986).

[35] *Coses evengudes*, II, paragraph 2854.

kingdom, the duke of Gandía, unable to pay his debts and protected by the crown against demands for the sale of his estates or at least for a more rigorous investigation of his accounts. In 1622 an agreement by a minority of creditors to accept a massive reduction of their claims was confirmed and made general by a royal decree. Porcar recorded bitterly in his diary the terms of this decree, especially the preamble in which Philip IV invoked all 'the fullness of his power ... which recognizes no superior on earth in all his realms for the purpose of backing up the duke of Gandía so that he may never pay what he owes his creditors'.[36] Throughout Porcar's diary one senses that the commonwealth is, indeed, in trouble – riven by a conflict between a popular party and a more powerful circle of men who have thrown in their lot with the *patria común* of the court.

The problem of the duke of Gandía and his creditors is merely one symptom of a broader problem: that very many, possibly a majority, of the feudal lords were bankrupt and, thanks to the protection of the crown, passing on the loss to clergy and honoured citizens who had lent them money. The great turning point in this whole drama was the expulsion of the last remnants of the *moriscos* (christians of Moorish descent) in 1609. The scale of this event is so huge, involving the displacement of nearly a third of the Valencian population, that it still defies the imagination despite the many studies devoted to it. The whole culture of Valencia had been shaped by the crusade against the Muslims, and the expulsion seems to have been initially quite popular. Francisco March, lord of the *morisco* village of Benamir, saw his revenues plummet from 1,000 to 100 ducats a year after 1609, yet he led the city of Valencia in commemorating the first anniversary of 'such a glorious triumph'. What all kings had aspired to since James I had been reserved by divine providence for Philip III, he told the Valencian public.[37] When Gaspar Aguilar, protégé of the duke of Gandía and one of the city's leading playwrights, published his 205-page poem celebrating the expulsion he included laudatory epistles from some lords who had lost *moriscos*, like Gaspar Mercader, count of Buñol, or the brothers Alvaro and Diego de Vich, barons of Llaurí.[38] These lords had dressed up as 'Moors' as recently as 1599 in the tournaments held to celebrate the marriage of Philip III in Valencia, and some of them, like the duke of Gandía, clearly enjoyed very good personal relations with the elders of the *morisco* communities

---

[36] Ibid., II, paragraph 2072. [37] Escolano, *Década primera*, X, p. 2002.
[38] F. Martí Grajales, *Ensayo de un diccionario ... de los poetas ... de Valencia hasta el año 1700* (Madrid, 1927), p. 22.

among whom they lived.[39] Yet the myth of being Valencian, especially in the cities, stressed difference from Islam. For Viciana and Escolano, the culture of their land was a legacy from Rome and owed nothing to Africa. The time had not yet come when culture would be interpreted more widely as family, house style, popular customs. Only then could a proper evaluation of the Islamic heritage be made.

If left to themselves the Valencians would have continued with the old imperfect, *de facto* coexistence with their *morisco* neighbours. The estate of the nobility protested against the expulsion in late September 1609, warning of the destructive economic consequences. They were overruled by the statesmen in Madrid, and one cannot help feeling that the events of 1609 represented a culmination of that opposition between 'state' and 'commonwealth' which Valencian writers like Cerdán and Furió were so good at discussing. Seen from Madrid the *moriscos* presented a twofold problem: military security and religious heterodoxy. The clash between state policy and local realities had already emerged starkly under Ferdinand the Catholic when Valencia, with its large Jewish as well as Muslim population, tried to block the introduction of the Inquisition. The Corts of the sixteenth century reflect a continuing struggle, with demands that the Inquisition limit its business to genuine cases of heresy, employ native Valencians, stop confiscating *morisco* land or fining *moriscos* since this harmed the rural economy, and take a more lenient view of *morisco* customs of marriage and feasts – for 'that is very useful for the service of Our Lord God and the salvation of the *moriscos*, and the quiet and repose of this kingdom'.[40]

Clearly it was dangerous to speak too openly on matters of faith, and a generation of religious and political pressure was transforming the attitude of the Valencians themselves to that coexistence with the other which was the very basis of their commonwealth. The transformation was a gradual one. When the leading Valencian patron of the arts don Diego de Vich (1584–1657) commissioned Juan Ribalta to paint thirty-one portraits of great Valencian figures these included not only stalwarts of the Catholic church like Saint Vincent Ferrer and Saint Francis Borgia but also the great humanists Ausias March, Luis Vives, Fadrique Furió Ceriol (whose *Bononia*, at the dangerously late date of 1556, had defended the diffusion of the Scriptures in the vernacular).[41] Vich was one of the numerous Valencian nobles – including the later president of the council of Castile, Cardinal

---

[39] F. Janer, *Condición social de los moriscos de España* (Madrid, 1857), pp. 293–4, letter from duke of Gandia to viceroy, 24 September 1609.

[40] R. García Cárcel, ed., *Cortes del reinado de Carlos I* (Valencia, 1972), *fur* 51 of 1552.

[41] Justo Pastor Fuster, *Biblioteca valenciana* (Valencia, 1827–30), I, pp. 253–4.

Gaspar de Borja — to have been brought up as a page at the court of Juan de Ribera, the archbishop of Valencia between 1568 and 1611 and one of the key figures in the Counter-Reformation in Spain. There Vich was introduced to the classics – Demosthenes, Cicero – as well as the religious art of Francisco Ribalta, Ribera's favourite painter.[42] The Valencian nobility were formed around 1600 in a culture that blended humanist interest in man with a mystical piety to judge, not least, by the flourishing Valencian school of painting at this time, which included Francisco and Juan Ribalta, Pedro Orrente and Jerónimo Jacinto Espinosa among others.

Valencia was chiefly notable, though, for its flourishing theatre. It produced Guillén de Castro (1569–1631), and gave an early welcome to Lope de Vega and Calderón. Here and in poetry Valencian talent seems to have found an important expression. Perhaps Escolano's comment about the 'sharp wits' of his fellow countrymen was drawn from his own experience as a member of the literary salon, the 'night owls' or *Nocturnos,* where nobles, priests and honoured citizens met from 1591 in the house of Bernardo Catalá de Valeriola to read spirited poems and essays to one another. The night owls engaged in what one might call a pastoral genre, expressing the ingenuity of the mind in exploring concepts of beauty or devotion.[43] A modern reader finds it all rather artificial, even stultifying. One of the most profound studies of the genre has taken as its focus the career of Gaspar Mercader, count of Buñol (1557–1631). Buñol had earned his title, it was rumoured, because of the dashing figure he had cut in the tournaments to celebrate Philip III's marriage in 1599. As Vich commented in his diary in 1631, on learning of his death, 'he was a lady's man, with a mischievous sense of fun, quick-witted, but extremely capricious, caring above all to make a name for himself'. In fact, he passed with ease from tilting with the lance to the poetic joust, winning a silver goblet in 1619 for his poem in honour of the canonization of yet another Valencian saint, Archbishop Villanueva.[44] Buñol, thought Vich, was the last of an older nobility which recognized no self-restraint. In one sense he was part of the city state, rubbing shoulders in the night owls with Escolano and the playwright Gaspar Aguilar, whose poem in praise of the expulsion of the *moriscos* we referred to earlier. It was a composite world, in which chivalric values still

[42] Ramón Robres Lluch, *San Juan de Ribera* (Barcelona, 1960), pp. 334, 339.

[43] Pedro Salvá and F. Martí Grajales, *Cancionero de la academia de los Nocturnos de Valencia* (Valencia, 1905–12).

[44] Martí Grajales, *Ensayo de un diccionario*, p. 18. Cf. Gaspar Mercader, *El prado de Valencia,* with introduction by Henri Mérimée (Toulouse, 1907), and Diego de Vich, *Dietario valenciano 1619–32*, ed. F. Almarche Vázquez (Valencia, 1921), p. 205.

mingled with the love of the local community. One senses this in Escolano, of course, but also in lesser figures like Aguilar. Son of a city councillor, Aguilar rose to become secretary to the duke of Gandía. His plays reflect some interest in the low pay and hard life of the peasants he may have met on the Gandía estates.[45]

But one of the features of seventeenth-century Valencia is surely the breakdown of that local commonwealth which could bring together men of different status, like Aguilar, Escolano, Vich, Buñol. The Buñol estate was ruined by the expulsion of the *moriscos*, and the count turned more to the court for pensions and office to help him survive. The lure of the court had, indeed, always been a fundamental undercurrent in Valencian culture. Already in 1563 Viciana tells us how he had loved to read the stirring tales of the old kings of Aragon. For him the prince was not only a governor – perhaps not even mainly a governor – but a moral influence on his people. Certainly this concept underlies his tributes to Ferdinand of Antequera, king of Aragon (1412–16), and Charles V, embodiments of virtue and chivalry. And he quotes an old adage approvingly: 'as is the king, so is his court; and as is his court, so will be his realm'.[46] Madrid, high up on the Castilian tableland, was a world away from Valencia, but increasing numbers of the local élite began to make the journey. Bernardo Catalá de Valeriola, friend of Escolano and founder of the night owls, was one, and his diary suggests rather vividly some of the hazards and travails of the enterprise. Born in 1569, he had gone to court for the first time in 1584. The great royal palace of the Escorial, recently completed, made its impression on this youth of fifteen: 'it is the best house there is in the world'. And when he returned in 1603, he walked through 'the whole palace' in Madrid, 'and I was really delighted, because it is a very good house, with a lot of pictures'. The journeys to Madrid and Valladolid were tedious and hazardous: at least a week on the road, with the risk of losing one's way in the storms which blew up suddenly in spring. But there were always Valencian friends to meet at one's destination – like the future duke of Lerma, who first presented him to Philip II in 1584. And Catholic ritual was everywhere familiar in an otherwise unfamiliar landscape. In the grim mountains of León, in May 1606, he lit a candle at the shrine of Our Lady of the Wayside.[47]

Catalá was no tourist; his frequent trips to court had the practical purpose of securing office for himself. One wonders how far this human migration

---

[45] *Poetas dramáticos valencianos* (Madrid, 1929), II, 'El Gran Patriarcha Don Juan de Ribera', act I (apparently referring, though, to the peasants of Badajoz, where Ribera had been bishop).

[46] *Crónica*, III, fo. 65.   [47] *Autobiografía*, pp. 2, 114 and 149.

began to alter concepts of the *patria*. Catalá had to make constant adjust-
ments to a different culture, not least in the sphere of language. His diary is
kept in Valencian, but it is intriguing how he lapses into Castilian after he
finally attains the honours of the court in 1604 – knighthood of Calatrava,
the office of *corregidor* of León. One of the bulwarks of the Valencian
identity had been its language. For Escolano there were three main linguistic groups in Spain: Basque, which was probably, he thought, the indigenous tongue of Iberia, to judge by the etymology of rivers and place
names; Castilian (including Portuguese), which had been 'of little account
until the time of the Catholic King Lord Ferdinand, keeping much of the
archaism of the hill country'; and finally the 'Limousin' or Occitan language, which stretched from Provence and Languedoc through Catalonia
into Valencia, the main literary medium of the Spaniards in the Middle
Ages.[48] Escolano, like Viciana and other Valencian writers of the time, was
profuse in his praise of the native tongue. On ceremonial occasions, such as
the commemoration of the reconquest, it was essential for preachers to
deliver the address in the vernacular. 'When I was a young man', recalled
one writer in 1640, 'we used to think so highly of the Valencian language
that when, in meetings of the city council, estates or other bodies, any
Valencian who was there began talking in Castilian, all the others would
rage against him, telling him to speak his own tongue.'[49] But, as the author
noted, all that had changed now. One can sense the transition in the formal
record of the Corts: whereas the *furs* of 1484–88 are drawn up in a lively,
vibrant Catalan, those of the sixteenth century have a rather hollow ring.
The traditional formulae are preserved, but the elasticity appears to have
gone out of the language. As Escolano put it, Valencian 'has come to lack
vigour and has stopped seeking refinement'. [50] A kind of vicious spiral had
set in during the sixteenth century: as fewer great writers, like Escolano
himself, chose to use Valencian, the tongue became slightly archaic, or a
debased oral medium. The blame could be attributed to the natural development of wider circles of communication within a multinational
monarchy: was Valencia not, after all, 'the *patria general* of all nations?'[51] To
speak only Valencian was to be provincial and to cut oneself off from that
wider world which was opening up with the union of Castile and Aragon.
Certainly the government made little attempt to unify the languages, preferring to word its decrees still in Valencian throughout the seventeenth
century. Rather, the pressure to adopt 'Spanish' was a cultural one, coming

---

[48] *Década primera*, I, pp. 88–97.   [49] Ortí, *Siglo quarto*, fo. 2v.
[50] *Década primera*, I, p. 96.   [51] Ortí, *Siglo quarto*, fo. 17v.

through the theatre, through the poetry of the night owls, through the pulpit.[52]

A generation of nobles educated at the court of the Andalusian archbishop Ribera and schooled in the classics would inevitably, like Diego de Vich, use Castilian (though since his diary only survives in edited fragments from the eighteenth century it is hard to be absolutely sure). But they might not feel themselves part of the wider *patria* of the court. Indeed, Vich's diary breathes undisguised hostility to a world of power from which he was excluded. Even the visits of Philip IV to Valencia in 1632 and 1645 failed to move him. As he records in his will, all he obtained from the latter visit was a suspension of the enquiry into the accounts of his grandfather, treasurer of the kingdom, in return for the sacrifice of two paintings by Sebastian del Piombo to the royal aesthete. In that year of revolution 1640 he had told the government he could not serve in the army in person since he was over 60 (he was actually about 55), and could not pay for a substitute since he had been ruined by the expulsion of the *moriscos*. Yet around this time he was paying Pedro Orrente and Jerónimo Jacinto Espinosa various sums to decorate the convent of Murta, his family mausoleum.[53] In the person of Diego de Vich one senses some of the best aspects of a traditional provincial culture: its cosmopolitanism allied with a strong sense of local community. Yet one will find it hard to define the political principles by which that older culture might defend itself against attacks from without.

For every Vich, whose life was bounded by the city of Valencia and the quiet Hieronymite retreat of Murta, there was a Bernardo Catalá or a Cristóbal Crespí de Valldaura (1599–1672). The latter, one of the dominant figures in Spanish political history as president of the council of Aragon and later one of the council of regency for Charles II, had started his career as spokesman for the estates of Valencia in 1626, making himself unpopular with Olivares by objecting to the Corts being held outside the kingdom. His cousin, the lord of Sumacárcer, was a ne'er-do-well, imprisoned on various charges of wounding and murder. Yet Crespí began to distance himself from that world of kinship and feud, studying law and rising to be a minister of the crown. His career recalls in some respects that of Tomás Cerdán de Tallada, who also had to choose between loyalty to his class, the knights of Valencia, and his profession. Crespí seems to have chosen early. In a letter of 1627 to his younger brother Juan, who was setting out for the army of Flanders, he enjoined him to 'shun the affections of a Micalete' (that is, a

---

[52] Joan Fuster, *Heretgies, revoltes i sermons* (Valencia, 1968), pp. 161–230.

[53] F. Almarche Vázquez, *Historiografía valenciana* (Valencia, 1919), pp. 190-251; Archivo del Reino de Valencia, Real 534, fo. 26, 11 March 1640.

faction leader), to be correct and friendly with all Valencians, but remember that 'the army has to be your *patria*'.[54] Cristóbal Crespí seems to have followed much the same prescription for his own career, taking a grim satisfaction in disappointing his compatriots who thought they had a special friend in Madrid. He came to be bitterly disliked in Valencia as an authoritarian minister who rode roughshod over native institutions and privileges. Though he was always formally respectful of the *furs*, he did go out of his way to uphold the majesty of his office, which he saw as fundamental to securing good government. The exercise of authority became in the seventeenth century a kind of political drama in its own right, as fear of losing control, or fear of confusion of private persons with public office, led the magistrate to surround himself with as many symbols of power as he could. Crespí's diary is a fascinating depiction of how armchairs, doors and antechambers can be used to make others feel uncomfortable.[55]

Though there were no revolts by the élite in seventeenth-century Valencia, there was a silent revolution under way which was preparing the country for the loss of its *furs* in 1707. In his survey of the chroniclers and diarists of the early modern period, published in 1922, Francisco Almarche Vázquez noted that the Valencian aristocracy appeared to have become servile to the court. His contemporary José Martínez Aloy charted the decline of Valencian liberties: 'We bless a thousand times the work of national unity carried out by the Catholic Monarchs', but an excessive centralization had 'gravely weakened the patriotism, vitality, economic life and way of government' of the peripheral kingdoms. Small wonder if the confusion produced by the change of dynasty led the Valencians to take up arms in 1705 against 'the Castilian preponderance', moved by the 'spirit of their country, attached to its liberties and hostile to the régime of absolutism'.[56] Almarche Vázquez and Martínez Aloy, like many others of the great Valencian historians around 1900, were influenced by what one might label a 'Carlist' historiography. Carlism had been strong in nineteenth-century Valencia, the voice of the clergy and the gentry in some of the poorer regions.[57] Like the Jacobitism of Sir Walter Scott's Waverley novels it lent itself to an idealization of a lost world of community, simple faith and personal loyalties. But, also like Scott, it had the merit of unconventionality, of standing against the facile idea of progress and questioning some of its assumptions. Against a historiography which laid emphasis on order and

---

[54] Eugenio de Ochoa, ed., *Epistolario español* (Madrid, 1856–70), II, pp. 63–5.
[55] 'Diario del señor vicecanciller Crespí', BNM, ms. 5742.
[56] *La diputación de la generalidad del reino de Valencia* (Valencia, 1930), pp. 255, 373–5.
[57] Evarist Olcina, *Carlisme i autonomia al país valencià* (Valencia, 1976).

rationalization, it stressed liberty, even if that word was written in the plural and sounded suspiciously like privileges.

Ultimately the Valencians of the Old Regime had defined themselves as a people in terms of the *furs*, those laws of the forefathers which seemed to embody the spirit of the local *patria*. For Escolano, 'the three estates ... propose and agree upon those laws and privileges which they judge benefi-cial to the commonwealth, and the king ratifies them by his decree'; and it was an impressive sight for Bernardo Catalá to see Philip III kneel at the high altar of Valencia cathedral in 1604 and, with both hands placed upon a crucifix, swear to uphold the decisions of the parliament of that year.[58] Yet, in retrospect, this would seem like the swansong of the old commonwealth. The beautiful fourteenth-century manuscript copy of the *furs* was printed in 1482 and an up-to-date version published in 1547, but that was the last. The Corts of 1564, 1604 and 1626 asked that revised editions should be produced, but, though a couple of useful summaries were composed, notably that by judge Tarazona in 1580, nothing substantial was achieved. Indeed, whereas the proceedings of individual Corts were traditionally printed within a couple of years, those of 1626 were delayed for nine years, and those of 1645 never saw the light of day.[59] Looking at the latter one can see why: they are an indigestible mass of particular and sometimes mutually contradictory petitions, which suggest that the old commonwealth of three estates was breaking down into its constituent parts of individual communi-ties. Whereas the proceedings of the Corts of Charles V and Philip II were a fairly manageable number of joint petitions from the three estates, in the seventeenth century the volume of petitions grew enormously. Instead of joint agreements by the three estates resulting in *furs* one had now more *actes de cort*, particular petitions of one or two estates. A classic example occurred in the Corts of 1626 on the vexed question of the debts of the nobility, with the clergy and the towns trying to secure a limitation of the alimony which the courts could assign to a bankrupt. An outraged noble estate protested that the others had invited the king to impose this solution on them 'by the plenitude of his power', without considering the damage which this would do to the kingdom's liberties.[60]

In the end, the king prudently referred the matter to the courts. No Habsburg sought a direct confrontation with Valencian liberties. The Corts

[58] *Autobiografía*, pp. 120–1; Escolano, *Década Primera*, v, p. 1077.
[59] E. Belenguer Cebrià, ed., *Cortes del reinado de Fernando el Católico* (Valencia, 1972), pp. vii–viii.
[60] Archivo del Reino de Valencia, Real 533, fo. 286 – apparently referring to *acte* 23 of Braços Eclesiástic and Real of 1626.

of 1626 and 1645, however, were hamstrung for a period over the question of whether the king was obliged to accept the petitions if he accepted the subsidy voted by the estates. The printed editions of the *furs* include even unsuccessful petitions, like the one from the clergy and towns on the debts of the nobility. One senses that their inclusion was a reflection of some uncertainty about the nature of law. Petitions were mostly couched in the form of references to good old custom. The clergy, towns and nobility took comfort in stating what they believed that custom to be, the polite formula by which the king turned down the petition was normally 'Let custom be maintained' – which left the door open for continued pressure on the king's ministers to conform to the estates' view of tradition. The trump cards were held by the ministers and judges who seem to have been transacting ever more business in the seventeenth century. One petition of the Corts of 1645 suggested that there ought to be a collected edition of the pragmatics or administrative orders issuing from the royal government.[61]

We need more study of the people behind this process, of the Valencian ministers, their social background and cultural formation. Those we have looked at briefly above, Crespí and Cerdán de Tallada, seem to have had a basic commitment to good order, to what Cerdán once called the 'spirit of the law', which had to be interpreted sometimes against the letter, especially if this was defended by powerful, privileged interests. Both Cerdán and Crespí came from one such privileged group, the local nobility. Both were sincerely attached to the Valencian *res publica*, but ultimately, perhaps, the institutions of the latter, marked out by the letter of *furs*, would have to be sacrificed to the overriding interest of the *estado real*, the new state. Could that state claim the affections of the Valencians? The complex ties of religion, human geography and tradition which made Valencia in the first place were not so easy to rearrange.

[61] Luis Guia Marín, ed., *Cortes del reinado de Felipe IV* (Valencia, 1984), p. 307.

8

The mental world of Jeroni Pujades

JAMES S. AMELANG

Jeroni Pujades was born in Barcelona in 1568. His father, Miquel Pujades, was a well-known lawyer and chronicler from Figueres, a town in the Empordà, a district in northern Catalonia bordering on France. Jeroni studied in Barcelona, and then in 1585 enrolled in the nearby university of Lleida, whence he emerged as a doctor in civil and canon law six years later. Upon returning to Barcelona he taught canon law in the municipal university, and soon married the daughter of a judge in the *Audiència*, or royal court of appeals. In 1604 the duchess of Cardona appointed him to the post of *Assessor del Comtat d'Empùries*, the chief legal officer for the seigneurial jurisdiction of the leading aristocratic family in the principality. His new job obliged him to leave Barcelona to take up his duties in the town of Castelló d'Empùries. He resigned in 1609, however, and returned to his native city.[1]

The next two decades found him immersed in the legal and political life of Barcelona: he served actively on the *Consell de Cent*, or city council, and held various minor posts in the municipal administration.[2] In 1621 he

Translations are by the author unless otherwise attributed.

[1] Biographical information on Pujades can be found in: F. Torres Amat, *Memorias para ayudar a formar un diccionario critico de los escritores catalanes* (Barcelona, 1836), pp. 509–15; Josep Maria Casas Homs' introduction to his edition of Pujades' diary, cited in note 4 below; and M. Pujol i Canelles, 'Aportació a la biografia de Jeroni Pujades. Una biblioteca particular del començament del S. XVII', *Annals de l'institut d'estudis empordanesos*, 18 (1985), 99–247, a thorough study of Pujades' private library as reported in his post mortem inventory.

[2] The contemporary (ca. 1608) political satire known as 'The Journey to Hell of the Peasant Pere Porter' mentions him (ironically?) as an *Advocat de Pobres*, charged with providing the

weighed into the controversy surrounding the legality of the viceroy's powers following the death of Philip III by publishing a brief favouring the royal cause. In the same year, however, he returned to Castelló. Both the profligate behaviour of his eldest son, and his failure to obtain compensation (such as a judgeship in the *Audiència*) for his efforts on behalf of the crown, had taken a heavy toll on the family economy. He died there in 1635. In his own words, he had lived a life 'neither in the grips of poverty (God be praised) nor very wealthy'.

His contemporaries knew Pujades above all for his writing. The official chronicler of the principality, he assembled a lengthy history of Catalonia from 213 BC to AD 1162, the first part of which was published in 1610.[3] The fruit of extensive documentary research in government and religious archives, it received official sanction through a hefty subsidy from Barcelona's city government. He also intervened in a variety of public literary competitions, such as the 'poetic tourneys' held during important civic celebrations like the canonization of St Raymond Penyafort (1601) and St Teresa of Avila (1622).

Jeroni Pujades was many things to many people: scholar, citizen, barrister, poet (of sorts), holder and seeker of minor office. He was deeply, even passionately, involved in the social and political life of early modern Catalonia, and it is hard to single out one of his roles over the others. He won greatest distinction in his time as a chronicler, but he is now best remembered for the diary he wrote from 1600 to 1630. A fascinating and obsessively detailed amalgam of family news, information about a wide variety of contemporary events, and uninhibited personal comment on the corruption and decline of morals of his times, his text is now recognized as the most important first-person source for the history of Catalonia during the crucial

---

poor with legal services; I have not been able to verify this appointment. See *Viatges a l'altre món*, ed. A. Pacheco (Barcelona, 1973), p. 67. It is not entirely clear whether Pujades was supposed to be in hell when the anonymous author referred to him.

[3] This work has a complicated history. Only a portion of it (to AD 714) was published in Pujades' lifetime, as the *Coronica universal del principat de Catalunya* [1609] (Barcelona, 1610). Pujades wrote the first volume in Catalan, but used Castilian for the other two parts. The original manuscripts were carried to France around 1650 by the scholar and diplomat Pierre de Marca, who incorporated in his own works (without attribution) many of the documents Pujades had collected. After circulating among different owners, the papers wound up in the Bibliothèque Royale in Paris, while copies made from the originals could be found in Barcelona beginning in the early eighteenth century (see, for example, Arxiu de la Corona d'Aragò, mss. Moderns 164). An abbreviated and poorly translated Castilian version was published in the *Diario de Barcelona* in 1777; the only complete edition is the *Crónica universal del principado de Cataluña*, ed. F. Torres Amat *et al.* (8 vols., Barcelona, 1829–32).

Jeroni Pujades

years of growing tension leading up to the war of the *Segadors*, which saw
Catalonia's secession from the Hispanic monarchy from 1640 to 1652.[4]

Pujades has usually attracted attention for his privileged observation of,
and rich commentary on, early modern Catalan politics and society. The
present essay examines him in a different light, within a cultural context,
and uses his diary to explore diverse aspects of the 'mental world' he
inhabited.[5] Not the least intriguing of the characteristics of this world was
an unusual abundance of autobiographical writings. I will try to suggest
reasons for this curious fact by situating his work within the larger corpus of
early modern Catalan first-person texts. I will also try to show that consideration of the different motives underlying the authorship of autobiography provides important clues to broader patterns of social and cultural experience, as well as to the more personal hopes and expectations of
an eloquent if bitterly disillusioned witness to a period of rapid change.

Strictly speaking, Pujades' text was not an autobiography. Instead, it was a
daybook in which he entered in strict chronological order notations of
varying length concerning a broad range of subjects. From a formal point of
view, his *dietari* mixed together several literary genres: diary, memorandum, chronicle and family register. Few aspects of contemporary life
escaped Pujades' attention, or his (usually disapproving) comment.
Violence was one favoured topic. Crimes of passion, vengeance and even
random brutality, along with factional conflicts, banditry and other, more
deliberately political, violence: all benefited from the impunity corrupt or
lazy judges accorded their perpetrators. The law itself – not his own practice
of it, but the endless disputes among rival authorities that found public
expression in constitutional claims and endless rounds of litigation – also
played a large role in his manuscripts. On a less sombre note, religion
appeared in many of his pages, especially colourful displays of devotion like
the processions in which all Barcelona turned out to honour the canoni-

[4] John Elliott was the first historian to draw attention to this text; he referred to it repeatedly in
The revolt of the Catalans: a study in the decline of Spain, 1598–1640 (Cambridge, 1963). See
p. 591 for a detailed description of the diary, and of how his discovery of a missing fragment
permitted him to reconstruct the chronological sequence of the dispersed manuscripts – an
episode he also mentioned in *Solemne investidura de doctor honoris causa al Profesor John
Elliott* (Barcelona, 1994), p. 28. The texts he read in manuscript have since been edited as the
Dietari de Jeroni Pujades, ed. J. M. Casas Homs (4 vols., Barcelona, 1975–76).
[5] Along the lines of John H. Elliott, 'The mental world of Hernán Cortés' (1967), now in his
Spain and its world, 1500–1700: selected essays (New Haven, 1989), pp. 27–41. For a similar
approach (and title) see D. D. Hall, 'The mental world of Samuel Sewall', in his *Worlds of
wonder, days of judgment: popular religious belief in early New England* (New York, 1989),
pp. 213–38.

zation of its native son Raymond Penyafort (1601). Pujades also noted events of significance within his family, his neighbourhood and his wide circle of friends and contacts. The reader can even follow him through the city, for he wrote down the names of those whom he saw and chatted with in the streets as he took his frequent walks.[6] Thus on 5 March 1602, for example, he noted that he heard a piece of juicy gossip directly from 'the archdeacon Duran, from the Seu d'Urgell, and canon Babau from Lleida, when I walked with them through St James' Square' (I, 179).

But what firmly held the centre stage in his tale was politics. From his reconstruction of the inner debates of the city council to the numerous libels and pasquins whose texts he copied word for word, it was politics, especially political conflict, that most interested him and roused him to his most impassioned remarks. Pujades reserved most of his copying and comments for local matters, but he also reported on a wide variety of events outside the principality. His work is an especially revealing source for news from the court in Madrid, unvaryingly interpreted as boding ill for the Catalans. His diary and others like it provide an interesting perspective from which to assess the way in which the periphery viewed the centre during these years of growing conflict, as well as the information and interpretive framework at the former's disposal.[7]

What impression does the author of this diary give of himself? First, he was, to the delight of future historians, meticulous to a fault. He loved to give exact figures, as during the Penyafort processions when, in addition to writing down the numbers from each confraternity that came to worship at the saint's tomb, he noted the 2764 maidens from the parish church of Santa María del Mar, the 2894 candles and torches used on the evening of 24 May 1601 and so on (I, 99, 121).[8] This passion for detail helps explain the text's length; the surviving portions of his diary total over 1200 folios.

Pujades also showed an acute awareness of his professional background.

---

[6] As one can with Samuel Pepys (1633–1703). See J. S. Pipkin, 'Space and the social order in Pepys' *Diary*', *Urban Geography*, 11 (1990), 153–75.

[7] A similar work is the diary of a parish priest from Valencia, Pere Joan Porcar's *Coses evengudes en la ciutat i regne de València. Dietari, 1589–1628*, ed. F. García García (abridged edition, Valencia, 1983). Needless to say, it would most interesting were someone systematically to study these and other texts to reconstruct the channels of communication of political and other news within the Hispanic monarchy, as well as the image they presented of the court and royal policy. For some useful general remarks, see H. Ettinghausen, 'The news in Spain: *Relaciones de sucesos* in the reigns of Philip III and IV', *European History Quarterly*, 14 (1984), 1–20.

[8] His obsession with record-keeping also included taking notes of sermons (e.g. II, 93), a practice apparently less frequent in Spain than in other parts of Europe. It also influenced the organization of the diary itself: significantly, starting with volume II, he cross-indexed its contents.

'I intend to talk about this like a lawyer', is a phrase he repeated in several of his works. In part, such references drew on his partaking, like others, in a broader corporate identity. Thus, toward the beginning of his diary, he approvingly recounted how Barcelona's lawyers triumphed over the honoured citizens and gentry in a dispute over their share of representation within municipal government (I, 218). Yet much of his attachment to the profession was personal. Unlike many of his contemporaries who possessed law degrees, Pujades had a thorough legal education, and did not hesitate to match his jurisprudence and erudition against the city's most prominent lawyers. It was no accident that he was frequently consulted as an antiquarian authority on issues of ceremonial precedence, and other legal and historical questions. In addition to tendering his advice on legal matters from his seat on the city council, Pujades was also retained by the municipal government as a consulting lawyer (*advocatus consulans*). Finally, thanks to his family connections, he was singularly well placed within Barcelona's legal hierarchy. He had close personal and kin ties with several judges on the *Audiència*, and one of his cousins served as legal counsel to the Franquesa/Lerma faction in Madrid.[9] All these factors help explain Pujades' pronounced self-consciousness as a participant in local politics, and his sense of being in the middle of things, even during his long periods of residence outside Barcelona in Castelló d'Empúries.

What comes across most clearly in the diary is the independent character of its author. Pujades was a man of strong opinions. For example, he thoroughly disliked and mistrusted foreigners: Italians, especially the Genoese; the English (because of their protestantism); Frenchmen; and above all Castilian officials, especially the viceroys, the instruments through which Madrid sought to reduce the principality's autonomy and privileges. He also had harsh words for his fellow Catalans, including the *diputats* or parliamentary deputies ('all thieves', III, 148), and the judges of the *Audiència* whom he knew so well. Nor did he spare vain aristocrats, dishonest merchants and hypocritical clerics. He reserved his harshest judgements for Catalans too willing to follow viceregal policies (e.g. I, 198), although in a 1622 entry he candidly admitted that had he stayed in Barcelona, he himself might have wound up the target of libels and attacks as a royalist due to his having taken a public stand favouring the recognition of the duke of Alcalá as viceroy (III, 124).[10] In short, his patriotism as a Catalan cannot be

---

[9] This was Francesch Mitjavila, who helped Pujades obtain his appointment from the Cardonas. He is frequently mentioned in the *dietari*. It is telling that even though Pujades does not devote much space to intimate family matters, he betrays constant awareness of kinship ties in his work.

[10] On this dispute, and Pujades' role in it, see Elliott, *Revolt of the Catalans*, pp. 148–81.

questioned. Nor can one doubt the depth of his xenophobia, or of the bitterness with which he judged those around him.

These latter traits are linked to a final point: Pujades' strongly voiced religious beliefs. He was a fervent catholic, describing himself as a 'good Christian and Catalan' (I, 143). The religious practices to which he seems most attached were traditional ones, like the veneration of relics and saints. Not surprisingly, his remarks on religious matters betray a militant and highly defensive awareness of being engaged in an endless battle against heresy. After Spain signed a peace in 1604 with the newly crowned James I (head of the 'evil sect' of protestants), Pujades railed against the government's allowing the English ambassador to bring protestant preachers with him into Spain: 'damn these reasons of state which are only cannon shots against the law of God' (I, 392). Further along he intoned 'All glory to the Lord who propagates and multiplies the Catholic faith and Holy Roman Church despite Englishmen, Germans and other barbarians who, blinded by their malice, refuse obedience to the apostolic Catholic Roman see' (II, 137) – an attitude which explains his (rare) expression of delight when he heard of a massacre of Huguenots in southern France in 1621 (III, 59). It is perhaps this, the dark side of Pujades for the modern reader, that best testifies to his role as spokesman for his times and for a mental world most would regard as better left behind.

Pujades' diary is unusual in terms of its length, its level of detail, and above all, its outspokenness, especially in regard to contemporary political issues. In other respects, however, his daybook represents merely one link in a long chain of autobiographical writing.

A word should be said about what is meant here by 'autobiography'. Few early modern texts were autobiographical in the modern sense of a retrospective, chronologically ordered account focusing on the inner personal life of the author. Despite some obvious exceptions (for example, spiritual autobiographies), early modern writing in the first person favoured the narration of activities and attitudes in the outer world. It relegated its more introspective moments to the margins of the text, through asides and brief, parenthetical comments, or to specific passages inserted within other, more impersonal works.[11] In this, the 'unautobiographical' character of his auto-

---

[11] As in the case of the master tanner Miquel Parets (1610–1661), who inserted a lengthy personal account of his sufferings during the plague of 1651 into a third-person chronicle of political and military events in Catalonia; see *A journal of the plague year: the diary of the Barcelona tanner Miquel Parets, 1651*, ed. and trans. J. S. Amelang (New York, 1991). For recent literary studies that focus on the relatively impersonal quality of early modern

biography, the Catalan barrister was no exception; Pujades was certainly no Pepys.

The literary context of this Barcelona diary – the corpus of what one could more accurately call 'personal documents'[12] – was both rich and complex. The authorship of first-person texts was a cultural practice with deep roots in medieval and early modern Catalan society. Persons from many walks of life took pen in hand to leave individual records of their existence in the form of diaries, memoirs and family chronicles.[13] Two features of this corpus are particularly striking. First, while most autobiographical writing originated in urban areas, where higher rates of literacy prevailed and the written word circulated with ease, a surprising number of personal documents hailed from the countryside as well, especially family chronicles from *masies*, or well established homesteads. Even more remarkable was the impressive representation of writers of humble origins – master craftsmen, peasants, even the occasional journeyman – among the ranks of autobiographers. First-person writing was resorted to on all sides of social boundaries, thus giving rise to a large and varied body of literary expression.

Who were these autobiographical authors? In the present state of knowledge, it would be impossible to provide a register of early modern Catalan personal documents, along the lines of, say, the thorough checklists available for contemporary Dutch autobiographical texts.[14] A recent survey has located over seventy such texts for Catalonia, and undoubtedly many more could be found.[15] Sixteenth- and seventeenth-century authors of *diotaris* similar to Pujades' included aristocrats and patricians like Perot Vilanova

autobiographical writing, see M. Levisi, 'Golden Age autobiography: the soldiers', *Hispanic Issues*, 2 (1988), 97–118, and A. N. Mancini, 'Writing the self: forms of autobiography in the late Italian Renaissance', *Canadian Journal of Italian Studies*, 14 (1992), 11–24. Also of interest is F. A. Nussbaum, 'Toward conceptualizing diary', in *Studies in autobiography*, ed. J. Olney (New York, 1988), pp. 128–40.

[12] While the term 'personal documents' is borrowed from the social sciences, my approach draws heavily upon the flexible definition of early modern autobiography informing recent work by Dutch and German scholars. See in particular R. M. Dekker, 'Ego-documents in the Netherlands', *Dutch crossing: a journal of Low Countries studies*, 39 (1989), 61–72, and *Ego-Dokumente*, ed. W. Schulze (Frankfurt, 1995).

[13] Overviews in Elliott, *Revolt of the Catalans*, pp. 590–2, and A. Simon i Tarrés, 'Memorias y diarios personales de la Cataluña moderna', *Historia social*, 2 (1988), 119–34.

[14] *Egodocumenten van Noord-Nederlanders uit de zestiende tot begin negentiende eeuw. Een chronologische lijst*, ed. R. Lindeman, Y. Scherf and R. Dekker (Rotterdam, 1993). I am grateful to Professor Dekker for providing me a copy of this valuable reference work.

[15] The most detailed inventory thus far can be found in M. Peña Diaz and A. Simon i Tarrés, 'La escritura privada en la Cataluña moderna', unpublished paper presented to the conference History under Debate, Santiago de Compostela, July 1993, which lists seventy-eight works for the sixteenth to eighteenth centuries.

(covering the years 1555–73), Jeroni Saconomines (1576–1603), Federic Despalau (1585–1600), Jeroni del Real (1637–83), Josep de Sullà (1640–49), Miquel Onofre Montfar i Sorts (1651–52) and his nephew Josep (1683–87); the judge Agustí Sala (1555–84) and a lawyer, Joan Baptista Sanç (1634–41); a physician, Onofre Monsalvo (1680–83) and the surgeon Jeroni Cros (1597–1639); the merchant Francesc Joan Ferrer (1640–41); clerics like Francesc Puig (1640–41), Sadurní Curb (1660– ca. 1675) and Jaume Avellà (1674–1711); notaries, including Francesch Vila (1591–1618), Pere Pasqual (1595–1644) and Joan Castanyer (1609–13); and the farmers Joan and Antoni Joan Guàrdia (1631–87), Bernat Roca (1654), Francesch Gelat (1687–1722) and Joan and Salvador Perai (1688–1709).[16] As this cursory list shows, authors of early modern Catalan personal documents can be found throughout the years in which Pujades wrote his diary. They hailed, moreover, from a broad range of social backgrounds – although, significantly, virtually all of them were male.[17] Finally, their ranks could be expanded considerably if one adds the references to personal, family and local events found in account books, chronicles and other documents from the period.

The abundance of autobiographical and semi-autobiographical texts in Catalonia found echo elsewhere outside the principality: Valencia and the Balearic Islands, especially Mallorca, also contributed to the production of personal documents.[18] On the whole, the writing of diaries and memoirs flourished more in the eastern part of the Iberian peninsula. There were, to be sure, exceptions to this rule, especially where spiritual autobiographies were concerned.[19] Still, first-person authorship was clearly more prevalent

[16] Many of these texts are available in published form, in a series of editions by Antoni Simon i Tarrés and Antoni Pladevall i Font. See *Guerra i vida pagesa a la Catalunya del segle XVII* (Barcelona, 1986); *Cavallers i ciutadans a la Catalunya del cinc-Cents* (Barcelona, 1991); and *Pagesos, capellans i industrials de la Marina de la Selva* (Barcelona, 1993).

[17] Several early modern Catalan women wrote spiritual autobiographies and diaries. See my 'Los usos de la autobiografía. Monjas y beatas en la Cataluña moderna', in *Historia y género. Las mujeres en la Europa moderna y contemporánea*, ed. J. S. Amelang and M. Nash (Valencia, 1990), pp. 191–212.

[18] Thorough bibliographic and archival checklists can be found in F. Almarche Vázquez, *Historiografía valenciana. Catálogo bibliográfico de dietarios, libros de memoria, diarios, relaciones, autobiografías, etc., inéditas, y referentes a la historia del antiguo reino de Valencia* (Valencia, 1919), and C. Simó, *Catàleg dels noticiaris mallorquins, 1372–1810* (Palma de Mallorca, 1990).

[19] See in particular Isabelle Poutrin's 'Les contemplatives et les pouvoirs religieux: autobiographies des mystiques. Sources inquisitoriales et hagiographiques, Espagne, 16e-18e S.,' PhD thesis, Université de Paris-X (Nanterre), 1991, in two volumes. I am indebted to the author and to Professor Bernard Vincent for allowing me to consult this work prior to its publication.

in the crown of Aragon, especially its maritime kingdoms. The abundance of personal documents in the Levant suggests some clues to what the writing of diaries meant to Pujades and to many of his contemporaries.

It may be easier to follow these clues by first pursuing the question of the geographical distribution of diaries and other first-person texts beyond the borders of Spain. By the seventeenth century autobiographical writing could be found in most parts of western Europe; nevertheless, it was not evenly distributed. Instead, it flourished more in certain cultural contexts than in others. England (and, by extension, New England) was clearly one of these areas. By the end of the seventeenth century, Germany (thanks largely to the Pietist impulse) was another, as was the Netherlands, whose rich tradition of personal documentation also drew upon, and to some extent antedated, similar protestant sources.

Autobiography prospered in parts of southern Europe as well. Its prominence during the late medieval and early modern periods was assured not only in the Mediterranean part of Spain, as mentioned above, but also in northern Italy and southern France. The broad geographical distribution of autobiographical foci notwithstanding, northern and southern Europe seem to have taken different paths toward the development of modern auto-biography. The prevalent form of self-writing in the three Mediterranean regions appears to have been family chronicles and memoirs. Late medieval Florence was the cradle of this sort of personal document, and *libri di famiglia* apparently spread from there to the Midi and the other maritime areas of the western Mediterranean.[20]

The roots of autobiography in northern Europe were somewhat different. There religious motives appear to have taken the lead in spurring the authorship of first-person texts. As a result, in the northern countries spiritual autobiography and other, more introspective approaches to the self prevailed among both laymen and clergy. Of course, many exceptions existed to this rule. Few northern European texts of the sixteenth century could match the powers of introspection of a Cardano, and it would be misleading to try to limit spiritual autobiographical writing to colder

---

[20] See in particular C. Bec, *Les marchands écrivains. Affaires et humanisme à Florence, 1375–1430* (Paris and The Hague, 1967); G.-M. Anselmi *et al.*, *La 'Memoria' dei mercatores: tendenze ideologiche, ricordanze, artigianato in versi nella Firenze del quattrocento* (Bologna, 1980); and A. Cicchetti and R. Mordenti, 'La scrittura dei libri di famiglia', in *Letteratura italiana. II. La prosa; III: Le forme del testo*, ed. A. Asor Rosa (Turin, 1984), pp. 1117–59, as well as their checklist *I Libri di famiglia in Italia* (Rome, 1985). Also useful is the anthology of *ricordanze* Vittore Branca edited under the title *Mercanti-scrittori. Ricordi nella Firenze tra medioevo e rinascimento* (Milan, 1986).

climes.[21] It obviously would be a mistake to devise a sort of Weber thesis of the evolution of autobiography, opposing the introspective north to the extrovert south. Nevertheless, clear differences – in genre preference, subject matter and patterns of circulation – separated what were, in at least some respects, distinct autobiographical cultures. In the specific case of spiritual autobiography, for example, important variants could be found among different religious cultures. Thus catholic spiritual autobiographies tended to be more exclusively mystical and more closely identified with female authorship than was the case in protestant countries like England, where masculine and non-mystical spiritual itineraries prevailed.[22]

To inquire after the causes of these differences would draw this essay too far from its concern with a single individual and the broader social and cultural spheres in which he participated. Yet it clearly would be fruitful to consider the diverse impulses behind autobiographical writing within Pujades' more immediate context. Sixteenth- and seventeenth-century Spanish autobiography found inspiration in many sources, including personal accounts of religious experience (missionary as well as mystical), the example of New World chronicles, and innovative forms of autobiographical fiction like the picaresque novel. None of these, however, appears to have directly influenced first-person records of daily life such as Pujades' diary. Instead, *dietaris* took root in social and cultural practices dating back several centuries.

The foremost among these, in terms of the number and antiquity of the texts to which it gave rise, was the keeping of accounts. Maritime cities like Barcelona had a long and distinguished tradition of commercial documentation.[23] Its adepts were not limited to merchant and administrative

---

21 See W. A. Christian Jr., 'Provoked religious weeping in early modern Spain', in *Religious organization and religious experience*, ed. J. Davis (London, 1982), pp. 97–114, for interesting remarks on habits of religious introspection and self-analysis in sixteenth-century Spain.

22 I know of no comparative survey of autobiography in early modern Europe, nor of any which attempts to contrast catholic with protestant forms of self-writing. An obvious starting point would be to study differences in autobiographical writing among different denominations within a plural religious culture. See, for example, J. Webber, *The eloquent 'I': style and self in seventeenth-century prose* (Madison, 1968), for remarks on the differences between Anglican and Puritan texts. Similarities and contrasts between Puritan and Quaker autobiographies are examined in G. A. Starr, *Defoe and spiritual autobiography* (Princeton, 1965); D. B. Shea Jr., *Spiritual autobiography in early America* (Princeton, 1968); O. C. Watkins, *The puritan experience: studies in spiritual autobiography* (New York, 1972); and K. von Greyerz, *Vorschungsglaube und Kosmologie. Studien zu englischen Selbstzeugnissen des 17. Jahrhunderts* (Göttingen and Zurich, 1990).

23 See, for example, A.-E. Sayous, *Els mètodes comercials a la Barcelona medieval*, ed. and trans. A. Garcia i Sanz and G. Feliu i Montfort (Barcelona, 1975).

élites. On the contrary, accounting was a habit widely distributed in late medieval and early modern urban society, especially in the Mediterranean. A recent preliminary survey of 3420 post mortem inventories registered in Barcelona from 1473 to 1600 found that 18 per cent of the men and 12 per cent of the women in the sample left private papers (above all, deeds and account books) among their belongings.[24] Clearly, diaries like Pujades' had their distant origins in this broadly diffused textual tradition.

Yet a significant distance, in terms of both form and content, separated *dietaris* from account books. In between them stood another genre, the family chronicle. *Libri di famiglia, livres de famille, llibres de memòria*: these are all names for a distinctive form of record keeping that began in northern Italy in the later Middle Ages. The family chronicle represented a transition from commercial to personal accounting, from the keeping of strictly business records to a broader effort to record information and more intimate reflections touching on non-business matters. This genre flourished in Tuscan cities in particular; although examples can be found from throughout Italy, there can be no question of Florence's pioneering role in the consolidation of this genre.[25] Tuscan merchants and patricians began to leave behind *libri di ricordanze* beginning in the thirteenth century. A broad range of social needs stood behind these intriguing documents. The obligation to render accounts for the administration of the family patrimony, and the need to keep track of the extensive web of credit and other micro-political relations in which most city dwellers participated, were but two of the motives underlying this intermediate stage in writing in the first person, both singular and plural.

A third autobiographical genre contributed to the development of the early modern *dietari*: the urban chronicle. While by the seventeenth century many cities (including Barcelona) could boast a proud tradition of anti-quarian research, it was above all the records of contemporary events within the urban context that constituted the closest parallel to diaries like Pujades'. Their circumscribed, local focus legitimated, even encouraged, intervention by the 'eyewitness' author. Unlike their royal and dynastic counterparts from the Middle Ages, the city chroniclers' sense of proximity provided substantial scope for personal expression. They thus brought the genre closer to a daybook of events that writers saw or overheard, or in which they directly participated.

---

[24] Peña Díaz and Simon i Tarrés, 'Escritura privada', p. 8.
[25] For some reasons why Florence took the lead in developing this genre, see J. Grubb, 'Memorie famigliari del Veneto', unpublished paper, November 1993. I am grateful to Dr Grubb for sharing the results of his extensive research with me.

Not surprisingly, many early modern diaries mixed the three genres of account book, family record and urban chronicle. Pujades' certainly did. In it he registered side by side real estate transactions, births and deaths and insider comment on local matters. He even sewed political pamphlets and legal briefs into its folds.[26] His motives in so doing, one may surmise, were equally mixed.

One aspect of the mental world of Pujades was the broader social and cultural practices he participated in with others. Shifting to his case in particular reveals the linkages between the purposes of an individual author and those permeating the wider context in which he lived and wrote.

Pujades specifically discussed his motives on the opening page of his diary:

In Psalm 77 the royal prophet David tells us that our children yet to be born and to come into the world will narrate and tell their own children what the Lord (that is, almighty God) had done with their fathers. And since our nature is mortal, as experience shows us, faith tells us, and St. Paul writes (1 Cor. 16, Heb. 9), and since we cannot live forever [*perpetuar-nos*] in order to tell and make known to our children and posterity what happened in our times, for all these reasons it is good to write and leave a record of what is now happening, so that by means of writing it will be known in the future. This is what moved Mr. Miquel Pujades, my father and lord, to write a diary of what happened in his time, which I continued until the hundredth year, which is the present year 1601. In this, since it is the beginning of a new century, and because the other [diary] was written partly in folio and partly in a [smaller] notebook, I wanted to start a new book ... [1, 67].

While many early modern diaries begin by mentioning the reasons that induced their authors to write, this is a singularly rich and complex statement of literary intention. Most striking is its emphasis on continuity among generations, product of the emulation of fathers by sons. In strongly Biblical terms, Pujades portrayed memory – more precisely, what will be known or remembered in the future – as the consequence of the filial act of recording. His particular case replicated the more general pattern, in that keeping a diary was a practice he inherited directly from his father.[27] At the

---

[26] As did other early modern diarists, like his near contemporary (and fellow barrister) Pierre de l'Étoile; see *The Paris of Henry of Navarre as seen by Pierre de l'Estoile: selections from his mémoires-journaux*, trans. and ed. N. Lyman Roelker (Cambridge, Mass., 1958). It is nevertheless worth remembering that Pujades referred in his diary to the existence of separate account books (e.g. II, 71), which suggests that he distinguished documentary genres by their functions, despite a certain amount of overlap in the contents of his different personal records. The latter is hardly surprising, especially given his overriding penchant for exactitude and detailed counting, as noted above.

[27] The elder Pujades' diaries have not been found, nor (to my knowledge) has anyone located his unpublished treatise in Catalan defending the rights and prerogatives of the kings of Aragon against France (mentioned in Torres Amat, *Diccionario*, p. 515)

same time, by inaugurating a new manuscript at the start of a new century, he formally committed his father's record to the past as he began one of his own. Literally turning over a new leaf, he claimed his own place within the chain of memory of his family and society at large.

This broader context is evoked by another characteristic of this work: the fact that Pujades wrote it at the same time he was working on his monumental chronicle of Catalonia. The link between the two works is significant. Pujades saw himself as a writer of history, not only of the remote past which served as a foundation for the present, but also of the present, soon to become the past of his descendants. His *dietari* was thus a sourcebook of contemporary events and of future history. The frank character of his political comments suggests that in its present form, its audience would most likely be restricted to more immediate family and friends. But that its main goal was to serve history in its different circles of reception can hardly be doubted.[28]

This impression is reinforced when one considers the prefatory remarks to the first volume of his chronicle, published in 1610. Two features of the introductory material stand out. First, its defensive tone, especially in his lengthy reply to an uncle who had criticized his writing history as an improper activity (whether for lawyers in general or Pujades in particular is unclear).[29] The second is the reference on the opening page to the failure of the Hebrew people to write its own history, despite the abundance of learned persons who could have undertaken this task. He referred in passing to Isaiah 41, which turns out on closer inspection to be a most intriguing verse:

Set forth your case, says the Lord; bring your proofs, says the King of Jacob. Let them bring them, and tell us what is to happen. Tell us the former things, what they are, that we may consider them, that we may know their outcome; or declare to us the things to come.

Here, in a familiar prophetic mode (this is hardly the last time Catalans would identify themselves with the people of Israel), the past appeared again as the key to the future, this time enshrouded in a language of case and proofs highly congenial to a legal temperament.

That scholars beginning in the seventeenth century would refer to Pujades' chronicle as a potpourri of primary documents lacking in developed historical analysis merely highlights the resemblances between the

---

[28] Hence one contemporary's assessment of the diaries as notebooks Pujades kept to help him write the history of his own times (reported in Torres Amat, *Diccionario*, p. 514).

[29] *Crónica*, pp. xviii–xxii. In the same preface he defends himself against the charge of 'idle tongues' that the chronicle is not his work, but his father's.

lawyer's two major literary endeavours. He wrote history as he wrote his diary: by rummaging and collecting texts, cutting and pasting them into a haphazard, uncritical miscellany. Yet there is no mistaking his deeper seriousness of purpose. The providential rhetoric, the repeated evocations of the prophets of Israel, perhaps even the ill-humour and bitterness of his frequent asides (qualities not unknown to prophets): all point to a vision of writing as eminently political and religious. For Pujades and many of his fellow diarists, authorship in the first person was not the act of affirmation of individualism and inner selfhood that standard teleologies of autobiography portray it to be. Authors affirmed their personal identity, to be sure, but as members of collectivities – familial, political, spiritual and professional – that endowed them with well defined (if at times conflicting) roles, rights and expectations. Writing a diary was not a withdrawal into a detached, self-consciously private world of the self. Instead, it was in many respects a way of participating in a larger *res publicae*, an extension of politics and piety by other means.

This is a large part of the explanation of the 'unautobiographical' nature of early modern autobiography, of the focus not on a deliberately isolated, Rousseau-like self, but the self in society. Pujades and his peers took the notion of participation and the rights and duties of citizens quite seriously. It is significant that the only speech of his own to the city council that he recorded in detail is one in which he outspokenly defended the traditional right of citizens from all estates to participate in municipal government. In so doing, he reported, he won the enmity of the honoured citizens and gentlemen, who threatened to refuse to sit in committees alongside citizens of inferior rank. Pujades' eloquence carried the day, however, and 'The people [*poble*] were very pleased with me' (I, 79).

This view of the diarist as citizen suggests important links between Pujades and the broader culture, or 'mental world', which he inhabited alongside many others. It also helps explain why early modern Catalonia, like Florence in earlier centuries, and like contemporary England and Holland, distinguished itself as a centre of autobiographical authorship. In part, as has been remarked, this practice was rooted in the commercial practices of maritime centres throughout the western Mediterranean area. That self-writing also extended to the countryside had more local roots, especially in the single-heir system of inheritance that contributed so directly to the strength of the principality's yeoman farmers (*masovers*) who made up the vast majority of rural authors of diaries.

Equally specific in character was the broad social distribution of the literary tradition of autobiographical writing in Catalonia. That craftsmen there should join notaries, liberal professionals and members of clerical and lay élites as authors of diaries, chronicles, family books and other personal documents owed much to local traditions of strong corporate organization and artisan representation in municipal government at a variety of levels. The political cultures of Catalonia, England, Holland and other foci of autobiographical writing rested to a large extent on broad notions of citizenship and the existence of certain widely extended rights, especially regarding participation in local decision making.[30] As the case of Pujades and many of his fellow first-person authors bears out, diaries often proved more a companion than a substitute for direct involvement in public life. For them, authorship was, among other things, an act of citizenship.[31]

Memory, history, duty, rights, citizenship – these are some of the clues which help explain the mental world of Jeroni Pujades, and the diverse ways his text conserved and configured not only personal and family events, but also a broader social and political record of past, present and future. His text is best understood not as a singular or isolated act of authorship; instead, it should be viewed as part of a widely diffused cultural practice linked to local traditions of citizenship and of framing what one might anachronistically label 'private' acts and interpretations in 'public' terms. The prevalence of such documents in early modern Catalonia also points to one of the key differences between Spain's centre and its Mediterranean periphery. In the latter area, notions of participatory government and a broadly focused 'citizen' discourse and collective memory were deeply rooted local traditions. They gave rise to a broadly based constitutionalism which formed a crucial part of the mental world Pujades shared with other Barcelonans.

---

[30] For England, Christopher Hill in particular has highlighted the broad social base underlying seventeenth-century political debate: see, for example, 'The Norman yoke', in his *Puritanism and revolution* (London, 1958), pp. 50–122. Similar emphasis can be found in B. Manning, *The English people and the English Revolution* (Harmondsworth, 1978), especially pp. 254–83, and D. Underdown, *Revel, riot and rebellion: popular politics and culture in England, 1603–1660* (Oxford, 1987). Two recent studies stressing extensive popular involvement in early modern English local administration are C. B. Herrup, *The common peace: participation and the criminal law in seventeenth-century England* (Cambridge, 1987), and V. Pearl, 'Change and stability in seventeenth-century London,' reprinted in J. Barry, ed., *The Tudor and Stuart town: a reader in English urban history, 1530–1688* (London, 1990), pp. 139–65. For Catalonia, see J. S. Amelang, *Honored citizens of Barcelona: patrician culture and class relations, 1490–1714* (Princeton, 1986), pp. 219–221, and E. Tello, *Visca el rei i les calces d'estopa! Realistes i botiflers a la Cervera set-centista* (Barcelona, 1990).

[31] I develop this argument further in my forthcoming study of artisan autobiographical writing in early modern Europe, which centres on a similar document, the *dietari* of Miquel Parets (see note 9 above).

Two years after Pujades began his diary, Ben Jonson introduced in his tragedy *Sejanus*[32] a 'writing fellow' who bears a remarkable resemblance to his Catalan contemporary. His name was Cremutius Cordus, and he passed the day gathering

notes of the precedent times and [making] them into annals; a most tart and bitter spirit, I hear, who under colour of praising those, doth tax the present state, censures the men, the actions, leaves no trick, no practice unexamined, parallels the times, the governments; a profest champion for the old liberty.

Significantly, in the next act Cremutius was arrested for publishing his annals, and was charged with the crime of 'comparing men and times'. No such misfortune befell Pujades. Then again, he never published his diary.

---

[32] *Sejanus*, II.2. For the circumstances surrounding the writing and performance of this play (the last one in which Shakespeare is documented as acting on stage), see D. Riggs, *Ben Jonson: a life* (Cambridge, Mass., 1989), pp. 99–105, and P. Thomson, *Shakespeare's professional career* (Cambridge, 1992), pp. 168–72. I first came across this passage in B. Stirling, *The populace in Shakespeare* (New York, 1949), p. 162.

9

Centring the periphery: the Cerdanya between France and Spain

PETER SAHLINS

In the early 1830s, the intrepid English traveller Richard Ford, wandering in the central Pyrenees between France and Spain, was struck by the animosity Spanish peasants expressed toward the French:

The [Spaniards'] hatred of the Frenchman ... seems to increase in intensity in proportion to vicinity, for as they touch, so they fret and rub each other: here is the antipathy of the antithesis; the incompatibility of the saturnine against the vain, the fickle, and the sensual; of the enemy of innovation and change, and the lover of variety and novelty; and however tyrants and tricksters may assert in the gilded galleries of Versailles that *Il n'y a plus de Pyrénées*, this party-wall of Alps, this barrier of snow and hurricane, does and will exist forever.[1]

More than a transparent description of social life in the borderland, Ford's revealing observation evokes an entire corpus of mythic representations and literary tropes from both sides of the Pyrenees. Indeed, the image of the Pyrenees as a natural frontier separating France and Spain has been part of a shifting repertoire in French and Spanish political and literary cultures since the eleventh-century *Chanson de Roland*. During the first half of the seventeenth century, at the height of the dynastic competition between the Bourbon and Habsburg monarchies, apologists and pamphleteers from both political centres produced a number of texts which compared the national

Translations are by the author unless otherwise attributed.
[1] Richard Ford, *Gatherings from Spain* (London, 1846), pp. 29–30.

and natural differences of Frenchmen and Spaniards, drawing often on contemporary and ancient theories of humours.[2]

To Ford, as to his seventeenth-century predecessors, it was the mountain chain of the Pyrenees which marked such national and natural differences. The Peace of the Pyrenees itself in 1659, signalling the end of the Bourbon–Habsburg phase of the Thirty Years' War and the formal political precedence of France over a Spain in decline, historicized the 'natural frontier' of the Pyrenees. The Treaty, which gave France the County of Roussillon and part of the Cerdanya valley, had declared that 'the Pyrenees mountains, which anciently divided the Gauls from the Spaniards, shall henceforth form the division of the two kingdoms'. Although the practical reality of defining 'which were the Pyrenees' produced further tortured diplomatic debates over the next two centuries, the image that the Pyrenees ought to divide the different nations of France and Spain persisted unchanged for centuries.[3] 'Truth on this side of the Pyrenees, error on the other', mused Blaise Pascal about the 'strange justice' of natural frontiers in the seventeenth century,[4] and Richard Ford only seemed to confirm this vision from the centre.

But what of the view of the people of the periphery, of the peasants, townsmen and nobles living in the borderland of Spain and France? Ford's description in the nineteenth century reveals more about the enduring stereotypes of national character than about the people of the borderland. Yet Ford none the less noted a significant feature of life on the frontier – the importance of perceived differences among rural and urban dwellers in proximity to each other. The history of the Franco-Spanish boundary and borderland is a history of difference, imposed not only by the two central states, of 'France' and 'Spain', but invented as well by the peasants, rural nobles, urban townsfolk and village communities in the borderland themselves. Indeed, the dialectical interplay of centre and periphery in the

---

[2] Carlos Garcia, *La oposicion y conjunción de los dos grandes luminares de la tierra, o la antipatía de franceses y españoles* [Madrid, 1617] (reprinted, Edmonton, 1979); Guez de Balzac, *Le Prince* (Paris, 1631), chapter 9. La Mothe le Vayer, *Discours de la contrairété d'humeurs qui se trouve entre certaines nations, et singulièrement entre la française et l'espagnole* (Paris, 1636); more generally, for Spain, see A. Gutierrez, *La France et le français dans la littérature espagnole. Un aspect de xénophobie en Espagne, 1598–1665* (Saint Etienne, 1977); and T. Calvo, 'Aspects d'une conscience nationale dans l'Espagne du XVIIe siècle', in *Le Sentiment National dans l'Europe Moderne*, Bulletin no. 15, Association des Historiens Modernistes (Paris, Université de Paris Sorbonne, 1991), pp. 65–85.

[3] Peter Sahlins, *Boundaries: the making of France and Spain in the Pyrenees* (Berkeley, 1989), pp. 25–53; Peter Sahlins, 'Natural frontiers revisited: France's boundaries since the seventeenth century', *American Historical Review* 95 (1990), 1423–1451.

[4] Blaise Pascal, *Pensées*, ed. L. Brunschvig (Paris, 1937), nos. 293–294.

borderland structured the emergence of distinct state territories and national identities of France and Spain between 1659 and 1868.

These dates correspond to the history of the political boundary itself. If the Peace of the Pyrenees gave France jurisdiction over the Roussillon and part of the Cerdanya, the two states did not delimit the boundary line itself until 1868: until then, no single series of boundary stones officially sanctioned by both states demarcated their separate national territories. The Pyrenees may have been one of the earliest boundaries to be enshrined in national images of difference; but the boundary itself was among the last to be delimited by the nineteenth-century European states. And when the two centres finally undertook the political process of delimitation, their efforts were greatly impeded by the implantation and adoption of national differences in the borderland.

Thus at the moment of the definitive delimitation and demarcation of the borderline, during the Bayonne Treaties of 1868, the village of La Carol in the French Cerdanya opposed a settlement of a border dispute with the neighbouring Spanish village of Guils which would have left the contested terrain in a condition of joint use. Claiming to want 'a dividing line to separate from now to eternity two villages of foreign nations and of different mores', the petitioners underscored their national differences as Frenchmen and Spaniards.[5]

The people of the borderland thus did voice the 'antipathy' noted by Richard Ford, but they did so in specific contexts and for specific reasons. That they did so in 1868 in the Cerdanya is none the less astonishing, since the inhabitants of the district were all Catalans, sharing a single ethnic and linguistic identity, while affirming their national differences as Spaniards and Frenchmen. In truth, they were invoking the material and symbolic resources of their respective states to empower themselves in local struggles. Still, far from erasing local differences and interests, as social scientists have been wont to inform us, the adoption of national identities affirmed and even deepened the attachment to local place.

Perhaps more importantly, the people of the periphery adopted identities as French and Spanish long before either centre developed the institutions and mechanisms for the dissemination of national culture from above. While the Old Régime monarchies in France and Spain concerned themselves with defining the territorial boundaries of sovereignty, the states did little to impose 'national' language or customs on the periphery. In France,

---

[5] France: Archives du Ministère des Relations Extérieures (FAMRE) Commission de Délimitation des Pyrénées (CDP), x, fo. 298 (letter to Callier, 20 June 1867).

it was not until long after the 1789 Revolution that nation building – gallicization – began in earnest.[6] In Spain, attempts to castilianize local Catalan society were even more limited and belated. Yet long before the central powers even considered such projects, villagers from both sides had been strategically deploying the discursive distinctions of national cultures to their own ends.

Much of the literature on the development of nations and states has told the story about the making of national boundaries and national identities in Europe as seen from the perspective of the centre, of Madrid and Paris. Few accounts reverse this lens, and consider the history, in this case, of France and Spain from the perspective of the periphery, of the borderland. The view from the periphery challenges us to rethink fundamental assumptions about territory and nationality, about state and nation. In particular, it forces us to consider how individuals and communities, as historical agents in their own right, make use of their boundaries and identities both against and in collaboration with distant political centres.

The eastern Pyrenean valley of Cerdanya, its several small towns and hundred or so villages with a mid-nineteenth century maximum population of nearly 22,000 inhabitants, presents itself as a remarkable laboratory in which to explore the intersection of centre and periphery. Before 1659, the counties of Cerdanya and Roussillon formed part of the principality of Catalonia, linked dynastically since the late fifteenth century, as part of the Aragonese crown, to the kingdom of Castile. Until the beginning of the eighteenth century, within this dynastic union, Catalonia retained its own laws, currency, political institutions, language and culture, with little attempt by the 'centre' to impose cultural unity on the 'periphery'.[7]

In 1659–60, France annexed the northern Catalan county of Roussillon and part of the adjoining valley of Cerdanya. The Peace of the Pyrenees in 1659 marked the final cessation and acquisition of territories and jurisdictions by Spain and France along the Pyrenees, ending the existence of the medieval states – notably Aragon and Navarre – which had spanned both watersheds, and creating what political scientists and historians have some-

---

6 Current received wisdom, following the work of Eugen Weber, *Peasants into Frenchmen: the modernization of rural France, 1870–1914* (Stanford, 1976), argues that not until the Third Republic in France did a consistent policy of 'nation building' emerge, one based on the extension of road and railway networks, military conscription and obligatory primary schooling. For a sustained critique of this view, with some comparative reflections on the Spanish case, see Sahlins, *Boundaries*.

7 John H. Elliott, *Imperial Spain, 1469–1716* (New York, 1963), pp. 17–43; and John H. Elliott, *The revolt of the Catalans: a study in the decline of Spain, 1598–1640* (Cambridge, 1963), pp. 1–48.

times described as one of the most stable and 'fossilized' boundaries of western Europe.[8] Yet much was to happen before the final delimitation of the boundary line in 1868, since the frontier which emerged from these treaties differed radically from that described more than two centuries later during the formal delimitation treaties of Bayonne, in 1866–68. The first set of treaties mark what contemporary geographers, following diplomatic usage, often call the phase of 'allocation' of the boundary, while the second constitute its 'demarcation' and 'delimitation'.[9] In fact, the commissioners in 1659 spoke of the 'delineation of the frontier' and understood that 'the line, which has to be almost mathematical, has necessarily to occupy a very narrow width'. They thus gave verbal form to the symbolic and ceremonial expression of the linear boundary established by Cardinal Mazarin and don Luis de Haro six months earlier. For when the two first ministers had negotiated the Peace of the Pyrenees, they had carefully chosen a 'neutral' site on an island in the middle of the Bidassoa River for their discussions. Cardinal Mazarin explained the proceedings:

Without further delay we had bridges built to link each side of our island [with the mainland] and plan to build equal lodgings, and a large room at the head of the island equidistant from the two lodgings, in which there will be two doors, one on his side, and one on mine, by which we can enter, each holding rank in the chairs which will be prepared for us on each side of the room, which we will take care to build and to furnish, each one his own half.

The symbolic equality still gave rise to competition between the two nations once the ministers and their entourages began to meet and later, during the marriage of Louis XIV and Maria Teresa (daughter of Philip IV) at the same site. More important, the ceremonial symmetry belied French strength at the bargaining table, as France, victorious on the battlefields, dominated the negotiations.[10]

When the plenipotentiaries and negotiators of the Peace and its two regulatory conventions of May 1660 spoke of and identified a linear boundary separating distinct sovereign polities, they were enacting an archaic and enduring notion which long preceded the modern territorial state, and which was affirmed during the negotiations of the Peace of the Pyrenees. Yet once the Peace and its conventions were signed, nothing was done to define the precise territorial boundaries of the kingdoms: no accepted set

---

[8] For example, J. Brunhes and C. Vallau, *La géographie de l'histoire* (Paris, 1921), p. 353; M. Foucher, *L'invention des frontières* (Paris, 1987), p. 128.

[9] S. B. Jones, *Boundary-making: a handbook for statesmen, treaty editors, and boundary commissioners* (Washington, 1945).

[10] Sahlins, *Boundaries*, pp. 25–9.

of boundary stones, no single line of soldiers or customs guards. Rather, as worked out in the further conferences held over the next few years in the town of Figueres, the two crowns established a series of jurisdictional frontiers corresponding to the different dimensions of royal administration, frontiers which failed to coincide. The ecclesiastical boundary was such that Llívia, along with the thirty-three villages ceded to France, remained dependent on the Spanish bishopric of Urgell. The maintenance of seigneurial jurisdictions on both sides of the boundary cut across the limits of judicial administration. The continuity of property ownership across the boundary and the constant insistence of both monarchies to fix taxes following the place of their proprietors' origins determined a distinct set of limits of fiscal sovereignty. Nor did the customs boundary coincide with the 'limits of France and Spain', since multiple 'internal customs' persisted long into the Old Régime.[11]

The history of the frontier from the beginning of the eighteenth century is that of the slow consolidation of multiple jurisdictional boundaries into a single territorial border line. The boundary line, as an imaginary and permanently defended division of two territorial states, only made its appearance beginning in the later eighteenth century, following a series of struggles over taxation and religious jurisdiction in the borderland. Spain's successful imposition of a cadastral tax in Catalonia in 1717, after the advent of the Bourbon monarchy, resulted in the first Spanish attempt to map the territorial limits of sovereignty. France's successful acquisition of temporal and spiritual authority over the parishes belonging to the bishopric of Urgell in 1732 brought the ecclesiastical frontier more in line with the political division of the two kingdoms.[12] Then, in the second half of the eighteenth century, the territorial notion of the state found its expression in both political theory (such as the work of the Swiss jurist Emmerich de Vattel) and in the failed attempt to delineate the Pyrenean frontier by the Caro-Ornano Commission in 1785.[13]

In many ways, the French Revolution (1789–99) was a dividing line, a frontier itself, out of which emerged the historical differentiation of national territories in the Cerdanya. Not only did the French revolutionaries invent the notion of territorial sovereignty in the creation of the departments, but at the same time the event marked the appearance of what Lucien Febvre

[11] Ibid., pp. 53–9.   [12] Ibid., pp. 77–89.
[13] J. Sermet, *La frontière des Pyrénées et les conditions de sa délimitation* (Lourdes, 1983); C. Desplat, 'Le parlement de Navarre et la définition de la frontière franco-navarraise à l'extrême fin du XVIIIe siècle', in J. F. Nail *et al.*, *Lies et passeries dans les Pyrénées* (Tarbes, 1986), pp. 109–20; and Sahlins, 'Natural frontiers revisited'.

called a 'moral frontier' between France and its neighbours.[14] During the eighty years between the Revolution and the delimitation of the Spanish-French frontier, Spain too experienced a series of revolutionary moments which led to an increasingly territorial understanding of national sovereignty. Indeed, the notion of a national boundary line emerged from the dialectic of revolutionary traditions in Spain and France. Thus, for example, in 1789, the Spanish government invoked the idea of a 'sanitary cordon' to stop its ideological contamination by French radical ideas.[15] Significantly, these positions were reversed during Spain's three-year experiment with liberalism in 1820–23, as the French Restoration monarchy, denying its revolutionary origins but preserving the Revolution's definition of national territory, established its own 'sanitary cordon' on the frontier.[16] The excuse was an epidemic in Catalonia, but the establishment of quarantine houses on the boundary had deep political significance for the two states and, as we shall see, important national implications for the local communities as well. In fact it was almost a half century later, coinciding with the invention of territory and nationality as part of the ideology of nationalism, that the ideal of a delimited national territory found expression in formal treaties between France and Spain (1866 and 1868).

The history of the formation of the political boundary between Spain and France can thus be told as one of diplomatic and military history, of international relations, of the history of struggles and disputes between two political centres. Yet it is a history which remains incomplete without the complementary perspective of the periphery, of the ways in which the central powers created the conditions for the possibility of both unity and difference of society and culture in the borderland, and the ways in which local historical agents played central roles in the determination of the final shape of the political boundary.

On the one hand, the imposition from Madrid and Paris of a set of military, fiscal, economic and ecclesiastical boundaries tended to unite the peasants and rural nobles from both sides of the boundary. Thus was a born a political culture of resistance in the borderland, a range of strategies and tactics which the people of the borderland used to oppose the frequently harsh presence of both states. Especially during the long second half of the

---

[14] '*Frontière*: the word and the concept', in P. Burke, ed., *A new kind of history and other essays: Lucien Febvre* (New York, 1973), p. 214.

[15] R. Herr, *The eighteenth-century revolution in Spain* (Princeton, 1958), pp. 253–4.

[16] J. F. Hoffman, *La peste à Barcelone* (Paris, 1964), esp. pp. 27–49; and for a first-hand description by the future prime minister Adolphe Thiers, see his journalistic account, *Les Pyrénées et le Midi de la France pendant les mois de novembre et décembre 1822* (Paris, 1823).

seventeenth century, a period of nearly continuous border skirmishes between French and Spanish troops in the Cerdanya, peasants, townsmen and nobles tended to unite in opposition to a common aggressor. More often than not, that enemy was 'the French', and the inherited antipathy of the Catalans was reinforced by the burdensome demands of taxes, foodstuffs and men requisitioned by the French troops. Beginning after 1721, however, as the two Bourbon crowns allied themselves in a series of Family Pacts and military demands became less oppressive, the people of the borderland continued to unite in opposition to the two states. Indeed, throughout the eighteenth century, the political boundary served not only as a source of livelihood – as peasants made a living and merchants made fortunes on an increasingly important contraband trade – but also as an instrument of resistance to state demands for taxes and militia.[17] In this context, and given the difference in fiscal régimes on the two sides of the border, family alliances and property ownership across the boundary actually increased substantially.[18] All this helped to maintain the ethnic and linguistic identities of the Cerdans as Catalans, identities which themselves further encouraged intermarriage across the boundary.

Paradoxically, the consolidation of the political boundary after the French Revolution created an even denser network of social relations among Catalans on both sides of the border. The economic and political differentiation of French and Spanish national territories in the early nineteenth century further encouraged an increasing rate of intermarriage and increased economic linkages across the boundary. As Catalan and Spanish political refugees and economic immigrants fled north, they began to settle in substantial numbers in the villages of the French Cerdanya. Indeed, the more the boundary became politically marked by the two centres, the more permeable it became in local society. Instead of dividing local society, the definition of the political borderland tended to bring the two sides of the Cerdanya in closer relationship, a relationship reinforced by common linguistic, family and religious practices.[19]

By the beginning of the Third Republic in 1871 – thus shortly after the

---

[17] For an overview of this 'culture of resistance' by the end of the eighteenth century, which none the less tends to exaggerate the effacement of the boundary in local life, see M. Brunet, *Le Roussillon. Une société contre l'Etat, 1780–1820* (Toulouse, 1986); and Sahlins, *Boundaries*, pp. 103–32.

[18] See my 'Nationality, residence, and the capitation tax in the 18th century French Cerdanya', in *Actes del Primer Congrés d'Història Moderna de Catalunya* (Barcelona, 1984), I, pp. 416–25.

[19] Sahlins, *Boundaries*, pp. 198–237.

boundary achieved its definitive shape in the Bayonne accords – no substantial or visible differences existed in language, religious practices, local customs or costumes between the French and Spanish sides. As the town council of Puigcerdà wrote in a petition of 1814, in a statement which all the evidence suggests was just as accurate fifty years later:

The peasants follow the same methods in cultivating their lands; the families of both sides are intertwined; landowners and proprietors from one Cerdanya own estates and properties in the other and vice versa; the people speak the same language, they dress alike, so that in seeing two individuals from the Cerdanya, one Spanish and the other French, it would be impossible to distinguish which is which without knowing them already.[20]

French military officials, political administrators and even less interested observers in the nineteenth century all concurred that this persistence of Catalan culture formed an obstacle to creating a national unity, to building the nation in the borderland.[21] Yet they were even more displeased with the way in which, when push came to shove, the Cerdans seemed to fail dramatically the political test of national identity and citizenship. Although there was much comment on the case of the Spanish Cerdans, it was on the French side that the contradictions between the central ideals and peripheral practices of national citizenship revealed the greatest slippage.

The idea of sacrifice to the nation – the willingness to fight and to die for the nation – is an ancient test of citizenship. Ernst Kantorowicz has shown how the Roman ideal of patriot, expressed in the sacrificial defence of the fatherland – *pro patria mori* – had died out by the second millennium in Western Europe, only to have been reborn within Christian theology as the ideal of the martyr. With the 'resecularization' of that concept in the twelfth century, the appearance of 'sentiments of semi-religious devotion' toward the *regnum* became part of the essential definition of Frenchness. To die for one's kingdom or, in the enlightened redefinition of sovereignty, for one's nation was the political test of Frenchness. From the revolutionary 'Defence of the Fatherland' to the military conscription of the Third Republic and twentieth-century ideals of nationalism, the idea of sacrificing local interests

---

[20] AHN, Est. lib. 674d, fos. 47–64 (petition of municipality of Puigcerdà, 14 July 1814).
[21] The memoranda and reports of French nineteenth-century military commanders and engineers are particularly revealing on this point, especially given their 'folkloric' preoccupations (or attention paid to details of language and local customs) within their military and strategic concerns: see the reports collected in France: Ministère de la Guerre. Archives de l'Armée de la Terre, Mémoires et Reconnaissances, esp. 1083–4 and 1221–3; see also Sahlins, *Boundaries*, chapter 6.

and concerns has been bound up in the essential ideal of French citizenship.[22]

These myths about Frenchness are important in the symbolic construction of national identity; but as historical models, they need to be tested critically through consideration of concrete instances. During the French Revolution, the peasants of the French Cerdanya had shown a singular lack of commitment to the new régime: when Spanish armies invaded the French borderland in the spring of 1793, many French Cerdans welcomed them as saviours. And in the two years of French military occupation which followed, many more young men fled to Catalonia to fight in the Catalan irregular troops *against* the French than responded to the 'Fatherland in Danger' and gave their lives to the nation.[23] The pattern continued under the Napoleonic régime, when much of Catalonia was annexed to the French empire. 'The first virtue of a good Frenchman', according to the interior minister in 1813, 'is to participate in saving his country from foreign domination.'[24] Yet by these criteria, the peasants and rural notables of the Cerdanya failed miserably. Recruitment was painful, and desertion endemic: the district of Sallagosa produced a greater percentage of deserters than nearly any other district in France.[25] Throughout the nineteenth century, the French Cerdans remained more engaged in the political struggles in Spain than those of France: the Carlist Wars mattered more than the Second Republic. And when France called them to arms again in 1870 and 1914, most Cerdans chose to flee across the border rather than fight – although by the First World War, the universal antipathy to serving the nation had somewhat dissipated.[26]

Yet if the Cerdans generally failed the test of national identity emanating from the centre, which was founded on the ideal of sacrificing local interests and a local sense of place to the nation, they none the less invented and affirmed national identities for themselves in other, more local contexts.

---

[22] E. Kantorowicz, *The king's two bodies: a study in medieval political theology* (Princeton, 1957), pp. 252–72; see also, for the medieval period, C. Beaune, *Naissance de la nation France* (Paris, 1985), esp. 324–35; and more generally, P. Contamine, 'Mourir pour la patrie, X–XXe siècles', in P. Nora, ed., *Les lieux de mémoire. La nation* (3 vols., Paris, 1986), I, pp. 11–43.

[23] ADPO, Q 38 (list of individuals designated mayors and councilors during the Spanish invasion, n.d. but ca. July 1793); AHP, Revolució francesa, esp. the list of 'Tercios del corregimiento de Puigcerdà,' 1795; and Sahlins, *Boundaries*, chapter 5.

[24] ADPO 3M(1) A/C 2, no. 88 (letter to prefect, 28 December 1813).

[25] Archives Nationales F(7) 3608 (prefect's reports of 1811–1813); see also Brunet, *Le Roussillon*, pp. 297–388.

[26] Sahlins, *Boundaries*, chapters 6, 8.

Indeed, the peasant communities of the Cerdanya and their local representatives on the municipal councils defined for themselves national identities without abandoning their sense of place, or their local interests. And
they did so despite their continued resistance to the state, as embodied in
the customs guards, soldiers and tax administrators stationed in the borderland. The peasant communities of the Cerdanya invented their own national
identities as Frenchmen and Spaniards while they continued to oppose the
authority of the two states, founding their new identities on motives antithetical to the ideals of the central governments and its agents.

For one thing, the affirmation of national identity in local terms was
grounded in an instrumental and practical use (and abuse) of the nation.
The Cerdans developed a rhetoric of national identity that masked their
interests and appealed to the ideals of government officials. Yet more than a
rhetoric, this evocation of national identity constituted a process of self-
fashioning whereby the Cerdans ended up taking seriously their affiliation
to France and convincing themselves of their identity as Frenchmen. What
began, then, as a strategic manipulation of identity grounded in local
interests, ended by defining a new identity from which a fresh set of
interests was to flow.

This complex movement originated in the process of drawing local
boundaries between an 'us' and a 'them' – that is, in the establishment of a
counter-identity against 'the other'. Such an oppositional model of national
identity can be examined in two distinct domains: the village affirmation of
national identity against other communities across the boundary; and the
collective self-definition of the village community against a range of individual outsiders.

On the first Sunday of July 1825, hundreds of peasants from the villages
of the French and Spanish Cerdanyas gathered in the capital town of
Puigcerdà, on the Spanish side of the boundary, to celebrate the annual
Feast of the Rosary. But instead of a festive rite of unity, the day turned into
a ritual 'massacre' of the French peasants who had come to feast and dine in
town. The festive atmosphere which began the day turned sour as the
town's gates were locked, and men, women and children from the Spanish
Cerdanya beat the French peasants screaming 'Kill the *gavatxos*, they have
ruled Spain for too long.'[27]

Gavatxos was the pejorative term in Catalan for 'foreigners', and specific-

---

[27] ADPO M non classée 1943: 'Rapport sur le rixe du 3 juillet 1825,' anon n.d., ca. August
1825; and letter of mayor of Carol to sub-prefect, 4 July 1825.

ally, for Frenchmen.[28] Used by the residents of the Spanish Cerdanya against their French neighbours, with whom they intermarried, it was matched by the derogatory designation of *Espanyols*, used by the French Cerdans to name their counterparts across the boundary. For residents of both Cerdanyas, the ethnic or cultural boundary of Frenchmen and Catalans had been pushed back to match the political boundary of France and Spain.

The events of July 1825 also suggest a remarkable intersection of local and national interests and identities. On the one hand, the riot was grounded in a communal dispute between Puigcerdà and the French villages of La Tour de Carol and Enveig. Puigcerdà drew its water from a canal which originated in France, and which passed through the two French villages. In a moment of agricultural intensification, first signs of an 'agricultural revolution', La Tour de Carol and Enveig had opened additional 'eyes' on the canal, and were irrigating their fields and meadows.[29]

Such disputes among village communities over forests, pastures and waters were endemic, part of the fabric of rural life for centuries. They have been recorded in the Cerdanya long before the political division of the valley between France and Spain, and they continued well into the nineteenth century, especially given the increased demographic pressure on already limited ecological resources, and the tendency for village communities to embrace more restrictive definitions of membership.[30] But the definition of the political boundary also transformed struggles among villages which it divided. Because of a lack of a common administration and judicial system to which both parties could appeal, fights among villages divided by the boundary tended to escalate, as communities took matters into their own hands. As the French customs director wrote to his finance minister in 1827, describing a state of affairs which was only to intensify over the next several decades in the Cerdanya,

Contiguous communities often have interests to fight out. When they are not under the same superior authority, their rivalries cannot be contained, their territorial

---

[28] The Castilian (Spanish) word was *gavachos*. The origin of the term is uncertain. Most scholarship notes its derivation from the Gévaudan region of France, a source of many migrants to Spain during the early modern period (see, e.g. J. Nadal and E. Giralt, *La population catalane de 1553 à 1717. L'immigration française* (Paris, 1960), p. 114); see also Gutierrez, *La France et les français dans la littérature espagnole*, pp. 94–121.

[29] AHP, 'Libre de Asequia' and 'Manuals d'Accords' for these years; see also ADPO M non-classée 1824/1.

[30] Peter Sahlins, 'The nation in the village: state-building and communal struggles in the Catalan borderland during the eighteenth and nineteenth centuries', *Journal of Modern History*, 60 (1988), 234–63.

encroachments cannot be stopped, and their usurpations of pasturing rights cannot be impeded. When local demands for protection remain without effect, the communities resort to armed struggle.[31]

Village communities appealed to their separate national administrations, evoking in their petitions as in their legal briefs the language of national identity. Written by village notables, sometimes with the assistance of hired lawyers, these petitions claimed to defend the interests of the nation as well as the community in preserving territorial integrity and punishing the usurpation of territorial sovereignty. Focusing on the defence of French territory against 'foreigners' – *Espanyols* and *gavatxos* – the petitions and demands for protection of the local community insistently emphasized the loyalty and national identity of the petitioners.

Of course, this language of national identity was evidently a rhetoric in the service of local interests. And as such, it intersected, during the nineteenth century, with the growing concern of the French state to protect itself against 'territorial violations'. In the 1820s, as we have seen, Spain undertook its first liberal experiment, while the French royalist government used the excuse of cholera in Catalonia to prevent the plague of liberal ideas from spreading into France. Erecting a 'sanitary cordon' which hermetically sealed the boundary, the French government affirmed the territorial character of sovereignty. From the perspective of local society, however, the sanitary cordon severely disrupted daily and local relations among villagers, and produced much opposition – sometimes in Catalan – to French and Spanish states. But it also produced, among the propertied classes and local political representatives, a vehement defence of the interests of the nation against the other.

Thus in February 1822, Llívia protested that the French community had taken advantage of their soldiers 'to usurp lands in contention', and argued that 'this town has always sought to protect the property rights of its fellow citizens and to uphold the integrity of Spanish territory'. From the extreme periphery of Spain came the most vociferous and militaristic nationalism, as Llívia argued how the Spaniards, valiant warriors who beat back 'the wings of the Eagle' (Napoleon), would always triumph 'despite treachery and intrigue'.[32] This is but one example of many: the 1820s and 1830s, in particular, were fertile years for the growth of national sentiment in the borderland. This is not to argue that the Cerdans on both sides of the

---

[31] FAMRE Limites, vol. 461, no. 31 (27 January 1827).

[32] Spain, Archivo del Ministerio de Relaciones Exteriores, Tratados y Negociaciones, 222–3 (memoir sent to the Cortes, 11 August 1820); Sahlins, *Boundaries*, pp. 233–7.

boundary, who spoke Catalan, practised the same local customs and inter-married freely among themselves, became Spanish or French. Rather, it is to point to the ways in which national identity were adopted and manipulated within local communities with their own local concerns.

In the course of the nineteenth century, and most evidently during the 1860s, the French and Spanish governments attempted to resolve once and for all the local disputes which seemed inevitably to lead to 'territorial violations'. Yet the village communities remained adamant in defence of a national territory against men, to repeat the phrase of La Tour de Carol in 1868, 'of foreign nations and different mores'. The village communities invoked such national differences when, in cultural terms, they would have been hard pressed to define the essential content of such differences. Moreover, they deployed national differences even when their own local interests in defending particular village territories were not at stake. By the 1860s, then, the claims of national identity had moved beyond the status of rhetorical flourish: the identity consistently invoked for strategic reasons had ended up being taken seriously, and the village communities adopted national identities from which a new set of interests would flow.

The self-definition of national identity took shape not simply as the expression of collective statements of opposition between communities divided by the national boundary, but also by the exclusion of outsiders from the village communities on both sides of the boundary. The village communities affirmed their national identities by ostracizing individuals who indiscriminately manipulated identities in the service of their private interests – that is, of people who not only used but abused the possibilities of manipulating identities in the borderland.

Consider the case of one Marc François Garreta, or Marcos Francisco Garreta or Marc Francesc Garreta, depending upon whom he petitioned. Born in the French village of La Tour de Carol in 1771, Garreta moved after the revolutionary disorders to the town of Llívia, a Spanish enclave completely surrounded by French villages. He married a Spanish woman, acquired property, and eventually held political office in the municipality of Llívia in the late 1820s and early 1830s. Then came rumbling of civil war in Spain, and Garreta decided to move back to France. He may have been pushed by the increased tax levies in the town or by fears for his physical safety as a prominent citizen. In November 1834, he requested confirmation of his French nationality:

I remained so long in Llívia because of business affairs and for no other reason: as a result, the Spanish authorities think that I am a Spaniard. I was elected mayor, and

I accepted because I was ignorant that it was against French law to hold office in Spain.[33]

In June 1835, the French minister of justice granted Garreta his petition, and returned to him the 'quality and rights of a Frenchman' which he had lost by holding public office in Spain.

But Garreta continued to live in both France and Spain. He was elected to the municipal council of the French village of Santa Llocaya in 1837, but less than a year later the town of Llívia confiscated some of his goods and imposed upon him a fine, claiming

that he had not returned to France to live as a Frenchman, but continued to live in this town behaving the same way and exercising the same functions as always, and he only left Llívia when the [Carlist] rebels invaded the Cerdanya, in order to flee from the hardship and taxes which good Spaniards had to suffer.[34]

Such manipulations of national identity proved disturbing to both French and Spanish officials alike. 'The right of nations has never allowed a foreigner to enjoy promiscuously the quality of being a citizen of his own and of another nation where he is living temporarily. Neither should the public order permit a foreigner to change his nationality when his interest so dictates, according to the principle of utility', wrote the civil governor of Barcelona in 1835. The Cerdanya abounds, he continued, 'in men who could be called amphibious in political society, because they will just as quickly wish to be considered French as Spanish'.[35]

Yet this characterization of an individual, echoed less eloquently about others by French officials of the time, had its origins in local society itself. It was the municipal councillors of Llívia, alongside the village councils of the French Cerdanya, who denounced Garreta's 'refined egoism' and gave him the label of 'political amphibian'. Garreta's differences with the municipality of Llívia resulted in a fistfight during a town meeting during March 1835, and he was subsequently involved in a number of other altercations which suggests his pariah-like status and social exclusion from the local community.[36]

Garreta's case was not isolated. In the earlier part of the century, those who were excluded from the community were frequently ex-nobles who

[33] ADPO M non classée 1883/2 (dossier on Garreta, esp. the decree of 17 June 1835).
[34] AMLL, letter of municipality to Puigcerdà governor, 16 July 1838.
[35] ADPO M non classée 1883/2 (letter to French consul in Barcelona, 23 April 1835).
[36] AMLL Manual d'Accords, 1832–43, fos. 119–22; see also AMLL (letter and memorandum of the municipality, 5 October 1838); and ADPO M non classée 1883/2 (French consul to prefect, 27 September 1842).

manipulated identities in the service of their propertied interests.[37] In the latter part of the century, as national conscription laws began to weigh more heavily on the French village communities, those who strategically evoked their Spanish ancestry and nationality were deemed 'selfish' and 'egotistical'. The village councils denounced them, seeing the 'public interest' threatened by 'those who do not fulfil their municipal obligations, but none the less want to enjoy all the advantages'.[38] The national governments tended to support such individuals who petitioned for French citizenship, taking seriously their rhetorical claims of loyalty and identity. But the communities acted otherwise, and by identifying these individuals as 'outsiders', they affirmed simultaneously their local and national identities.

It is worth stressing again the extent to which in both cases this contextual affirmation of national identity involved neither the abandonment of local identities nor the loss of local interests. In both cases, the village communities defined for themselves, against either a collective or singular other, the identities of their constituent members as Spaniards or Frenchmen. This process – the contextual and oppositional definition of national identity at the periphery – took place long before the two states imposed their ideals of national unity from the centre: by the late nineteenth century, the Cerdans had already defined for themselves a meaningful sense of nationhood.

[37] Sahlins, *Boundaries*, pp. 222–5.
[38] Municipality of Err, quoted in Sahlins, *Boundaries*, pp. 227–8.

Part III

Spain and its empire

10

David or Goliath? Philip II and his world in the 1580s

GEOFFREY PARKER

The coronation of Philip II as king of Portugal at Tomar on 16 April 1581 created the first empire upon which the sun never set. Nevertheless, the king did not look forward to the ceremony: 'As you know', he confided in a letter to his daughters, 'they want to dress me in silk brocade, very much against my will'; but, on that historic day, he rose to the occasion. Putting aside the mourning that he had worn since the death of his fourth wife, six months before, 'The king came in clothed in silk robes of crimson, with a long train... Crowned, with the sceptre in his hand, he looked like King David.'[1]

Philip's accession to the throne had already been announced to the outposts of the Portuguese empire: thus in November 1580 the king ordered the city of Goa to obey his orders thenceforth, and the governor proclaimed him in September 1581, sending on news to Malacca, the Moluccas and other distant territories.[2] The only resistance to the Spanish succession

Many thanks for references to David Coleman, Benedict Kiernan and Sanjay Subrahmanyam, and for suggestions and comments to Fernando Bouza, Richard Kagan and Nancy van Deusen. I also acknowledge the inspiration of John Elliott's study 'The Spanish monarchy and the kingdom of Portugal 1580–1640', in M. Greengrass, ed., *Conquest and coalescence: the shaping of the state in early modern Europe* (London, 1991), pp. 48–67. All translations are mine unless otherwise attributed.

[1] F. J. Bouza Alvarez, ed., *Cartas de Felipe II a sus hijas* (Madrid, 1988,) p. 43, Philip II to his daughters, Tomar, 3 April 1581; L. Cabrera de Córdoba, *Historia de Felipe II, rey de España*, II (Madrid, 1877), pp. 633–4.

[2] J. H. da Cunha Rivara, ed., *Archivo Portuguez-Oriental (APO)*, fasc. I, livro I (2nd edition, Nova Goa, 1877), pp. 90–1, Philip II to the city of Goa, 7 November 1580; D. do Couto, *Da*

arose in the Azores, but amphibious expeditions conquered first São Miguel in 1582 and then, with a force of ninety-eight ships and 15,000 men, Terceira in 1583. Philip's possessions now ran from Madrid through Mexico, Manila, Macao and Malacca to India, Mozambique and Angola and so back to Madrid.

A practical demonstration of the monarchy's new global reach occurred during the lunar eclipse of 17 November 1584: the newly founded Academy of Mathematics in Madrid sent out in advance a dossier of instructions, including a semi-circle of the same size for recording observations, not only to Antwerp, Toledo and Seville, but also to Mexico City, Manila and perhaps even Macao.[3] In addition, to ensure the most accurate results, in 1583 the council of the Indies also despatched the noted astronomer, Jaume Juan of Valencia, to Mexico along with special instruments to observe the eclipse, and thus (the council hoped) to establish the exact longitude of the capital.[4] Even before the union of crowns, a Spanish astrologer had commented on the fact that the 'banners and standards' of his sovereign 'have crossed more than one third of the world, from Sicily to Cuzco and to the province of Quito, a distance which includes nine hours of difference, for when it is nine o'clock at night here it is midday there. And if we measure its extent, from north to south, it covers one quarter of the earth.'[5]

Intoxication with Habsburg power was nothing new. The election in 1519

Asia. Decada X (Lisbon, 1788), book I, pp. 17–19. A ship from Portugal brought the news to Malacca in November 1581, but Macao only heard in March 1582 via Mexico and Manila – an interesting indication of the relative speed at which news travelled from Europe to the Far East.

[3] See the sheets for Mexico in Archivo General de Indias, Seville, *Mapas y planos. Mexico*, 34, 'Observación del eclypse lunar que aconteció el año de 1584 a 17 días de noviembre'. See also U. S. Lamb, 'The Spanish cosmographic juntas of the sixteenth century', *Terrae incognitae*, 6 (1974), 56–62, at 60 (although with the date 'October 1584'). D. C. Goodman, *Power and penury: government, technology and science in Philip II's Spain* (Cambridge, 1988), p. 67, records that observations were also coordinated with colleagues in China. An attempt to establish the longitude of Mexico had also been attempted during the lunar eclipse of 1577: see C. Fernández Duro, *Disquisiciones náuticas. IV: Los ojos en el cielo* (Madrid, 1879), pp. 309f., G. B. Gesio to Philip II, 18 January 1579.

[4] AGS, Guerra Antigua 155/149, consulta of the council of the Indies, 5 February 1583, and fo. 150, 'Instructions for Jaume Juan', 13 December 1582 (note the commendable foresight: almost two years ahead of the predicted eclipse). Unfortunately, when the moon first became visible in Mexico on the night of 17 November 1584, the eclipse had already begun and so Juan and his fellow observers could only fix a time for the end; and, of course, given the inaccuracy of the clocks available – one 'a counterweight clock of great accuracy' the other 'a well-constructed clock with wheels' – they could not be sure of the exact time anyway, although that was the whole point of the exercise.

[5] BL, Egerton ms. 592/38-48v, 'Discurso astronómico' (anonymous), at fo. 44. In fact only six 'hours' separate Madrid and Cuzco, but the idea of using time zones to measure size seems strikingly modern.

of Charles V as Holy Roman Emperor gave rise to a spate of polemics calling upon the new ruler to imitate the achievements of his namesake Charlemagne and unite all Christendom; and Charles's coronation by the pope in 1530 unleashed a fresh torrent of prophetic pamphlets in which the emperor appeared as a second Augustus. Juan Ginés de Sepúlveda, later appointed tutor to Philip II, wrote one of the more extreme of these imperialist tracts and no doubt tried to pass his ideas on to his young charge.[6] Somewhat later, Prince Philip's journey from Spain to the Netherlands in 1548 occasioned a further literary effusion urging the Habsburgs to acquire the 'Universal Monarchy'.[7] Before long, some of Philip II's subjects saw this in global terms. No sooner had a small party, commanded by Miguel López de Legazpi, landed at Cebu in the Philippines than Friar Martín de Rada dreamed of using the archipelago as a base from which to conquer China – a suggestion enthusiastically endorsed by others: by Andrés de la Mirandola, the royal factor in Manila, in 1569; by the Augustinian Diego de Herrera, a member of Legazpi's expedition, in 1570; and by Legazpi's successor as governor, don Francisco de Sande, in 1576. Only two or three thousand European troops would be required, Sande claimed, and only one mainland province needed to be attacked, because 'in conquering one province, the conquest of all is made'.[8] Shortly afterwards, Giovanni Battista Gesio, an expert on geography at the Spanish court, argued that the Philippines should become a military base 'like Italy and Flanders, with a garrison of

---

[6] See A. Losada, *Juan Ginés de Sepúlveda a través de su 'Epistolario' y Nuevos Documentos* (2nd edition, Madrid, 1973), pp. 64ff. and 94ff.; O. Niccoli, *Prophecy and people in Renaissance Italy* (Princeton, 1990), pp. 113–20 and 168–88; J. M. Headley, 'The Habsburg world empire and the revival of Ghibellinism', in S. Wenzel, ed., *Medieval and Renaissance Studies*, VII (Chapel Hill, 1978), pp. 93–127; and J. M. Headley, 'Rhetoric and reality: messianic humanism and civilian themes in the imperial ethos of Gattinara', in M. Reeves, ed., *Prophetic Rome in the High Renaissance period: essays* (Oxford, 1992), pp. 241–69.

[7] These publications are surveyed by F. Bosbach, 'Papsttum und Universalmonarchie im Zeitalter der Reformation', *Historisches Jahrbuch*, 107 (1987), 44–76; F. Bosbach, *Monarchia Universalis. Ein politischer Leitbegriff der frühen Neuzeit*, Schriftenreihe der historischen Kommission bei der bayerischen Akademie der Wissenschaften, 32 (Göttingen, 1988), chapter 4, and pp. 166–7 (a list of works on the subject published during Philip II's lifetime); and A. Pagden, *Spanish imperialism and the political imagination* (New Haven, 1990), pp. 2ff. and 37ff.

[8] L. Diaz-Trechuela, 'Consecuencias y problemas derivados del Tratado en la expansión oriental', in L. M. Enciso Recio and L. A. Ribot García, eds., *El Tratado de Tordesillas y su época* (forthcoming); E. H. Blair and J. A. Robertson, eds., *The Philippine Islands, 1493–1898* (55 vols., Cleveland, Oh., 1903–9), XXXIV, pp. 222–8, Rada to the Viceroy of Mexico, Cebu, 8 July 1569; and IV, pp. 21–93, Sande's 'Relación' of 7 June 1576 (see pp. 58–9 and 62–3). For more of the same, see L. Bourdon, 'Un projet d'invasion de la Chine par Canton à la fin du 16e siècle', in *Actas do III Colóquio internacional de estudos Luso-Brasileiros*, II (Lisbon, 1960), pp. 97–121, at p. 101.

numerous experienced troops' because the islands could serve as a launching pad for the conquest and conversion of Japan, divided and weakened by
civil war, and perhaps also of China.[9] The council of the Indies, however,
sharply rejected these wild ideas: 'It seems to us here', a royal order of April
1577 declared, 'that it is inappropriate to discuss the conquest of China at
this time.'[10]

The Spanish government could still be seduced by other imperialist
dreams, however. The coincidence of the spectacular victory of Lepanto
over the Turks with the birth of a son and heir to Philip II in 1571 provoked
a veritable torrent of letters from the king's chief minister, Cardinal Diego
de Espinosa, drawing the attention of anyone who would listen to these
indubitable signs of God's special providence towards Spain 'which leaves
us with little more to desire but much to expect from His divine mercy'.
Espinosa even compared Lepanto with the drowning of Pharaoh's army in
the Red Sea, while the king commissioned a vast commemorative canvas of
the two events from Titian, the foremost painter of the age. Meanwhile in
Italy, many speculated that Philip would continue in God's grace to re-
conquer the Holy Land and revive the title 'emperor of the east'.[11] A few
years later, yet another spate of 'universalist' polemics followed the death in
1578 of the childless King Sebastian of Portugal at the battle of Alcazar-
quivir – a circumstance in which some detected God's hand, 'because
Divine Providence would not have permitted such a remarkable event
without a great cause'.[12] In the rhetorical phrase of the Dominican
preacher, Fray Hernando del Castillo:

Uniting the kingdoms of Portugal and Castile will make Your Majesty the greatest
king in the world ... because if the Romans were able to rule the world simply by
ruling the Mediterranean, what of the man who rules the Atlantic and Pacific oceans,
since they surround the world?

---

[9] IVDJ, 25B carpeta 22, n.p., Gesio to Philip II, 23 and 24 February 1576. For more of the
same, see ibid., Gesio to Philip II, 23 April 1577.

[10] See Diaz-Trechuelo, 'Consecuencias y problemas'; and Blair and Robertson, *The Philippine
Islands*, IV, pp. 94–5.

[11] BL, Add. 28,704/270v-1, Espinosa to the duke of Alva and don Juan de Zúñiga, 4 December
1571, on the victory 'la mayor después de la del Vermejo'. On 'The allegory of Lepanto', see
E. Panofsky, *Problems in Titian, mostly iconographic* (New York, 1969), pp. 72f., and M.
Tanner, *The last descendant of Aeneas: the Hapsburgs and the mythic image of the emperor*
(New Haven, 1993), pp. 216f. On the messianic ambitions of the Spanish court at this time,
see H. Jedin, *Chiesa della storia* (Brescia, 1972), pp. 703–22; and E. Garcia Hernán, 'Pio V y
el mesianismo profético', *Hispana Sacra*, 45 (1993), 83–102.

[12] R. Cueto, '1580 and all that ...': Philip II and the politics of the Portuguese succession',
Portuguese Studies, 8 (1992), 150–69, at 156: Cristobal de Moura to Philip II, 25 November
1578. Cueto provides many more examples on pp. 156–7.

The unification of the peninsula soon came to be seen as a vital step on Spain's road to global mastery. According to Giovanni Battista Gesio, acquiring Portugal 'would be the principal, most effective, and decisive instrument and remedy for the reduction of the Dutch [rebels] to obedience', as well as a useful means of controlling England. In the terse phrase of Hernando del Castillo 'The gain or loss [of Portugal] will mean the gain or loss of the world.'[13]

However, not all observers welcomed this expansive vision. William Cecil, Lord Burghley, chief minister of Elizabeth I, observed in 1584 that, with the Portuguese empire under Philip II's belt 'I know not what limits any man of judgment can set unto his greatness.' England would surely now become a prey to Philip's 'insatiable malice, which is most terrible to be thought of, but most miserable to suffer'; while the following year, Henry of Navarre likewise expressed his fear of 'the ambition of the Spaniards who, having acquired domination of so many lands and seas, believe no part of the world to be inaccessible to them'.[14] Even within Spain, some felt misgivings about the union with Portugal. In February 1580 the Jesuit Pedro de Ribadeneira warned one of the king's ministers about the evils of wars which 'pitted Christians against Christians, catholics against catholics', and lamented the high taxes which already meant that 'although the king is so powerful and so feared and respected, he is not as well liked as he used to be'. A war for Portugal might expose new and unwelcome tensions in Spain, and allow the king's enemies abroad to find and exploit a 'fifth column' of discontented subjects within the peninsula.[15]

Nevertheless, Ribadeneira conceded, the only thing worse than fighting to secure Portugal would be to let someone else acquire it! Even though uniting the peninsular kingdoms would threaten the European balance of power (just as Charles V's election as Holy Roman Emperor had done in 1519), allowing the Lusitanian inheritance to pass to someone else would

---

[13] Quotations from F. J. Bouza Alvarez, *Portugal en la monarquía hispánica (1580–1640). Felipe II, las Cortes de Tomar y la génesis del Portugal Católico* (2 vols., Madrid, 1987), p. 82 (Castillo); BSLE, ms. P. I. 20, fos. 44–5, Gesio to Philip II, 16 November 1578. See also the equally forceful views of Pedro Salazar de Mendoza and of Philip II himself quoted in L. Pereña Vicente, *La teoría de la guerra en Francisco Suárez* (Madrid, 1954), I, pp. 76f.

[14] Quotations from W. Scott, ed., *The Somers collection of tracts* (London, 1809), pp. 164–70; W. T. MacCaffrey, *Queen Elizabeth and the making of policy 1572–1588* (Princeton, 1981), p. 339; and G. Groen van Prinsterer, ed., *Archives ou correspondance inédite de la maison d'Orange-Nassau*, 2nd series, I (Utrecht, 1857), p. 11, Henry of Navarre to the earl of Leicester, 8 May 1585.

[15] *Monumenta histórica societatis Iesu*, LX, *Ribadeneira* (Madrid, 1923), pp. 22–9, Ribadeneira to Cardinal Quiroga, 16 February 1580. See also the other 'opponents of empire' discussed by Anthony Pagden: pp. 316–33 below.

point a dagger at the heart of Spain itself. The central question facing Philip II and his ministers after 1580 was therefore how to ensure that the assets conferred by the new inheritance outweighed the liabilities.

Initially, the government tried to foster a new spirit of integration. Just twelve days after the 'governors' of Portugal had recognized his claim to the throne, but before securing the kingdom itself, Philip II issued an edict that abolished the *puertos secos*, the sixty or so customs posts in Castile which (since 1559) had collected a 10 per cent duty on all goods crossing the frontier; and at the Cortes of Tomar in 1581 he abolished them on both sides of the frontier.[16] Much subsequent legislation, particularly economic measures, henceforth applied to all the Iberian kingdoms: thus the various orders to embargo north European shipping, from 1585 onwards, went to Lisbon and Oporto as well as to Bilbao, Valencia and Seville.[17] The king even went to live in Portugal for almost three years, from 1580 to 1583, and took steps to 'castilianize' the royal palaces: Juan de Herrera and Filippo Terzio came from the Escorial with orders to do 'everything necessary to complete the work on Your Majesty's palaces' in the kingdom, while experts from Castile were summoned to put the royal gardens 'in the same order and perfection as those at the Casa del Campo and Aranjuez'. At the same time, labourers and engineers toiled to make the Tagus navigable from Lisbon to Toledo.[18]

An atlas of twenty-one manuscript maps of the entire Iberian peninsula, conserved at the Escorial library, offers perhaps the best surviving example of the desire to harmonize Philip II's old and new realms after 1580.[19] Pedro de Esquivel, professor of mathematics at the University of Alcalá de

---

[16] Bouza Alvarez, *Portugal en la Monarquia hispánica*, pp. 652–6; H. Lapèyre, *El comercio exterior de Castilla a través de las aduanas de Felipe II* (Valladolid, 1981), part I.

[17] For example, see J. Calvar Gross *et al.*, *La Batalla del Mar Océano (BMO)*, II (Madrid, 1989), pp. 135–6, for the *cédula* of 5 May 1586 for Castile; and AGS *Secretarías Provinciales*, lib. 1550, fo. 255, 'O Cardeal' to Philip II, 31 May 1586, for Portugal (see also the protest of the Lisbon merchants in ibid., fos. 395–7, partly published in *BMO*, II, pp. 282–3).

[18] F. Checa, *Felipe II. Mecenas de las artes* (2nd edn., Madrid, 1993), p. 270; IVDJ 99/208, 'Lo que Rodrigo Alvarez portugués pretende'; ibid., fo. 137, Juan de Ibarra to Mateo Vázquez, 3 February 1582, announcing the safe arrival at Aranjuez of Juan Bautista Antonelli in a boat from Lisbon 'de que se an maravillado'.

[19] BSLE, ms. K.I.1: each map measures approximately 30 by 45 centimeters. The relationship between Esquivel's survey and the Escorial atlas is inferred from the following data. The calligraphy and cartography of the Escorial atlas clearly date from the reign of Philip II. The maps in the atlas, except the one for Portugal, appear to have no precursors and must therefore be the result of some special ground survey carried out by triangulation. Such a survey would have taken several years and could only have been undertaken with a licence from the crown. Only Esquivel is known to have undertaken such a survey during the reign of Philip II.

Henares and an expert in surveying, had begun work on a map of Spain in the 1560s. According to one observer:

One could say without exaggeration that it was the most careful, diligent and accurate description ever to be undertaken for any province since the creation of the world ... There is not an inch of ground in all of Spain that has not been seen, walked over or trodden on by [Esquivel], checking the accuracy of everything (insofar as mathematical instruments make it possible) with his own hands and eyes.

Although Esquivel died in 1575, he left 'the greater part' of the map done.[20]

This implies that Esquivel was working on a single map, which had not quite been completed by the time of his death. However the Escorial atlas contains twenty-one maps, the first (and most complete) of which covers the whole peninsula, rather than just Spain. The rest form a series of sectional surveys done to the same scale, in which Portugal is the best covered and Aragon and Catalonia the worst.

The inclusion of Portugal as a fully integrated part of the main map is striking, since until 1580 it was an independent state into which Esquivel and his team could not have penetrated. Moreover, the Portugal map in the collection must derive from a separate and superior survey, for there is a clear disparity in standard: thus the rivers that cross the frontier are shown in far more detail on the Portuguese than on the Spanish side. Given the similarity in scale and technique employed for both Castile and Portugal (perhaps due in part to the role of the brilliant Portuguese cartographer João Bautista de Lavanha in preparing the Spanish maps) it seems likely that, although research for the sectional maps of the Escorial atlas may have been complete before the Spanish conquest of Portugal in 1580, they were only plotted afterwards. Thanks to the combined cartographic resources of Spain and Portugal, the Iberian peninsula now enjoyed better representation in maps than any other European area of comparable size: at 1:430,000, the Escorial atlas contains by far the largest European maps of their day to be based on a detailed ground survey.[21]

Philip II had no intention of effecting a total integration of his peninsular

[20] F. de Guevara, *Comentarios de la pintura* [ca. 1564] (Madrid, 1788), pp. 219–21; A. de Morales, *Las antegüedades de las ciudades de España* (Alcalá de Henares, 1575), fos. 4v–5.

[21] For a fuller discussion of the Escorial codex, see G. Parker, 'Maps and ministers: the Spanish Habsburgs', in D. Buisseret, ed., *Monarchs, maps and ministers: the emergence of cartography as a tool of government in early modern Europe* (Chicago, 1992), pp. 124–52, at pp. 130–4. In 1583, the royal cosmographer Juan López de Velasco suggested that the *Relaciones Topográficas* circulated in Castile during the 1570s should now be extended to the crowns of Aragon and Portugal, but nothing came of the plan: see F. J. Bouza Alvarez, 'Monarchie en lettres d'imprimerie. Typographie et propagande au temps de Philippe II', *Revue d'histoire moderne et contemporaine*, 41 (1994), 206–20, at 213.

dominions, however. To take a tiny but representative example of his respect for autonomy and tradition, in August 1581 one of his secretaries drew up a warrant in favour of a Venetian ambassador intending to return home overland, calling upon the authorities of each community along the way 'from this city of Lisbon to Madrid and from there to Barcelona' to provide the travellers with lodging and transport 'at just and reasonable prices, without charging them any more than these things cost locally'. But after the king signed this routine order, probably one of scores to cross his desk that day, he had second thoughts, scratched out his signature and added:

This order, saying 'From here to Madrid and from there to Barcelona' will not do. It must read 'from the frontier between the kingdoms of Portugal and Castile to Madrid, and from there to the frontier between the kingdoms of Castile and Aragon'. Let it be done that way.[22]

The king realized that protocol and local privileges required separate orders for both Portugal and the crown of Aragon.

This solicitude for the particularist sensibilities of his new subjects began to wane after 1583, when Philip returned to Castile.[23] Now the king's administrative contact with Portugal centred on the weekly package of letters concerning matters that required royal decisions sent by the viceroy to Madrid. Those for the year 1586, for example, which survive intact in a fat register of 728 folios, dealt *inter alia* with a request from the archbishop of Goa for 'some relics, and especially wood from the True Cross'; the possibility of lifting the ban on card games; a *junta* to be established 'to codify the laws of this kingdom into a single corpus'; 'the importance of expelling the Jews from Lisbon'; the machinations of 'Duarte Lopes, ambassador of the king of Congo'; and the need to appoint a bishop for, and found Christian churches in, Japan.[24] However, side by side with these spiritual and material issues, almost half of the letters in the volume concerned defence: sending a naval squadron to the Azores in order to protect the returning East Indiamen against possible attack by English pirates, and building fortresses in Brazil, Africa and the Atlantic islands,

---

[22] BL, Add. 28357/498, cédula of August 1581.

[23] Although, admittedly he made it seem that his absence would be brief, and left behind his favorite nephew, Albert, as regent: see *APO*, I, part I, pp. 93–4: Philip II to the city of Goa, 2 February 1583.

[24] AGS, Secretarías Provinciales, lib. 1550, fos. 46 (Goa: 1 February), 89 (card games: 15 February); 351 and 472 (legal codes: 12 July and 10 September); 416 and 675 (expulsion of Jews: 9 August and 15 November); 534 (Congo: 18 October); 72, 569 and 596 (Japan: 7 February, 1 and 8 November 1586).

likewise against the English.[25] It was the shape of things to come. Though English (and, to a lesser degree, French) merchants and mariners had occasionally challenged Portugal's monopoly on seaborne trade with Asia and Brazil, and though England and Portugal had suspended commercial relations briefly after 1568, the two nations had composed all their differences in 1572.[26] During his circumnavigation between 1577 and 1580, Francis Drake took care not to harm Portuguese property. The story during Drake's West India raid of 1585–86, however, was quite different: first he harried Spanish Galicia and then attacked the Portuguese Cape Verde islands before moving on to ravage the Spanish Caribbean.[27]

Although none of the letters from Lisbon during the year 1586 bears an apostil or any other evidence of the king's personal attention, Philip II took Drake's depredations as a *casus belli* and plunged his entire monarchy into a bitter war with England which lasted until 1604. The chronicler Pero Rois Soares of Lisbon significantly entitled his account of 1585: 'Chapter 82, which gives the reason why war broke out with England, the cause of so many evils for this kingdom, as you shall hear.'[28]

At first, however, the government's aggressive stance proved popular, and drew upon the new imperialist spirit bred in various parts of the peninsula by the union of crowns. The iconography of the king's ceremonial entry into Lisbon in 1581, for example, reflected a newly confident spirit of expansion. Thus one of the triumphal arches showed Janus surrendering the keys of his temple 'as if to the lord of the world, who holds it securely under his rule'; while another bore the legend 'The world, which was divided between your great-grandfather King Ferdinand the Catholic and your grandfather King Manuel of Portugal, is now linked into one, since you are lord of everything in the East and West.'[29] Meanwhile, in Castile, the verses of the soldier-

---

[25] Ibid., fos 2 (escort: 4 January); 128 (defence of Cape Verde Islands and Arguim: 8 March); 320 (Brazil: 12 July); 572 (Minha: 25 October 1586); and many more.

[26] See, for an English attempt at piracy against the Portuguese, William Towerson's fight in 1557: J. F. Guilmartin Jr., *Gunpowder and galleys: changing technology and Mediterranean warfare at sea in the sixteenth century* (Cambridge, 1974), pp. 85–94; for the 'embargo' see A. J. Crosby, *Calendar of State Papers Foreign of the reign of Elizabeth, 1569–71* (London, 1874), pp. 3, 25, 149f. and 578f.; and ibid., *1572–4* (London, 1876), pp. 1f. (draft treaty between England and Portugal, 1 January 1572).

[27] Compare N. J. W. Thrower, ed., *Sir Francis Drake and the famous voyage, 1577–1580* (Berkeley, 1984), pp. 60–77 (one brush with a Portuguese galleon off the Celebes: p. 70), with M. F. Keeler, ed., *Sir Francis Drake's West Indian Voyage, 1585–86* (London, 1981), pp. 27f. (the sack of Santiago in the Cape Verde islands).

[28] P. Rois Soares, *Memorial*, ed. M. Lopes de Almeida (Coimbra, 1953), p. 230.

[29] Details from Checa, *Felipe II*, pp. 271–2 and 486. Yet more imperialist examples appear in those locations.

poets Fernando de Herrera, Alonso de Ercilla and Francisco de Aldana, which circulated widely in the 1580s, all displayed a self-intoxicating rhetoric which called for Spain to conquer the world.[30] A medal struck in 1580 made the same point more concisely – it showed the king with the inscription PHILIPP II HISP ET NOVI ORBIS REX (Philip II, king of Spain and of the New World) on the obverse, and on the reverse, around a terrestrial globe, the uncompromising legend NON SUFFICIT ORBIS (The world is not enough).[31] Another Portuguese medal design of the same year, in a conscious attempt to go beyond the famous PLUS ULTRA motto of his father, displayed the zodiac with the phrase ULTRA ANNI SOLIS-QUE VIAS ('Beyond the solar circuit of the year': a slight emendation of Vergil's formula for the Roman Emperor Augustus in the *Aeneid*) 'because God has given him [Philip II] a greater inheritance; and with his great power he could be lord of Cambodia and China and of other vast provinces if he wished'.[32]

Equally ambitious suggestions flowed in from the periphery of the empire. In 1583, at the suggestion of the first bishop of Manila, Domingo de Salazar, Governor Gonzalo Ronquillo Peñalosa of the Philippines once again urged his master to sanction an expedition to conquer China. The following year in September 1584 the devout but pragmatic Matteo Ricci in China wrote scathingly of the pusillanimity of his hosts,

Because when two or three Japanese warships come and land on the coast of China, they burn their boats and capture villages and even large cities, putting everything to

[30] See the brilliant analysis of the 'messianic imperialism' of these three writers by A. Terry, 'War and literature in sixteenth-century Spain', in J. R. Mulryne and M. Shewring, eds., *War, literature and the arts in sixteenth-century Europe* (London, 1989), chapter 4. See also the other imperialists discussed in F. Fernández Armesto, 'Armada myths: the formative phase', in P. Gallagher and D. W. Cruickshank, eds., *God's obvious design: papers of the Spanish Armada Symposium, Sligo, 1588* (London, 1990), pp. 19–39; P. Fernández Alba-ladejo, 'Imperio de por sí. La formulación del poder universal en la temprana edad moderna', in G. Signorotto, *L'Italia degli Austrias. Monarchia cattolica e domini italiani nei secoli XVI e XVII* (Mantua, 1993), pp. 11–28; and Pereña Vicente, *Teoría*, p. 68.

[31] The device was in widespread use by 1586, when Drake's men found in the governor's house in Santo Domingo a 'scutchion' of the royal arms of Spain which contained a globe and a scroll 'wherein was written these words in Latin "NON SVFFICIT ORBIS" – a very notable marke and token of the vnsatiable ambition of the Spanish King and his nation'. From 'A summarie and true discourse of Sir Francis Drake's West Indian Voyage' (1589), in Keeler, *Sir Francis Drake's West Indian voyage*, p. 245 (see also the small reproduction of the device in plate Vb). For the medal: see F. J. Bouza Alvarez, 'Retórica da imagen real. Portugal e la memória figurada de Filipe II', *Penélope*, 4 (1989), 20–58, at 39.

[32] IVDJ 62/916, Duarte Nunes de Leão to Gabriel de Zayas, 8 August 1585. Although Checa, *Felipe II*, pp. 281f., cites the document, my reading of the text – and above all of the Latin inscription (which Checa gives as ULTRA OMNI SOLISQUE VIAS) – differs from his.

the torch and sack, without anyone offering resistance . . . It is true that the Chinese have many fortresses, and the towns all have their walls with which to resist the fury of the pirates; but the walls are not of geometric design [i.e. they lacked bastions] nor do they have traverses or moats.[33]

Others were quick to draw the obvious conclusions. Thus the recipient of Ricci's letter, Juan Bautista Román, added a covering note which alleged that 'With less than 5000 Spaniards Your Majesty could conquer these lands [China] and become lord of them, or at least of the maritime areas, which are the most important in all parts of the world. And with half-a-dozen galleons and as many galleys you would be master of all the coast of China and the adjacent provinces.'[34] That same year, 1584, João Ribeiro Gaio, bishop of Malacca, advocated pooling the resources of Spain and Portugal in order first to secure the simultaneous conquest of south-east Asia, and then to annex southern China. The bishop envisaged an expeditionary force of 4,000 Portuguese troops leaving Goa to attack and destroy the hostile Sultanate of Acheh in Sumatra, while simultaneously 2,000 Spanish soldiers would sail to, and occupy, first Patani and then Siam before moving on effortlessly (and, he seems to have assumed, without casualties) to conquer the city of Canton, 'so rich and sumptuous, and all those other regions of the south [of China], which are many, and very great and very wealthy. And thus His Majesty will be the greatest lord that ever was in the world.'[35] The following year, one of Philip II's judges at Manila, Melchor Dávalos, went even further and called for the king 'to evict and expel the Muslims from all the Philippine islands, or at least to subject them and make them pay tribute, vanquishing those in Java, Sumatra, Acheh, Borneo, Mindanao, Solo, the Moluccas, Malacca, Siam, Patani, Pegu and other

---

[33] P. Torres Lanzas and F. Navas del Valle, eds., *Catálogo de los documentos relativos a las Islas Filipinas existentes en el Archivo General de Indias de Sevilla*, II (Barcelona, 1926), pp. clxxxiii–iv; and F. Colin and P. Pastells, *Labor evangélica de los obreros de la Compañia de Jesús en las islas Filipinas*, III (Barcelona, 1902), pp. 448–52, Matteo Ricci to Juan Bautista Román, 13 September 1584. On Ricci's acute military sense (and contempt for Chinese military skills), see J. D. Spence, *The memory palace of Matteo Ricci* (London, 1983).

[34] J. Guillén Tato, ed., *Museo Naval. Colección de documentos y manuscritos inéditos compilados por Fernández de Navarrete*, XVIII (Nendeln, Kraus Reprint Co., 1971), fos. 146–60, 'Relación dirigida por Juan Bautista Román', Macao, 28 September 1584, after receiving Ricci's letter (at fo. 159v). On the terror which paralysed maritime China, see K. W. So, *Japanese piracy in Ming China during the sixteenth century* (East Lansing, Mich., 1975).

[35] From Ribeiro Gaio's 'Derrotero y Relación' of 1584, in the *Codex Boxer*, now in the Lilly Library of Indiana University at Bloomington, quoted, along with other 'universalist' projects of the day, in C. R. Boxer, 'Portuguese and Spanish Projects for the Conquest of Southeast Asia, 1580–1600', in Boxer, *Portuguese conquest and commerce in southern Asia, 1500–1750* (London, 1985), chapter 3, pp. 118–36.

kingdoms which venerate Mohammed'. And in 1586, a 'general assembly' of the Spanish inhabitants of the Philippines, led by the bishop and the governor, drew up a lengthy memorandum urging the king to undertake the conquest of China and sent Father Alonso Sánchez, S.J., to Spain with orders to present their arguments to the king.[36]

Meanwhile, in Europe, jubilation at the marquis of Santa Cruz's conquest of the Azores in 1582 reached such heights that, according to some *madrileños*, 'even Christ was no longer safe in Paradise, for the marquis might go there to bring him back and crucify him all over again'.[37] Nor did the celebrations stop at verbal hyperbole: a bowl commemorating the Terceira campaign of 1583 (found among the wreckage of one of the Spanish Armada vessels that foundered off Ireland) shows Spain's warrior patron saint with new attributes. He still rides a charger, with his sword arm raised to strike down his foes; but these foes are no longer cowering infidels. Instead they are the swirling waves of the ocean, waves now subdued by Spain along with the human enemies who sought refuge amongst them.[38] The euphoria even affected Santa Cruz who in August 1583, flushed by his success in the Azores, pointed out to the king that:

Victories as complete as the one God has been pleased to grant Your Majesty in these islands normally spur princes on to other enterprises; and since Our Lord has made Your Majesty such a great king, it is just that you should follow up this victory by making arrangements for the invasion of England next year.

The marquis recommended using the newly expanded Iberian resources of his master to concentrate an expeditionary force of overwhelming strength in preparation for a rapid descent on the English coast as close to London as possible.[39]

Gradually, the conquest of England – just like the conquest of Portugal a few years before – came to be seen as the only means of assuring imperial

---

[36] Colin and Pastells, *Labor evangélica*, III, pp. 32–3: Melchor Dávalos to Philip II, Manila, 20 June 1585; Blair and Robertson, *The Philippine Islands*, VI, pp. 197–229.

[37] Bibliothèque Nationale de Paris, Fonds français, ms. 16108/365, M. de St Gouard (French Resident at the Court of Philip II) to Catherine de Medici, 20 August 1582.

[38] See the reproduction of the bowl, dated 1583, in C. Martin and G. Parker, *The Spanish Armada* (London, 1988), colour plate 25. For a discussion of new ways of portraying St James at precisely this time, see IVDJ 62/917, Duarte Nunes de Leão to Zayas, 17 August 1585.

[39] *BMO*, I, pp. 395f., Santa Cruz to Philip II, 9 August 1583 (see also the king's reply dated 23 September, ibid., p. 406). By a curious coincidence, Pope Gregory XIII attempted at precisely this moment to rekindle the king's interest in invading England: see ibid., pp. 406–9, Philip II to the count of Olivares, his ambassador in Rome, 24 September 1583 (with supporting documents), in reply to the pope's letter of 16 August proposing the enterprise of England.

security. An important strategic assessment prepared in 1585, just after Francis Drake raided Galicia, argued that 'to fight a purely defensive war [against England] is to court a huge and permanent expense, because we have to defend the Indies, Spain and the convoys travelling between them'.[40] Even the prudent duke of Medina Sidonia, when asked his opinion in 1586 on mobilizing a fleet against England, urged 'that this should be set in hand at once, and in earnest, and let it be understood that it will not suffice simply to oppose what the English send: it will need to go into the Channel'.[41] The central government agreed. Early in 1587, 'with the English established in Holland and Zealand, together with their infestation of the Americas and the high seas, it seems that defensive measures cannot deal with everything. Rather, it obliges us to put their house to the torch.' And if that 'house' could not be England, 'then let us take from them Ireland, which could be used as a pawn to exchange for the places they hold in the Netherlands, that voracious monster which gobbles up the troops and treasure of Spain'. By the spring of 1588, with 130 ships and 25,000 men ready at Lisbon, the government believed that 'all our wars and affairs afoot today are reduced to this one enterprise': the invasion and conquest of England.[42]

But such an exclusive and expensive policy – the Armada cost 30,000 ducats a day and tied down all the naval and military resources of the peninsula – gravely affected the other parts of Philip II's vast empire. Thus in February 1588, the king rejected the request of his viceroy in Goa, Dom Duarte de Meneses, for the dispatch of 'more troops, ships and munitions than normally leave [for India] each year' in order to attack Acheh because 'The large number of ships of all sorts, troops, munitions and military equipment' assembled for the descent on England 'consume so much that it was not in any way possible (even though we have tried very hard) to send more than five ships' to Goa. But Acheh might still be assaulted with the help of a miracle, Philip continued:

---

[40] IVDJ 32/225, 'A Su Magestad, del Comendador Mayor' [don Juan de Zúñiga], undated but late 1585.

[41] Library of Congress, Manuscript Division, Sir Francis Drake Collection, 3, Medina Sidonia to Philip II, 25 October 1586, minute, point 13. See the similar views of the merchants of Seville in H. Lapèyre, *Une famille de marchands. Les Ruiz* (Paris, 1955), pp. 422–3.

[42] G. Maura Gamazo, duke of Maura, *El designio de Felipe II y el episodio de la Armada Invencible* (Madrid, 1957), p. 167, don Juan de Idiáquez to the duke of Medina Sidonia, 28 February 1587; and E. Herrera Oria, *La Armada Invencible*, Archivo Documental Español, II (Valladolid, 1929), pp.148f., same to same, 20 February 1588.

For what cannot be done now may still happen, if Our Lord wishes to provide the occasion by doing something over here that would be so much for his service, and of such general and such great importance for Christianity, and for the general and particular good of all my kingdoms and lordships.[43]

Now an element of 'providentialism' of this sort lurked in the strategic thinking of almost all states in the century following the Reformation, as religious and political issues became ever more tightly intertwined and the Bible came to serve as a guide to secular as well as spiritual salvation. Most nations in this period regarded themselves as the new 'chosen people', granted a special mandate for empire by God. Thus Philip II's arch-enemies, the English and the Dutch, also regarded their victories as the result of direct divine intervention (such as the famous inscription on a Dutch medal struck to celebrate the destruction of the Spanish Armada: 'God blew and they were scattered'). Likewise they saw their history as predetermined by providence, and viewed wars against enemies of their faith as a crusade.[44] But these sentiments ran particularly strongly in the Iberian peninsula. In the early sixteenth century, King Manuel of Portugal believed himself destined to become emperor of the east, as did his con-temporary Ferdinand of Aragon (who already boasted the title 'king of Jerusalem').[45] Later in the century, many felt that only providence could have created the Habsburg empire through a complex sequence of dynastic accidents (by premature deaths and infertile unions as well as by judicious marriages) and made Charles V lord of Mexico and Peru. Friends and foes alike regarded the Spanish monarchy as an almost supernatural force. More than all other states, wrote Tommaso Campanella, 'it is founded upon the occult providence of God and not on either prudence or human force'; and

---

[43] *APO*, III, pp. 130–1, Philip II to Viceroy, 23 February 1588.

[44] Various 'providentialist' medals of 1588 are reproduced in M. J. Rodríguez Salgado, ed., *Armada 1588–1988* (London, 1988), pp. 276f. For examples of English and Dutch 'providentialism' see M. McGiffert, 'God's controversy with Jacobean England', *American Historical Review*, 88 (1983), 1151–74; C. Z. Wiener, 'The beleaguered isle: a study of Elizabethan and early Jacobean anti-Catholicism', *Past and Present*, 51 (1971), 27–62; D. R. Cressy, *Bonfires and bells: national memory and the Protestant Calendar in Elizabethan and Stuart England* (Berkeley, 1989), chapters 7, 9 and 10; D. R. Woolf, *The idea of history in early Stuart England: erudition, ideology and 'the Light of Truth' from the accession of James I to the Civil War* (Toronto, 1991), pp. 4–8; and G. Groenhuis, *De Predikanten. De Sociale Positie van de Gereformeerde Predikanten in de Republiek der Verenigde Nederlanden voor 1700* (Groningen, 1977), pp. 77–107.

[45] On Manuel, see L. F. F. R. Thomaz, 'Factions, interests and Messianism: the politics of Portuguese expansion in the East, 1500–21', *Indian Economic and Social History Review*, 28 (1991), 97–109; on Ferdinand, see L. Suárez Fernández, 'La política internacional de España en la época de los Reyes Católicos', in Enciso Recio and Ribot Garcia, *El Tratado de Tordesillas*.

the whole of its history came to be seen as a heroic progression in which disasters – even the Moorish conquest of 711 and, eventually, the Spanish Armada of 1588 – became mere episodes in Spain's almost miraculous advance toward world monarchy.[46]

A unique aura of 'messianic imperialism' came to pervade the court of Philip II. Officials justified difficult political choices on the grounds that they were necessary not only for the interests of Spain but also for the cause of God, attributed victories to divine intervention and favour, and rationalized defeats and failures either as a divine test of Spain's steadfastness and devotion or else as a punishment for momentary human weakness.[47] From the 1570s, the government organized a gigantic prayer-chain throughout Castile seeking divine guidance and protection for the king, as principal defender of the catholic faith. Thus the archbishopric of Seville (for example) was divided into 1,100 separate prayer stations, each of which had three days assigned annually – in strict rotation – for the special collect.[48]

Philip II felt entirely comfortable with this providential vision and constantly equated his own interests, and those of the lands that he ruled, with those of God. Thus in the 1560s he refused to moderate the heresy laws in force in the Netherlands because he believed that 'if the catholic faith is lost, my estates will be lost with it'; and he urged his advisers 'To tell me in all things what you think is best for the service of God, which is my principal aim, and so for my service'. Before long, the two had become inseparable: 'You are engaged in God's service and in mine – which is the same thing', he loftily reassured one of his dispirited commanders in 1573.[49]

This total identification in Philip II's mind between the cause of God and his own interests sometimes led him to adopt extreme positions and take extreme risks. On several occasions he declared himself ready to sacrifice all his dominions, if necessary, rather than imperil the integrity of the catholic faith. In 1585, after his commander in the Netherlands (Alexander Farnese,

---

[46] Campanella quoted by Pagden, *Spanish imperialism*, p. 51. On Spain's history as a cycle of alternating disasters and miracles, see the penetrating remarks of P. Gallagher and D. W. Cruickshank, 'The Armada of 1588 reflected in serious and popular literature of the period', in Gallagher and Cruickshank, *God's obvious design*, pp. 167–83.

[47] See the classic discussion of the origins of Spanish 'messianic imperialism' in the 1520s in M. Bataillon, *Erasmo y España. Estudios sobre la historia espiritual del siglo XVI* (2nd edition, Mexico, 1950), pp. 226–31; and F. Yates, *Astraea: the imperial theme in the sixteenth century* (London, 1975), pp. 1–28.

[48] See details in Bouza Alvarez, 'Monarchie', pp. 214f.

[49] Est. 527/5, Philip II to Gonzalo Pérez, undated [March 1565]; and Bibliothèque Publique et Universitaire, Geneva, ms. Favre 30/73v, Philip II to don Luis de Requeséns, 20 October 1573, copy of holograph original: 'Spero en Dios. . .que os dara mucha salud y vida, pues se empleara en su servicio y en el mío, que es lo mismo.'

duke of Parma) had persuaded several rebellious cities to surrender in return for limited religious toleration for a period, the king expressed regret about the concessions, because 'I believe it would be better to forfeit all that I have rather than compromise for a moment my constancy where religion is concerned.'[50]

Likewise, in 1586, when the king sanctioned Spanish intervention in France to uphold the catholic faction, he noted on a document:

Truly, I have only agreed to this because it seems to be the only way available to remedy the religious state of that kingdom. It may mean that we shall encounter other difficulties arising from what we are doing, but the cause of religion is the most important thing of all.

Four years later, to justify committing a major army to the support of the Catholic League in France, the king reiterated that 'upholding the faith has been and still is my principal objective in all that has been and is being done'.[51] It might have been imperialism dictated by sincere religious convictions, but it was imperialism none the less.

The same certitude that he could read God's mind better than anyone else even influenced strategy on a practical level. In 1587–88, as he planned the overthrow of Elizabeth Tudor, Philip II had no doubt that, at the critical moment, God would intervene directly to provide the desired outcome in spite of all the odds. So when the commander of the invasion fleet complained about the danger of launching the Armada against England in midwinter, the king replied serenely:

We are fully aware of the risk that is incurred by sending a major fleet in winter through the Channel without a safe harbour, but. . .since it is all for His cause, God will send good weather.

Again in June 1588, after a storm had damaged some of the ships, driven others into Corunna, and scattered the rest, when a minister suggested that these reverses might be a sign from God to desist, the king replied:

---

[50] Letter to the duke of Parma quoted (with other similar ones) in J. Zarco Cuevas, 'Ideales y normas de gobierno de Felipe II', in F. Pérez Mínguez, ed., *Reivindicación histórica del siglo XVI* (Madrid, 1928), pp. 151f. See also the celebrated letter to Pius V in 1566, printed in L. Serrano, *Correspondencia diplomática entre España y la Santa Sede durante el pontificado de S. Pío V*, I (Madrid, 1914), p. 316: 'rather than suffer the least damage to the Catholic church and God's service I will lose all my states, and a hundred lives if I had them'.

[51] AGS, Est. K 1448/43, royal apostil on a letter from don Juan de Idiáquez to don Bernardino de Mendoza, 27 April 1586, minute; Zarco Cuevas, 'Ideales', pp. 151f, Instruction to don Diego de Ibarra, 18 November 1590.

If this were an unjust war, one could indeed take this storm as a sign from Our Lord to cease offending Him; but being as just as it is, one cannot believe that He will disband it, but rather will grant it more favour than we could hope.

'I have dedicated this enterprise to God', the king concluded. 'Get on, then, and do your part!'[52] Upon such rocks of intransigence, rational calculations of Spain's strategic advantage foundered.

The humiliating failure of the Armada, however, forced Philip II to adopt a more defensive policy, and to make hard strategic choices. New initiatives for further expansion were now either vetoed or else compromised for lack of central support. Some, like the various projects for the invasion of China, no doubt lacked merit – although the remarkable success of a small combined operation of Spanish and Portuguese soldiers and missionaries in Cambodia between 1596 and 1599 indicates what luck – combined with a total lack of scruple – could do.[53] Others, however, like the repeated Portuguese efforts to conquer Sri Lanka after 1594, or the efforts of the Philippines government to occupy Taiwan after 1597, might have succeeded in creating secure bases had those concerned received adequate funding.[54] Within Europe, Philip II's failure to provide substantial and sustained support to Tyrone's rebellion in Ireland ranks as perhaps the greatest lost strategic opportunity of the 1590s.[55] Worse, the king's inability to defend his subjects' interests at home while his resources were fully committed against his enemies abroad led to grave material losses. Direct English assaults on the peninsula came in 1589 (on Corunna), and 1596 (on Cadiz) while the English fleet maintained a semi-permanent predatory presence off

---

[52] Quotations from AGS, Est. 165/2-3, Philip II to Archduke Albert, 14 September 1587; and Oria, *Armada Invencible*, pp. 210–14, Philip II to Medina Sidonia, 1 July 1588.

[53] On the first see Bourdon, 'Un projet d'invasion de la Chine'; on the second, B. Bierman, 'Los portugueses y españoles en Camboja al fin del siglo XVI', *Archivo Ibero-Americano*, 38 (year 22) (1935), pp. 261–70; B. P. Groslier and C. R. Boxer, *Angkor et le Cambodge au XVIe siècle d'après les sources portugaises et espagnoles* (Paris, 1958), pp. 34–62; and M. Phoeun, ed., *Chroniques royales du Cambodge (de 1594 à 1677)* (Paris, 1981), pp. 72–5. Boxer, 'Portuguese and Spanish projects', noted both escapades.

[54] On Ceylon, see T. Abeyasinghe, *Portuguese rule in Ceylon, 1594–1612* (Colombo, 1966); and G. D. Winius, *The fatal history of Portuguese Ceylon: transition to Dutch rule* (Cambridge, Mass., 1971). On Taiwan, see P. Torres y Lanzas, ed., *Católogo de los documentos relativos a las Islas Filipinas existentes en el Archivo General de Indias de Sevilla*, IV (Barcelona, 1928), pp. lxxviii–lxxx; and Boxer, 'Portuguese and Spanish projects', p. 132. In the end Spaniards from the Philippines did maintain settlements on the north coast of Taiwan between 1624 and 1642: see R. G. Knapp, ed., *China's island frontier: studies in the historical geography of Taiwan* (Honolulu, 1980), 13f.; and J. L. Phelan, *The hispanization of the Philippines: Spanish aims and Filipino responses, 1565–1700* (Madison, Wis., 1967), pp. 138–9.

[55] See H. Morgan, *Tyrone's rebellion: the outbreak of the Nine Years' War in Tudor Ireland* (London, 1993), pp. 206–13; and J. J. Silke, *Kinsale: the Spanish intervention in Ireland at the end of the Elizabethan wars* (Liverpool, 1970).

the Iberian coast. Although the Royal Navy itself scored but few spectacular successes – most notably the capture of the India carracks *Madre de Deus* in 1592 and the *São Valentim* in 1601 – English privateers scored far more.[56] In the three years following the Armada, 1589–91, English vessels took at least 299 prizes, worth perhaps £400,000 (equivalent to the government's entire annual revenue) and well over £100,000 annually thereafter. Nine-tenths of the value of this English plunder came from ships sailing from India, Africa and America to the Iberian peninsula, with 'Brazilmen' (vessels carrying sugar and brazilwood from Pernambuco to Portugal) as the commonest prize of all.[57]

The effect of prolonged war with England and the Dutch on Iberian overseas commerce soon proved devastating. During the first eight decades of the *carreira da India*, between 1498 and 1586, not a single ship of the hundreds sailing between Portugal and India fell prey to pirates; but during the next decade, between 1587 and 1596, no fewer than five carracks were either captured or burnt by enemies. Furthermore, the constant diversion of shipping and materials to operations in the North Atlantic after 1585 both reduced the number of vessels available for trade with India and complicated the task of preparing the outward voyages, with the result that the carracks left in smaller numbers and set sail dangerously late. Whereas before the union of crowns only one vessel in ten foundered en route between Lisbon and Goa, between 1580 and 1610 the total soared to one ship in four; moreover, whereas between 1500 and 1579 only six ships sailed from Lisbon too late to catch favourable winds to India, between 1580 and 1608 fourteen 'lost their voyage'. Overall, shipping arriving in Goa from Portugal declined by 25 per cent between 1580 and 1600.[58] Likewise the trade between Spain and the Americas fell dramatically in 1587–88 and scarcely recovered until peace with England came in 1604.[59] In the 1590s the Dutch, too, began to trade and loot in Africa, South America and, eventually, Asia, plunging the colonial administrations of both Castile and

---

[56] For the *Madre* see K. R. Andrews, *Elizabethan privateering: English privateering during the Spanish War 1585–1603* (Cambridge, 1964), p. 73; for the *Valentim*, see Public Record Office, London, Audit Office 1/1691/39 and 1/1692/42 (accounts of Fulk Greville and William Ryder for the sale of the cargo – which brought in £44,000, more than the entire cost of the navy for a year!).

[57] See Andrews, *Elizabethan privateering*, pp. 124–34.

[58] J. C. Boyajian, *Portuguese trade in Asia under the Habsburgs, 1580–1640* (Baltimore, 1993), pp. 24–5; and L. de Figueiredo Falcão, *Livro em que se contem toda a fazenda e real patrimonio dos reynos de Portugal* (Lisbon, 1607; reprinted, 1859), pp. 194–6. (Note that the carrack listed as lost in 1586 was the *São Phelipe* captured by Drake in 1587.)

[59] See the tables and commentary in H. and P. Chaunu, *Séville et l'Atlantique, 1504–1650*, III (Paris, 1955), pp. 398ff., and VIII, part 2 (Paris, 1959), pp. 753ff.

Portugal into a frenzy of defence spending – from escorts and convoys to fortresses and garrisons, and from Mombasa and Macao to Manila and Callao. Although the financial state of the *estado da India* had given some cause for concern before the union of crowns, the detailed fiscal surveys of 1581, 1588, 1607 and 1609 all showed a healthy surplus, despite the almost constant state of war that existed between the Portuguese and some of their neighbours.[60] However, the arrival of the English and Dutch ('os enemigos de Europa' as the viceroys always termed them) both reduced the profits from the various trades on which the *estado* thrived and increased the cost of defence, as one outpost after another required expensive new fortifications.[61] By the 1630s, the revenues of Portuguese India fell far short of the costs of administration and defence, while its unsecured debts stood at 4 million cruzados.[62] The evolution of the imperial budget in Spanish America followed a similar path: although remittances to Seville remained high until the 1610s, the cost of defence soared – and not only the defence of the long coastline of the islands and mainland of the Americas but also of the Philippines. Indeed, between 1618 and 1621 the Royal Treasury in Mexico sent more money to the Philippines than to Spain, and by 1640 it spent one-third or more of its revenues on defence.[63]

[60] See details in A. Teodoro de Matos, 'The financial situation of the State of India during the Philippine period (1581–1635)', in T. R. de Souza, ed., *Indo-Portuguese history: old issues, new questions* (New Delhi, 1985), pp. 90–101. For some doubts concerning the solvency of the Portuguese Asia, see M. N. Pearson, *Merchants and rulers in Gujarat: the response of the Portuguese in the sixteenth century* (Berkeley, 1976), p. 56. The constant state of war in which the *estado da India* existed appears clearly in the reports of the viceroys to Lisbon between 1605 and 1622 printed in R. A. Bulhão Pato and A. da Silva Rego, eds., *Documentos remettidos da India ou Livros das Monções* (10 vols., Lisbon, 1880–1975).

[61] The magnificent survey carried out in 1633–5 by A. Bocarro, *O livro das plantas de todas as fortalezas, cidades e povoações do Estado da Índia Oriental* (3 vols., new edition, Lisbon, 1992), records and depicts the new fortifications begun at Mascate (1588), Mombasa (1593), Damão (1615), Diu (1634) and so on.

[62] On the apparent surplus of 1635 see Teodoro de Matos, 'The financial situation', p. 93; however, the budget omitted the cost of equipping the return fleet that year (a point made to me by L. F. F. R. Thomaz). Moreover in 1634 Viceroy Linhares expressly stated that the revenues of the *estado* did not suffice to cover ordinary expenditure and defence: see Historical Archive, Goa (HAG), ms. 1162/128-9, Asiento of the council of finance, 16 August 1634. HAG, ms. 26/69v-70, Linhares to Philip IV, 7 December 1634, copy, put the debt at 'mais de cuatro milhaões [cruzados]'.

[63] See P. Bakewell, *Silver mining and society in colonial Mexico: Zacatecas 1546–1700* (Cambridge, 1971), p. 232; M. A. Burkholder and L. L. Johnson, *Colonial Latin America* (Oxford, 1994), p. 150; J. A. Calderón Quijano, *Fortificaciones en Nueva España* (Seville, 1984); G. Guarda, *Flandes Indiano. Las fortificaciones del reino de Chile, 1541–1826* (Santiago de Chile, 1990); P. E. Hoffman, *The Spanish crown and the defense of the Caribbean, 1535–85: precedent, patrimonialism and royal parsimony* (Baton Rouge, 1980); and G. Lohmann Villena, *Las defensas militares de Lima y Callao* (Seville, 1964).

Fernand Braudel's classic study of Philip II and his world saw the years 1578–83 as 'the turning point of the century', which marked a decisive shift in Europe's centre of gravity from the Mediterranean to the Atlantic. In political terms, between 1577 and 1581 Philip II disengaged from his long-running struggle with the Ottoman Turks and (although he continued to encourage Safavid Iran to fight on) instead concentrated his resources – both those of the Portuguese empire and the fast-rising remittances from America – in 'a great battle for control of the Atlantic and world domination'.[64] And when that bid foundered, as it did in the 1580s and 1590s, those whom the Habsburg monarchy had failed to vanquish sought their revenge.

But would the north Europeans have tried to overturn the Iberian intercontinental trading monopolies anyway? After all, they had challenged them long before 1580: the French in Canada, Brazil and Florida; the English in Guinea, the Caribbean and (during Drake's circumnavigation of 1577–80) in the Pacific too. Although it is notoriously difficult to predict the might-have-beens of history, a brief consideration of the ventures that immediately followed the defeat of the Spanish Armada in 1588 may be instructive. For although the profits of Philip II and his subjects from their overseas empires declined, those of their enemies did not soar. Although the capture of individual carracks proved extremely profitable, the expense of fitting out expeditions, and later of maintaining bases overseas, absorbed almost all the gains made from commerce. The Dutch East India Company – the most profitable overseas enterprise mounted by Philip II's enemies – until 1630 landed annually at Amsterdam cargoes well under half the value of those landed at Lisbon, and paid only thirteen dividends in cash.[65] The Dutch West India Company, founded in 1622 to break into the lucrative Iberian trades with Africa and the Americas, despite heavy subsidies from the government had run up debts of 18 million florins by 1640 and was declared bankrupt and liquidated by 1674.[66] The early financial history of the various English companies founded to trade in Asia and the Americas likewise lacked lustre: even Drake's West India raid of 1585–86 made a loss of 25 per cent; the Virginia Company failed; and the English East India Company

---

[64] F. Braudel, *The Mediterranean and the Mediterranean world in the age of Philip II*, II (London, 1973), p. 1176; S. A. Skilliter, 'The Hispano-Ottoman armistice of 1581', in C. E. Bosworth, ed., *Iran and Islam* (Edinburgh, 1971), pp. 491–515.

[65] See Boyajian, *Portuguese trade*, p. 128; G. Parker, *Spain and the Netherlands, 1559–1659* (London, 1979), pp. 193–5; and M. A. P. Meilink-Roelofsz., *Asian trade and European influence in the Indonesian archipelago between 1500 and about 1630* (The Hague, 1962), p. 386.

[66] Parker, *Spain and the Netherlands*, pp. 195–6.

(which lacked any fixed capital) experienced constant cash flow problems until the 1650s.[67]

It therefore seems unlikely that, on commercial grounds, merchants from northern Europe would have chosen to make the heavy investment necessary for even modest success in intercontinental trade had they been able to secure the colonial produce they desired within the Iberian peninsula – as they had done until the embargoes of 1585–86. After that, however, in order to secure the spices, silks, silver and other luxuries from the Far East and the Far West, the English and Dutch had no alternative but to sail to the source and get it themselves. In this context, had the embargoes affected Spain but not Portugal – that is to say, had Philip II not been king of Portugal – the financial and the political incentives for the northerners to organize their own trade with Asia would both have been lacking.[68]

In the end, therefore, the annexation of Portugal in 1580 weakened rather than strengthened the monarchy of Philip II: the liabilities ultimately outweighed the assets – principally because the union threatened the prevailing balance of power in Europe. And yet, as Pedro de Ribadeneira had written at the time, what else could the king have done except enforce his claim to the Portuguese succession? The consequences for Philip II's Monarchy had either dom Antonio (an illegitimate cousin of King Sebastian who enjoyed French and English support) or some other hostile claimant gained control of Portugal can easily be imagined: the cost of defending the long land frontier and the vital sea lanes would soon have proved crippling. The dilemma bore a curious resemblance to that facing Philip's great-grandson, Louis XIV, in 1700. Carlos II, the last of the Spanish Habsburgs, bequeathed all his territories to Louis's grandson; if Louis refused the inheritance, it would pass intact and entire to the Austrian Habsburgs; and if they refused, it would go to the duke of Savoy. Louis and his ministers, just like Philip II and his advisers, rated the risks attached to allowing the adjacent inheritance to pass to another claimant higher than the possibility that joining together two great empires would prove unacceptable to the other major powers and so precipitate, sooner or later, a general European war. They accepted the poisoned chalice.[69]

---

[67] Keeler, *Sir Francis Drake's West Indian voyage*, p. 56; B. Bailyn, *The New England merchants in the seventeenth century* (Cambridge, 1955), pp. 2–5; K. N. Chaudhuri, *The English East India Company: the study of an early joint stock company, 1600–1640* (London, 1965).

[68] On the significance of the embargoes, see G. Parker, *The grand strategy of Philip II* (New Haven, 1996), chapter 5.

[69] On Louis XIV's reluctant decision to accept the will of Carlos II, see the brilliant elucidation in A. Lossky, *Louis XIV and the French Monarchy* (New Brunswick, 1994), pp. 260–2.

In the event, the union of crowns in 1580, like the Spanish succession in 1700, unleashed an international crisis. It provoked a major conflict with other European states – several of them possessing imperial aspirations of their own – and brought war to almost every corner of Philip II's monarchy, imperilling its integrity and threatening its future. As a senior diplomat shrewdly put it, shortly after the king's death:

Truly, sir, I believe we are gradually becoming the field where the whole world wants to shoot its arrows; and you know that no empire, however great, has been able to sustain many wars in different areas for long. If we can think only of defending ourselves, and never manage to contrive a great offensive blow against one of our enemies, so that when that is over we can turn to the others, although I may be mistaken, I doubt whether we can sustain an empire as scattered as ours.[70]

The empire on which the sun never set had become a target on which the sun never set; and the central government always seemed to lack the resources to do more than respond to each attack with half-measures. In the withering assessment of one of Spain's leading naval commanders:

I have been much grieved for some years past to see that, for motives of economy, expeditions are undertaken with such small forces that they principally serve to irritate our enemies, rather than to punish them. The worst of it is that wars thus become chronic, and the expense and trouble resulting from long continued wars are endless.[71]

So, thanks to the strategic overstretch caused by the union of crowns, Philip II, who on his coronation day at Tomar in 1581 had seemed like David, by the time of his death in 1598 had begun to resemble Goliath.

[70] IVDJ, 82/444 duke of Sessa (Spanish ambassador in Rome) to don Balthasar de Zúñiga (Spanish ambassador in Brussels), 28 September 1600, minute. The occasion for this outburst was the rumour that an envoy of the Sharif of Morocco had gone to London to forge an alliance with Elizabeth of England.

[71] M. A. S. Hume, ed., *Calendar of Letters and State Papers relating to English affairs preserved in ... Simancas: Elizabeth,* IV (London, 1899), p. 690, don Pedro de Padilla, Adelantado of Castile and commander of the abortive Armadas of 1596 and 1597, to Philip III, 10 December 1601.

II

※

Olivares, the Cardinal-Infante and Spain's strategy in the Low Countries (1635–1643): the road to Rocroi

JONATHAN I. ISRAEL

In terms of territory and dependencies, the Spanish monarchy in early modern times was essentially a Mediterranean and trans-Atlantic empire. It extended across the southern flank of Europe and included an immense portion of the New World. Yet, paradoxically, during most of the age of Spanish greatness, the principal strategic pivot and main military base of the monarchy was located far from both the main territorial blocs of which the empire was composed – in northern Europe. In the opening decades of Spain's ascendancy down to the 1530s, its principal armies operated in Italy or the Iberian peninsula itself. But from the 1540s onwards, for well over a century, the Spanish crown chose to concentrate its military might, resources and expenditure, and thus its capacity to influence international affairs, in the Low Countries. This remarkable enduring strategic posture ceased only with the peace of the Pyrenees (1659) when Spain definitively lost its place at the head of the European powers, to France, and turned its efforts to attempting to recover Portugal.

There were several reasons for this, at first sight, rather illogical choice of main strategic base but the most compelling, during much of this long period, was the need to combat French power and influence, France being Spain's chief rival for hegemony in Europe. For France proved to be much more vulnerable to pressure from the Low Countries than to Spanish power

I would like to express my gratitude to both editors and also to Robert Oresko and Fernando González de León for their assistance with various matters discussed in this article. Translations are mine unless otherwise attributed.

Figure 3   Spain's strategy in the Low Countries, 1635–1643

exerted in the south. Of course, there were intervals when France was not the foremost danger facing the Spanish monarchy, such as the early 1560s when the spread of Ottoman power in the Mediterranean posed the chief threat, or the 1570s and 1580s when the rebellion in the northern Netherlands was the main preoccupation, or the opening years of the Thirty Years' War when the challenge to Habsburg ascendancy in the Holy Roman Empire seemed most urgent. But taking the period from 1540 to 1659 as a whole, France was, and was perceived to be, Spain's chief rival and the principal threat to Spain's preponderance in Europe.

For well over a century, then, the Netherlands was Spain's main strategic base or, as it was expressed then, *plaza de armas*. This is a point worth emphasizing for not a few historians, and generations of history students, have been convinced that (at least down to the fall of Breisach, in 1638) France was boxed in, all but encircled by Spanish and other Habsburg territories. A glance at a map of sixteenth- or early seventeenth-century Europe might indeed suggest precisely that; but such notions overlook the fact that the Franche-Comté (or Spanish Burgundy) was virtually indefensible and useless as a strategic base. Spanish Lombardy was a valuable possession and effective barrier, excluding French power from most of Italy, but was hardly suitable as a launching pad for Spanish offensives against, or any kind of intervention in, France, being separated from that monarchy by Piedmont and the Alpes Maritimes. Furthermore, the parts of Catalonia, Aragon and Navarre bordering on France, regions less densely populated and developed than southern France, were also for the most part weak links in what was, all considered, an exceedingly precarious chain. In fact, there was only one strong point among the Spanish territories adjoining France and that was the Spanish Netherlands. But so formidable and impenetrable was that bastion to sixteenth- and seventeenth-century armies, owing to the dense clustering of walled towns and new style fortifications, and the large number of rivers, dikes and canals to be found there, and so well-suited was that region to the maintenance of a large standing army, and the logistics of equipping and provisioning troops, that it served, on its own, to tip the strategic balance between Spain and France in such a way as to place France at a constant and appreciable disadvantage. Given that the Spanish Netherlands were difficult to invade from France, while on the French side the terrain lay invitingly open and Paris itself was only a short distance from the borders of Artois and Hainault – St Quentin, then just over the border in France being already over half way on the road from Brussels to Paris – Spain was, for as long as it possessed at least one large and well-equipped army, and stationed it in the Netherlands, capable of paralysing French offensives towards Italy or Spain, and pinning France helplessly to the defensive, whenever it chose. Whatever the position elsewhere, the Spanish army in the Netherlands could usually force the French to drop everything, and concentrate on defending the heart of the French monarchy merely by setting foot across the border. In this way, the Spanish Netherlands, though far from the two main territorial blocks of the empire, became what has been described as 'both the hammer and anvil of the Spanish Monarchy'.[1]

Consequently, during the war of 1635–59, the longest and most gruelling contest between Spain and France, there was never, at any stage, the slightest possibility that Spain's main army would be stationed anywhere other than in the south Netherlands. But there is a very real question as to when, precisely, the main Spanish effort came to be directed against France. It has been generally assumed that at the outset of this great struggle, Philip IV's chief minister, the count-duke of Olivares, was fully resolved on a large-scale offensive against France. However, it is open to doubt whether this was anything more than a momentary impulse if it was even that.[2] Since 1621, the Spanish army of Flanders had been locked in an arduous, slow moving war of sieges and counter-sieges with the Dutch. Did Spain now simply abandon, or give greatly reduced priority, to a struggle in to which such vast resources had been poured, over so many years, to turn its might against France which (at least on land) was undeniably its most powerful adversary? This is, indeed, a crucial question about Spanish strategy in 1635 and subsequent years, down to the battle of Rocroi (1643), the years in which Spain was still capable of mounting powerful offensives. When, and by what stages, did Spain scale down its war with the Dutch and unleash its principal effort against France?

By and large historians have simply taken it for granted that the Dutch front must have been relegated to secondary importance in Spanish strategic councils from 1635 onwards, and most general histories of the Thirty Years' War firmly give this impression. Even books which specifically deal with Spain's European strategy assert that this was the case. Thus, one historian claims that the Spanish–Dutch war 'faded into the background, ceasing to be a "hot war" (except in the maritime theatre) and by default, conditions approximating to those of armistice held sway until the Treaty of Mün-

---

[1] J. I. Israel, *The Dutch Republic and the Hispanic world, 1606–1661* (Oxford, 1982), pp. 251–2.
[2] John H. Elliott, *The count-duke of Olivares: the statesman in an age of decline* (New Haven and London, 1986), pp. 494–5.

ster'.[3] Admittedly, what I shall call the conventional view that Spain now gave priority to the French war, reversing its previous strategy in the Netherlands, appears to be vindicated by the fact that in 1636 the army of Flanders did enter France. In that year, the governor-general of the Spanish Netherlands, Philip IV's younger brother, the Cardinal-Infante, penetrated as far as Corbie, causing panic in Paris. Usually this episode is viewed as part of a massive, long-planned and major Spanish offensive. Moreover, this almost universally postulated 'great offensive' against France has been written about in rather dramatic terms. One scholar asserts that 'in 1636 the offensive directed by the Cardinal-Infante Ferdinand from the Low Countries had almost reached Paris', that Olivares at this juncture pressed the emperor 'to join in a decisive attack on France' and that the 'Cardinal-Infante together with Piccolomini and Gallas at the head of the Imperialist forces began a campaign directed at the very heart of France'.[4]

This interpretation remains predominant in recent publications. We are told of the 'offensive stage of the war against France' in the years 1635–7 and that the 'joint Spanish-Imperial invasion of France, at first promising much, petered out in 1637'.[5] Another scholar assures us that 'in 1635 the Cardinal-Infante took the offensive against France, striking hopefully from the Low Countries towards Paris; by August 1636 his army had reached Corbie'.[6] Yet another, in a widely read general work, claims that in 1635 Olivares 'planned the triple invasion of France in the following year' and that the 'conquest of an area as large as France was ... beyond the military capacities of the Habsburg forces' which, however, 'briefly approached Paris'.[7]

I have already made some attempt to challenge this prevailing interpretation and show that it has little or no basis in fact.[8] My purpose in this present essay is to restate my views of the matter in a more developed form and with more reference to the strategic relationship between Spain and France, arguing that there was no large-scale, concerted Spanish offensive against France in the years 1635–7, or subsequently (until the early 1640s),

---

[3] R. A. Stradling, *Europe and the decline of Spain: a study of the Spanish system, 1580–1720* (London, 1981), pp. 103–4.

[4] J. V. Polišenský, *The Thirty Years' War* (2nd edition, London, 1974), p. 219.

[5] R. A. Stradling, *Philip IV and the government of Spain (1621–1655)* (Cambridge, 1988), pp. 80, 130, 162.

[6] J. Lynch, *The Hispanic world in crisis and change, 1598–1700* (Oxford, 1992), p.140.

[7] Paul Kennedy, *The rise and fall of the great powers* (Lexington, Mass., 1987), p. 40; more guarded, but still to an extent giving the same impression, is R. J. Bonney's section 'France's war by diversion' in Geoffrey Parker, ed. *The Thirty Years' War* (London, 1984) pp. 144–53.

[8] Israel, *The Dutch Republic and the Hispanic world*, pp. 250–62.

ordered from Madrid or anywhere else. I hope to show that the 'French' front was not given priority over the 'Dutch' front, by Madrid or Brussels, in 1635–7 and that, furthermore, Olivares was as convinced as anyone of the need to concentrate Spain's main effort against the Dutch rather than the French and, over the winter of 1635–6, insisted on this in the most categorical terms. But, above all, my object is to explain the logic of Spanish strategic thinking in the later 1630s, the priorities which shaped Olivares' approach, the true reasons for the hastily improvised thrust to Corbie and, lastly, why, after 1640 Spanish ministers finally decided to drop the predominantly 'Dutch strategy' of the previous years and launch Spain's main effort against France.

It has been claimed, as recently as 1986, that Olivares' grand plan to attack France in 1635–7 was 'surely the most ambitious military conception of early modern Europe', that 'Olivares was relying to a significant extent on a rapid removal of France from the list of his enemies' and that the 'Cardinal-Infante was ordered to be prepared for all-out war with France'.[9] The same author admits that the reality was less grandiose than the concept but still insists on 'how close Olivares came to the outright defeat of France when a year later and considerably reduced in scale he actually launched his offensive'.[10] But in reality the Cardinal-Infante received no orders to attack France, following the French declaration of war and, during the early months of 1635, before the joint Franco-Dutch invasion of the Spanish Netherlands of that summer focused his mind instead on a plan to capture Philippine, one of the key Dutch strongholds around the Scheldt estuary.[11] Nor was Spain's principal ally, Philip IV's cousin, the Holy Roman Emperor Ferdinand II (1619–1637) either planning, or ready to contribute to, a major offensive against France at this stage.[12] Furthermore, it should not be forgotten that the original reason why the Cardinal-Infante was sent to the southern Netherlands with a powerful army in 1634 was not to fight France, or strike, from Flanders, into Germany, but for a different and very specific purpose: to restore Spanish power and authority in the Low Countries following the humiliating and disastrous setbacks at Dutch hands in 1629–33 and the severe weakening of the army in Flanders resulting from Spanish involvement in the

---

[9] R. A. Stradling, 'Olivares and the origins of the Franco-Spanish war, 1627–1635', *English Historical Review*, 101 (1986), 90–1; ironically Stradling criticizes John H. Elliott for not giving more emphasis to Olivares' plans to invade France.
[10] Stradling, 'Olivares and the origins', p. 91.   [11] Israel, *The Dutch Republic*, p. 252.
[12] E. Straub, *Pax et Imperium. Spaniens Kampf um seine Friedensordnung in Europa zwischen 1617 und 1635* (Paderborn, 1980), p. 471.

War of Mantua (1628–31).[13] By 1633 Spanish prestige in the Low Countries stood lower than at any time since the disastrous collapse of the late 1570s, during the governorship of don Juan de Austria, and its aftermath, so that for Olivares and Philip IV restoring Spain's might and *reputación* in the Netherlands was a priority of the utmost and overriding urgency. Given the extent of territory and large number of towns lost in the years 1629–33, it was inherent in this task of restoring Spain's position in the Netherlands that at least some of the strategically important lost towns and fortresses – which included Maastricht, Venlo, Roermond, Helmond, Eindhoven, Rheinberg, Wesel, Sittard, 's-Hertogenbosch and Limburg – should be recovered.

There were no orders, then, to concentrate against France. On the contrary, in a special meeting held in Madrid on 2 February 1635, before the French declaration of war (19 May 1635), but at a time when it was clearly pending, the count-duke and five other ministers, including the marquises of Leganés and Villahermosa, agreed on the necessity to launch an offensive against the Dutch and recapture Limburg and Maastricht as soon as possible, and then also Venlo, Roermond, Grave and crossing-points on the Lower Rhine, so as to restore Spain's strategic position in the chief river valleys of the Low Countries and revive its capacity to intervene in the German conflict.[14] On 18 March, the Cardinal-Infante wrote from Brussels confirming that he would follow his orders to concentrate against the Dutch and, if the expected quick successes were achieved, try to secure the now desperately needed truce with the Republic and thereby halt the escalating overseas conflict, above all in Brazil, and free Spain to confront France.[15]

In the event the Cardinal-Infante accomplished nothing in the interval before the Franco-Dutch invasion of June 1635. The advancing French and Dutch armies joined forces in the Maas valley in July, while the Cardinal-Infante fell back to cover Brussels. The invading army, some 60,000 strong, captured Diest, Tienen and several smaller places in Brabant before setting siege to Leuven (Louvain). But poor organization and logistics and the spread of sickness among the French, soon weakened the besieging army and this, together with their failure to make any impact on the walls of

---

[13] Israel, *The Dutch Republic*, pp. 238, 245, 250–1; Elliott, *The count-duke of Olivares*, pp. 453–4.

[14] AGS, Est. 2050. 'Junta particular sobre algunos propuestos de lo que se podría obrar este año con las armas en Flandes', Madrid, 22 February 1635; see especially Olivares' observations on fo. 5.

[15] AGR, Brussels, SEG, vol. 212, fo. 269. Cardinal-Infante to Philip, Brussels, 18 March 1635.

Leuven, rapidly transformed the strategic position.[16] Before long the Spaniards had regained the initiative and both French and Dutch were forced into a headlong retreat northwards towards the United Provinces.

The Cardinal-Infante could now counter-attack in whichever direction he chose but opted (in accordance with his general instructions) to launch his offensive towards the north.[17] After recapturing Diest and Tienen, he advanced north-eastwards, towards the Rhine. Then, in late July, came the sensational news that a small Spanish column, operating further north, had succeeded in taking Schenckenschans (or Schenck or, in Spanish Esquenque), one of the most vital Dutch fortresses on the Lower Rhine, guarding a major route of access into Gelderland from the east. Schenck had not the slightest relevance to any conceivable attack on France but Olivares and Philip IV were not just gratified on hearing the news: their spirits soared. Over the next months Olivares was nothing less than euphoric. For he was convinced that the capture of Schenck opened the way to much greater strategic gains at Dutch expense than had been projected in the spring of 1635. Schenckenschans provided, or so it seemed, a heaven-sent opportunity to revive Spanish power on the Lower Rhine in dramatic fashion and tip the balance in the Low Countries back in favour of Spain. Philip and Olivares ordered the Cardinal-Infante to advance further north, pour troops and resources into the Lower Rhine area and do everything possible to secure his lines of communication with Schenck: 'so that from there we can make war in the heart of Holland and, I hope, if we proceed thus and, as you say, if we clear the enemy from the Maas, and with this fortress, you will be able to make the peace or truce [with the Dutch] that we want'.[18] Once confirmed, the Spanish public were told of the Cardinal-Infante's glorious triumph against the 'Dutch' by means of a printed account published in Seville.[19] The Dutch public, by contrast, was deeply disturbed by the unpalatable news. The Stadholder, Frederik Hendrik, decided to keep his field army out in the open around Schenckenschans all

---

[16] AGR, SEG, vol. 213, fo. 1. Cardinal-Infante to Philip, Brussels, 11 July 1635.

[17] Diego de Luna y Mora, 'Relación de la campaña del año de 1635', in *Colección de documentos inéditos para la historia de España* (113 vols., Madrid, 1842–95), LXXV, p. 398; Henri Lonchay, *La rivalité de la France et de l'Espagne aux Pays-Bas (1635–1700)* (Brussels, 1896), pp. 76–7.

[18] BL, Add. 14007, fo. 53. 'Copia de carta de s.Magd. para el señor Infante Don Fernando', Madrid 25 October 1635: 'para que de alli se pueda poner la guerra en el coraçon de Holanda, y si se hace asi, espero, que con limpiar la Mosa, como decéis, y con este fuerte, avéis de hacer la paz o tregua que quisieremos ...'

[19] *Breve y verdadera relación de como por parte de su Magestad Católica ... se ganó el fuerte llamado de Eschenk* (Seville, 1635).

winter, to ensure recovery of the vital point of access at the earliest opportunity.[20]

During August and September 1635, a Spanish army of 20,000 men occupied the duchy of Cleves (technically part of Brandenburg) and joined forces with an imperialist contingent sent to assist. The plan was to create a strategic wedge on the Lower Rhine, straddling the Dutch-German frontier linking Schenck with the main body of the Spanish Netherlands.[21] The Cardinal-Infante in person quartered, for over a month, at Goch, several miles across the German border, supervising the activity of his commanders in Cleves, northern Brabant and on the eastern side of Schenck. In a letter to the king, he apologized for not spending the entire winter in Cleves, explaining there was an acute shortage of provisions and forage in the area.[22] During October, don Fernando fortified the town of Gennep on the Maas (far to the north of Venlo) thereby creating a strategic cordon connecting the Habsburg wedge in Cleves with Spanish Brabant, isolating Dutch-held Venlo, Roermond, Limburg and Maastricht. At the same time, though, he began preparing the king and Olivares for the possibility that Schenck might not be secured. He assured Philip that Gennep was being fortified in such a fashion that it would shortly be 'one of the best places which Your Majesty possesses in these provinces ... and it is of incomparably greater significance than Schenck because it can be supplied and held whereas the latter can not'.[23] Rounding off their success, in early November, Spanish troops took the fortress town of Limburg and localities of Valkenburg and 's-Hertogenrade, thereby transforming the strategic situation in the Maas valley.[24] For with these gains, the Spaniards liquidated most of the Dutch wedge which had separated Spanish Brabant from the Rhine valley since 1632 and cut off the Dutch garrison in Maastricht.

On releasing his field army to winter quarters and returning to Brussels in mid-November, don Fernando left 1,500 crack troops in Schenckenschans with supplies for 'seven months', 2,000 men under don Francisco Toralto at Cleves, and strong supporting garrisons in the positions between Cleves and

---

[20] J. J. Poelhekke, *Frederik Hendrik, Prins van Oranje: een biografisch drieluik* (Zutphen, 1978), pp. 451–2.

[21] Ibid., p. 451; see also J. I. Israel, 'Olivares and the government of the Spanish Netherlands, 1621–1643', in J. I. Israel, *Empires and entrepots* (London, 1990) pp. 183–4.

[22] AGR, SEG, vol. 213, fo. 89. Cardinal-Infante to Philip, Goch, 20 August 1635.

[23] Ibid., fo. 166. Cardinal-Infante to Philip, Gennep, 11 October 1635: 'es incomparablemente de mayor importancia que el Esquenque porque este se puede socorrer y mantener y aquel no'.

[24] W. Jappe Alberts, *Geschiedenis van de beide Limburgen* (2 vols., Assen, 1972–4) II, p. 4; J. A. K. Haas, *De verdeling van de landen van Overmaas, 1644–1662* (Assen, 1978), p. 5.

Schenck and at Gennep, Straelen and Geldern.[25] Additional forces were deployed around Limburg and Maastricht. Olivares and the king, however, were not convinced that don Fernando had done all he could to extend, and strengthen, Spain's newly won enclaves in the Maas valley and Cleves. In his instructions of 11 December 1635, the king instructed his brother to hold Schenckenschans 'at whatever cost', strengthen the Spanish positions between Schenck and Cleves and fortify Helmond so as to secure his line of communications across northern Brabant.[26]

The king's orders, and Olivares' strategy, could not have been clearer or more emphatic. Spain's effort was to be concentrated against the Dutch. There are no grounds for claiming 'that the government at Madrid was divided on whether it was preferable to concentrate the war effort on France or the Dutch Republic'.[27] It has been asserted that the French boundaries were more vulnerable to invasion and so the decision was taken to concentrate military action there. In 1636, the army of Flanders reached Corbie on the Somme, about eighty miles from Paris. The Spaniards also invaded from Franche-Comté in the east; and had their planned invasion of [sic] Catalonia not been deferred until 1637, this triple offensive might have knocked France out of the war...[28]

But the truth is that neither Olivares, nor the king, nor the Cardinal-Infante, nor any important minister – either over the winter of 1635–6, or at any point during the first five months of 1636 – proposed launching an offensive, major or minor, against France. Nor, as we shall see, did the Spaniards invade France from Spanish Burgundy – on the contrary the Spaniards almost lost the territory that year and there were no preparations of any kind for an invasion of France from Catalonia until the following year.[29]

Moreover, Olivares was the most categorical of all in insisting that Spain's efforts in 1636 should be concentrated against the Dutch. 'Your Majesty', he advised the king on 16 November 1635, 'may rest assured that neither your father, nor grandfather, had the opportunity which you now

25 AGR, SEG, vol. 213, fo. 89. Cardinal-Infante to Philip, Brussels, 22 November 1635.
26 Ibid., fos. 396–8. Philip to Cardinal-Infante, Madrid, 11 December 1635: 'aquello [Esquenque] se ha de mantener a qualquier precio'; Israel, 'Olivares and the government of the Spanish Netherlands', p. 184.
27 R. Bonney, The European dynastic states, 1494–1660 (Oxford, 1991), p. 210.
28 Ibid,. pp. 210–11.
29 Paul Henrard, Marie des Médicis dans les Pays-Bas (1631–1638) (Brussels, 1876), p. 564; on the absence of preparations for an invasion of France from Catalonia in 1636, see John H. Elliott, The revolt of the Catalans: a study in the decline of Spain (1598–1640) (Cambridge, 1963), pp. 313–16.

have to settle the affairs of Holland with advantage and reputation, because God has been pleased to place the master-key in Your Majesty's hands.'[30] At the meeting of the council of State in Madrid, on 7 December, the count-duke again urged a maximum effort to secure and exploit Spain's gains on the Lower Rhine and in northern Brabant.[31] In one of his most insistent letters, in March 1636, Olivares assured the Cardinal-Infante that 'without Schenck we have nothing even if we were to capture Paris; and with it we have everything, even if we should lose Brussels and Madrid'.[32]

The Dutch, for their part, spared no effort to retake Schenckenschans. The fortress, on an island in the Rhine, was bombarded relentlessly from both shores, and by a flotilla of river gun-boats, a scene recorded subsequently on a large painting by Gerrit van Santen commissioned by the States-General. Finally, on 30 April 1636, the 600 survivors of the garrison, battered beyond endurance, surrendered to the Stadholder. The entire United Provinces erupted in jubilation and thanksgiving services. By contrast, the count-duke when he heard the news was beside himself with exasperation and grief. 'For I see', he wrote to the Cardinal-Infante, on 25 May 1636, 'that we have lost the best jewel which the king, our master, possessed in those states with which to settle his affairs successfully.' It was, he averred, a 'great blow for the king and all Spain'.[33]

The loss of Schenckenschans was a severe setback to Spanish hopes and to Olivares and the king. But it by no means nullified all the gains of the previous autumn or invalidated the logic of the offensive against the Dutch. If no offensive against France was planned during the winter of 1635–6, neither was there any talk of invading France, in Madrid or Brussels, in the aftermath of the fall of Schenck. There was, of course, a re-appraisal of Spain's strategy in the Low Countries in both capitals during May and June 1636. But in Spain, Olivares (and the king's other principal advisers) simply re-affirmed that the Dutch front was to have priority and that on the French side the army should fight purely defensively.[34] The count-duke continued to focus his attention on northern Brabant and the Lower Rhine, railing

---

[30] Quoted in Elliott, *The count-duke of Olivares*, p. 493.

[31] AGS, Est, 2050 consulta 7 December 1635, 'voto del Conde Duque'.

[32] Bayerische Staatsbibliothek, Munich, Cod. hisp. 22, fo. 12v. Olivares to Cardinal-Infante, Madrid, 14 March 1636: 'que sin el Squenque, no ay nada, aunque se tome a Paris, y con el, aunque se pierda Bruselas y Madrid, lo ay todo'.

[33] Ibid., fo. 17v. Olivares to Cardinal-Infante, Madrid, 25 May 1636: 'pues veo, señor, que se ha perdido la mayor joya que el rey nuestro señor tenia en esos estados para poder acomodar sus cosas con gloria ... grande golpe, señor, para el rey nuestro señor, grande para toda Espana'; see also Elliott, *The count-duke of Olivares*, p. 504 and Israel, 'Olivares and the government of the Spanish Netherlands', p. 184.

[34] AGS, Est. 2051, consulta of 17 June 1636.

about the vital importance of securing Helmond and Eindhoven and the failure to post enough Spaniards and Italians, the monarchy's best troops, in and around Schenck.

In the spring of 1636, the army of Flanders was a formidable engine of war, officially totalling 69,703 officers and men.[35] But, until late May, it was still the Dutch, and not France, that it was preparing to attack. In the event, however, the army of Flanders did not fight offensively against the Dutch Republic in the summer of 1636. Instead the decision was taken not in Madrid but at Brussels, late in May, to suspend this offensive and, instead, launch a secondary thrust, or 'diversion' as it was called, into France. Writing to the king, explaining this change of plan, on 26 May 1636, the Cardinal-Infante was at pains to stress that he and his commanders had been intending to launch a major attack against the Dutch, as the king and Olivares had instructed, but that the dramatic change in circumstances had persuaded him to switch to a French strategy.[36] For his, and the king's, plans had been based on the assumption that France would that year be pinned to the defensive by the projected imperialist invasion of eastern France with 40,000 men. Since the withdrawal of the Swedes to the northern fringes of Germany and the departure of the protestant electors from the war under the terms of the Peace of Prague (30 May 1635),[37] the emperor's position in Germany had indeed been greatly strengthened (albeit only temporarily) and a decision had been taken in Vienna, to strike at what now appeared to be the emperor's sole major enemy operating in the empire – France. But during May it emerged that logistical and financial difficulties had prevented the emperor's commanders amassing sufficient forces on the Rhine for them to invade France on their own; they informed Brussels they could only now do so in conjunction with the army of Flanders and to this don Fernando had agreed. In other words the Spanish invasion of France in the summer of 1636 was an entirely makeshift, secondary operation, improvised at exceedingly short notice, which had nothing what-soever to do with any grand Spanish design to invade France from several directions, in massive force, and which was decided on in Brussels purely in response to pressure from Vienna and the imperialist generals and because the Cardinal-Infante decided that he should not forgo the opportunity to combine his forces with those of the imperialists. . . .

Furthermore, even while announcing this change of plan, the Cardinal-

---

[35] Ibid., consulta 12 April 1636, citing figures sent the previous February by the *contador* Diego de Hernani.
[36] AGR, SEG, vol. 214, fos. 449–61v. Cardinal-Infante to Philip, Brussels, 26 May 1636.
[37] Polišenský, *Thirty Years' War*, pp. 216–17; Parker, *Thirty Years' War*, pp. 158–60.

Infante continued to reiterate that, as far as Spain was concerned, it was better to concentrate against the Dutch rather than France and that this was the view of his advisers in Brussels as well as of ministers at Madrid. Interestingly, one of the principal arguments advanced in Brussels for giving priority to the Dutch front, rather than the French, were the sentiments of the inhabitants of the Spanish Netherlands themselves. These, reportedly, had so great a preference for fighting the protestant Dutch, rather than the catholic French, that they would rather win a single mile of territory back from the United Provinces than entire provinces from France.[38]

Meanwhile, it is evident that Philip IV and Olivares were still expecting, as late as the second week of June 1636, that the main effort of the army of Flanders that year would be directed against the Dutch. Writing to the Cardinal-Infante, on 13 June 1636, Philip IV ordered him to advance into northern Brabant, fortify Helmond and Eindhoven and try to retake Schenck.[39] When they learnt of the change of plan, though, Philip and Olivares readily accepted that it was better to thrust into France together with the imperialists than invade Dutch territory without imperialist assistance, and without an imperialist attack on France, and all the more so since they now knew that a French army of 14,000 men, under Condé, had invaded Spanish Burgundy, during May, and set siege to its capital, Dôle.

Since no preparations of any kind were made for a thrust into France, from the Spanish Netherlands, before late May 1636, there was never any possibility of the invasion being coordinated with attacks by Spanish armies operating from Italy or Catalonia. The invasion turned into the sensational episode it did solely because of the unexpected weakness of the opposition and its extraordinary effect in France. The Cardinal-Infante, assured by his intelligence service that the Dutch were unprepared to assail him in his rear,[40] left Brussels at the end of June and gathered, at Mons, a lightly equipped invasion army of 18,000 men, a high proportion of which consisted of cavalry, including an imperialist contingent under Octavio Piccolomini.[41] He also published a manifesto in French blaming the war on France and accusing France of destabilizing the Holy Roman Empire and having brought in the Swedes which was cited as the cause of the devastation of

---

[38] AGR, SEG, vol. 214, fos. 254–60.

[39] AGR, SEG, vol. 214, fo. 565. Philip to Cardinal-Infante, Madrid, 13 June 1636.

[40] René Delplanche, *Pierre Roose, chef-président du Conseil-Privé des Pays-Bas (1586–1673)* (Brussels, 1945), p. 100.

[41] Henrard, *Marie des Médicis*, pp. 564–7; Lonchay, *La rivalité*. p. 83; see also David Parrott, 'Richelieu, the *Grands*, and the French army', in J. Bergin and L. Brockliss (eds.), *Richelieu and his age* (Oxford, 1992), p. 166.

Germany and sacking of innumerable catholic churches and monasteries as well as the destruction of the catholic faith in whole areas.[42] The French monarch was further accused of aiding and abetting the Dutch 'rebel vassals of His Majesty of Spain', usurping the lands of the duke of Lorraine, and persecuting his own mother, Marie des Médicis.

Advancing from Mons, via Avesnes, the Spaniards set siege to the key French frontier fortress of La Capelle. To their amazement, its large garrison, unnerved by the exploding shells fired by the Cardinal-Infante's siege mortars, a recent innovation as yet unfamiliar to the French, surrendered after only four days. The Cardinal-Infante was soon again astonished when Le Câtelet, one of the strongest fortresses in all France, capitulated – again after only three days.[43] His victorious troops then occupied Guise, Vervins and Bohain in rapid succession. As the Spaniards continued to advance westwards, towards the Somme, Louis XIII, in a state verging on panic, returned from Fontainebleau to Paris. On reaching the Somme, the imperialist contingent crossed over and captured Roye from where Piccolomini marched into a wide swathe of territory around Compiègne, causing utter consternation in Paris. On 7 August, the Cardinal-Infante set siege to Corbie – a vital fortress town on the Somme, certainly, but no great distance into France from the then Spanish Netherlands frontier – setting a large part of the town alight with his mortar bombs. Corbie surrendered a week later.

Meanwhile, on 8 August, the day after the commencement of the siege of Corbie, Louis XIII wrote to Condé, who was progressing with his siege of Dôle, ordering him (after making a final attempt) to abandon the siege and withdraw towards Paris to help preserve the heart of the French state.[44] But by the time Condé received these instructions, made his final unsuccessful attempt to take Dôle and withdrew from Spanish Burgundy, several more

---

[42] Juan Antonio Vincart, 'Relación y commentario de los sucessos de las Armas de S.M....d'esta Campaña de 1636', in *Colección de documentos inéditos*, LIX, p. 8; much of this propaganda had already appeared in the *Declaration de son Altèze touchant la guerre contre la covronne de France* (Brussels, 24 June 1635).

[43] Vincart, 'Relación y comentario', pp. 17–18.

[44] Louis XIII to Condé, Paris, 8 August 1636 in D. L. M. Avenel (ed.), *Lettres, instructions diplomatiques et papiers d'état du Cardinal de Richelieu* (Paris, 1853–77), V (1635–1637), pp. 534–5: 'Mon cousin, c'est avec beaucoup de deplaisir que je suis contraint de vous mander que le siège de Dôle tirant de longue, il est nécessaire de le lever pour retirer l'armée que vous commandez auprès de moy et conserver le coeur de l'estat, mais, comme j'estime que votre mine s'en va en estat de faire son effect, je désire qu'auparavant que vous leviez ce siège vous la faciez jouer, et faciez un dernier effort pour tascher à emporter cette place, qui porte tel coup à mes affaires qu'elle est capable de conserver ma réputation et mon royaume.'

weeks had elapsed and, by that time, the danger posed by the army of Flanders was already receding. At the French court, it was expected, after the fall of Corbie, that the Spaniards would penetrate further, though not necessarily towards Paris. On 17 August Richelieu confided to an underling: 'I do not know what the enemy will do but it is my view that they will advance on Abbeville or Amiens.'[45] Piccolomini was eager to advance further. He did his best, as he reported to Gallas, on 18 August, to persuade the Cardinal-Infante not to halt, urging that there would never be a better opportunity, such was the enemy's disarray, and that the Spanish army could cross the Somme with relatively little risk, but the Cardinal-Infante was firmly resolved to withdraw.[46] He had planned only a minor operation. He felt that he lacked the forces for anything more ambitious and should not risk the royal army. His army was also hampered by constant bickering among his generals.[47]

Consequently, by the time the Cardinal-Infante received definite word of the raising of the siege of Dôle, in early September, he was already back in Cambrai and the bulk of his invasion force had left France. Ironically (but typically in seventeenth-century conditions), the imperial army, under Gallas, despite the French evacuation of Spanish Burgundy (and having been handed the initiative on a plate) were, at that point, still not ready to launch their own thrust from the east. Condé raised the siege of Dôle on 15 August. Gallas' invasion force (which consisted of imperialists and Lorrainers but no Spanish troops) did indeed eventually cross Spanish Burgundy and penetrate into French Burgundy. But the main imperialist invasion of France from the east (such as it was) did not begin until mid-October – a whole month and a half after the Spanish withdrawal from the Somme.[48] This new invasion succeeded in taking Mirebeau after which the army's high command was riven by dispute. Charles, duke of Lorraine, whose duchy had been seized by the French king and who was striving to regain it through his alliance with Spain, urged an advance on nearby Dijon. But the slow and excessively cautious Gallas insisted on setting siege to the minor

[45] Ibid., v, p. 549. Richelieu to Chavigni, Paris, 17 August 1636: 'Je ne scay pas ce que feront les ennemis, mais ma pensée est qu'ils iront à Abbeville ou à Amiens.'
[46] Vincart, 'Relación y comentario', pp. 46, 50, 65; O. Elster, *Piccolomini-Studien* (Leipzig, 1911), pp. 70–1.
[47] See Fernando González de León, 'The road to Rocroi: the duke of Alba, the count duke of Olivares and the high command of the Spanish Army of Flanders in the Eighty Years' War, 1567–1659' (PhD thesis, The Johns Hopkins University, Baltimore, Md. 1991), pp. 166–8. (I am extremely grateful to Dr González de León for allowing me to see the relevant sections of his thesis.)
[48] Edmond de Vernisy, *L'invasion de Gallas. Tricentaire de l'invasion allemande en Bourgogne en 1636* (Paris, 1936), pp. 49,57.

fortress town of Saint Jean-de-Losne, west of Dôle, only a few miles across the French frontier. The invasion was destined to proceed no further. Saint Jean resisted tenaciously until, on 3 November, the imperialists were forced to raise the siege and retreat back to Spanish Burgundy by the approach of Condé's relief army.[49] In other words Gallas' invasion from the east was a fiasco which failed even to pose a serious threat to Dijon let alone to the 'heart of France'. Shortly after Gallas' undignified evacuation of the tiny morsel of France he had overrun, the Spanish garrison of Corbie capitulated to its French besiegers. On 17 November, Richelieu wrote triumphantly to the king, exclaiming that he hardly knew how to express his joy at the sudden and dramatic turnaround of the situation.[50] Olivares, for his part, was deeply distressed by the loss of Corbie, lamenting in a long missive to the Cardinal-Infante that the main Spanish force had been withdrawn from the Somme too soon and that not enough had been done to secure 'a place of such importance'.[51]

Yet the count-duke had also been greatly impressed by the general impact of the march to Corbie and the profound shock administered to the French court and all France. Consequently, it was at this point that Madrid and Vienna began planning a grand offensive against France. This time Olivares did indeed intend a large-scale invasion with the army of Flanders coordinating with the Spanish armies in Italy and Catalonia. Since the main attack could only be launched from the Spanish Netherlands, arrangements were made to send substantial reinforcements to the Cardinal-Infante from Naples as well as Spain, adding 8,000 Spaniards and Italians to the 65,000 men officially in the army of Flanders at the end of 1636.[52] The army of Lombardy was expanded to about 40,000 men. The plan was for the Cardinal-Infante to invade from the north, this time with some 30,000 men while the army of Lombardy crossed Savoy, entered Provence and thrust towards Marseilles, while the third and smallest of the three Spanish invasion armies, some 15,000 men based in Catalonia, penetrated the Languedoc.[53] For his part, the Emperor Ferdinand planned to send

[49] Ibid., pp. 116, 132–3.
[50] Richelieu to Louis XIII, Paris, 17 November 1636 in Avenel, *Lettres, instructions*, p. 681: 'Je ne scaurois assez témoigner à Vostre Majesté la joye que j'ay de voir qu'elles [ses affaires] changent de face. La prise de Corbie et le levement du siège de Saint-Jen-de-Losne, assiegé par toutes ies forces de l'Empire, et ensuite la retraite de Galasse sont deux pièces de grande considération.'
[51] Bayerische Staatsbibliothek, Munich, Cod. hisp. 22, fo. 39v. Olivares to Cardinal-Infante, Madrid, 13 December 1636.
[52] AGS, Est. 2051, consulta 8 February 1637, fo. 5; Elliott, *The count-duke of Olivares*, p. 523; see also Elster, *Piccolomini-Studien*, pp. 72–4.
[53] Elliott, *The count-duke of Olivares*, pp. 522–4; Elliott, *Revolt of the Catalans*, pp. 324–5.

Piccolomini from the Spanish Netherlands into the Champagne, towards Rheims, while the imperialist army on the Rhine attacked the French in Alsace.

During the early months of 1637, there was unanimous agreement among the members of the council of state in Madrid that Spain should that year adopt an offensive strategy against France and fight defensively against the Dutch.[54] The duke of Albuquerque, at the meeting on 25 February, warmly seconded the count-duke's opinion that the army of Flanders should invade France that summer as swiftly and vigorously as possible, that this strategy best served Spain's interests both with regard to the war and 'the peace for which we hope', and that France should be invaded without any designs, or diversions, being attempted in the Netherlands, or any reserve forces being kept there beyond what was essential for defence against Holland.[55] He added that should Spain launch an offensive against the Dutch it would mean hazarding everything, including Spain's position in Italy, for little purpose.

And yet the strategic key, as always, lay in the Spanish Netherlands and, at Brussels, the Cardinal-Infante and his advisers continued to equivocate between the strategy of 1635–6 and what was now proposed. The Cardinal-Infante's trusted secretary, don Miguel de Salamanca, arrived in Madrid early in February 1637 and participated, expounding his master's views, in the crucial strategic debates of that month. He emphasized – and the relevance of this was to become plainer as the months passed – that the Cardinal-Infante's preference had all along been, and still was, for an offensive war against the Republic rather than France.[56] The Cardinal-Infante was inclined to a 'Dutch' strategy partly because this would be more popular with the inhabitants of the south Netherlands (by which was meant the Dutch speaking population of Flanders and Brabant rather than the inhabitants of Artois and Hainault), partly because towns and districts captured from the Dutch belonged to the king and would not be automatically returned (as would be anything taken from the French) and, finally, because the Dutch had been weighed down by war with Spain for many years and it was best not to give them any respite, especially as the king of France, with his present difficulties, was in no position to assist them. By concentrating Spain's might against the Republic, the Dutch could be brought to an 'acceptable' truce and Spain would then be far better placed to deal with France.

---

[54] AGS, Est. 2051, consultas of 25 and 26 February 1637.
[55] Ibid., consulta 25 February 1637. 'Voto del duque de Albuquerque', fos. 2v–3.
[56] Ibid., consulta of 8 February 1637. 'Voto' of Miguel de Salamanca, fo. 3.

Olivares insisted on a three-pronged assault on France in 1637 but not much, indeed practically nothing, came of it.[57] The small army operating from Catalonia crossed the French frontier on 29 August but, a month later, on 27 September, was routed by the French at Leucate. The army of Lombardy, embroiled in the fighting in Piedmont, was unable to cross into France at all. The council of State in Madrid approved the Cardinal-Infante's plan to strike deep into France, but no sooner did the army begin to mass on the French border than it had to be recalled owing to the descent of a Dutch field army of 18,000 men, under the Stadholder, on the northern borders of the Spanish Netherlands. After encamping for several weeks, poised to invade Flanders – he had hoped to be able to strike at Dunkirk – Frederik Hendrik marched into northern Brabant and set siege to Breda, taking advantage of the fact that much of the Cardinal-Infante's army was still in Artois and Hainault.[58]

Exploiting Frederik Hendrik's descent on Breda and the consequent transfer of Spanish forces northwards, the French then invaded from the south. In August, just a few days before the army of Catalonia entered the Languedoc, Olivares and the king received the unpalatable news that Breda was besieged, since 21 July, and that the French had captured Landrecies, a few miles to the east of Cambrai.[59] What made the siege of Breda so galling was that it was precisely Olivares' 'French' strategy which had given the Dutch their opportunity to dig in and complete their siege fortifications. For previously, while the main Spanish forces had been based in Brabant and Flanders, Frederik Hendrik's attempts to descend on Breda had each time been thwarted by a swift Spanish response.[60]

Thus, at the very moment that Olivares' grand three-pronged assault on France was supposed to begin, the bulk of the army of Flanders was recalled from the French frontier and concentrated against the Dutch.[61] Nor, from late August 1637 onwards, for the rest of that campaigning season, was there any question in the count-duke's mind that the Dutch front had to have priority. In the first place Breda with its garrison of over 3,000 men made up

---

[57] Elliott, *Revolt of the Catalans*, pp. 325–6; Elliott, *The count-duke of Olivares*, p. 523; see also José Alcalá-Zamora y Queipo de Llano, *España, Flandes y el mar del Norte (1618–1639)* (Barcelona, 1975), p. 365.

[58] A. Waddington, *La République des Provinces-Unies, la France et les Pays-Bas espagnols de 1630 à 1650* (Paris, 1895), I, pp. 295–6; Israel, *Dutch Republic and the Hispanic world*, p. 257.

[59] BL, Add. 14007, fo. 69. 'Copia de carta de S. Magestad para el Infante', Madrid, 25 August 1637.

[60] AGS, Est. 2052, consultas of 7 September and 7 October 1637 and the enclosed 'Discurso en que se pondere lo que se ha dejado de hazer y pudiera haver hecho en el socorro de Breda'.

[61] AGS, Est, 2052. Cardinal Infante to Philip, Antwerp, 28 July 1637.

of Spaniards, Italians and Walloons and Burgundians, was one of the most important strongholds of the Spanish Netherlands and a pillar of the king's *reputación*, representing as it did one of the most glorious successes of the early part of his reign. In the second place, the loss of slices of Brabant and Flanders to the protestant Dutch had a more disturbing impact on the States of Brabant and Flanders, the two principal contributing provinces of the Spanish Netherlands, than did loss of towns and districts to the French in Artois and Hainault.

Unable to relieve Breda, the Cardinal-Infante marched eastwards with 17,000 men, and opened an offensive against the Dutch in the Maas valley. After a few days' heavy bombardment, Venlo's garrison of 1,200 surrendered. Next, the Spaniards bombarded and forced the capitulation of Roermond. After this, don Fernando considered besieging Grave, Nijmegen or perhaps Maastricht but then, on the advice of his military commanders – but against that of the principal civilian minister in his entourage, Olivares' special confidant, the president of the Secret Council at Brussels, Petrus Roose – he ceased his attack on the Dutch and turned back, alarmed by reports that the French were now making rapid progress in Artois, Hainault and Luxemburg.[62] Breda capitulated to the Dutch on 7 October. However, on 26 October, a Spanish column sent from Geldern scaled the walls of, and almost succeeded in capturing, the Dutch-arrisoned Rhine port of Rheinberg, in the electorate of Cologne.

The question of whether or not don Fernando judged correctly in turning back, in September 1637, was intensively debated both in Madrid and Brussels. At the gathering of the council of state on 7 October, Olivares strongly criticized the Cardinal-Infante's decision, insisting that he should have continued 'capturing places' from the Dutch and might, by this means, have forced Frederik Hendrik to raise the siege of Breda.[63] The king then wrote to his brother, instructing him to keep up the pressure on the Dutch, try to take Rheinberg so that Spain should again have a crossing-point on the Lower Rhine, and also tighten the blockade of Maastricht.[64] The Cardinal-Infante was also ordered, when campaigning ceased, to quarter his army for the winter over on the Dutch side, away from the French, so as to cover Antwerp which (since the loss of Breda) had now become more vulnerable. In addition, he was instructed to strengthen the garrisons of Gennep, Stevensweert, Geldern, Roermond and Venlo and improve the fortifications of Helmond, Eindhoven and Lier.

[62] AGR, SEG, vol. 217, fo. 382. Cardinal-Infante to Philip, Brussels, 1 November 1637.
[63] AGS, Est. 2052, consulta 7 October 1637. 'Voto del Conde Duque', fo. 1.
[64] AGR, SEG, vol. 217, fos. 353–v. Philip to Cardinal-Infante, The Escorial, 22 October 1637.

Olivares and the king aspired to make the army of Flanders stronger than ever in 1638. It was planned to send no less than 4,700,000 ducats to the Spanish Low Countries and expand the army there to over 80,000 men.[65] But how should Spain's main strike force be used? Scarcely surprisingly, after the fiasco of his grand, three-pronged, assault on France the previous year and the abrupt reversion to a 'Dutch' strategy since August 1637, the count-duke was now more convinced than ever that the Dutch front should have priority. At the meeting of the council of state on 8 January 1638, he declared that, ideally, it would be best to fight offensively against both France and the Republic but that since this was impossible 'and it is necessary to choose it is certain that concentrating against the Dutch is best'.[66] At the gathering of the council of state on 7 March, most ministers present openly disagreed, warning that if the king decided on 'offensive war' against the Dutch, and 'defensive' against France this would leave France with a free hand which could have disastrous consequences for Spain and Italy as well as the Spanish Netherlands.[67] But the count-duke, never one to be deterred by the objections of his colleagues, remained adamant. In his instructions to the Cardinal-Infante of 17 March 1638, the king stressed the urgency of settling with the Dutch while at the same time insisting that no settlement with the 'rebel' provinces would be acceptable unless they agreed to abandon their conquests in Brazil and restore Breda, Maastricht, Rheinberg and Orsoy.[68] The last two, crossing-points over the Lower Rhine, were deemed essential to Spain's standing in Germany. Obviously no such settlement would be attainable without subjecting the Dutch to massive new pressure. In the gathering of the council of state of 11 May 1638, Olivares again stressed that the most urgent priority now was to break the Franco-Dutch alliance by securing a favourable 'truce' with the Dutch and that the only way to accomplish this was to press them hard by both sea and land.[69] Already Olivares had his eye on the great armada he was amassing in Spain and which he was to send against the Dutch the following year, and how best to combine this pending maritime offensive with Spanish strategy on land.

Thus, for the campaign of 1638 Spanish strategy was again one of offensive war against the Dutch and a purely defensive effort against the French. In the event, however, neither Olivares' preference for a Dutch

---

[65] Ibid., fo. 462.

[66] AGS, Est. 2156, consulta, 8 January 1638. 'Voto del Conde-Duque': 'pero haviendo de escoger es cierto que es lo mejor (guerra offensiva) a Olanda, siendo flaquisima la razón de dezir que a olandeses siempre se les tiene alli...'

[67] AGS, Est. 2053, consulta of the *junta de estado*, 7 March 1638, fos. 6–11.

[68] AGR, SEG, vol. 218, fo. 455. Philip to Cardinal-Infante, Madrid, 17 March 1638.

[69] AGS, Est. 2053, consulta 11 May 1638, fos. 11v–12.

offensive, nor the disagreement among ministers at Madrid, made much difference since the Spaniards were pinned to the defensive by coordinated Dutch and French attacks. Nevertheless, it should be noted that the main military effort still had to be made against the Dutch rather than the French, because Antwerp was a great deal more important to the Spanish crown than St Omer. For many weeks the French border was left with only a skeleton defence. To the great joy of Olivares and the king, the Cardinal-Infante's defensive campaign of that year was exceptionally successful. The Dutch did indeed make a determined thrust towards Antwerp but their vanguard was caught in the open, at Kallo, by a crack force of Spanish troops, in what was the only pitched battle of the second part of the Eighty Years' War, and overwhelmed. The Spaniards captured 2,500 prisoners, eighty-one river barges and a good quantity of Dutch artillery. Writing to the king shortly afterwards, the Cardinal-Infante described his success rather grandly as the 'greatest victory which you Majesty's arms have achieved since the war in the Low Countries began'.[70] Soon after, the French army besieging St Omer was routed by a joint imperialist-Spanish force under Piccolomini.[71] During August, the focus of the war shifted north-eastwards to the Maas valley. Frederik Hendrik encircled Geldern with 16,000 men but was forced into a humiliating and costly retreat by the Cardinal-Infante's counter-thrust which was again backed by Piccolomini whose troops remained in Cleves, over the winter of 1638–9.[72]

During 1639, the army of Flanders was again pinned to the defensive. But it was still a uniquely well-entrenched and powerful force of some 70,000 men and the expectation was, in both Brussels and Madrid, that the Cardinal-Infante would be able to resume the offensive in 1640, given a measure of imperialist support, and assuming that the reinforcements which were sent on the huge armada (100 ships; 2,000 guns; 20,000 men), under Antonio de Oquendo, reached their destination safely. The Cardinal-Infante was told, in late July, to expect 9,000 'Spaniards with some Italians' for his army.[73] In the event, the armada which set sail from Corunna on 6 September met with disaster at the hands of the Dutch fleet in the Channel. But before Tromp ordered the final Dutch attack which destroyed the bulk

---

[70] AGR, SEG, vol. 219. fo. 255v. undated June 1638: 'la mayor victoria que han tenido las armas de Vuestra Magestad después que se començo la guerra en Flandes'.
[71] Lonchay, *La rivalité*, p. 91.
[72] F. Nettesheim, *Geschichte der Stadt und des Amtes Geldern* (2nd edition, 1963), pp. 214–15; O. Elster, *Die Piccolomini-Regimenter während des 30 jährigen Krieges* (Vienna, 1903), pp. 73–4.
[73] BL, Add. 14007, fo. 71. 'Copia de carta de S.Magestad para el Infante,' Madrid, 30 August 1639; Israel, *The Dutch Republic*, p. 317.

of the ships, at the Downs, some three-quarters of the Cardinal-Infante's reinforcements were successfully ferried across to Flanders from England.[74] By December 1639, the Cardinal-Infante had 77,000 men, of high quality, poised for action against either the French or Dutch.[75]

From August 1639, before the armada set sail, and in anticipation of striking a major blow at Dutch sea power, as well as reinforcing the army of Flanders, a new phase began in the strategic debate in progress since 1635 at Madrid and Brussels. Olivares and the king wanted an early offensive – to begin in March 1640 – launched before the French and Dutch were in a position to react. But how should the army of Flanders be used? One might readily suppose, with the mounting pressure of Spain's Catalan front, following the fall of the vital fortress of Salces to the French, on 19 July 1639, and the subsequent determined efforts on the Spanish side to regain the stronghold, that the obvious strategy would be to invade France from the Spanish Netherlands thereby relieving the pressure in the south. Yet, once again, this is not how Olivares and the king viewed the situation – they hoped to recover Salces before the onset of the main campaign season of 1640 in any case, and neither during 1639, nor over the winter of 1639–40, was any decision taken in Madrid to launch 'a general assault on France'.

What then was the strategy adopted by Spain for 1640? Setting out the available options in his instructions to the Cardinal-Infante of 30 August 1639, the king emphasized that the crucial thing was to achieve some notable success, either against the French or their Dutch allies, which would demonstrate the revived offensive capacity of the army of Flanders, and therefore of the Spanish monarchy as a whole, and enhance *reputación* sufficiently to facilitate the obtaining of the 'peace we desire so much [*la paz que tanto se desea*]'.[76] On balance, the king expressed a slight preference for a thrust into France, provided the Cardinal-Infante was reasonably sure he could capture one of the major strongholds along the Somme – Abbeville, Amiens, Péronne, Saint Quentin or Corbie – and this time hold it. If this seemed unattainable, the Cardinal-Infante was ordered to strike at the Dutch and specifically at one of five key strongholds which Olivares and Philip were anxious to regain – Sluis, on the Scheldt estuary, was their first choice but if this appeared too difficult, then Grave or Maastricht, on the Maas, or Rheinberg or Wesel, on the Rhine.[77] Madrid's preference, after

[74] Alcalá-Zamora, *España, Flandes y el mar del Norte*, pp. 444–5.
[75] Geoffrey Parker, *The military revolution: military innovation and the rise of the West, 1500–1800* (Cambridge, 1988), pp. 40,168.
[76] BL, Add. 14007, fos. 73–4v. Philip to Cardinal-Infante, Madrid, 30 August 1639.
[77] Ibid., fo. 74.

Sluis, was for Rheinberg. Should neither offensive seem feasible then the Cardinal-Infante was to try to recover the (only two) major strongholds the French had thus far managed to capture in the Spanish Netherlands – Landrecies and Hesdin (taken in 1639).

The Cardinal-Infante replied, from Dunkirk, on 7 October, in a less than optimistic tone. He was dismayed by the emperor's decision to recall Piccolomini and his troops, due to the revival of Swedish power and Swedish advances in Silesia and Saxony, remarking that 'if he goes, it will be a miracle if Your Majesty does not lose these states in the coming year'.[78] But should the emperor relent, and imperialist support be forthcoming, then there would be the possibility of an early offensive. He firmly ruled out, however, any attack on the Somme line, explaining that this year large French forces had gone into winter quarters near enough to the Somme to react quickly to any surprise thrust.[79] It would be too dangerous to attempt any of the French towns specified in Madrid. If he were to invade France, don Fernando suggested that Charleville-Mézières, far to the east, in the Meuse valley, a tiny independent sovereignty under the Nevers branch of the House of Gonzaga, would be both an easier, and safer, target and yet also one which would yield worthwhile strategic dividends. For, from there, Spanish troops would be able to bring the whole of the Champagne under threat of attack and render Rheims (a city which was not fortified) insecure. There was also the prospect, with the Spanish army operating in the area, that Louis, count of Soissons and other local malcontents might rise against their king.[80] Nevertheless, all considered, he and his advisers still thought it best to launch the offensive against the Dutch. For there were better, and more important, strategic gains to be made by thrusting to the north. Sluis, though, was definitely ruled out. 'What everyone here considers most suitable', he wrote, 'and I above all, is that we attempt Maastricht, because it is a place in the centre of these lands from where the Dutch range over Brabant, Luxemburg, Namur, Limburg and Geldern, raising contributions from the villages and unfortified places as much as they want, without our being able to stop it, something which causes much discontent in the land.'[81] Maastricht, he urged, would also be an excellent base from which to attack Grave and Rheinberg.

---

[78] Ibid., fo. 76. 'Copia de la respuesta que hico el señor Infante', Dunkirk, 7 October 1639.
[79] Ibid., fo. 77.
[80] On Soissons, see John H. Elliott, *Richelieu and Olivares* (Cambridge, 1984), pp. 89, 146.
[81] BL, Add. 14007, fo. 78: 'señor son tantas las razones que ay para librarse de una vez de este embarazo, que mi opinión es, deve precede el emprender esta plaza a todas las demas, y se podra yntentar con mucha facilidad en el tiempo que V.Magestad quiere, que se salga en campaña por la comodidad que havra en las prebenciones de todo...'

The basic pattern, and logic, of Spanish strategy in the Low Countries in the years 1635–9 was only finally broken by the (for Spain) catastrophic events of the year 1640. The Cardinal-Infante was unable to strike in March, partly owing to the late arrival of remittances from Spain but also because Piccolomini was withdrawn.[82] In May 1640, the Spanish Netherlands were invaded by both the French and the Dutch. The French set siege to Arras but, as in the previous year, the Cardinal-Infante had to give priority to the Dutch front, rather than the French,[83] so that no real effort was made to save Arras. Frederik Hendrik advanced cautiously from Flanders, probing the defences of Bruges. Finding no gap, he next tried to invest the Spanish forts facing Sluis and then attempted Hulst, each time being checked by Spanish counter-movements and a series of clashes. On 3 July 1640, the Frisian Stadholder, Hendrik Casimir, was killed in a fight on a redoubt near Hulst.

By this time, with the Cardinal-Infante boxed in between the French and the Dutch, Olivares and the king were confronted by a rapidly deteriorating situation both on the Italian front and in Catalonia. As disaster followed disaster, the year 1640 effectively removed all prospect of gaining the upper hand against the French or Dutch. Catalonia slid from sullen disobedience into open rebellion. On 7 June armed insurgents seized Barcelona and murdered the viceroy of Catalonia as he sought to escape, on the shore. Arras fell to the French on 9 August. On 24 September, the Catalan rebels officially requested a military alliance with the French king against the king of Spain.[84] Early in November, the victorious French entered Turin, re-establishing the authority of the pro-French claimant to the duchy, duchess Marie-Christine. Then, and most disastrous of all, on 1 December, a *coup d'état* toppled the Habsburg régime in Lisbon and all Portugal rose against the Spanish crown. To round off this catalogue of disaster, on 26 January 1641, a combined Catalan–French force decisively repulsed the Castilian army which Olivares and the king had sent to subdue Catalonia, at Montjuich, outside Barcelona.

Such massive setbacks as the rebellions of Catalonia and Portugal inevitably administered a severe shock to the entire Spanish monarchy and weakened it fundamentally. The strategic position of Spain was transformed and, in the following months, the standing and prestige of Spain were heftily marked down in all the capitals of Europe. Spain's enemies

[82] Elster, *Die Piccolomini-Regimenter*, pp. 70, 75.
[83] Waddington, *La République*, pp. 316–17.
[84] Elliott, *Revolt of the Catalans*, pp. 500–4

were encouraged by the spectacle to expect greater and more rapid gains at its expense, while many of Spain's friends and allies began to distance themselves from the court at Madrid which, in turn, further debilitated Philip IV's overall strategic position. Hitherto, one of Spain's most useful allies in the war with France had been duke Charles of Lorraine who, besides much else, had, as we have seen, played a major role in the campaigns in Burgundy in 1636. But Lorraine, from March 1641, entered into dealings with Richelieu and even though the duke subsequently played something of a double game he had, from this point on, to be largely discounted as an ally of Spain.[85]

But what strategy did Spain now adopt? Just as one would expect, Madrid's initial response was to raise armies in the peninsula and seek to crush the rebels as swiftly as possible. Owing to its proximity to France, priority had to be given to the Catalan front so that while repeated efforts to subdue Catalonia failed, no significant pressure was exerted on Portugal.[86] Hence, as the year 1641 unfolded, Olivares and the king had to decide whether now to divert most of Spain's military spending, and its best troops, from Flanders, giving priority to the new Iberian fronts, or continue with the old strategy of concentrating Spain's military muscle in the Netherlands. No one at the Spanish Habsburg court was in any doubt as to the extreme seriousness of the situation they now faced in the Iberian peninsula. Nothing was plainer than that the French would do their upmost to exploit the gaps which had opened up in Spain's defences, bolstering both rebellions and especially that of the Catalans.

Yet it was precisely because the Spanish monarchy was in such a dangerous conjuncture that Olivares and the king re-affirmed their strategy of keeping their principal army, their best troops and the bulk of their military spending in the south Netherlands.[87] The remittances sent from Madrid to the Spanish Netherlands in the years 1640–2 were indeed astonishingly high, among the largest ever seen.[88] It was not until the year 1643 that the adverse impact of the Catalan and Portuguese revolts on the monarchy's fortunes was reflected in a serious reduction in the flow of royal funds to

---

[85] Waddington, *La République*, I, p. 330.
[86] Elliott, *The count-duke of Olivares*, pp. 604, 612, 635–7.
[87] Israel, 'Olivares and the government of the Spanish Netherlands', pp. 186–7.
[88] Ibid.; according to official figures recorded in Brussels, the royal treasury in the Spanish Netherlands received 4,746,000 ducats from Spain in 1640, almost as much in 1641 and only somewhat less in 1642, with a large drop in 1643: see Rafael Valladares Ramirez, 'La peninsula y Europa. Los Habsburgos españoles y la alianza anglo-portuguesa (1640–1670)' (doctoral thesis, University of Madrid, 1992), p. 129.

Flanders. Even after the catastrophe at Rocroi, the official strength of the army of Flanders, as late as December 1643, was still 77,517 men.[89]

It was basic to Spain's European strategy in the years 1641–3 to use its principal military bastion to exert such pressure on France as to prevent Louis XIII and Richelieu sending the bulk of their forces to Catalonia and other southern fronts. What had changed fundamentally is that there was now no longer any question of giving priority, at least as regards offensive action, to the Dutch war. From the summer of 1640 onwards there was no more talk, in Madrid or Brussels, of besieging Maastricht, Sluis or Rheinberg, securing northern Brabant, or compelling the Dutch to relinquish their conquests in Brazil. Henceforth, the point of concentrating Spain's military might in the Low Countries was to pose a convincing strategic threat to France and, by this means to thwart the French offensive in southern Europe. The Spanish monarchy was now in a desperate plight. Yet the army of Flanders was still an impressive force. In a memorandum which he wrote at Douai, in October 1640, Miguel de Salamanca could still, with some justification, list the superior 'valour and military experience' of Spain's officers and soldiers in the Netherlands as a major strategic asset in the war against the French.[90]

In the years 1641–2 both the Catalan and Portuguese revolts prospered. French intervention was slowly stepped up. In the spring of 1642, a powerful French army reached Lérida from where it proceeded to invade Aragon, capturing Monzón in June. On 10 September 1642, the key Spanish border fortress town of Perpignan surrendered to its French besiegers. On 7 October, a combined Catalan–French army decisively defeated the Castilian counter-offensive at Lérida.

Logistical difficulties, inexperienced troops, lack of up-to-date fortifications and sheer incompetence all contributed to the repeated failures of Spanish arms in Catalonia, Aragon and against Portugal.[91] As defeat followed defeat and humiliation was heaped on humiliation, it became ever plainer that the only feasible way to redeem the honour and *reputación* of Spain and its king, raise morale in Castile and at court, and restore Spain's standing in Europe both strategically and diplomatically was to strike into France from Flanders. It is thus a mistake to view Olivares' refusal to concentrate Spain's military might within the peninsula as misplaced obstinacy. Given the overall situation, it made good strategic sense to preserve the army of Flanders and keep it where it was.

---

[89] Geoffrey Parker, *The Army of Flanders and the Spanish Road, 1567–1659* (Cambridge, 1972), p. 272.

[90] BL, Add. 14007, fo. 100.   [91] Elliott, *The count-duke of Olivares*, pp. 635–8.

The Cardinal-Infante having been carried off by smallpox in November 1641, at the age of 39, the destiny of the army, and of the Spanish Netherlands, lay in the hands of his successor as governor-general, don Francisco de Melo, soon to become marquis of Tordelaguna. He was in no doubt as to what was expected of him. Philip IV and Olivares instructed Melo to take the field early in 1642 and stay on campaign for as long as he could, making the 'greatest effort possible in the Netherlands to divert (the French king) from his design' of pouring his armies into Spain and Italy.[92] He was to be helped in his task by the imperialists, whose approach on the Lower Rhine sufficed to cover Geldern (which Frederik Hendrik was still endeavouring to take) and force the Dutch to spend the summer fruitlessly shielding Rheinberg and Orsoy. For much of the summer Melo thus had a fairly free hand. He was also given exceptionally wide powers to determine strategy and make decisions.[93]

His original plan was to invade France and try to penetrate to the Somme; but finding his path blocked, he advanced westwards from Douai to attack the French garrisons in Artois.[94] He recaptured Lens on 19 April and then besieged the important fortress of La Bassée. The 2,400 survivors of its original 3,000 man garrison surrendered on 11 May. Melo next marched, via Inchy, to tackle two French armies approaching from the south. He succeeded in surprising and inflicting a heavy defeat on the 'army of Champagne', under the maréchal de Guiche, on 26 May, at Honnecourt. The French reportedly lost over 4,000 casualties killed and wounded and another 3,000 men taken prisoner. Enthusiasts in the Spanish Netherlands ranked the battle the best Spanish victory since Nördlingen. Guiche himself escaped but Melo captured all his artillery and banners and twenty-two marquises, counts and barons. The army of Flanders next blockaded the French garrison at Landrecies but then had to march far to the east to meet another threat. By September, though, Melo was back at La Bassée with his full field army and from there he recovered and fortified Bouchain, Lillers and Aire.[95] In all, he was in the field for seven months, throwing his whole strength into harassing French garrisons and the French border, pursuing a strategy which had not, at any time, been pursued in the years 1635–40.

But the very success of the army of Flanders' campaign of 1642 lured it to disaster. For it lulled Melo into a false sense of his, and his army's,

---

[92] Juan Antonio Vincart, 'Relación de la campaña de 1642', in *Colección de documentos inéditos*, LIX, pp. 118–19.
[93] González de León, 'The road to Rocroi', p. 172.
[94] Vincart, 'Relación de la campaña de 1642', pp. 120–6; Lonchay, *La rivalité*, pp. 101–2.
[95] Vincart, 'Relación de la Campaña de 1642', pp. 195–6, 201.

capability and exerted an immense pressure on him to perform similar feats in 1643. Olivares ensured that he had even wider powers than before.[96] Within the Iberian peninsula the Spanish crown was now in desperate straits. The governor-general of the Spanish Netherlands had the money and troops and was now the only Spanish commander with the means to deliver the French a stinging blow. His strategy in 1643 was to invade France, in full force, via the valley of the Oise.[97] Advancing from Namur, with 17,000 men, he crossed into France and set siege to Rocroi. But expecting to capture the town in a few days and supposing Condé, with his relief army, to be further away than he was, he simply encamped around its walls without digging elaborate entrenchments, and erecting the siege fortifications used for a full-scale siege.[98] It was to prove a fatal error. Condé arrived on the scene, on 19 May, with some 23,000 men, and at once advanced to attack. The army of Flanders just had time to draw up in battle formation. The ensuing battle lasted six hours for much of which the outcome hung in the balance. Finally some of the non-Spanish contingents of the army of Flanders wavered and broke. The day ended with the core of the army, the proud Spanish veterans, being cut down where they stood.

Rocroi marked the end of an era, destroying the reputation of the army of Flanders for invincibility in the field. The bulk of Melo's high-grade troops were killed or captured. But the wider significance of the battle can only be properly grasped if it is viewed in the context of the new and peculiarly difficult strategic situation in which Spain found herself following the revolts of Catalonia and Portugal. The disaster resulted from attempting to strike hard into France at a time of overall military weakness, a strategy for which there was mounting pressure, from Madrid, on the governor-general of the Spanish Netherlands in the early 1640s. But this should be regarded as an entirely new phenomenon which arose only after, and as a consequence of, the catastrophic developments of 1640. Throughout the earlier phase of the Franco-Spanish conflict (1635–40) very different strategic priorities had prevailed leading, in the main, to a concentration of Spain's offensive power not against France but against the Dutch.

Finally, Rocroi marked the end not only of a legend but also of a strategic phase. For after 1643, it was no longer possible for Spain to launch an offensive from the Spanish Netherlands into France – not even, to any significant extent, when France in turn was gravely weakened, in the years

[96] González de León, 'The road to Rocroi', pp. 173, 208–9.
[97] Lonchay, *La rivalité*, p. 114.
[98] Henri d'Orléans, duc d'Aumâle, *Histoire des princes de Condé pendant les XVIe et XVIIe siècles* (Paris, 1889–96), IV, pp. 66, 79–80.

1648–53, by the Frondes. Yet Rocroi by no means ended the Spanish Netherlands' role as Spain's principal military bastion and base. This the region was to continue to be for another sixteen years, until the conclusion of the great war with France, in 1659.

12

✳

Conquest after the conquest: the rise of
Spanish domination in America

PETER BAKEWELL

The Spanish military conquests on the American mainland between, roughly, 1520 and 1540, are justly famous, or infamous, episodes in the history of European expansion. In those two decades a small number of Spaniards, probably not above 10,000 even if late-comers and people behind the front lines are counted, overcame native polities containing many millions in central and southern Mexico, Central America and the regions of South America we now know as Colombia, Ecuador, Peru, Bolivia and Chile. Great and sometimes acrimonious controversy still surrounds the question of how many millions of Indians there were. The answer will probably never be known for certain. The most sober study of the Peruvian case suggests a range of 4–12 or even 15 million;[1] and for central and southern Mexico, serious arguments have been made for figures from 6 to 25 million.[2] These are the best-studied regions – the heart of the Inca empire, and almost the whole of the Aztecs'. The pre-conquest populations of other areas are still less precisely (if that is the word) known. For understanding the conquests, the numbers in any case do not matter much. Whether high or low estimates are taken, the invaders were still outnumbered by thousands to one.

All translations are by the author unless otherwise attributed.

[1] N. David Cook, *Demographic collapse: Indian Peru, 1520–1620* (Cambridge, 1981), pp. 113–14.

[2] William M. Denevan (ed.), *The native population of the Americas in 1492* (2nd edition, Madison, 1992), p. xxi.

Controversy abounds, too, over the means of conquest, though it is less heated, and has more to do with the ranking of explanations than with identifying them. Nearly all agree that some combination of the following can account for the rapid Spanish victory over the high- and middle-ranking native cultures: superiority of weapons, tactics and strategy; fatal political divisions on the native side; disease introduced, unwittingly but devastatingly, from Europe; disastrous misapprehension by the natives of the Spaniards' intentions, ambitions, procedures, identity and strength; and, behind this misunderstanding, a psychological mismatch between, on the one hand, peoples inhabiting an animistic world in which human and divine fused together in a mesmerizing blur and, on the other, attackers who, though convinced of the divinely directed rightness of their actions, were also brilliant practitioners of the purposive pragmatism of the late Renaissance – 'the practical truth of things rather than...fancies'.[3] At an early skirmish in the Mexican campaign, according to Cortés' eulogizing biographer, Francisco López de Gómara, the apostles James and Peter appeared to aid the Spanish. Bernal Díaz del Castillo, a foot soldier in the Aztec conquest, and later its leading chronicler, was not so sure. He had been in the battle. Gómara had not. 'It might be', Díaz conjectured, 'that I, because a sinner, was unworthy to see them.'[4] But, he went on, 400 other soldiers had also failed to notice these agents of divine aid. He remained sceptical.

Those two decades of military conquest have understandably drawn more attention over the years than any other episode in Spanish American history, with the possible exception of the Wars of Independence. They hold great drama, heroism, tragedy – and mystery. For the Spanish victory, it seems, however endlessly analysed, still resists final elucidation. How could so many fail to crush (perhaps literally) so few? This fascination with the military phase of the conquest has in turn obscured the fact that, in the creation of the Spanish American empire as it came to be, the campaigns of Cortés, Pizarro and their lesser, but still remarkable, imitators, were only the end of the beginning. They gave, of course, crucial control of territory, and yielded an apparently cowed native population. But it was not at all clear that the submission would last and, accordingly, the territory remain controlled.

Nor, in the whirl of the conquests, could the Spanish gain more than a broad impression of what the mainland contained, or of the nature and organization of its peoples. The campaigns left, certainly, an alluring

---

[3] Niccolò Machiavelli, *The prince*, trans. Daniel Donno (New York, 1966), chapter 15.
[4] Bernal Díaz del Castillo, *Historia verdadera de la conquista de la Nueva España* (Mexico City, 1950), I, p. 146.

impression of great possible wealth in gold and in the productive capacity of abundant native labour. This impression was crucially important because it drew more Spaniards to America. But what precisely the combination of that labour and that land might yield remained to be discovered. The military conquests can quite reasonably be seen as a case of smash and grab. But once what was immediately at hand had been grabbed, more durable sources of wealth had to be created. Doing so took time, and diverse sorts of new effort. For native populations to be made permanently beneficial to both state and individuals, it soon became clear that their political, religious and social arrangements had to be known. An administrative machine had to be created and installed to govern them (and, it soon became clear, to control settlers who threatened to gain from America at the state's expense). Information had to be gathered about who and what was on the land, and then assembled into a useful picture. These activities, mental and physical, added up to a process of domination of America that took place mostly after the military conquests were over, and that was far slower and less definite than they had been. And domination was never, of course, complete. But by the end of the sixteenth century remarkable progress had been made towards achieving it. Perhaps, indeed, Spanish America was never again as firmly under the thumb of the metropolis as it was for a few decades before and after 1600.

The most obvious tool of domination was the administrative apparatus that Spain began installing in America within years of Columbus' first arrival. The admiral soon revealed an ineptitude or lack of interest in governing that gave the Catholic Monarchs an opening to insert their own bureaucratic agents in Columbus' fief of Hispaniola. By 1500 he had lost his administrative powers. In 1502 Spanish presence in the Caribbean was in effect recreated with the arrival in Hispaniola of the first fully fledged royal governor, Nicolás de Ovando. He had brought across the Atlantic a fleet carrying some 2,500 colonists, among them the first families to leave Spain for America.

The continuing influx of settlers, and the outward movement from Hispaniola to the other large islands and the isthmus of Panama that began in 1508, brought a need for more comprehensive administration. The year 1511 marks the appearance in Spanish America of what was to become the basic building block of colonial government, the *audiencia*. The first of these regional courts of appeal was set up in Santo Domingo in that year and, despite the presence now of Columbus' son Diego as titular viceroy, soon became in reality the source of administrative orders as well as of legal judgement. A brief interruption in the *audiencia*'s rule came between 1517 and 1520, when for an experimental and unique period government of the Spanish Indies was entrusted to churchmen – three Jeronymite friars named by Cardinal Cisneros acting as regent of Spain in the opening months of Charles I's reign.

The friars proved no more able as administrators than the secular officials preceding them. Thus, as Cortés advanced in 1520 in the conquest of the Aztecs, power was returned to the *audiencia* of Santo Domingo, and the scene was set for the transfer to the mainland of the controlling institutions that two decades of experience in the Greater Antilles had produced.

With the advance to the mainland that the Mexican conquest brought, a vision of a Spanish American empire began to take form. From the first Mexico obviously far exceeded in population, wealth and cultural and geographical complexity anything previously encountered in the Caribbean. It presented an immense administrative challenge. Initially there was little choice but to leave Cortés with the power he had acquired as conqueror, risky though that clearly was. The risk was immediately demonstrated in the grants he made to his men of *encomiendas* – allocations of the tribute and labour of groups of native people. This practice had proved immensely harmful to the Caribbean natives, and Charles had called in 1520 for an end to *encomiendas*. Cortés himself had seen the harm done, and wished to avoid its repetition in Mexico. But practical politics left him no choice – or so he argued to the king – but to reward participants in the conquest with these grants.

In reality, everywhere on the mainland the *encomienda* proved a useful, indeed essential, transitional form of government. While royal officers were still few and far between, it at least gave a large number of private settlers a binding interest in the places where their Indians lived. Those who held *encomiendas*, the *encomenderos*, also played a large economic role in survey-ing America for productive potential. They did so not as a result of any planned administrative scheme, but simply because they wanted to know what they could demand in tribute, and to what use their people's labour could be put. Further, in the 1520s and 1530s in Mexico and Central America, and in the 1530s and 1540s in South America, *encomenderos* or their agents were the only Spaniards, apart from priests, with whom many native people had contact. For better or worse, they were the *de facto* colonial authority in much of the countryside.

The era of the *encomendero* soon passed in most of the empire. The system threatened to give excessive wealth and local power to what came quickly to be seen, and to see itself, as a nascent colonial aristocracy. In the 1540s and 1550s law and a rising bureaucracy reined in the *encomenderos*, though not without violent resistance in Peru and rumblings elsewhere. Holders of encomiendas there long continued to be after then, but shorn of economic and political, if not social, influence.

The administrative need for the *encomienda* lasted for what was, given the immensity of the governmental task facing Spain, a remarkably short time. In Mexico, officialdom was sufficiently rooted barely a decade after the conquest for the *encomenderos'* role as representatives of colonial power to become redundant. Cortés, who apart from being governor was the supreme *encomendero*, holding tens of thousands of Indians, was the first to go – removed from office and deprived of many of his tributaries in the late 1520s. At the same time an *audiencia* was set up in Mexico City, the first on the mainland. In the early 1530s began, if slowly, the appointment of *corregidores*, the salaried administrators of local, rural districts. Then, in 1535, Mexico received its first viceroy. This was evidence of recognition in Spain that here was indeed a place worthy to be ranked as a separate *reino*, or realm, of the Habsburg monarchy. Now the essentials of a bureaucratic panoply were in place. Much remained to be done in completing the apparatus, expanding it as Spanish occupation of Mexico spread (an *audiencia* in Guadalajara in 1547, for example), and adjusting it to meet developing needs. By mid-century it was functioning well, ready to respond to the rising fiscal demands that Spain would impose on the American colonies from then on.

Broadly speaking, the same happened elsewhere on the mainland. Conquerors were briefly entrusted with government, then replaced by *audiencias* (and in the case of Peru, by a viceroy as well, in 1544). *Encomenderos* yielded slowly to *corregidores*. Besides the *audiencias* in Santo Domingo and Mexico City, nine others were created at Panama (1538), Guatemala City and Lima (1543), Guadalajara and Bogotá (1547), La Plata (now Sucre, 1559), Quito (1563), Concepción (Chile, 1565–75, restored at Santiago, 1603) and Manila (1583).[5] The more peripheral the area, the later the date of its court's foundation. None the less, only three other *audiencias* were added to the eleven created before 1600: Buenos Aires, Caracas and Cuzco, all in the 1780s. Three of the sixteenth-century *audiencias* (Mexico City, Bogotá and Quito) were sited at centres of pre-conquest political authority. These places are now the capitals of national states. Their political and administrative role extends back, through the *audiencias*, to the fifteenth century or earlier.

---

[5] For the founding dates, Ernst Schäfer, *El consejo real y supremo de las Indias*. II: *La labor del consejo de Indias en la administración colonial* (Seville, 1947), second appendix, pp. 443 ff.

If there was some continuity of place from native administration to colonial government, there was naturally an even stronger link between governmental practice in Spain and that of America. The viceroyalty was a device used by the Aragonese monarchy to control its provinces in the peninsula and in the Mediterranean and Italy. The American *audiencia* had its origins in the *chancillerías* (high courts) of Castile. Both the *corregimiento* and the *encomienda* had Iberian precedents. All these, and other, institutions of course underwent adaptation to American demands and conditions. Early viceroys were given extraordinary freedom of executive action, to enable them to respond to problems with minimum need for consultation with Spain. *Audiencias*, especially those more distant from the two viceregal capitals, became more important as executive councils than as law courts. Lower executive officers, such as *corregidores*, had also to wield considerable judicial authority as first-instance magistrates, given the size of America and the general remoteness of their districts from the *audiencias*. In general, American conditions led quickly to the fusing in single offices and governing bodies of executive, judicial and legislative powers. That early trait of colonial government has proved difficult to modify in the national history of Spanish American states.

Continuity and adaptation also marked the all-important tie of church with state in the Indies. Isabella, especially, had drawn the two tightly together in Castile for her political ends. But the influence over the colonial church that the monarchy gained through various papal concessions soon after her death went much further. In return for Spain's undertaking to evangelize American natives, Rome gave the crown control over tithes, the right to nominate candidates for church offices at all levels, regulation of movement of clergy across the Atlantic, and veto powers over papal despatches to America. In principle, and broadly speaking in practice too, all this made the colonial church an arm of the state. The early decades on the mainland, though, were not without tensions. The crown's decision to entrust evangelization to the regular clergy was certainly justified by the spiritualizing reforms that they, particularly the Franciscans and Dominicans, had recently undergone in Spain. But, as corporate bodies, the religious orders could resist direction much more firmly than the secular church might have done, and tended to follow their own courses of action. It was mainly from the evangelizing regular clergy that calls came for protection of Indians from the demands of settlers, and sometimes even for a rigid separation of native people from Europeans. Such notions might now and then appeal to the royal conscience; but in general they threatened the prospect of profit from America, which became an ever more potent determinant of colonial policy. Rather like the *encomenderos*, the missionary friars were indispensable for the early taming of the mainland. There was no one else available to do the job. But like the *encomenderos* they proved as much a problem as a solution. In the mid-century came increasing reports from royal officials that the friars were in fact achieving the separation of Indians from colonists that they had long advocated. They had done so by making themselves the secular as well as spiritual authorities in their parishes (particularly in the countryside), even acting as judges, and punishing offenders in jails they had themselves built. Coming on top of earlier sorts of refractoriness, this intrusion by the friars into royal jurisdiction – the central function of the Castilian monarchy – was intolerable. From the 1560s Philip II's government moved with some success to curb the religious orders' autonomy and to replace them in parish work with priests from the secular hierarchy. Philip was helped in this by the fact that his complaints about the regulars were those also of the Council of Trent. He welcomed the Council's determination to subject the regulars to the episcopal hierarchy.[6] The religious orders in America resisted stoutly. Many of their members long remained in parish work, but now without the freedom of action they had enjoyed in the early decades. The parish priesthood, whether secular or regular, increasingly became a conduit through which the Spanish state could control and observe communities in the Indies, both native and European.[7] A parallel channel with some of the same functions was added ca. 1570 when the Inquisition was extended to America.

Whatever the disputes between crown and clergy in the first decades over procedures, and even the form that colonization should take, it is still true, of course, that both pursued the broad aim of 'civilizing', which was tantamount to hispanizing, the American natives. Christianity was the ideology of domination. For the indigenous peoples, royal officials and friars were both invaders, one group just more obviously aggressive than the other. Further, the friars knew that the better their acquaintance with the object of their efforts, the more quickly and fully christianization would come. Learning and recording native language was an obvious and practical early step; as was investigation of religions. Many of the missionary friars had been well prepared for such tasks by a thorough humanistic education in Spain; and some of them were led by well-sharpened intellectual curiosity to look beyond what was practically needed for spreading the Word, and to

---

[6] See Demetrio Ramos, 'La crisis indiana y la junta magna de 1568', *Jahrbuch für Geschichte von Staat, Wirtschaft und Gesellschaft Lateinamerikas*, 22 (1985), 8ff., and particularly 14–15.
[7] Cf. Karen Spalding, *Huarochirí: an Andean society under Inca and Spanish rule* (Stanford, 1984), p. 250.

study native culture for its intrinsic anthropological interest. If they had not done so, much less would now be known about Aztecs, Incas and others. But, again, however purely intentioned the efforts of these scholar-friars of the sixteenth century, their work was inevitably to an extent political in that it increased Spanish knowledge of native people, and hence confidence in dealing with them. Colonial control thus became surer footed. Understanding is in itself a form of domination, and one whose practical utility is not hard to find. There were Spanish administrators who saw this well. One was Juan de Ovando, president of the council of the Indies in the early 1570s, who blamed earlier faults in the government of America on the poor quality and quantity of information received by the council. Both he and the king in those years strove to correct the deficiency by, among other things, creating the post of Chronicler of the Indies in 1571 (first held by Juan López de Velasco), and calling for bigger and better reports from the colonies. Their interest in Indian affairs is very clear. So it is odd indeed to find Philip in 1577 suddenly ordering the confiscation of the greatest of all ethnographic works on Indians in the empire, Fray Bernardino de Sahagún's *General history of the things of New Spain*, and banning further writing and publication on indigenous religion, history and life. The removal of Ovando's influence with his death in 1575 is perhaps part of the reason. Without that moderating force at hand, Philip may have been inclined – especially when facing crises at home such as state bankruptcy in 1575, and mutiny in the army of Flanders together with Turkish successes in the western Mediterranean in 1576 – to take a more impatient, even brutal, line in American administration. What Indians were or had been was perhaps now less important than what they must do as the colonies' major work force to provide the income Spain needed to fight its European battles. Knowledge of their past glories of polity and culture might raise objections to their broad use as labour. Investigation of their religion now seemed, perhaps, likely only to muddle or block their christianization, which was necessary if they were to be truly subject to Spain and Spanish colonists. Beyond all this, much of the work on native culture had been done by Franciscans, prime among them Sahagún himself. Franciscans were suspect as champions of the Indians. And as the chief proponents of a millenarian interpretation of Spain's enterprise in America, they were implicit foes of a utilitarian view of the empire's function.[8] Whatever the reasons for Philip's ruling, the late

---

[8] For the decree of 1577 and its circumstances: D. A. Brading, *The first America: the Spanish monarchy, creole patriots, and the liberal state, 1492–1867* (Cambridge, 1991), pp. 120–1; and Georges Baudot, *Utopía e historia en México. Los primeros cronistas de la civilización mexicana (1520–1569)* (Madrid, 1983), pp. 471–502.

1570s saw enquiry into Indian culture and history severely cut back. It was a reduction in the mental engagement with America that had previously, in the final analysis, only contributed to Spanish control.

The combined pressures of state, church and settlers produced severe changes in native societies in the sixteenth century. The clearest is a compression of social ranks. This was especially obvious in the high cultures, of course; the less developed were more egalitarian in the first place. The military conquests removed immediately the supreme leadership of the great polities. This is literally true. In 1532, Pizarro seized Atahualpa in Cajamarca twenty-four hours after the Spaniards first met that final Inca monarch; and Cortés took Moctezuma II captive only a few days after entering Tenochtitlan in 1519. By the end of the fighting, in both cases, the leading native nobility, which also embraced the high priesthood, was largely disbanded. Almost all high-status holders of power in the native polities thus disappeared within, at most, a few years; the exceptions were those who had allied with the Spaniards.

There followed an interlude of three or four decades of stability of native social ranking, in part corresponding to the period in which *encomenderos* were the main agents of Spanish authority. These years show a reversion to native political and social conditions as they had been before the rise of the great, but very late, pre-conquest states. Those states had conquered and incorporated many smaller and older polities, which re-emerged, after the Spanish conquest, as the largest surviving units of native socio-political organization. Their ruling lineages retained a deeply rooted authority in them. The early Spanish administration found these locally prominent families indispensable for controlling the mass of the population, and extracting tribute from it. Local lords – whom the Spanish generically called *caciques*, though that term belonged only in the Greater Antilles – knew what tributes their people had given to the Aztecs and Incas. In return for political and economic rewards (being left in power, free to feather their own nests) they would collaborate with the Spanish in the provision of tribute in goods and labour. Connections between *caciques* and *encomenderos* were sometimes close, for mutual benefit. If Spain could hardly have controlled the mainland colonies without *encomenderos* in the 1520s and 1530s, it was scarcely less dependent on the *caciques*.

The *caciques'* respite was, though, brief. As the Spanish bureaucracy, and knowledge of America, grew, the intermediary role of the local Indian lords shrank. Besides that, tribute revenues dropped as the native population fell before the onslaught of epidemics. At the same time, Spain's reliance on America to meet its fiscal needs was rising. The outcome in the middle decades of the century was an enlargement of the tributary net, mainly to bring in large numbers of personal dependants and servants of the *caciques* who had hitherto been exempt from tribute payment. This had, first, the effect of simplifying the structure of native society by levelling up its lowest segments to the now almost universal category of common tribute-payer; and, second, that of depriving *caciques* of much of their material support, as well as of their status as masters of many retainers.[9] Though the function and position of *cacique* survived throughout the colonial era, after the mid-sixteenth century the pre-conquest lordly lineages weakened, or at least sought to adapt to colonial conditions by hispanizing their behaviour. Some lords became, for example, remarkably enterprising businessmen, producing goods for Spanish consumption in an effort to replace the economic base they had lost in the reforms of the mid-1500s.

Though the emphasis of recent research has been on the resistance of native cultures to, or their self-protective assimilation of, Spanish influence[10] – and much certainly survived, as the briefest visit to southern Mexico, northern Central America, or the central Andes shows – this self-defence undeniably took place in societies that were structurally less complex than what had existed before 1500. By the mid-sixteenth century Spaniards in America were well on their way to regarding the native peoples as an undifferentiated mass whose function was to provide tribute for the state and cheap labour for the colonists. And that was not merely a practically convenient concept for the Spanish to adopt. In the ways described, and others, the previously ranked societies of the advanced cultures had lost their upper and lower strata. The surviving near-unitary mass was settling, and being depressed, into the position of the labouring common people at the base of the new colonial society.

As this social domination was proceeding, Spaniards were busy also mastering the territory of America in various ways. Much exploration took place during the conquest years. Cortés reconnoitred central Mexico before and during his conflict with the Aztecs; and Pizarro spent several years in intermittent exploration of the north-west coast of South America before advancing in 1532 into the Inca heartland of the Peruvian Andes. After

[9] Cf. Susan Ramírez, 'El *Dueño de Indios*: thoughts on the consequences of the shifting bases of power of the *Curaca de los viejos antiguos* under the Spanish in sixteenth-century Peru', *Hispanic American Historical Review*, 67 (1987), 575–610.

[10] E.g. James Lockhart, *The Nahuas after the conquest: a social and cultural history of the Indians of Central Mexico, sixteenth through eighteenth centuries* (Stanford, 1992); or, more briefly, Lockhart, 'Postconquest Nahua society and culture seen through Nahuatl sources', in his *Nahuas and Spaniards: postconquest central Mexican history and philology* (Los Angeles/Stanford, 1991).

these major confrontations, lesser leaders and late-comers moved out from the newly created Spanish bases in search of similarly alluring targets elsewhere. None was found. But these efforts led to the start of permanent occupation of many regions in the late 1520s and 1530s: Guatemala and elsewhere in northern Central America; New Granada (now Colombia); Quito (now highland Ecuador); Chile. The pace of exploration by Spaniards seeking high cultures to conquer, for wealth and glory, was astounding. Many of the central mainland towns of colonial, and national, times were founded by the early 1540s, from Guadalajara in western Mexico to Santiago in central Chile. After then, exploration was driven especially by the search for precious metals. The gold accumulated over centuries by various native cultures had soon been looted. And it quickly became clear that America had more to offer in silver ores than it did in unexploited deposits of gold. That prospect rapidly pulled explorers outward from established centres. The result was the discovery at Potosí in 1545 of the largest concentration of silver ore found in the first half of the colonial era. That find led not only to the presence of an enormous town (of over 100,000 by 1600) on an otherwise extremely improbable site high in the Bolivian Andes, but also to the appearance of a constellation of supporting settlements over a very large area around it. The rise of Potosí, indeed, caused much of the Spanish settlement of what is now highland Bolivia. The region had, before the conquest, held a number of moderately advanced native groups forming a transition between the high-culture area of southern Peru and the simpler tribes of the interior lowlands of South America. The rise of silver mining in and around Potosí now made that same zone (present highland Bolivia) an integral part of Peru, the central area of Spanish culture in South America.

Silver had a similar, but much more pronounced, influence in northern Mexico. There, the discovery of many large ore bodies from 1546 onwards brought a wide scattering of mining towns into existence over the next fifty years. It also brought, until almost 1600, a grinding conflict between the nomadic tribes of the northern plateau and Spanish settlers. The final outcome was the disappearance, partly by absorption, of the nomads, and the incorporation of the *altiplano* – the high plateau – into the main current of Mexican existence essentially for the first time. The replacement of elementary hunting-gathering native tribes in the north by distinctly Spanish towns (tightly linked to central Mexico by silver exports and other trade) was certainly the most startling change in cultural geography that Spanish colonization produced in Mexico, and one that it is difficult to match in South America.

By the late sixteenth century, exploration and the expansion of settlement following from it had yielded an enormous amount of information about Middle and South America. Spanish officialdom made notable contributions to its gathering. Royal officers in the mature bureaucracy of the final third of the century were keen to report on human and natural resources, partly for the state's benefit, and partly, like some of the early friars, out of simple fascination with the New World. And from the 1580s much of this information was encapsulated in a series of formal reports, the *Relaciones geográficas*, prepared area by area by local officials by order of the council of the Indies, and sent to Madrid. Thus, for the first time, a corpus of knowledge, mainly geographical and economic, about an enormous segment of American territory was gathered into one place. The *Relaciones* served the purposes of Spanish control; they continue to serve historians.

The collection of information both reflected and promoted the growth of Spanish economic domination of America. By the end of the sixteenth century this was remarkably advanced. Mining had led the way. Most of the mining centres were in areas too high or too dry for production of the foodstuffs and animals needed to feed the workforces and provide power for machinery. Certainly, wherever possible around the mining towns – in places, in fact, that would seem barely cultivable – farming appeared: in high but sheltered Andean valleys; along seasonal watercourses in the semi-desert of the Mexican *altiplano*. Freight costs to remote mining sites were severe enough to encourage use of whatever nearby land could be persuaded to produce food. But inevitably much had to come from afar: mules and cattle to the Potosí district from the central plains of present Argentina, maize and wheat to northern Mexico from the fertile valleys, once lake beds, in the centre of the colony. Mining led, then, to the growth of medium- and long-distance internal exchange, on a scale, and between regions, far different from what had occurred even in the largest native polities. Not all trade, of course, was the outcome of demand from mining populations. The rise of large administrative and ecclesiastical centres, such as the viceregal and *audiencia* capitals, also evoked local and distant production of food, and of raw materials for the considerable variety and number of artisans who were at work by the end of the first century. Craft production drew on both Spanish and indigenous traditions, with perhaps some African component in metal working.

Trade was also a response to the growth of regional specialization of agricultural production as the Spaniards, starting from native practice but adding their own expanding knowledge, discovered what would grow where. The Spanish addition was particularly notable in the case of introduced crops. Wheat, being their staple and preferred cereal, they tried everywhere they went. It succeeded in temperate regions, such as central Mexico and central Chile, where great wheat farms developed. Elsewhere the colonists slotted wheat into any suitable ecological niche they could find. Certain valleys in the central Andes, up to 10,000 feet or so, were one such type of site. Other, more exotic, examples are sugar cane and grapes. Cane did well in the Caribbean, in various parts of southern Mexico, and in the irrigated river valleys crossing the arid north coast of Peru. Grapes were planted successfully in various parts of Mexico, but proved to do best of all in southern Peru. Wine made from them was traded not only by land (to Potosí, for example, and other high cities in the Andes) but by sea to Mexico, and by the end of the sixteenth century was supplanting imports of Spanish wine. Sugar likewise went by sea down the west coast of South America. Trade between colonies, as well as within them, was well established before the sixteenth century was out and grew after that time. With few exceptions, such as central Mexican trading with Yucatán or northern Central America, or the state-directed movement of food and cloth in the Inca state, there was no native precedent for exchange over such distances.

Much of the economic innovation and organization achieved in the sixteenth century derived from the introduction of European technology. If weapons new to native Americans, made of unfamiliar metals, had played a crucial role in the military conquests, new techniques, machines and other artefacts were no less important in the processes of domination at work during the rest of the century. The list could be long. It includes durable paper, phonetic writing and the printing press for rapid and accurate recording and storing of information; carts and ships for long-distance trade; water-wheels and mechanical mills for processing grain, cane and silver ores; iron and steel tools for farming; and a variety of artisanry. Most striking of all was the use, developed in Mexico in the 1550s from small-scale European precedents, of mercury to refine silver by amalgamation. This technique was the foundation of colonial Spanish America's vast silver output, and hence the root also of much of its internal and external trade. The contrast between the technological armoury of even the highest cultures in 1500, and what was in general use a century later, is overwhelming. No native culture had put the wheel to any practical use; only the central Andeans possessed, in the llama, an animal capable of carrying more than a human could, and no use was made of the llama to pull loads; planting was nowhere done with anything more advanced than a digging stick.

The Spaniards introduced non-military technology on the mainland very soon after the conquest, especially for handling products that were themselves imports. Mechanical mills for grinding wheat and crushing cane were early examples. But it seems likely that the pace of technological installation was accelerated by the rapid decline of native population that also followed the conquests, as, in essence, lost labour had to be replaced by capital.

Though the pre-conquest numbers of the native Americans are hotly disputed, all agree that those numbers dropped vastly over the following century (or more, in some regions). In the mid-sixteenth century the Spanish began to count native people for the purposes of the state's tribute collection; and those enumerations, though fraught with interpretive problems, provide a surer basis for calculation than anything available for earlier times. These records suggest that the native population of central and southern Mexico (the best-studied region) fell from somewhere in the 3.5 to 6.3 million range ca. 1548 to a low point of 0.73 million ca. 1625. In what is now the territory of Peru, native numbers went from 1.3 million ca. 1570 to 0.67 million ca. 1620 (though some of the apparent decline there may have been the result of migration).[11] And the low point in Peru may not have come until the 1720s. Since there is no reason to doubt that some decline took place between the first Spanish–native contact in any region and the time when the colonial government began to count Indians – reports of epidemics in the early decades, for instance, are frequent – it seems clear enough that native population losses were generally very high: probably over 90 per cent, for example, in central and southern Mexico. No large, central region seems to have been spared. There is consensus that the main cause of the decline was disease originating in the Old World: certainly smallpox and the plague; and probably typhus, measles, mumps and influenza. A recent modelling of the native demographics in the Valley of Mexico (the densely populated basin in which Mexico City lies) concludes that disease alone can account for the great losses evident there in the sixteenth century.[12] Some evidence exists, though, for a decline in native birth rates after the conquest. Some of the apparent 'loss' of population, then, may consist of those who were never born, rather than those who died.

The disastrous slump in native numbers changed the nature of Spanish imperial enterprise in America. The expectation was, as the great mainland conquests began, that the apparently endless numbers of native people who had created the great and prosperous high cultures would be able to support

[11] For the higher Mexican figure, Sherburne F. Cook and Woodrow Borah, *Essays in population history: Mexico and the Caribbean* (Berkeley and Los Angeles, 1979), III, pp. 1, 100; and, for the lower, Rudolph A. Zambardino, 'Mexico's population in the sixteenth century: demographic anomaly or mathematical illusion?', *Journal of Interdisciplinary History*, 11 (1980), 10–14; for Peru, Cook, *Demographic collapse*, p. 253.

[12] Thomas M. Whitmore, *Disease and death in early colonial Mexico: simulating Amerindian depopulation* (Boulder, 1992), p. 214.

Spaniards in the same way – with tributes in labour and goods. The demographic subsidence made this impossible, especially because from the start the numbers of settlers expecting support from Indians grew; and because, from the accession of Philip II in 1556 onwards, Spain adopted a policy of maximizing America's contribution to the state treasury.[13] A variety of measures were tried to increase the 'yield' of the remaining Indians, some of them already recounted here: censuses of the tributary population, cuts in the number of exemptions from the tax, congregation of remaining natives into fewer communities for easier collection of tribute (a policy implemented in Mexico in the 1550s and in the central Andes in the 1570s) and, naturally, increase in tributary tax rates. None of these sufficed to preserve the tribute-based empire.

The outcome on the state's part included a diversification of taxes and conscious stimulation of American production, mainly through the organization of systems of forced native labour for tasks considered of public utility. These, principally, were food production, public works such as roads and bridges, and silver mining. From the 1550s Indian workers had been drafted *ad hoc* by colonial administrators for particular tasks. But in the 1570s broad and regularized systems were set up: the *repartimiento* in Mexico and the *mita* in the central Andes. Each, initially at least, obliged a small fraction of native men to work for a set time yearly in one of the tasks judged deserving of forced labour. They received a statutory, if very low, wage from the Spanish employer to whom they were assigned. The authorities most closely associated with these arrangements were don Martin Enríquez in Mexico (viceroy from 1568 to 1580), and don Francisco de Toledo in Peru (viceroy from 1569 to 1581); both systematized and extended prior practices rather than creating drafts *ex nihilo*.

Silver, being in essence money, was obviously the American product of most urgent interest to a Spanish government faced, as Philip II's was, with constantly growing European commitments. Hence silver offers the clearest example of conscious economic stimulation by the state. One of the tasks given to Viceroy Toledo before he left Spain was to bring about the transfer of amalgamation technology from Mexico to Peru. Again he worked, once in Peru, with a process that was already in motion. By early 1572 amalgamation was beginning to appear in Potosí. Its rapid adoption from then on, in combination with cheap *mita* labour, led to a four- or five-fold increase in Potosí's production between the early 1570s and the early 1580s, and to a

---

[13] Carlos Sempat Assadourian, 'La despoblación indígena en Perú y Nueva España durante el siglo xvi y la formación de la economía colonial', in *La formación de América Latina. La época colonial*. Lecturas de historia mexicana, VIII (Mexico City, 1992), p. 70.

continued rise until 1592, the year of highest silver output at any time in Potosí's history. Paralleling the extension of amalgamation to the central Andes was the creation of a royal monopoly in the production and distribution of mercury, to ensure that silver refiners had a reliable and affordable supply of that crucial reagent.

Colonists, meanwhile – particularly new arrivals who had not seen America in the early post-conquest days – took to working themselves in the entire range of occupations that existed in Spain, from farming to long distance trade. They preferred, it is true, to supervise rather than to put their own hands to the tools; but Spaniards' refusal to do physical work in America is a myth. Many of them wanted, none the less, native workers. When the state's system of drafts failed to supply their needs, as it often did in the areas of dense Spanish settlement, they hired Indians for wages under individual contract, or, if prosperous, bought African slaves. The productivity of these workers (and also real returns to labour) grew as employers invested in capital goods. Farmers, often working land fallen vacant because of the disappearance of natives once dependent on it, built storage barns and irrigation works, and bought teams of oxen to pull metal-bladed ploughs, increasing the proportion of food grown in the colonies by European-style extensive techniques. Textile producers installed mechanical, if crude, looms and spinning wheels in primitive mills. Freighters invested in mule teams, and, where the terrain allowed, in heavy carts and draft oxen. Shippers built vessels on the Pacific coast of Middle and South America to carry intercolonial trade.

Some of this would doubtless have happened in any case. But the Spaniards' direct involvement in production in the colonies was increased and accelerated by the shrinking of the supply of native labour and of tributary products.[14] By pushing colonists into productive activity, the demographic losses had the broader effect, also, of forcing them into closer contact with America – making them, in some cases, literally put their hands to the earth, and in general come to grips with its lands, climates and resources more fully than would otherwise have been necessary, or likely. Without a great native population to support them, and in a sense to act as buffer between them and the land, colonists were forced to Americanize themselves in the second half of the sixteenth century. Thus, in more than a purely and obvious numerical sense, the native population collapse

[14] This line of thought was first advanced by Woodrow W. Borah, in *New Spain's century of depression* (Berkeley and Los Angeles, 1951). Various others have pursued it since, recent among them Sempat Assadourian, in 'La despoblación indígena'.

following the military conquests worked to intensify Spanish economic domination of America. (At the same time, though, that Americanization was part of the rise of *criollo* feeling, or the self-identification of American-born Spaniards with their regions of origin in the New World. And that identification was soon to lead to a loosening of Spain's administrative and fiscal hold on the Indies.)

Similar outcomes of depopulation may be argued for the other forms of domination, besides the economic, suggested here. The drop in native numbers undermined the established economic bases of *caciques*, making it easier for Spaniards, both official and private, to push these local leaders aside in the mid-century when their use as middlemen was becoming less crucial. This contributed to the simplification of native social structure that the colonizing state pursued. The decline also both created a need for, and simplified, the congregation of natives in new towns and villages. This regrouping brought social and, in all probability, psychological disruption. Once again, the Indian social fabric was weakened, to the benefit of the colonizers.

Further, administration, in a limited bureaucratic sense, can only have been simplified by the decline of the native population, and Spanish control thereby strengthened. Though the demographic losses forced profound adaptations on the Spaniards of the sort suggested earlier here, the administrative task of governing the indigenous population surviving in, say, 1600 was surely simpler and cheaper, than it would have been if the original numbers, several times larger, had still been in place. The same could be said of the church's missionary work.

Consideration of religion, however, raises questions about the limits of Spanish domination. Even though evangelizing the unconverted, and maintaining the faith of those already evangelized, should have become an ever more practicable task as the native population shrank, what struck, and increasingly worried, churchmen in the final third of the sixteenth century was the degree to which native religion persisted. Christianity had been incorporated into prior beliefs, rather than displacing them. In part, this concern (or, in some priests, anger and even despair) was the result of a broad shift in attitude towards native culture. The first generation of friars had been predisposed, by humanistic education and immediate awareness of the splendours of the high cultures, to view Indians positively. Later missionaries, more rigidly minded products of the Counter-Reformation, and knowing Indians only in their reduced colonial state, were more likely to be critical. An inclination to seek parallels between native religion and Christianity gave way, after ca. 1560, to condemnation of Indian cults as devilry and violent efforts to uproot them.[15] But, changes in perception aside, there could be no doubt in the late sixteenth century that evangelization had failed – in the sense that it had not been able to extirpate indigenous religious belief and practice.

As with religion, so, clearly and unsurprisingly, it was with other contents of the native mind. American languages remained in common use throughout the colonial period. Few Indians besides leaders and officials learned much Spanish. Although Spanish infiltrated native languages, it did so slowly;[16] and language provided a barrier behind which native mentality could retreat. Native modes of thinking did not, with rare exceptions, become europeanized. In some central Mexican communities, to take a single illustrative example, the military conquest itself and its leaders had by the late seventeenth century been woven seamlessly into a characteristically myth-like story of their past, in which the European invasion was seen as no more significant than other interference before it by local outsiders.[17]

The control that Spaniards developed, therefore, over natives' bodies, largely stopped short of their minds. And, indeed, control over bodies, though considerable, proved less sure as time passed than had been hoped: for example, Indians tended to abandon the new places in which they had been congregated and returned home; some slipped out of the draft labour systems and into waged work; some took advantage of a legal loophole to avoid draft labour and tribute, by leaving their home community and taking up residence in another native place as *forasteros*, or outsiders.[18] But the native mind was predictably the most difficult aspect of America for Spaniards to penetrate. And the mental isolation of the native people may have increased as, after the mid-sixteenth century, the Spaniards sought to relegate them as a largely undifferentiated mass to a servile role at the base of society. Earlier efforts to educate at least the leaders along European lines, and to understand a broad range of indigenous practices, lapsed. Abandoned mentally, as it were, by the Spaniards, Indians perhaps found it easier to maintain a mental privacy.

The mind of the native apart, however, Spain – settlers, church and state – in the sixteenth century achieved a remarkable domination of Middle and

---

[15] Cf. Inga Clendinnen, *Ambivalent conquests: Maya and Spaniard in Yucatan, 1517–1570* (Cambridge, 1987), chapter 6; and Sabine MacCormack, *Religion in the Andes: vision and imagination in early colonial Peru* (Princeton, 1991), chapter 6.

[16] Lockhart, *The Nahuas*, chapter 7.

[17] Lockhart, 'Views of corporate self and history in some Valley of Mexico towns, late seventeenth and eighteenth centuries', in *Nahuas and Spaniards*, p. 59.

[18] Ann M. Wightman, *Indigenous migration and social change: the forasteros of Cuzco, 1520–1720* (Durham, N.C., 1990).

South America. The process was, in its persistence, its comprehensiveness and its interconnections, just as remarkable as the military conquests and, judged by some criteria, even more so. Few regions, apart from what was physically impenetrable or absolutely without economic interest, were left unexplored. Settlement spread fast and wide. Where secular colonists found no attraction, missionaries often went. Economic resources were surveyed and developed, often through the application of imported technology. Economic connections over longer spans than had ever existed before were in place before the century was done. Private and bureaucratic effort combined to achieve these results. Spanish officials sometimes referred to the American empire as a *máquina*. By 1600 the machine was installed, huge beyond precedent, blemished here and there with *ad hoc* parts, full of frictions making it creak and groan; but undeniably running.

One basic function of the machine, which it performed rather well before 1600, considering the physical difficulties, was simply to provide a set of linkages – administrative, defensive, economic, ideological – between the home country and the empire, between the centre of the Spanish world and its New World periphery. While the colonial structure can hardly be described as centralized in the sixteenth century, since much had to be left for decision on the spot, still the growth of the American empire can properly be seen as a remarkable outcome of that concentration of power achieved in Spain by Isabella and Ferdinand in the last quarter of the fifteenth century, and reinforced in the sixteenth by Charles V and Philip II. The dilution of that power in the seventeenth, so obvious in Spain's internal and European history, naturally had its American effects, and some degree of American cause, as well. The difficulty with at least the social components of the Indies machine was that they were organic, and controllable only in some respects by government. There was no means by which the monarchy could stop either increase in the white colonial population, or, even less, the growth in that population of feelings of American identity. Spanish officials were worried by the potential problem of these American-born whites, known in Peru as *criollos* as early as the 1560s, well before the sixteenth century was out. By 1600, though the populations are not known precisely, creoles undoubtedly far outnumbered *peninsulares* in America, and were becoming insistent that more of the colonies' honours and wealth than they were receiving were properly theirs. Over the next century and a half they gradually got their way – through persistence, through bargaining with the administration, through disregard for the law, and particularly through purchase of office, which by the 1640s made them powerful in the treasury system, and by 1700 in the highest levels of the *audiencias*. By these means and others this new white variety of native American proved capable of doing what Indians had never been close to accomplishing, of halting and even reversing the current of Spanish domination. It is true, of course, that this current flowed much less strongly after 1600 than before for many reasons, and so was more easily resisted. It is also true that creoles were to a degree Spaniards, and had no thought of breaking up the colonial system to achieve their own goals. They would, rather, work within its limits as they could stretch them. None the less, between the America of 1600 and that of a century later, there is a vast difference in the efficacy and reach of Spanish control; and for that difference, the rise of creoles in numbers, ambition, self-awareness and confidence is in good part responsible. Future attempts to return these white American natives to a state of domination akin to that of the sixteenth century would only, after 1800, lead them to a definitive break with Spain.

13

Heeding Heraclides: empire and its discontents, 1619–1812

ANTHONY PAGDEN

I

Heraclides of Byzantium, ambassador of Antiochus, presented himself to Publius Scipio and warned him: 'Let the Romans limit their Empire to Europe, that even this was very large; that it was possible to gain it part by part more easily than to hold the whole.' Scipio was unimpressed. 'What seemed to the ambassador great incentives for conducting peace', Livy tells us, 'seemed unimportant to the Romans.'[1] But Heraclides' words would return to haunt later European empire-builders who could, with hindsight, see all too clearly that Scipio should have been a little more attentive to what the ambassador had told him.

None of the early modern European empires were, perhaps, more conscious of this than the Spanish and none more prone to self-doubt and to self-reflection. The reasons for this are not hard to find. Spain was driven for longer and more consistently than its French, British and later Dutch, rivals by an ideology of evangelization, an ideology which demanded continual re-assessment of both the behaviour and the motives of those engaged

The title of this essay borrows, of course, from Freud's essay *Das Unbehagen in der Kultur* (1929), usually translated as 'Civilization and its discontents'. The loan is not merely frivolous. Freud's argument that, as 'culture' expands it necessarily imposes restraints upon the individual – the 'super-ego' – which can only result in discontent has certain clear structural affinities with the arguments against the exponential increase of empire which I discuss here. All translations are mine unless otherwise attributed.

[1] Livy, *Ab urbe condita*, XXXVII, p. 35.

in the colonizing project. It was also simply the largest – larger, as its ideologues rarely tired of stressing, even than Rome itself been; its territories were the most widely distributed and embraced the greatest number of different cultures. Uniquely, it also possessed an extensive European base. From the accession of Charles V to that of Philip V, the centre of the 'Spanish monarchy' – for as John Elliott has frequently reminded us, if this was an 'empire' in fact, it never was in name – was always Europe: the Netherlands, Portugal between 1580 and 1640 and above all Italy, 'the garden of the Empire', as Mercurio de Gattinara, echoing Dante, once called it.[2] These factors underpinned the claims, made in one idiom or another from the days of Charles V to those of Charles II, for the supposed, and always hoped for integrity of an *imperium,* one in which in the words of St John's Gospel as used by Ariosto, 'there shall be one flock and one shepherd'.[3] The Spanish overseas empire had come into being as a part of the Holy Roman Empire, and although in 1558 the empire itself had passed to the Austrian Habsburgs, the universalism which had marked Charles V's reign persisted, in one form or another, until the final demise of the dynasty. Spanish and Italian understanding of the political and legal identity of the monarchy remained deeply influenced by its imperial origins. By contrast, therefore, with the other European empires (whose overseas possessions were only ever colonies or plantations, sources of wealth for the metropolis with semi-independent legal identities), the Spanish monarchy conceived of itself as what its French and English critics feared. what was described in the language of the time as a 'Universal Monarchy'. No Castilian king ever entertained the illusion that he might make himself master of the entire world. Nor perhaps, with the exception of the Neapolitan magus Tommaso Campanella, did many of their ideologues.[4] But if they were unwilling to take Ariosto's encomium literally, they still thought of the monarchy, as they had thought of the empire, as a single political, if not yet cultural, community beneath a common rule of law. In practice this community was governed very much according to local laws and customs, particularly in Europe, but the monarchy as a whole was widely conceived as the embodiment of a *ius,* or, in the language of the Roman law which had been adopted

---

[2] Quoted in F. Chabod, *Storia de Milano nell'epoca di Carlo V* (Milan, 1961), p. 101.
[3]   E vuol che sotto a questo imperatore
      Solo un ovile sia, solo un pastore.
Quoted in Frances Yates, *Astraea* (London, 1975), p. 26.
[4] See Anthony Pagden, *Spanish imperialism and the political imagination* (New Haven and London, 1990), pp. 37–63.

by the empire, a *ius commune*, which was itself a romanized version of what Aristotle had called a *koinos nomos*, a universal law for all mankind.[5]

The acquisition and the maintenance of this conglomerate was never, however, regarded by Castilians as an unequivocal good. After the 'Spanish Empire' had, with the abdication of Charles V, been detached from the Holy Roman Empire, the Spanish kings had always looked upon Castile as the centre of their domains and the rest of the monarchy, even on most occasions Aragon, as the periphery. This was, at least, one of the causes of the war in the Netherlands; this was why Philip II built his capital in Madrid, not in Lisbon. As the fortunes of the monarchy began to decline, however, this periphery demanded ever greater sacrifices from the centre, and as it did so the voices of discontent increased in number and in volume. As John Elliott pointed out in a lecture given in 1977, by the early seventeenth century the empire had come to seem, even to the count-duke of Olivares, to be a 'poisoned chalice which had sapped their [the Castilians'] vigour and aggravated their ills'.[6]

In this essay, I wish to explore some of the ways in which Spaniards responded to what they understood to be their persistently over-extended monarchy's greatest dilemma: the need to balance preservation against expansion and to provide, by the most rational means possible, for the good of all its constituent parts. In the course of this debate a powerful argument emerged which claimed, as Antiochus' ambassador had effectively done, that all extended empires were by their very nature bound to outrun their origins in ways which would inevitably be disastrous for all those who lived in them.

II

The earliest objections to the scale and extent of the Spanish monarchy had, paradoxically, come from a group of theologians and jurists who were very close to the crown. These men, Domingo de Soto (1494–1570), Diego Covarrubias y Leyva (1512–1567) and, most remarkable of all, the humanist bureaucrat Fernando Vázquez de Menchaca (1512–1569), to name only the most influential, were all broadly speaking anti-imperialists. They were so, however, not, as so many historians have supposed, because of their horror

---

[5] *Rhetoric*, 1.12 (1373^b), and see P. A. Blunt, 'Laus imperii' in P. A. Garnsey and C. R. Whittaker, eds., *Imperialism in the ancient world* (Cambridge, 1978), pp. 159–91. The association of Roman law with Aristotle's *Koinos nomos* was the work of Aelius Aristedes.

[6] 'Spain and its empire in the sixteenth and seventeenth centuries', now printed in *Spain and its world 1500–1700* (New Haven and London, 1989), pp. 25–6.

at the human suffering which the Spanish colonizers had inflicted upon the colonized – although that horror was real enough – but because of the threat that all extended empires posed to what they conceived to be the true nature of the civil community. All had powerful legal and moral reasons for believing that no universal empire could possibly fulfil the function of a true civil society, nor adequately provide for the security, welfare and happiness of all its members. Since all maintained that society had been instituted by God for the collective good of its members, all insisted that *imperium* (sovereignty) could only be exercised legitimately over areas which were small enough to allow the ruler the authority he required in order to care for the interests of what Vázquez calls his *cives et subditi*, his 'citizens and subjects'. All larger political communities were not merely inconvenient. They were also unnatural. 'All things', wrote Domingo de Soto in his great treatise on rights, *De Iustitia et Iure*

which do not change, have fixed limits to their size, for an ant cannot reach the height of a man, nor a man the size of an elephant. It therefore follows that neither can a prince spread his warmth throughout a society [*respublica*] which extends across all regions and all peoples, so that he can know, emend, correct and dispose of what happens in each individual province . . . Consequently, as power exists in order to be exercised [*potestas sit propter usum*], and its exercise is impossible over such extended territory, it would follow that such an institution is vain. But God and nature never do anything in vain [*nihil fecit frustra*].[7]

The seas, said Vázquez de Menchaca echoing an ancient topos which was to be employed again and again in the anti-colonial literature of the eighteenth century, had been created precisely to keep men apart. Those who violated these natural limits did so to the ultimate detriment both of themselves and of all those whom they encountered. It was, he argued, precisely the existence of the New World 'situated in the most remote and unknown regions which are difficult of access' and which could only be reached by crossing 'immense and tempestuous seas' which had effectively undermined any claim on the part of the Castilian crown to possess natural rights in the Americas. 'After the discovery', he wrote,

it now appears with much greater clarity to be absolutely impossible that the right to rule [*dominium*] over so many regions, peoples and provinces separated from one another by such enormous distances, could reside with one man.[8]

---

[7] *De Iustitia et iure* (Salamanca, 1556), p. 306.
[8] *Controversiarum illustrium usuque frequentium, libri tres* [1563], ed. Fidel Rodriguez Alcalde (Valladolid, 1931), II, p. 25.

The arguments of Soto and Vázquez, like those of their great predecessor Francisco de Vitoria (ca. 1485–1546), were limited to a concern with the legitimacy of extensive empire. Although part of their argument was that such societies could not be justified because they could not be made to work in practice, they were very largely unconcerned with the realist implications of their claims.[9] As the political and economic 'decline' of Spain became increasingly evident, however, even those who were untroubled by questions of sovereignty and who had placed their faith in some kind of universal order because it seemed to offer the only guarantee of stability, began to question the wisdom of maintaining an empire as far flung and as disparate as the Spanish had become. It was, said Sancho de Moncada, professor of Sacred Scripture at the University of Toledo in 1619, now a commonly held view derived from Livy, that God and nature had placed a limit on all empires beyond which 'they have to return back as do the waves'. Like the Romans, the Castilians had made a crucial error when they abandoned their natural frontiers. The prudent ruler was one who, knowing exactly when he had reached those limits, chose to maintain his state by closing its borders. Had the Romans remained within Italy their empire there would have survived forever. 'The very nature of Your Majesty's Monarchy', wrote Moncada,

extended to so many and such distant provinces . . . The conquest of remote nations in the Indies and the conservation of the Royal patrimony in the kingdoms of Naples and Sicily and the Duchy of Milan, and the states of Flanders, have been a natural cancer in the body of Spain.[10]

The majority of those who warned in this way against the dangers inherent in over-extension were the writers within the tradition of 'reason of state'. This term, which is generally associated with Machiavelli and Tacitus, had wide circulation in Spain, despite attempts by nearly all Spaniards to detach the concept from any direct association with Machiavelli himself. The possibility of a science of politics governed by the notion of *interests* held out great attractions for those, in particular the professional administrators and diplomats, who had for long struggled to understand the workings of a political culture over which religious ideologies exercised such a decisive influence. In this they were helped by the Piedmontese former Jesuit, Giovanni Botero, the first person to write a book

---

[9] I discuss these arguments at length in a forthcoming book, *Lords of all the world: ideologies of empire in Spain, Britain and France 1530–1830* (New Haven and London, 1995), chapter 2.

[10] *Restauración política de España* (Madrid, 1619), pp. 1r–v. Moncada, however, did not share this view.

with the title *On the reason of state (Della ragion di stato)*.[11] This was first published in 1589 and proved to be enormously influential in Spain, where it was translated into Spanish by the historiographer-royal, Antonio de Herrera in 1603.[12] (Herrera's great *Historia general de los hechos de los Castellanos en las Islas i Tierra Firme del Mar Oceano* may itself have been an attempt to meet Botero's objection that although its achievements 'far surpass those of the Greeks and the Macedonians', Spain, alone of all the great imperial powers had 'never had these deeds recorded by men worthy of the theme'.)[13]

Botero set out explicitly to construct a theory of politics which would 'correct' the insights of the impious Machiavelli and the pagan Tacitus against the 'truths' of Christianity.[14] His wider project, furthermore, was, as Richard Tuck has described it, an attempt to locate 'the principles of *ragion di stato* not in the parochial politics of Italy but in the Catholic imperialism of the Habsburgs'.[15] Botero had little doubt that 'the human race would live more happily' under a universal – or at least pan-European – political order, of the kind which the empire had been under Charles V.[16] The 'majesty' and immensity of such a world order would, he thought, approach the divine. He also recognized, however, that such orders if not impossible to create, were, as the Spanish case had shown, virtually impossible to sustain. Their continuing success depended upon cooperation and trust, but no actual extended state had ever been able to engage the interests of all its members equally. In terms of feasibility, a system of mutual antagonism, a balance of powers (*l'arte de contrapesare*), might be the only solution to Europe's current ills, above all the threat of encroaching Calvinism and of Turkish invasion. 'We', he concluded sadly, 'are moved more effectively through fear of evil, then desire for the good.'[17]

'Reason of state' – the need to assess in this way the likely behaviour of agents according to assumptions about the nature of their interests – was, as Botero said, principally concerned 'most nearly with preservation and more

---

[11] The best bio-bibliography of Botero is the entry by Luigi Firpo in *Dizionario biografico degli italiani*, XIII (Rome, 1971), pp. 352–62.

[12] In Sancho de Monacada's project for a 'nueva y importante universidad en la corte de España' which would teach the science of politics to Spaniards, the two main set texts were to have been Botero and Thomas More's *Utopia*. *Restauración política*, pp. 11–12.

[13] Giovanni Botero, *The reason of state*, trans. and ed. P. J. and D. P. Waley (London, 1956), p. 190.

[14] Ibid., p. xiii.

[15] Richard Tuck, *Philosophy and government 1572–1651* (Cambridge, 1993), p. 66.

[16] *Relatione della republica venetiana* (Venice, 1605), pp. 9r–10v.

[17] 'Discorso dell'eccelenza della monarchia', in *I Capitani del signor Giovanni Botero benese* (Turin, 1607), p. 237.

nearly with the extension' of empires.[18] And of all the European empires none presented the dual problem of how to balance the former against the claims of the latter in such acute form as the Spanish. For the Spanish monarchy was, he pointed out, 'not only wide but also vast' not only extended, but also divided, and divided 'not simply by rivers and inlets from the sea, but by the Ocean itself . . . with so great a variety of peoples, differing from one another in languages and customs in religion and in every other quality'.[19]

The preservation of a domain of this kind required of the ruler a constant adjustment between internal and external causes, since with the acquisition of each new territory, the shape of the whole polity necessarily changed. Preservation, as Botero warned, once again echoing Antiochus' ambassador, is more difficult than conquest. 'He who conquers and enlarges his dominions', he wrote, 'has only to labour against the external causes of ruin; but he who strives to maintain what he already holds has to contend with both external and internal causes. Territory is acquired a little at a time, but it must be preserved together as a whole.'[20]

The difficulty, however, was that as each new territory entered the empire, the empire as a whole was compelled to change both its political structure and, in some never very clearly specified sense, its image of what kind of society it was. In this way the loss or decline of any single part would inevitably result in the transformation and possible decline of the whole. Spain, said Botero, had, only next door, the dismal example of Portugal whose own empire had been brought down through the decay which resulted from luxury which had been introduced into the metropolis by 'the soft ways of the Indies'.[21]

By the end of the sixteenth century, the distinction between expansion and preservation – and Botero's formulation of it – had become the key terms in what now seemed the inevitable progress of all 'extended empires'. The difficulty, however, was that in the typology of sixteenth-century political thinking, 'preservation' belonged to the domain of 'prudence', expansion to that of 'valour'. As Benjamin Constant, looking back much later over the ruins of the Napoleonic empire, was to point out, these, in fact, corresponded not to two competing 'virtues' but to two distinct phases in the development of societies.[22] Most sixteenth- and seventeenth-century

---

[18] *The reason of state*, p. 3.   [19] 'Discorso dell'eccelenza della monarchia', p. 236.

[20] *The reason of state*, pp. 5–6.

[21] Ibid., p. 70.

[22] 'The spirit of conquest and usurpation and their relation to European civilization', in *Political writings*, ed. Biancamaria Fontana (Cambridge, 1988), pp. 52–3. Constant's distinction is between the ages of war and those of commerce.

theorists were, of course, highly sensitive to the kind of historical causality to which Constant was referring and, much as many of them distrusted Machiavelli, to the force of sheer contingency in all human affairs. Even so fierce a providentialist as Campanella allowed considerable scope in the affairs of men to the operations of *fortuna*. Their overwhelming concern with a supposedly unchanging human psychology meant, however, that they were unable to provide any compelling theoretical account of how an empire which had begun as one kind of project could transform itself into another.

It is not simply that the acquisition of empire demanded, in the first instance at least, only force, whereas preservation required acts of legislation, cultural cohesion and the establishment of binding relationships between the various parts of which the empire was composed. It is also the case, noted Baltasar Alamos de Barrientos in his 1594 commentary on Tacitus, that since all political communities exist in time and possess the attributes of other natural organisms, they are all committed by their very nature to exponential growth 'from the natural greed of men to increase their own grows as the greatness of the empire grows'.[23] Spatial and temporal immobility is no more an option for states than it is for single individuals. As Botero himself had recognized, although he did not attempt a solution to the problem, halting the process of expansion could not be a simple act of will. It would require a reconceptualization of the structure of the whole far greater than that required each time a new territory had to be incorporated into it. Most rulers were simply not wise enough for this task, which is why, Lycurgus, the wisest of them had tried to arrest the whole process at the start.[24]

Since the Spanish monarchy had been created, and continued to be sustained, by the 'spirit of conquest', any attempt to transform its nature without some re-ordering of the political culture which sustained it could only result, not in the preservation of what already existed, but instead in the loss of everything. This was, indeed, as the diplomat Diego Saavedra Fajardo recognized in 1639, 'the danger of monarchies ... that in seeking repose, they become unsettled. Wishing to cease, they fall. In ceasing to work, they become ill.'[25]

As the Spanish royal secretary Pedro Fernández Navarrete, observed in 1621, when an empire appeared to be successful men were inclined to

[23] *Aforismos al Tácito español*, ed. J. A. Fernández-Santamaría (Madrid, 1987), p. 129.
[24] Botero, *The reason of state*, p. 6.
[25] *Empresas políticas. Idea de un príncipe político-crisitiano*, ed. Q. Aldea Vaquero (Madrid, 1976), p. 604.

believe that the wealth and reputation gained by conquest were in themselves sufficient for their own preservation. This, however, was clearly false. But even those who could see that conquest and preservation were two distinct kinds of political goods, and that of the two preservation was the more worthy ('because it is part of prudence and wisdom, virtues superior to force'), were generally compelled to concede that it was force or 'valour' which 'more readily wins the common approval'. In the Spanish case, for instance, it would have been wise for the king not merely to cease all further expansion, but even to abandon some of those territories he already had – a clear reference to the Netherlands. 'Were it not', Fernández Navarrete concluded, 'that reputation obliges her [Spain] to preserve them.' The ruin of monarchies, he knew only too well, 'usually has its origin in their own greatness'.[26] No empire, with the sole (and unrepresentative) exception of China, had ever succeeded in redirecting its energies from expansion into preservation.[27]

'Preservation', furthermore, required not only different political virtues from the ones which had been responsible for the creation of the empire – prudence rather than valour, wisdom instead of force – it also required different kinds of rulers, and different concepts of the nature of the states over which they ruled. It was clearly the case, however, that few of those who had given their support to their rulers precisely because they possessed the qualities needed to create great and extensive empires, were likely to transfer that allegiance willingly to those who knew when to stop and how to preserve. The Romans, observed Botero, had called Fabius Maximus the shield of the Republic, and Marcellus the sword, and wisely they had 'rated Fabius above Marcellus'. Yet in practice this honour had been purely formal for, he concluded, it was a melancholy truth that people always give greater honour to conquerors, just as they 'prefer a tumbling torrent to a calm river'.[28] In this respect, said Saavedra Fajardo, all empires were like 'living beings or vegetables'; the larger they grew the closer they came to their end.[29]

The tragedy of all empires was that not only did their rulers not know when to stop: in a very real sense, they *could* not stop. As Charles III's reforming minister of finance, Pedro Rodríguez Campomanes, explained in 1775, the 'spirit of conquest', which provides the 'principle' – to use

[26] *Discursos políticos* (Barcelona, 1621), pp. 60–5.
[27] Botero, *The reason of state*, pp. 6–7. On Botero's conception of *prudenza* see Gianfranco Borelli, *Ragion di stato e leviatano. Conservazione e scambio alle origini della modernita politica* (Bologna, 1993), pp. 63–94.
[28] *The reason of state*, pp. 6–7.   [29] *Empresas políticas*, p. 598 and cf. p. 822.

Montesquieu's term – for all empires, necessarily blinds men to the very fact that every state has limits imposed upon its territorial expansion by nature. 'The unbridled desire to expand', he wrote of Spain, 'obscured the imagination, so that no-one could see that this expansion was the true cause of [its] ceaseless debilitation.'[30]

For all these theorists the problem of the evolution of empires presented, in its most intractable form, the perennial question of how to sustain certain kinds of cultural values over time. Martial valour, they knew, once it ceased to have anything to act upon either turned against the society which had nurtured it, or declined into idleness, vanity and display. Aristotle had taught them that radical cultural change of the kind which the transition from 'expansion' to 'preservation' demanded, the effective transformation of an entire people's ethos, could only be achieved from outside. But to stand outside oneself was rarely if ever possible. The age of the great law-givers, who had been great precisely because they possessed this quality, had long since passed. The most that the modern monarchies of Europe could hope for would be to deflect the energies of their would-be conquerors into other, analogous, but less destructive activities. And these, too, were likely to prove a temporary diversion or the pastimes of men who had grown finally weary of battle. Even Saavedra Fajardo, who was more sanguine than most about the possibility for the endurance of the martial spirit, could, in the end, offer only the somewhat improbable suggestion that the war-like properties which had created the Spanish empire might now be deflected from conquest into building and science. Augustus, he claimed had prevented 'his fiery spirt' from becoming 'covered in ashes', by re-ordering the calendar and calculating the movements of the planets. With the same objectives in mind, Philip II, had 'raised up that great work, the Escorial, in which he succeeded in overcoming the wonders of Nature with art, and of demonstrating to the world the greatness of his mind and his piety'.[31] But, as Saavedra Fajardo knew full well, neither of these men had been able to prevent the further expansion of their states, or their ultimate decline. The Spanish monarchy, it seemed, was destined to follow the course of all previous empires. The famous *declinación* of the monarchy, which had been evident since at least the early seventeenth century, was not merely an economic catastrophe no one seemed able to remedy, nor even the consequence of a historical vision which assumed too great a similarity

---

[30] *Discurso sobre la educación popular de los artisanos y su fomento* (Madrid, 1775), p. 411.
[31] *Empresas políticas*, pp. 604–5.

between living organism and states.[32] It was an inescapable part of the psychology of imperialism itself.

III

By the early eighteenth century, however, this psychology had changed. With the conclusion of the War of the Spanish Succession in 1714 the monarchy had been stripped of all its remaining dominions in Europe, and with them had gone many of the ideological underpinnings which had sustained its former aspirations to universalism. Spain and its overseas empire now looked very much more like Britain and France and their overseas empires: no longer a single community bound by a common law, but a metropolis and a number of distant, and increasingly independent, colonies. As Montesquieu observed as early as the 1730s 'The Indies and Spain are two powers under the same master, but the Indies is the principal one, and Spain is only an accessory. It is useless for politics to attempt to reduce the principal to the accessory, for the Indies will always draw Spain to themselves' (*les Indes attirent toujours l'Espagne à elles*).[33]

By the time Montesquieu wrote these words, however, the obvious need to reform the monarchy had become far more than the quest for an economically productive and politically compliant association of dominions – the attempt to 'reduce the principal to the accessory'. It had become, as Franco Venturi has rightly observed, a 'quest for a more general need, an insistent search appearing under different forms, for the mission of Spanish life of the past and the future ... The crisis of reform was developing into a crisis of identity.'[34]

And a change of identity was precisely what the 'enlightened' Spaniards who came to power under Charles III and Charles IV hoped to bring about. Like most of its European critics, these men – Campomanes, Jovellanos, José del Campillo y Cosio, Bernardo Ward, the counts of Floridablanca and Aranda – believed that Spain was trapped by an archaic mental condition, what had for long been captured by the phrase 'the spirit of conquest'.

In the sixteenth century, argued José del Campillo y Cosio in one of the most influential projects for reform, the *Nuevo sistema de gobierno económico*

---

[32] On this see the now classic article by John Elliott, 'Self-perception and decline in early-seventeenth-century Spain', in *Spain and its world 1500–1700*, pp. 241–61.

[33] *De l'esprit des lois*, XXI, 22. *Oeuvres complètes*, ed. Roger Caillois (Paris, 1949–51), II, p. 648.

[34] *The end of the Old Regime in Europe, 1776–1798*, trans. R. Burr Litchfield (trans. of parts 1 and 2 of volume IV of *Settecento riformatore*) (Princeton, 1991), I, p. 237.

para la América of 1743,[35] conquest had been both legitimate and, to a certain degree, profitable for the crown. It had been in keeping both with the martial spirit of the times and with the immediate need to subjugate large numbers of Indians. But those times had passed very rapidly, and the following century which should have been a Golden Age had been instead a 'century of disgrace and loss', as the Spaniards, rather than consolidating their hold over what they had already gained, and diversifying the colonial economy, had simply gone on conquering.[36] The *conquistadores* and their heirs, concerned as they were to perpetuate an archaic society based upon martial valour, had failed to grasp that wealth depends upon a political order directed towards development not rapine. Look, said Campillo, at the Great Khan: with less able ministers than the king of Spain and less territory, he none the less has a greater income and, Campillo added darkly, 'neither are his vassals so oppressed'. The Americas had been laid waste by their European conquerors. What 'in the hands of the natives' – and Campillo was not inclined to be sentimental about them – 'and in the midst of their barbarity' had been, 'a discreet and political nation' was now, 'so many uncultivated, uninhabited, and almost entirely annihilated provinces, which could be the richest in the world'.[37]

Campillo hoped that now, and by the application of his *Nuevo sistema*, it might be possible to change the ideals and assumptions which had in this way framed the early empire. At no previous moment in its history had Spain been so well placed to transform the whole balance of its empire, to exchange 'expansion' for 'preservation', without collapsing as all previous commentators had believed she must in 'luxury' and 'decadence'. Campillo and Campomanes, Jovellanos and Ward, the servants of a Bourbon king, were free to ascribe Spain's ills to a dynasty which had now come to be seen as foreign – 'Austrian' – and which, ever since the *comunero* revolt had systematically destroyed Castile's constitutional traditions. What Campomanes described bitterly as 'the two brilliant reigns of Charles V and Philip II' had, he believed, destroyed Castile.[38] The principles by which the Habsburg monarchs had ruled had been transformed into an ideology

---

[35] The full text was only printed in 1798. But it circulated widely in court circles before that date, and a modified version appeared as Part II of Bernardo Ward's *Proyecto económico* in 1779. For an account of the relationship between the two texts see the introduction by Antonio Elorza to his edition of Campillo's *Lo que hay de mas y menos en España para que sea lo que debe ser y no lo que es* (Madrid, 1696), pp. 11–16.

[36] *Nuevo sistema de gobierno económico para la América* (Madrid, 1789), pp. 6–7.

[37] Ibid., p. 3.

[38] *Cartas político-económicas* (to the count of Lerena), ed. Antonio Rodríguez Villa (Madrid, 1878), p. 15.

which, he observed sarcastically, was 'all that one could desire from the lordship of the Ottoman constitution'. The 'tyrannical maxims of the Empire' which had sustained this ideology had in turn been 'adopted as principles of the civil law, which for so many centuries have ruled in our universities, and which have therefore triumphed in [royal] councils composed of men of mediocre birth, mediocre wealth and mediocre understanding'.[39]

Successive and progressively weaker Habsburgs had in this manner transformed a powerful tyranny into a crumbling edifice which could not be reformed as it stood. 'I compare our monarchy in its present state', Campomanes wrote to the count of Lerena in 1790, 'to an ancient house sustained by the force of remedies in such a way that the same materials which are used to shore up one side, pull down another, and it can only be improved by tearing it all down and building it again.'[40]

The means by which it was to be built again was free trade. For Campomanes, however, *comercio libre* became not merely an economic doctrine, a means to palliate the worst effects of the mercantilist policies of the previous reigns. It became too, a means to reform the entire structure of the society. For 'free trade' implied the political liberty which the more enlightened British and French political economists had long urged upon their respective monarchs. 'To extend to a people the liberty which prudence demands', he told Lerena, 'is the soul of commerce and of the happiness of the nation'.[41] Commerce would, in this way, be responsible for the creation of what Bernardo Ward described as 'a new being' (*nuevo ser*) for the entire Spanish empire.[42]

Campomanes, however, also recognized that the kind of reforms which would be necessary to remake the Spanish empire in the image of the British or the French ones would, as he put it, 'be morally – by which he meant culturally – impossible'. Because the Spanish *imperium* had been grounded upon the image of a single, culturally varied political order, ruled according to a codified body of laws and founded upon a unified set of religious beliefs, it had always been a closed society. Free trade meant creating a polity which was potentially open to foreign political influence, and that also meant exposing the colonies, and through the colonies metropolitan Spain itself, to the potential influence of heresy. The Spanish empire under Charles III

---

[39] Ibid., pp. 66–7.   [40] Ibid., p. 21.   [41] Ibid., p. 21.

[42] *Proyecto económico en que se proponen varias providencias, dirigidas a promover los intereses de España, con los medios y modos para su plantificación* [1762] (Madrid, 1799), p. 253. Campillo y Cosio's version of this phrase is 'dar un nuevo esfera a la América' (*Nuevo sistema de gobierno económico para la América*, p. 70).

and Charles IV was in many significant respects a very different society from the one it had been in the reigns of Charles V and Philip II. But even the relatively enlightened Charles III could not entirely abandon the belief that Spain's greatness, Spain's very survival, depended upon maintaining its political and cultural integrity.

Free trade also implied another, more immediately tangible kind of threat. The most widely accepted account of the decline of the Spanish economy in the late sixteenth century had been based upon the altogether plausible assumption that an over-dependence upon bullion had led to a decline in manufacturing industries, and consequentially to an over-dependence upon foreign industry, foreign supplies and, because of spiralling inflation, foreign bankers. This was an economy which, if never quite so dismal as the portrait Jovellanos, Campomanes and others were later to paint of it, was nevertheless very largely dependent upon staples, exporting agricultural produce and vast quantities of bullion, in exchange for foreign manufactured goods. Furthermore, unlike some other staple dependent economies it produced few, if any, of what Albert Hirschman has called backward and forward linkages.[43] Throughout much of the sixteenth and seventeenth centuries, even the sacks in which merino wool, one of the mainstays of the Castilian economy, was exported were themselves imported. By the early eighteenth century, only the policy of restricted trading regulations and tight import controls, which goes under the name of mercantilism, seemed to provide the theoretical possibility of a check on the ceaseless haemorrhage of national resources. To some extent these policies also worked. Public revenue, which had stood at a mere 5 million pesos in 1700, had already risen to 18 million pesos by the 1750s, and continued to rise throughout the 1760s and 1770s. To have abandoned this in favour of the *laissez-faire* economic principles which modern, and predominantly French, economic theory demanded seemed to most Spaniards, attracted though they were by the intellectual brilliance of the new economics, merely to be returning to the deregulation and the chaos of the reign of Charles V.

In 1762, Campomanes offered his own solution to both these problems in a treatise entitled, *Reflexiones sobre el comercio español a Indias*. This was principally a reply to the observation on the Spanish empire in Sir Josiah Child's *A new discourse on trade* of 1665 and Montesquieu's remarks in Book 21 of *De l'esprit des lois*, these two texts being, in Campomanes' view, the most perceptive ever written on the state of Spanish America.[44]

---

[43] *A bias for hope: essays on development and Latin America* (New Haven, 1971).

[44] 'Juzgo, que de todos los estrangeros, después de Josías Child, es él [Montesquieu] que con mayor attención ha observado la constitución de nuestras colonias en América y la calidad

Child had argued for the removal of all the restrictions currently imposed upon the colonies. This, he believed would not only put an end to the crippling contraband trade, it would also make the colonies themselves more productive as they sought to produce a wider range of goods for hugely increased markets. Above all it would encourage the colonists to turn away from the simple production of bullion to agriculture which, for Child, as for most contemporary political economists, constituted the true source of wealth in all colonial societies. From this process both the colonies and the metropolis would necessarily benefit.

In responding to these claims Campomanes was driven to redescribe the old distinction between the 'kingdoms of the Indies', and the various dominions within Europe itself. He was one of the first to speak consistently of the American 'colonies', and to treat them, not as a distinct although dependent part of Castile, but as communities comparable with the colonies which France and Britain had established in North America, communities which had been created by, and existed very largely in the commercial interests of, the mother country. The mistake of the Castilian crown, he believed, had not been, as both Child and Montesquieu had insisted, to place extensive trade restrictions on the American colonists, but rather to limit access to the American trade to Castilians. The Spanish Empire constituted in effect a vast internal market, so vast that it could operate its own global economy. Yet in 1596, Philip II had denied the Portuguese any share in the American trade, and in 1634, Philip IV had prevented them for trading in the Philippines.[45] The same limitations had been applied to Flemings, Italians and in some cases Aragonese. Similar attempts had been made to ban trade between the colonies, in particular the lucrative exchange of luxury commodities and bullion between Mexico, Peru and the Philippines. As everyone knew, the effect of this legislation had been to drive the trade into the hands of the *contrabandistas*. Campomanes' project would have opened up the American markets not to 'foreigners', but to all the subjects of the Castilian crown irrespective of their origins and, crucially, it would have deregulated the trade between them. From such beginnings Campomanes believed, the ethos of the commercial society would come slowly to replace the older order of domination. And with the establishment of free trade between all its various far-flung regions, he was confident that 'Spain would change its nature [*ser*] without need for the complicated

del comercio que hacemos en ellas', *Reflexiones sobre el comercio español a Indias* [1762], ed. Vicente Llombart Roas (Madrid, 1988), p. 359.
[45] *Reflexiones sobre el comercio español a Indias*, p. 62.

operations proposed by [Jerónimo] Uztariz, [Bernardo] Ward and [Nicolas] Arriquivar'.[46]

Campomanes' project was only ever implemented in part. The *comercio libre* decree of 1778, which abolished the fleet system and deprived the port of Cadiz of the monopoly it had exercised over all colonial trade, did, however, produce a brief upsurge in American commerce until the British naval blockade of 1796.[47] The more general economic and social reforms which took place under the ministries of Jovellanos, Campomanes, Florida-blanca and Aranda effectively transformed the entire political and cultural image of the monarchy. By the 1780s the 'kingdoms of the Indies' had been replaced by 'the Ultramarine provinces'. Gone, too, was any notion of a trans-Atlantic community, of a *ius commune* embodied in the legal person of the king. Indeed, the king's advisers edged their ruler as close as they dared to the image of a constitutional monarch, of the ruler as magistrate not a judge, of one bound by the laws he himself had ratified.

The final transformation of the Spanish monarchy would have been one in which an 'empire' became a federation of allied states. This would have been based not upon the now archaic concepts of *imperium* and *dominium* which had dominated all previous debates over the legitimacy of the empire in America, and of the legal relationship between the metropolis and the colonies. It would, instead, have been founded upon voluntary allegiance. The Spanish crown, wrote Turgot, in a characteristically perceptive *mémoire*, written in April 1776, if it was to avoid the difficulties which the English were now experiencing in their America colonies, had to cultivate the 'principles of fraternal liaisons based upon an identity of origins, of language, of customs, without conflict of interests'; and, in the interests of all its subjects, it had to learn 'how to offer liberty as a gift, instead of allowing it to be dragged by force from an empire that can no longer be sustained'. 'Wise and happy', he wrote, 'would be the nation which, the first to bend its politics to new circumstances, would consent to see its colonies as allied provinces, and not as subjects to the metropolis'.[48] With this end in mind, the count of Aranda, an acquaintance of Voltaire and Raynal, and president of the council of Castile, prepared a memorandum on the possible dismemberment of the American colonial system. 'Your Majesty', he wrote

---

[46] *Cartas político-económicas*, p. 23.
[47] See David Brading, 'Bourbon Spain and its American empire', in the *Cambridge History of Latin America*, ed. Leslie Bethell (Cambridge, 1984), I, pp. 409–24.
[48] *Mémoire sur les colonies américaines, sur leurs relations politiques avec leurs métropoles, et sur la manière dont la France et l'Espagne ont du envisager les suites de l'indépendance des Etats-Unis de l'Amérique* [6 April, 1776] (Paris, 1791), pp. 32–3.

to Charles III, 'should dispossess himself of all his dominions in both Americas', preserving only the islands of Cuba and Puerto Rico, as a basis for Spanish trade. All the rest, Aranda suggested, should be transformed into three independent kingdoms (corresponding to the three viceroyalties) ruled in loose federation, not under a Spanish monarch but, as the title had been conceived during the days of Charles V, a Spanish emperor.[49] Such a federation would, Aranda believed, yield more to the Spanish treasury in trade, than the colonies now did in taxation. Emigration from Spain – still believed to be a drain on the human resources of the metropolis – would cease and, once united, the three kingdoms would be far more capable, and politically more inclined, to resist the kind of external threat which Aranda, like most Spaniards, believed, not without reason, the new United States posed to the independence of the southern colonies.[50]

Nothing, of course, came of this. Charles III and Charles IV could imagine themselves as the rulers of a modern commercial empire. They could accommodate themselves to the idea, actively pursued by Charles III, of a new universal society in which *criollos* and Castilians might have equal rights to public office in both the metropolis and the colonies.[51] They could even accept, as the British had, a high degree of local legal autonomy for the colonies. What they could not contemplate, however, any more than could George III, was the kind of trading federation which Aranda, Turgot, Adam Smith and Richard Price had seen as the only possible future for the older European overseas empires.[52]

Neither, in the end, could the *criollo* population of the Americas. All the reforming projects of the Spanish Enlightenment had worked on the assumption that it would be in the long-term interests of both the Castilian crown and the colonists to remain united. True, the kind of union which Campillo, Campomanes and their successors had envisaged had been based

---

[49] 'Exposición del conde de Aranda al rey Carlos III sobre la conveniencia de crear reinos independientes en América', Andrés Muriel, *Gobierno del señor rey Carlos III* [1838], ed. Carlos Seco Serrano, Biblioteca de autores españoles, 115 (Madrid, 1959), pp. 399–401. The undated text was probably written in 1783.

[50] On the fears of both Aranda and Floridablanca, which were widely shared at the time, see Juan Hernández Franco, *La gestión política y el pensamiento reformista del conde de Floridablanca* (Murcia, 1984), pp. 329–50.

[51] Price, who corresponded extensively with Turgot on the subject, also believed that some kind of federation was the only possible relationship between the European monarchies and their overseas possessions. See, 'Observations on the nature of civil liberty, the principles of government and the justice and policy of the war with America', in D. O. Thomas, ed., *Richard Price: political writings* (Cambridge, 1991), pp. 34–5.

[52] On Charles III's system of union and equality see Richard Konetzke, 'La condición legal de los criollos y las causas de la independencia', *Estudios americanos* 11 (1950), pp. 31–54.

upon reciprocity. It came close to what had been, in Campomanes' political imagination, the kind of ancient constitutional arrangements which had existed in Spain, before the (largely fictional) common law rights of Castilians had been usurped by their imported Habsburg rulers. But it never allowed for the possibility of a fully independent Spanish America. The colonists might be permitted to enjoy free and equal rights with the inhabitants of Castile, but the colonies continued to exist entirely for the benefit of the metropolis. The settler populations themselves, however, as they gradually developed their own sense of identity, came increasingly to believe that political autonomy was the only form under which their ambitions could be realized. For all the striking intelligence, and the breadth of vision, of men like Campillo and Campomanes, the reformers never fully grasped that by the late eighteenth century 'preservation', no matter what shape it might ultimately take, could no longer be a shared objective for all the peoples of the Spanish monarchy. With the apparent exception of Aranda, they had not seen, as Turgot and Smith had seen, that the only possible form of 'preservation' now open to them, was dissolution.[53]

---

[53] Great Britain, wrote Smith, should 'voluntarily give up all authority over her colonies', in that way, 'turbulent and factious subjects' would be transformed into 'our most faithful, affectionate and generous allies; and the same sort of parental affection on the one side, and filial respect on the other, might revive between Great Britain and her colonies, which used to subsist between those of ancient Greece and the mother city from which they descended'. He recognized, however, as Turgot had done, that 'The most visionary enthusiast would scarce be capable of proposing such a measure, with any serious hope of its being adopted.' Adam Smith, *An inquiry into the nature and causes of the wealth of nations*, eds. R. H. Cambell and A. S. Skinner, textual editor W. B. Todd, (Oxford, 1976), II, p. 61

14

Why were Spain's special overseas laws never enacted?

JOSEP M. FRADERA

> But, Mr Figaro, today I find that in Havana they have not only not
> sworn allegiance to the Constitution, but that they are not supposed to
> swear allegiance to it; that the Government, which I respect so much,
> has ordered the people not to swear allegiance to it, and that those
> inhabitants of the island of Cuba who have sworn allegiance to it are
> rebels; that it seems as if the Constitution is not an overseas matter,
> much less an absolute good, but rather a relative one. In a word, it is
> like a hat which sits well only on the head for which it was made, and
> therefore in the Peninsula alone can it fit.
>
> Mariano José de Larra, *Figaro a los redactores de El Mundo*, 1836.

The Spanish Constitution promulgated on 8 June 1837 included two
additional articles of special importance. The first referred to the jury
system in the Spanish judicial process, something which still does not exist;
the second clearly stated that 'the overseas provinces will be governed by
special laws', but offered no further particulars. Eight years later, a new
constitutional text, written and passed by the moderate Liberals, suppressed the first of the additional articles of the previous constitution but
said nothing about the other, concerning how Spain's overseas provinces
should be governed. The commitment to endow Cuba, Puerto Rico and the
Philippines – the last remnants of Spain's overseas empire – with special
laws therefore persisted.

In 1869, less than one year after the Liberal parties formed a new provisional government, a fresh constitution was promulgated. This document declared that 'the constituent *Cortes* [parliament] will reform the present system of government in the Overseas Provinces after the delegates from Cuba and Puerto Rico have taken possession of their seats, in order to extend to the said Provinces, with any modification that may be deemed necessary, the rights assigned in the Constitution'. It indicated more fully in the next paragraph that 'the regime governing the Spanish provinces situated in the Philippine Archipelago will be reformed by a law'. Then in 1876, after the democratic experience of the First Spanish Republic of 1868–74, yet another constitution declared in its thirteenth chapter that 'the overseas provinces will be governed by special laws; however, the government is authorized to apply to the said provinces, with any modifications it deems suitable and duly informing the parliament, the laws enacted or to be enacted for the Peninsula. Cuba and Puerto Rico will be represented in the Cortes in a manner to be determined by a special law, which could differ for each of the two provinces.'[1]

Thus, between 1837 and 1876, different governments kept postponing the enactment of the oft-promised 'special overseas laws'. Though in fact never passed, this special legislation hovered like a spectre over all discussions of the political regime of the colonies. The purpose of this essay is to analyse the reasons which led to the formulation of the promise of special laws for Cuba, Puerto Rico and the Philippines, as well as to indicate the factors which prevented their enactment in the decades that followed.

Understanding the motives underlying Spanish policy toward the political regime in the colonies requires a digression which begins with the break up of the empire at the beginning of the nineteenth century. During the imperial period, the specificity of American legislation was well established: from its origins at the start of the sixteenth century, a complex institutional system, itself an adaptation of older Castilian juridical and political traditions, governed Spain's American empire. The monarchy administered the colonies through a network of viceroys, military officers, and judicial personnel; and the laws and ordinances which applied to the Americas were codified in the so-called *Leyes de Indias*. For almost three

Translation by James L. McCullough, who is also responsible for the translation of quotations unless otherwise attributed.

This essay is a progress report on the research project entitled *El imperio insular. Política colonial y cambio económico y social en las Antillas españolas y Filipinas (1759–1868)*, financed by the DGICYT, Ministry of Education and Science, Spain.

[1] Texts of the constitutions are cited from the compilation by S. Cánovas Cervantes, *Pugna entre dos poderes*, Barcelona, n.d.

hundred years, this system remained intact; the separate, and dependent, status of the colonies was left untouched.[2]

This situation changed dramatically with the wars of independence in the second decade of the nineteenth century. The decisive factor was the affirmation of Liberal principles of government on both sides of the Atlantic during the Napoleonic invasion of Spain (1808–14), accompanied not only by a crisis in the structure of the state, the absolute monarchy, but also by a crisis concerning the relationship between centre and periphery, namely in the institutional and legal arrangements that had kept the Spanish empire intact for over three centuries.

During the Napoleonic years, the monarchy's subjects on both sides of the Atlantic realized that the old system of relations between the metropolis and its colonies had run its course.[3] These sentiments found early expression in the *Manifiesto a los españoles americanos* of 10 May 1809, issued by the regency government established while King Ferdinand VII was detained in France by Napoleon. The manifesto declared that in future the American subjects of the Spanish monarch were to enjoy not only good government but also strict equality with metropolitan Spaniards. Nor was this recognition of the equal rights of Spaniards and Americans mere rhetoric: it represented a sincere effort on the part of the regency to come to grips with the secessionist sentiments of various parts of the empire, notably Argentina and Venezuela. It also constituted the first formal recognition that the overseas possessions could no longer be ruled through the existing *Leyes de Indias*.[4]

In spite of the good intentions exhibited in this document, however, the royal order of 29 January 1810 which convoked the constituent Cortes of Cadiz only allowed the American colonies to send twenty-six delegates as compared to more than two hundred from the peninsula. Furthermore, given the length of time required for these American delegates to arrive in Cadiz, the colonies had to be represented by proxies appointed by the Americans already resident in Spain. Nevertheless, in Cadiz, in theory at

---

[2] A general overview of this question, with a focus differing from that of this essay, can be found in François Xavier-Guerra, 'The Spanish-American tradition of representation and its European roots', *Journal of Latin American Studies*, 26 (1994), 1–35.

[3] On the Americans' participation in the Cortes of Cadiz see Marie Laure Rieu-Millan, *Los diputados americanos en las Cortes de Cádiz* (Madrid, 1990); and Maria Teresa Berruezo, *Los diputados americanos en las Cortes de Cádiz* (Madrid, 1986).

[4] Manuel Morán Orti, 'La formación de las Cortes (1808–1810)', in *Las Cortes de Cádiz, Ayer*, ed. Miguel Artola (Madrid, 1991), I p. 34. On the legislative aspects of the elections during the Cortes, see Pilar Chavarri Sidera, *Las elecciones de diputados a las Cortes generales y extraordinarias* (Madrid, 1988).

least, the Americas possessed equal rights to Spain. It was, moreover, assumed that this equality could 'without obstacles be increased for future [Cortes]'. A royal decree of 15 April 1810 further guaranteed equal rights between Spaniards and 'American Spaniards' and also declared that 'the Spanish dominions in both hemispheres form a single, united Monarchy, a single, united Nation, and a single family, and that as a result those who are native to the aforementioned overseas dominions are equal in rights to those of the Peninsula'.

The invocation of equal rights was underscored a year later through an initiative that would have enormous consequences for the future: a decree issued by the Cortes on 19 March 1811 established, among other things, equal proportional representation for peninsular inhabitants and Americans in the Cortes itself. The presence of these American delegates embodied the concept of a single nation as opposed to a nation and its colonies. The decree was in this sense designed to appeal to Americans at a moment when demands for independence could readily be heard overseas.[5] According to this decree, moreover, the nation became the only source of political rights, and these rights were guaranteed to all 'American Spaniards' regardless of racial or ethnic origin. The goal of equal rights also led the delegates gathered at Cadiz to abolish those institutions which derived from the right of conquest, along with the servitude it implied.[6] Thus on 7 January 1812 the Cortes issued a decree abolishing Indian taxes and Andean conscription. Although this decree would never be implemented, its good intentions were clear: '... the positive acts of inferiority peculiar to the peoples overseas, monuments of the old system of conquest and colonies, should disappear before the majestic idea of perfect equality, of reciprocal love and of the union of interests with those of the Peninsula, which has been so solemnly proclaimed by the Cortes.'[7]

---

[5] In a speech to the Cortes on 17 December 1811, Agustin Argüelles declared, 'With respect to the other point of the American colonies remaining governed according to the colonial system, I only appeal to the justification of the Congress. A Constitution which grants equal rights to all free Spaniards, which establishes a national representation which has to meet every year to sanction laws, levy taxes and raise troops, which requires a Council of State composed of Europeans and Americans, and which establishes the administration of justice in such a way that under no pretext do the latter have come to the Peninsula in order to litigate – is a Constitution which rests on these bases compatible with a colonial regime?' On Argüelles's attitudes toward America, see Albert Dérozier, 'Argüelles y la cuestión de América ante las Cortes de Cádiz de 1810–1814', in *Homenaje a Nöel Salomon. Ilustración española e independencia de América*, ed. Alberto Gil Novales (Barcelona, 1979), pp. 159–164.

[6] *Diario de las sesiones del congreso de diputados* (DSCD), Madrid, s.d., 26 October 1811.

[7] Indigenous tribute was abolished in March 1811, an action which immediately raised the question of payments to the parish clergy who depended on it. See DSCD, 12 March and 20

Yet the prospect of the end of vassalage and, even more importantly, the creation of a single unified nation that did away with the unequal relationship between the metropolis and its colonies in the end proved more than the legislators gathered in Cadiz could stomach.[8] At a time when parts of the empire had already seceded, even the most liberal legislators became reluctant to undertake any initiative that might undermine imperial unity further. For this reason, the organization of the new political framework along liberal principles coincided with military and diplomatic attempts to regain control over Buenos Aires and Venezuela.[9] The Cortes' desire to maintain the empire intact translated into a studied ambiguity between two manifestly different political options. On the one hand, the peninsular delegates defended a vision of the kingdom's body politic which studiously ignored the social and territorial ambitions of the American representatives. These ambitions were grounded in part in a theory of 'natural fatherlands', which held that political authority ought to be vested in local or at least regional institutions. The peninsular delegates, however, embraced the more liberal principle of a fatherland based on the concept of national sovereignty, single and indivisible.[10] Equally problematic for the peninsular delegates was the issue of equality itself, especially as it related to the so-called 'coloured castes'.[11] In this respect, the Cortes which gathered to draft the first Spanish constitution attempted to find the language needed to proclaim the principle of a single, unified nation that encompassed both sides of the Atlantic but which at the same time guaranteed metropolitan supremacy in the new state.

June 1811, and 13 December 1812. The abolition of the *mita*, or labour conscription, proposed by the Guatemalan delegate, Castillo, a constant and sincere defender of the Indians, was discussed and passed in the session of 12 August 1812: DSCD, pp. 3530–3. It is interesting to note that the proposal was attacked by Ostolaza, a Peruvian by birth and confessor of Ferdinand VII, who was determined to maintain all types of levies on the indigenous population. One of the topics discussed in the sessions of 21 October 1812, was whether to exempt the Indians from personal services and from forced labor on public works. On this subject, see Mario Rodríguez, *The Cadiz experiment in Central America, 1808 to 1826* (Berkeley, 1978), pp. 80–1 (which places special emphasis on the interventions of the Central American delegates), and Carlos Díaz Rementería, 'Las Cortes de Cádiz y el indio americano. Las normas y su incidencia: el caso andino', *Revista de historia del derecho Ricardo Levene (Buenos Aires)*, 27 (1990), pp. 79–97.

[8] See Michael P. Costeloe, *Response to revolution. Imperial Spain and the Spanish Revolutions, 1810–1840* (Cambridge, 1986).

[9] For these military measures, see Edmundo A. Heredia, *Planes españoles para reconquistar hispanoamérica* (Buenos Aires, 1974).

[10] See J. Varela Suanzes-Carpegna, *La teoría del estado en los orígenes del constitucionalismo hispánico (Las Cortes de Cádiz)* (Madrid, 1983), p. 427. See also the excellent work by Xavier Arbós, *La idea de nació en el primer constitucionalisme espanyol* (Barcelona, 1986).

[11] The most detailed studies of this topic, although not always convincing, are Magnus Mörner, *Race mixture in the history of Latin America* (Boston, 1967), and *Region and state in Latin America's Past* (Baltimore, 1993).

The political distance separating the royal order of 15 April 1810 from the Constitution decreed by the Cortes of 1812 is palpable.[12] The former unequivocally upheld the principle of equality between Spain and the American colonies. In contrast, the language used in the new Constitution was more qualified. Although it stated that 'the Spanish nation is the union of all Spaniards from both hemispheres', a single body from which all sovereignty derived, composed of 'all free-born men residing in the domains of Spain, and the children of these men', other articles of the Constitution cast doubt on the equality of the Americas.[13] Thus article 3, which was devoted to the composition of the Cortes, specified that 'the basis of national representation is the same in both hemispheres'; but this equality of representation was contradicted by the stipulation that, of the forty individuals who were to comprise the new council of state, only twelve would represent America.[14] In addition, the Constitution established sharp restrictions on the political rights of Americans. Article 5 tacitly recognized the legitimacy of slavery and also made it difficult for the 'coloured castes' to become Spanish citizens. Further, it limited the rights of domestic servants by establishing minimum property requirements for political office.[15] It also specifically defined citizens as 'those Spaniards who, through both lines, derive their origin from Spanish dominions in both hemispheres and have their residence in any town'.[16] The Constitution of 1812 thus deprived all people of African ancestry – almost one-third of the Spanish American population – of the basic rights of citizenship.[17]

---

[12] The best work on this question is still James F. King, 'The colored castes and American representation in the Cortes of Cadiz', *Hispanic American Historical Review*, 33 (1953), 33–64., and *Mexico and the Spanish Cortes, 1810–1822*, ed. N. L. Benson (Austin, 1966).

[13] Cánovas Fernández, *Pugna entre los poderes*, p. IV.

[14] On this particular topic, see Francisco Tomás y Valiente, 'Los derechos fundamentales en la historia del constitucionalismo español', *Códigos y constituciones (1808–1978)* (Madrid, 1989), pp. 153–5.

[15] On these exclusions, see Manuel Pérez Ledesma, 'Las Cortes de Cádiz y la sociedad española', *Las Cortes de Cádiz, Ayer*, pp. 167–206.

[16] On this question, see the work of J. F. King cited in note 12. Of lesser interest is Cesáreo Armellada, *La causa indígena en las Cortes de Cádiz* (Madrid, 1959).

[17] No one in Cádiz knew for certain what proportion of the population was white, Indian, or 'coloured', so the delegates consulted Alexander von Humboldt's *Tablas geográficas y políticas del reyno de Nueva España* (1804) and his *Ensayo político sobre el reino de Nueva España* (published in French between the years 1808 and 1811). The only other available source for New World population was the error-ridden census of 1797. In view of its imprecision, the Cortes commissioned Ciriaco González Carvajal, former *oidor* of the Philippine and Mexican *audiencias*, later member of the Council of the Indies, to conduct a new census. See Sylvia Vilar, 'Une vision indigéniste de l'Amérique en 1812. Trente-six questions élaborées par les Cortes de Cádiz', *Mélanges de las Casa de Velázquez*, 7 (1971), 399–404, and her 'Ultimas proyecciones coloniales de la España ilustrada: dos "interrogatorios" de Indias inéditos (1760–1812)', *Hispania* 31 (1971), pp. 617–55.

The contradictions of the Constitution of 1812 were such that it was doomed to failure. On the one hand, it attempted to guarantee equal rights and equal representation for all Spaniards, regardless of whether they lived on the eastern or western shore of the Atlantic. On the other hand, it established restrictions that prevented any effective transfer of power to the American representatives by reducing them to the status of a permanent minority in the Cortes. In light of these contradictions, it is not surprising that some of the delegates who helped draft the constitution seemed to be walking a tightrope, conceding political rights to the Americans while simultaneously ensuring the pre-eminence of the metropolis. Typical in this respect were the gyrations of Alvaro Flórez Estrada, an outspoken Liberal delegate from Asturias. In principle he disliked the inequality inherent in colonial status:

No overseas possessions, not just those of Spain, but also those of other powers, have ever been considered an integral part of the nation to which they belonged. The attitude of every metropolis has been to impose on their possessions a harsh dependency that not only prevents them from prospering but also from acquiring the resources they would need in order to contemplate – let alone succeed in – throwing off their yoke.

Flórez Estrada therefore disapproved of the measures taken by the Cortes to place strict limits on American representation in the future Spanish state. Yet even he could not avoid the anti-American prejudices exhibited by most other peninsular delegates.

America, whose population is estimated at barely fifteen million, has eight million Indians, four million Blacks, and the rest Creoles and Europeans. The Indians and Blacks are in such a state of barbarism that surely they cannot be considered capable of making good use of the right to representation. Without education, without any cultivation of their intellectual faculties, and, even more, without good customs, it is (to say the least) very doubtful whether they should be granted the right to national representation. Such a right would not serve any other purpose than to allow all the benefits to accrue to the Creoles and Europeans, since surely the Blacks and the Indians would not elect their fellows; nor even if they were to elect them, could such people be useful to the nation. Surely those who feign a love for liberty have few reasons to lament the lack of these representatives in order for us to believe their votes to be sincere.[18]

---

[18] A. Flórez Estrada, *Examen imparcial de las disensiones de América con España, de los medios de su reconciliación, y de la prosperidad de todas las naciones* (Madrid, 1950), pp. 12, 31.

Compounding the Spanish delegates' lack of knowledge about the Americas, and the prejudices they displayed towards its coloured castes, was a deep mistrust of the political loyalty of the creole elite, even those representing territories that had remained loyal to the monarchy and to the Cortes.[19] Another crucial point of disagreement between the Spanish and the American delegates was the alleged uniqueness of the political conditions in America: those differentiating factors of race and culture which, in the opinion of the Spaniards, prevented the new political order from being immediately established in the American parts of the monarchy, that is, in the former colonies. In fact, the alleged 'specificity' of the Americas – in other words, its racial stratification – continued to dominate colonial politics even after Spain's dominions overseas were reduced to the island outposts of Cuba, Puerto Rico and the Philippines.

Americans and Europeans in the same monarchy: some more equal than others

The political equality promised to Spain's American subjects by the royal decree of 1810 never materialized. It was diluted by exceptional measures initiated during the two constitutional periods of 1810–14 and 1820–23 in which otherwise Liberal principles of government held sway. On more than one occasion, Liberal colonial policy deviated from the terms of the recently proclaimed equality, forcing even those Americans who wished to remain Spanish citizens to accept restrictions that, in law or practice, implied a relationship of subordination to metropolitan interests. This policy prefigured the manner in which later Spanish governments dealt with the remaining colonies.

Even in 1810, the Americas were severely underrepresented in the Cortes, while the colonial delegates present can hardly be said to have been representative of their constituents. Thus, the American-born Joaquín

---

[19] Agustín Argüelles' distrust of the American representatives in the Cortes is noteworthy: 'In regard to the principles and general resolutions, which in the abstract favoured liberty, the Liberal delegates from overseas did not diverge from those of Europe. On this point, all interests were the same. But, in their practical and immediate application to all the cases in which we tried to maintain the supreme authority of the state, give strength and vigour to the government of the motherland, and sustain the unity and coherence of such distant and vast provinces, one could see in the American delegates a certain reservation or turning away, one could note a kind of caution: in sum, it was impossible to ignore the fact that they were heading towards another goal, that they were guided by rules that were different, if not contrary, to those which served as norms for the Peninsular delegates'; *Examen histórico de la reforma de Cádiz* (Madrid, 1970), p. 245.

Mosquera and Ignacio Rodríguez de Rivas, both members of the regency government, had little in common with the majority of the American delegates.[20] Also at issue was the question of American representation in the newly planned council of state. Both the terms of the debate and the intervention of Agustín Argüelles, an outspoken Liberal and the most authoritative voice among the Spanish delegates, are quite revealing, especially since the issue touched less on abstract matters of political theory than on the eventual distribution of power. The constitutional commission proposed, as we have seen, the establishment of certain criteria for membership in the council, including the stipulation that a minimum of twelve out of a total of forty councillors should be non-Europeans.[21] The Americans interpreted this clause as discriminatory, since it was based on criteria other than proportional representation. Argüelles, in contrast, defended it, arguing that in this instance 'the commission departed from the principle of equality in order to ensure that over the course of time there could never be any combination that would exclude the corresponding number of Americans. It indicated that there be at least twelve'.[22] Yet, for all his good intentions towards the Americans, Argüelles did nothing to help increase the proportion of overseas delegates in other government offices. Even on the constitutional commission formed in December 1810, Americans only accounted for three representatives against ten from the peninsula. This imbalance was so scandalous that, at the request of the commission itself, two more Americans were admitted in March 1811.[23]

In addition to the question of colonial representation in the Cortes and government offices, Americans and Spaniards disagreed about the organization of political power in the empire and, in particular, about the capacity of the metropolitan government directly to intervene in local affairs overseas. Underlying this disagreement, as mentioned above, was a deep ideological split that originally surfaced at the Cortes of Cadiz.[24] In contrast to the centralized concept of monarchy held by the peninsular delegates, the Americans envisaged a monarchy based on geographical and historical natural fatherlands – and, consequently, a more decentralized state. Natur-

---

[20] Marie Laure Rieu-Millan, *Diputados americanos*, p. 294.   [21] DSCD, 31 October 1811.

[22] DSCD, 5 November 1811. Let us leave aside the fact that, in 1837, Argüelles would have a great deal to do with the 'combination' that would remove the Cuban delegates from the Cortes.

[23] M. Cristina Diz-Lois, *Actas de la comisión de constitución (1811–1813)*, Madrid, 1976, pp. 20–21.

[24] J. Varela Suanzes-Carpegna, *La Teoria del estado*, pp. 423–34.

ally these delegates held out for a re-organization of government that would transfer at least some decision making from Spain to America.[25]

The decisive moments in this power-struggle took place during the debates over the organization and powers of the *diputaciones* (provincial assemblies) and of the *jefe político* (the institutional and personal representative of the central government at the provincial level). In both cases, Peninsular delegates upheld the principle of restricting local or provincial autonomy. They also rejected the possibility of integrating into the Constitution of 1812 a distinctly American organization of power, different from that of the European part of the Monarchy, and instead sought to establish laws which reinforced metropolitan control over overseas institutions.

The Spanish delegates' idea of control derived from the latent tension between political representation – a political space wherein it was impossible to avoid creole demands – and the development of the administrative structure of the Liberal state, whose watchwords were unity and hierarchy. Their basic idea was to ensure peninsular monopoly over the executive apparatus in America, mainly by asserting control over key offices in the existing colonial administration, including viceroys, captains-general, governors, intendants and the like. In essence, the Spaniards fought to maintain the institutional apparatus of the Old Regime and to resist any and every attempt to grant additional powers to local and provincial institutions overseas, especially the *diputaciones*.[26]

The resolution of these questions by the Cortes of Cadiz and the parliamentary sessions of the Liberal government of 1820–23 illustrates clearly the reticence of the peninsular representatives towards the Americas. Admittedly, when the Mexican representative Ramos Arispe suggested separating political and military control in the overseas territories, Argüelles not only supported the proposal but sought to implement it in the peninsula.[27] But most peninsular delegates opposed this separation of powers in the Americas on the grounds that any attempt to weaken colonial authority would favour secessionist tendencies.[28] Secondly, the Americans regarded as excessive the powers accorded to the office of the *jefe político*, a

---

[25] Ibid., pp. 432–3.

[26] Mario Rodríguez refers to the reticence during the Liberal *Trienio* of 1820–1823 regarding the provincial assemblies in 'The "American question" at the Cortes of Madrid', *The Americas*, 8 (1982), 297.

[27] On these questions for Spain specifically, see the excellent works of Roberto L. Blanco Valdés, *Rey, Cortes y fuerza armada en los orígenes de la España Liberal, 1808–1823* (Madrid, 1987), and Pablo Urbano Casado, *Las fuerzas armadas en el inicio del constitucionalismo español* (Madrid, 1982).

[28] See Ramos Arispe's comments in DSCD, 19 December 1812.

key official in the colonial administration which the Cortes of Cadiz un-
successfully tried to create. According to Ramos Arispe, a strong *jefe politico*
would undermine the authority and independence of the provincial assemblies which embodied, via the concept of collective representation, the
Americans' desire for self-government.[29]

The peninsular delegates' fear of the possible autonomy of the Americas
underlay the constitutional debate over the *diputaciones*.[30] The debate
between Ramos Arispe and the delegate from Guatemala Larrazábal on one
side, and Argüelles and the count of Toreno on the other, is highly representative of the different orientations of the peninsular and American
politicians. In a speech on 12 January 1812 Ramos Arispe argued that the
jefe politico, an office which was to be reserved for native-born Spaniards,
was endowed with excessive, indeed arbitrary power. Specifically he
rejected the notion that the office should serve as the sole conduit for
communications between the provincial assemblies and the central government. He also feared that the *jefe's* power to oversee the correspondence of
municipal governments and to suspend the members elect of the assemblies
would curtail the development of new provincial organs. The *jefe politico*, in
his view, would enjoy more power than had the viceroys under the *Leyes de
Indias*. Ramos also expressed fears about the right of the royal intendant, the
crown's chief financial officer in the colonies, to attend the sessions of the
diputaciones. Since these assemblies were to be small, Ramos argued that the
presence of the intendant would unfairly favour the central government in
provincial affairs.[31] Underlying Ramos' objections to the intendants was a
basic question: what would be the true powers and prerogatives of the
provincial assemblies within the monarchy itself?

A decade later, during the Liberal era (1820–23), the Cortes was still
debating this important issue. On 15 March 1821, fourteen overseas delegates presented a proposal to expand the number of overseas *diputaciones*,
but this apparently innocuous measure provoked heated debate.[32] For the
Americans, the assemblies constituted a symbol of self-government; but for
many peninsular delegates they represented a threat to the notion of central-

29 M. Turrado Vidal, 'El jefe político. Diseño de su institución en las Cortes de 1811 a 1814',
   Boletín de Documentación, 114 (1988), pp. 49–80.
30 A. Martínez Riaza, 'Las diputaciones provinciales americanas en el sistema Liberal
   español', *Revista de Indias*, 52 (1992), 647–91.
31 Ramos Arispe went so far as to declare, referring to the intendants: 'I expect that the
   wisdom of His Majesty will someday free us from this semi-French institution, simplifying
   the administration of the Treasury, and thus the term 'Intendant' will be substituted by the
   title of 'Leading Official of the Provincial Treasury'; DSCD, 12 January 1812, p. 2607.
32 DSCD, 30 April 1821, pp. 1357–63.

ized government which stood at the foundation of the Liberal state. The Spaniards therefore sought to guarantee the presence of state officials in the provincial assemblies, whether new or old. As Martínez de la Rosa put it: 'in order to compose the provincial assembly, there must be two officials appointed by the Government: one, the *jefe político* of the province, who is the highest official; the other, the Intendant.'[33] Confronted by the Americans' desire to endow their assemblies with the maximum degree of autonomy, the peninsular delegates did everything in their power to prevent this. Some, including the count of Toreno, even went so far as to argue that these assemblies, for all their democratic pretensions, did not truly represent the areas they were meant to serve.[34]

Continuing tensions between the Spaniards and the Americans over these and related issues had important consequences for the future of Spain's remaining colonies. Fundamentally, they reinforced the metropolitan rulers' support for a new constitutional framework which kept autonomy at a minimum. The Spaniards' idea was to convert institutions such as viceroyalties, captaincies-general, governorships and intendancies, into the executive branch of the administration and to make certain that new ones, such as *diputaciones*, were so structured as to ensure Madrid's control over all matters of local government. In the short term, the consequences of this principle of restriction in America remained limited, since the effective

---

[33] Ibid., p. 1361. On Martínez de la Rosa's position on American questions, see C. Pérez Bustamante, 'Martínez de la Rosa y la independencia de la América española', *Revista de Indias*, 21 (1991), 385–404.

[34] Argüelles defended an even more forceful position:

These bodies (the assemblies) have been formed with the laudable objective of having the provinces prosper; but, it is necessary to look for balance so that the government, which is responsible for the peace of the *pueblos*, can and should take the opportune measures, and this is my answer to Mr. Arispe, who is against the jefe político and the intendant having a vote in the assemblies. The action of the government without this would be null on many occasions: and the seven individuals representing the province would maintain their preponderance.

It is equally necessary to counter any idea of representation that can be offered in lieu of the provincial assemblies. Perhaps the opinions of some gentlemen derive from this mistaken principle. The diputaciones are elected by the people in order to combine the trust and removability of their members with subordination to the government, which avails itself of them for the execution of its orders. National representation can not be more than one, and this, embodied by the Cortes alone, is the only [institution] that can express the will of the people, and thus the provincial assemblies do not have, nor through their nature can they have, any representative character except in the economic area, and with absolute submission to the supreme authority. Each Diputación is like a council uniting everybody from the province in one place, and maintaining unity, performing in this the same functions that the *Acuerdos* of the *Audiencias* performed before (DSCD, 12 January 1812, p. 2610).

implementation of the reforms decreed by the Cortes of Cadiz and during the 1820s was slow, late and imprecise.[35]

During the two constitutional periods under discussion here, the powers of the captains-general in America increased, allegedly because the critical circumstances of war in the peninsula and in the Americas made this policy unavoidable.[36] Civil and military authority in America remained unified in the figure of the viceroys and captains-general and, while legislation regulating provincial governments specified that the *jefe político* would not wield military powers, it allowed the government temporarily to unify civil and military authority when exceptional circumstances obliged.[37] In the parts of empire not under viceregal authority, like Cuba, Puerto Rico, the Philippines and Venezuela, where the institutionalization of the new figure of the *jefe político* threatened to curtail the powers granted to the captains-general, this process did not get very far owing to the metropolitan government's policy of granting the latter the powers of the *jefe político*'s office.[38] This occurred in Puerto Rico in 1811, after a half-hearted attempt at secession.[39]

[35] In Puerto Rico, for example, the provincial assembly did not meet until 5 May 1813, a few months before the restoration of absolutism. The return of Ferdinand VII meant the end of elected city councils on the island, although the previous increase in their number was left unchanged. See A. Gómez Vizuete, 'Los primeros ayuntamientos Liberales en Puerto Rico (1812–1814 y 1820–1823)', *Anuario de Estudios Americanos*, 47 (1990), 581–615. The article by de los Angeles Hijano Pérez on the Cuban municipalities, 'El régimen municipal de Cuba en la segunda mitad del siglo XIX', *Anuario de Estudios Americanos*, 50-2 (1993), 243–77, is very disappointing.

[36] These exceptional attributes were extended whenever special circumstances made them advisable. Hence the late decree of the Cortes of 28 June 1822, which authorized the government to 'proceed with respect to the business of the overseas provinces as it sees fit, and as demanded by the different circumstances in each of the territories in which it is necessary to impose its influence and authority, or to use other more energetic and active resources to sustain our enterprises'. One should note that the decree did not refer to political or military powers but rather to those relating to business, scientific expeditions, the risk of invasion, etc., although the wording was deliberately ambiguous.

[37] Marie Laure Rieu-Millan, *Diputados americanos*, p. 300.

[38] It should be remembered that the Cuban delegates, for example, demanded the resignation of the Island's highest authority, the marquis of Someruelos, in the secret session of the Cortes of 21 January 1811, alleging that he had committed manifest abuses of power. Their petition was clearly a consequence of the harsh treatment by the captain-general of those implicated in the failed attempt at secession by Basave and Aponte the previous year. See Allan J. Kuethe, *Cuba, 1753–1815: crown, military and society* (Knoxville, 1986); also, Larry L. Jensen, *Children of colonial despotism: press, politics, and culture in Cuba, 1790–1840* (Tampa, 1988).

[39] On the political background of events in Puerto Rico, see the excellent book by Jesús Raúl Navarro García, *Control social y actitudes polticas en Puerto Rico (1823–1837)* (Seville, 1991). The speeches by the Puerto Rican delegate, Ramón Power, are in DSCD, 20 August 1811, pp. 1661–3. Power's address to the Cortes demanding the revocation of the royal order can be consulted in Aida R. Caro de Delgado, *Ramón Power y Giralt. Diputado*

In addition, the authority of the viceroys in America was reinforced when they assumed the powers of the superintendents, a transfer which gave them authority over the civil treasury and its judicial responsibilities. Although the Liberal government in 1820 revoked the viceroys' power to control the treasury, Spain tended, whenever possible, to concentrate maximum authority in the hands of its chief officers abroad.[40] This policy was, of course, moot in the case of those colonies that declared their independence during the 1820s, but it had important repercussions for Cuba, Puerto Rico and the Philippines.

From equality in theory to inequality in practice

Spanish colonial policy during the years immediately following the death of Ferdinand VII in 1833 was dominated by the definitive resolution of the problems raised in the two previous constitutional eras. The first indication of the road colonial politics would follow was the metropolitan government's refusal to allow Cuba to implement measures designed to separate political and military powers and to establish a provincial assembly.

In November 1833, the minister of the interior, Javier de Burgos, proposed the establishment of a number of 'subdelegations', the institutional basis of what would eventually become the *jefes políticos* or civil governors in each of the Spanish provinces.[41] Even earlier, a royal decree on 23 October 1833 called for the establishment of a subdelegation in Cuba.[42] Along the same lines, de Burgos commissioned the Cuban Arango Parreño to formulate a plan for the establishment of a civil government on the island. Arango soon proposed the restriction of the powers of Havana's captain-general together with other reforms that amounted to Cuba's transformation from a colony into a province equal in political status to those of the peninsula. Arango was well aware of the implications of his proposals for Cuba's future and hastened to declare that 'in our American domains, we should fortify the superior authority of the head [captain-general] of the province; but

---

puertorriqueño a las Cortes Generales y Estraordinarias de España, 1810–1812 (Compilación de documentos) (San Juan, 1969), pp. 1546–64.

[40] This disposition relating to New Spain was promoted, once again, by the delegate Ramos Arispe: see DSCD, sessions of 5 and 7 April. On the discussions of the viability of the intendency during the reign of Charles IV, see Luís Santiago Sanz, 'El proyecto de extinción de las intendencias de América y la Ordenanza General de 1803', *Revista de historia del derecho*, 5 (1953), 123–85.

[41] On Javier de Burgos' initiatives, see M. Ballbé, *Orden público y militarismo en la España constitucional (1812–1823)* (Madrid, 1983).

[42] F. J. Ponte Rodríguez, *Arango y Parreño. Estadista colonial* (Havana), 1937, p. 235.

why should we not make those divisions which, instead of weakening it, could perhaps contribute to its greater decorum?'[43] Not surprisingly, Arango's project provoked fierce opposition from the captain-general of Havana as well as a certain reticence from the minister of the interior in Madrid. In May 1835, the captain-general of Cuba, Miguel Tacón, expressed to the government of Madrid his complete opposition both to the creation of a 'civil governor' and to Arango's suggestion that he relinquish some of his powers.[44] Even before this letter arrived in Madrid the government issued two decrees, dated 21 and 26 March 1834, that strengthened Tacón's powers; and on 18 February 1835 it suspended Arango's commission and simultaneously confirmed the captain-general of Havana as Cuba's supreme military and political authority.[45]

Madrid's refusal to accept political reforms in Cuba following the death of Ferdinand VII led to an unprecedented crisis in the relations between the Cuban ruling class and the metropolis. In the course of the 1830s Spanish obstinacy on this issue placed the Havana creoles in a difficult position. They possessed enormous economic and social power, thanks to an expanding slave economy producing sugar and coffee and the weak international position of the metropolis, but they had no voice in the island's government and could do little more than attempt to influence policy by lobbying either the powerful Cuban intendancy or the government in Madrid.[46] This was not much to show for such an accumulation of wealth and power. In the eyes of Liberal Spanish governments of the 1830s, however, the only way to retain control of the Antillean colonies was through an efficient military policy and strict control of colonial institutions. They consequently granted more power to the captains-general of Cuba, Puerto Rico and the Philippines – who were delighted to take it – and simultaneously subjected the institutions of the old imperial framework, such as the *audiencias* and the intendancies, to their authority – and thus to the authority of the metropolis.[47] This transformation of colonial power left

---

[43] A little earlier Arango had expressed to the secretary of state his disappointment regarding the attitude of the captain-general. See the *Obras de Francisco de Arango y Parreo* (Havana, 1952), II, pp. 629–30.

[44] Ibid., p. 626.

[45] J. Pérez de la Riva, *Correspondencia reservada del Capitán General Don Miguel Tacón con el gobierno de Madrid, 1834–1836* (Havana, 1963), p. 154.

[46] On the nineteenth-century Cuban intendancy, see Violeta Serrano, *La Intendencia de hacienda en Cuba* (Havana, 1990).

[47] I have explored this process, crucial to the Spanish Liberals' colonial policies, in an unpublished paper: 'El colonialismo Liberal, 1810–1868 (Politica y hacienda en Cuba, Puerto Rico y Filipinas del Imperio al "imperio insular")', 1992.

no space in the three colonies for the development of home rule, let alone for local institutions of the kind that had been developing in the peninsula.

Under these conditions, the only reminder of the participation of the Americans in the Liberal Cortes of 1808–14 and 1820–23 was the annoying presence of a group of Cuban delegates in the *Estamento de Próceres* (Estate of Notables) in 1834 and in the Cortes of 1835–36. When a majority of Liberal delegates decided to take charge of colonial policy, following the uprising of La Granja in Spain and the insurrection of Lorenzo in Santiago (Cuba) during the summer of 1837, the expulsion of the Antillean representatives became inevitable.[48] It was to avoid rubbing salt into these wounds that 'special laws' were promised – even though, as we know, they were never enacted. The promise of this legislation was thus the product of the frustrated development of institutions along Liberal lines in Cuba, Puerto Rico and the Philippines. It also represented the premeditated prolongation and accentuation of the almost unlimited power of the colonial authorities in Spain's remaining possessions. The 'special laws', in reality, meant on the one hand the absence of laws, special or ordinary, adapted specifically to the colonies and, on the other hand, the extension to the colonies of laws enacted for Spain itself, once the changed context of the nineteenth century invalidated the old *Leyes de Indias*.

---

[48] On the insurrection of Lorenzo, see Jesús Raúl Navarro García, *Entre esclavos y revoluciones. (El colonialismo Liberal de 1837 en Cuba)* (Seville, 1991). The best guide to the dense and complex political history of Spain in this period, with special attention to the events of 1837, remains Josep Fontana, *La Revolución Liberal (Política y hacienda, 1833–1845)* (Madrid, 1977).

Index

Abarca, Pedro, 182
Acheh, 255, 257
Agreda, Sor María de, 46, 50, 71
Aguilar, Gaspar, 202, 204, 205
Alamos de Barrientos, Baltasar, 63, 68, 130, 141, 323
Alarcón, Antonio de, 70
Albia (or Alvía) de Castro, Fernando, 93, 97, 135, 155
Alcántara, 93
Alcocer, Juan de, 110, 118–20
Alcocer, Pedro de, 88–9, 90
Alfonso X, The Wise, of Castile, 74, 77, 197
Alfonso IV, The Benign, of Aragon, 191
Alicante, 190, 195
Almarche Vásquez, Francisco, 208
Alvarez de Toledo, Francisco, 107
Alvarez Zapata, Juan, 106, 107–8
America, 14–15, 22–4, 264, 319, 327
    administration and domination of, 298–302, 307, 314
    central control of, 346–9
    church and state in, 301–3
    creoles in, 312, 314–15, 332, 340–1
    disease in, 297, 304, 309
    equal rights for, 336–9
    exploration of, 305–7
    and free trade, 330–1
    friars in, 299, 301–3, 312
    language and culture in, 313
    legal system, 335–6
    means of conquest of, 297

mining in, 306–7, 310–11
native religion in, 312–13
population of, 296, 309
and racial differences, 340–1
relationship with Spain, 331–3
representation in Cortes, 341–7
role of colonists in, 311–12
studies of native life in, 303–4
taxation of, 310
technology in, 308–9, 310
trade and agriculture in, 307–8
and tribute payments, 304–5, 310
Andalusia, 54, 134, 137, 153–5
Anne of Austria, 35
Annius of Viterbo, 77
Antwerp, 285, 287
Apianus, Peter, 84
Aquinas, Thomas, 29, 31, 57, 59, 61
Aragon, 19, 94, 132, 136–7, 139, 141, 153, 190, 230, 292, 318
    Castilian hostility to, 133–4
    concept of liberty in, 169–75
    defence of liberties of, 175–80
    ecclesiastical liberties, 174
    feared union with Castile, 167–8
    histories of, 82–4, 154
    and laws of Sobrarbe, 164–6, 169, 174, 181–2
    liberties of the nobility, 174
    new political currents in, 180–1
    preservation of civic liberty in, 163–4
    re-affirmed *fueros*, 184

reconciled liberty with authority, 185–7
reputation for liberty, 160–1, 166
resistance theory in, 176–9
suppression of, 162
and union with Spain, 148–9
uprisings in, 172–3, 178–9
Aranda, count of, 331–2
Arango Parreño, 347–8
Arévalo, Fray Juan de, 144
Argensola, Bartolomé Leonardo de, 94, 166, 179–80, 181
Argensola, Lupercio Leonardo de, 168, 179–80
Argentina, 307, 336, 338
Argüelles, Agustín, 341n, 342–4, 345n
Arista, Iñigo, 169
Aristotle, 30, 87, 90, 318, 325
Arroyal, León de, 73–4, 96, 99
Asia, 255, 261–2, 264–5
Asturias, 154–5
audiencias, 298ff.
Auñon, marquis of, 144
autobiography, 213, 216–20, 224–5
Avila, 53, 88
Avila, Melchor de, 51
Ayala family, 106–7, 116
Ayora de Córdoba, Gonzalo, 87–8
Azores, 246, 252, 256
Aztecs, 296, 299, 303–5

Bacon, Francis, 27–8
Baltasar Carlos, Prince, 184
Barajas, count of, 140
Barbosa Homen, Pedro, 66
Barcelona, 87, 193, 211, 212, 214, 290
account books in, 220–1
chronicles of, 221
constitutionalism of, 226
Barco de Avila, 92–3
Bardaxi, Ibando de, 164n, 170, 176
Basque Country, 181
Bayonne treaties of 1868, 229, 231
Beuter, Anton, 88, 98
Biondo, Flavio, 87
Blancas, Jerónimo de, 165, 170–1, 177
Bodin, Jean, 172
Botero, Giovanni, 60, 320–4
Brabant, 273, 275, 277, 283, 285, 292
Brazil, 273, 286
Breda, 284–5, 286
Bujalance, 93
Buñol, count of *see* Mercader, Gaspar
Burghley, Lord, 160–1, 166, 184, 249
Burgos, 54, 68–9, 87, 91–2, 151, 153, 154
Butterfield, Herbert, 3, 10

Cabrera de Córdoba, Luis, 32, 83, 93–4, 179
caciques, 304ff.
Cadiz, 331, 336–8
Calatayud, 93
Calderón de la Barca, Pedro, 156, 197, 204
Cambodia, 254, 261
Camos, Marco Antonio, 32
Campanella, Tommaso, 145, 258, 317, 323
Campillo y Cosio, José del, 326–7, 332–3
Campomanes, P.R., 326–33
Cantabria, 154
Cardinal-Infante, Ferdinand, 271–89
Caribbean, 298–9, 308
Cascales, Francisco de, 91–2, 95
Castiglione, 31
Castile, 15, 19, 22, 63, 167, 177, 230, 248, 250, 253, 318
chorography of, 88
as community of cities, 137
composite monarchy of, 136
comunero movement in, 134
concept of community in, 127–31
and conflict with Aragon, 82–3
conscience and theology in, 48–51
and consent to taxation, 59, 61
converso middle class in, 104–5
debates on taxation, 68–71
destroyed by Habsburgs, 327
hispanization of, 137–41
histories of, 138, 144
hostility to Aragon, 133–4
lack of unity in, 136–7
lacked exclusive rights, 140
and military organization, 153
nationalism in, 126, 131–7, 144
price rises in, 115
provincialization in, 151–5
relationship to Spain, 126–7, 130–1, 137–8
resented burdens of empire, 141–3
and resentment of foreigners, 149–50
resisted integration, 132
and royal history, 74–7, 82
silk trade in, 108
and Spanish unity, 145–51
teritorial expansion of, 103
weakness of national sentiment in, 158–9
Castillo, Fray Hemando del, 248–9
Castrillo, count of, 48–9, 70–2, 130
Catalá de Valeriola, Bernardo, 204–7, 209
Catalonia, 4, 5, 20, 136–7, 141, 181, 189, 211, 239, 276, 282
autobiographical writing in, 213, 217–18, 225
and Cerdanya, 229–30, 232ff.
French invasion of, 182–3, 230, 236
histories of, 84

Catalonia (*cont.*)
 nationalism in, 126
 Pujades' history of, 212, 223
 revolt of, 3, 14, 22, 45, 83, 85, 149, 150,
   185, 290–2
Catholic Monarchs, see Ferdinand and
   Isabella; see also Spanish monarchy
Ceballos, Jerónimo de, 59–60, 63–6
Cecil, William see Burghley, Lord
Cedillo, count of, 106
Central America, 296, 299, 306, 313; see also
   America
centre and periphery, 18–19, 24, 103, 225
 in Cerdanya, 229–30, 233–4, 242
 crisis of, 336
 dialogue between, 14–15, 21
 and history, 74, 83
 and nationalism, 126
Cerdán de Tallada, Tomás, 65–6, 198–200,
   203, 207, 210
Cerdanya, 21
 divisions in, 228–9
 national identities in, 229–30, 236–7,
   239–42
 and Pyrenean boundary, 230–4
 resisted France and Spain, 234–6
Céspedes, Andrés García de, 86
Céspedes y Meneses, Gonzalo de, 83
Ceuta, 150
Charles, duke of Lorraine, 281, 291
Charles I, of Castile; see Charles V
Charles II, 148, 152, 158, 184–5, 265
Charles III, 326, 328–9, 332
Charles IV, 326, 329, 332
Charles V, 75, 77, 79, 80, 88, 131, 134, 171,
   200, 205, 249, 258, 299, 314, 318, 321,
   327, 329
 and Aragon, 167–8
 coronation of, 247
 and royal favourite, 31–2
 universalism of, 317
Chelva, 90, 189
Child, Sir Josiah, 329, 330
Chile, 306, 308
China, 247–8, 254, 255–6, 261, 324
chorography, 18, 19, 74, 84–99
Chronicles, urban, 87, 221–22; see also
   history
cities
 chronicles of, 221–2
 and civic liberty, 163
 and civic pride, 155–6
 and metropolis, 156–7
 as political communities, 127–9, 137
 and provincial awareness, 151–2
Cleves, 275–6

Colón, Fernando, 86
Colmenares, Diego de, 90, 94
colonies see America; see also Overseas
   Provinces
Columbus, Christopher, 15, 298
community, 155–7, 162
 in Castile, 127–31
 consciousness of, 125
 and *patria*, 158
 types of, 128–9
 and villages, 237–40
 see also cities; nation
comunero revolt, 88, 90, 103, 134
Conchillos, Joseph, 98–9
Condé, Henri II of Bourbon, Prince of, 279,
   281, 282, 294
Constant, Benjamin, 322–3
constitutionalism, 58, 60–2, 63–4, 66, 162,
   166, 177–8, 226
Constitutions, 334–5, 339–40
Contreras, Antonio, 70
conversos, 18–19, 104–5, 111, 114, 123–4
Corbie, 271, 272, 276, 280, 282
Cordoba, 52–3, 70, 73, 94, 120–1
Cortés, Hernando, 297, 299, 300, 304–5, 349
Cortes of Aragon, 161, 163–4, 175–6, 178–9,
   184–5
Cortes of Cadiz, 23, 336–9, 342–6
Cortes of Castile, 134, 136–7, 148, 150, 154
 cities and provinces in, 151–2
 and taxation, 48–9, 51–2, 59, 61, 64, 68–71
Costa, Juan, 163, 168, 182
councils, 139–40
counsellors, 30, 31–3, 43; see also royal
   favourite
Covarrubias, Diego de, 57–8
Covarrubias, Sebastian de, 84–5
creoles, 312, 314–15, 332–3, 341
Crespi de Valldaura, Cristóbal 207–8, 210
cronista del rey, 74–5, 76–7, 81
Cuba, 23–4, 334, 336, 346–9

Dénia, 190
diaries, 222, 225; see also Pujades, Jeroni
Díaz del Castillo, Bernal, 297
Dôle, siege of, 279, 280, 281
Dormer, Diego José, 201
Drake, Francis, 253, 257, 264
Dutch, 81, 160, 249, 262–3
 overseas empire, 264–5
 war with Spain, 270–95
 see also Low Countries; Spanish
   Netherlands

Elche, 93, 96
Elizabeth I, 160, 161, 249

Elliott, Sir John, 14–16, 18, 126, 132, 162,
    317–18
  life and works, 1–13
empire, British, 328, 330
empire, Spanish
  expansion of, 324–5
  opponents of, 23, 318–20
  overseas, 317
  preservation of, 320–5
  as universal, 247–9, 254–6, 258–9, 317,
    319
encomenderos, 299ff.
England, 85, 90, 95, 147, 160–1, 162, 186,
    195, 219, 220, 225, 249
  attacked Portuguese ships, 252–3
  overseas trade, 264–5
  war with Spain, 253, 256–7, 260–3
Enveig, 238
Escolano, Gaspar, 191–2, 194–5, 196–8, 200,
    203–6, 209
Espinola, Bartolomé, 52
Espinosa, Gabriel de, 141
Espinosa, Jerónimo Jacinto, 204, 207
Esquivel, Pedro de, 250–1
Europe
  autobiographical writing in, 219–20
  and Spanish empire, 267, 269, 317
Extremadura, 153–5

family chronicles, 219, 221–2; *see also*
    autobiography
favourite *see* royal favourite
Febvre, Lucien, 11
Feijóo, Fray Benito, 157–8
Ferdinand and Isabella, 75, 76–7, 103,
    105–6, 115, 132, 133, 167, 171, 203,
    258, 298, 301, 314
Ferdinand II, Emperor 272, 282
Fernández de Medrano, Juan, 33, 35
Fernández Navarrete, Pedro, 59, 65–6, 130,
    144, 146, 323–4
Fernández de Oviedo, Gonzalo, 75
Fernández-Santamaría, J.A., 51
Figueres, 211, 232
fiscal theory, 56–66; *see also* taxation
Flanders, 141, 149, 184, 283–5
  army of, 270, 271, 276, 278, 282, 286–7,
    293–4
  see also Spanish Netherlands
Florence, 219, 221, 225
Flórez Estrada, Alvaro, 340
Ford, Richard, 227–8
France, 21–2, 35, 47–8, 70, 83, 85, 134, 149,
    172, 177, 181, 195, 219, 239, 260, 264,
    267, 294
  and free trade, 328–9

grand offensive against, 281–3
invasion of Catalonia, 182–3, 230, 236
as main rival to Spain, 269–70
nationalism in, 235–6
and Pyrenean boundary, 227–34
  Spanish attack on, 270–3, 278–80, 282–4,
    293
Franche-Comté, 269, 276, 279, 280–2
Frederick Hendrik, Stadholder, 274, 284–5,
    287, 290
French Revolution, 232, 234, 236
friendship, 27–33, 38–42; *see also* royal
    favourite
Fuensalida, count of, 106–7
Fuente, Diego de la, 110–11, 114
Fuente, Juan de la, 110–11
Fuente, Rodrigo de la, 110, 112
fueros, 164–87; *see also* liberty
Fuertes Biota, Antonio, 182, 187
Furió Ceriol, Fadrique, 30, 161, 199–200,
    203

Galicia, 153, 154, 253, 257
Galíndez de Carvajal, Lorenzo, 75–6, 137
Gallas, Matthias, 271, 281, 282
Gándara, Miguel Antonio de la, 158
Gandía, 190, 202
Garreta, M.F., 240–1
Gennep, 275–6, 285
Genoese, 120
geography, 84, 86, 247, 251
George, St, 178, 196
Germany, 219, 272, 274–5, 278, 280, 286
Gerona, 150
Gesio, Giovanni Batista, 249
Ginés de Sepúlveda, Juan, 247
Goa, 245, 252, 255, 257, 262
Gómara, Francisco López de, 297
Gómez de Sandoval y Rojas, Francsico *see*
    Lerma, duke of
González, José, 70
González Dávila (or de Avila) Gil, 40, 84
González de Cellorigo, Manuel, 60, 65, 130,
    138, 145, 147
Gracián, Baltasar, 94
Granada, city of, 53–5, 63, 98, 107
  silk trade in, 108
  Torre family in, 117–20
Granada, kingdom of, 18–19
  reconquest of, 103
  tax-farming of silk rents in, 109–21
  toledanos in, 105–6ff.
  see also Granada, city of
Greater Antilles, 299
Guajaras, 107
Guaras, Antonio de, 160–1, 166

Gudiel y Peralta, Luis, 70
Guicciardini, Francesco, 80–2, 161
Guils, 229
Guimerá, count of, 177, 181

Habsburgs, 17, 131, 246–7, 258, 265, 269, 321
Haro, Luis de, 22, 46–7, 231
Helmond, 273, 276, 278, 285
Henry of Navarre, 249
Herrera y Tordesillas, Antonio de, 79, 80, 81, 144, 321
Hispaniola, 298
history, 17–18, 74–84, 93, 95–6, 138, 144, 154–5, 157, 223–4; see also chorography
Holland see Dutch
Holy Roman Empire, 278–9, 317–18
Hotman, François, 161, 177
Howell, James, 21
Huesca, 91
Hurtado, Fernando, 110–11
Hurtado, Guiomar, 111, 114, 117
Husillo family, 112–14

Incas, 296, 303–5, 308
India, 262
Indians
  and depopulation, 309–12
  languages of, 313
  mental isolation of, 313
  religions of, 312–13
  studies of, 303–4
  tribute payments from, 304–5, 310
Indies, 148, 263, 299, 326, 331
  Council of the, 247–8, 303, 306
  see also America; Indians
Inquisition, 19, 103, 105, 107, 111–12, 123, 203, 302
Ireland, 256, 257, 261
Isabella, Queen of Castile; see Ferdinand and Isabella
Islam see Muslims
Italy, 134, 141, 149, 150, 219, 221, 247, 248, 267, 269, 282–3, 290, 317
Ivars, Joan Lluch, 192–3

Jaén, 52, 53
James I of Aragon, 190
James I of Valencia, 196–8
James, St, 89, 145, 196
Japan, 248, 252
Jews, 90, 203; see also conversos
John II of Castile, 40, 74–5
Jonson, Ben, 226
Jovellanos, G.M. de, 326–7, 329, 331
Jover Zamora, J.M., 146–7

Juan, Jaume, 246
justice, 57–9, 61–2, 199; see also law

La Alberca, 93
La Tour de Carol, 229, 238, 240
Lancina, J.A. de, 129
Lanuza, Juan de, 178
Lanuza, Vicencio Blasco de, 167
Larrea, Juan de, 60
Las Casas, Bartolomé de, 128, 130
law, 60–1, 68, 164–6, 170, 180–1, 197–8, 208–10; see also justice
Laynez, Joseph, 60, 62–3, 65
Legazpi, Miguel López de, 247
León, Luis de, 56
Lepanto, victory of, 248
Lerma, duke of, 17, 45, 205
  announced as royal favourite, 33
  appointed sumiller de corps, 37
  defence of, 39–42
  downfall, 43
  opposition to, 39, 42–3
  power of, 38
Leuven (Louvain), 273–4
liberty, 19, 168–9, 186
  in Aragon, 160–2, 163–6, 169–72, 184–7
  and authority, 182–3
  ecclesiastical, 174
  of the nobility, 174
  and Saragossan Privilegio, 175
Limburg, 273, 275–6
Linz, Juan, 50
Lipsius, Justus, 180
Lisón y Biedma, Mateo, 55, 63–4, 65, 68
Llanos Ribera, Antonio Fernández de, 143
Llívia, 232, 239–41
Logroño, 93, 97, 135, 154–5
Lombardy, 269, 282, 284
Lombay, marquis of, 173
López de Mendoza, Francisco, 201
López de Toledo, Diego, 106
López Galván, Juan, 168
López de Velasco, Juan, 303
Louis XIII, 280, 292
Low Countries, 22, 160–1, 172, 184, 219, 225, 257
  heresy laws in, 259
  and Spanish attack on Dutch, 274–5
  as Spanish power base, 267, 269
  see also Spanish Netherlands
Luna, Alvaro de, 40
Lupián, Antonio, 181

Maas, 274, 285
Maastricht, 273, 275–6, 285–6, 289
Macao, 246, 263

Machiavelli, 169, 320–1, 323
Madariaga, Fray Juan de, 67
Madrid, 156–8, 193, 205, 246
Malacca, 245, 255
Malaga, 109
Maldonado, Juan, 133, 135
Maldonado, Pedro de, 39–41, 45
Mallorca, 218
Manila, 246, 254, 263
Maravall, J.A., 126, 127, 155
Marca, Pierre de, 181
March, Francisco, 191–2, 193, 202
Mares, Vicente, 90, 189
Mariana, Juan de, 46, 58–9, 63, 68, 79, 80, 98, 130, 138, 161
Marineo Sículo, Lucio, 77, 82, 86
Márquez, Fray Juan, 59, 60–2
Martínez Aloy, José, 208
Martínez de Silíceo, Juan, 123
Martínez de Villar, Miguel, 93
Mártir Rizo, Juan Pablo, 128
Martyr of Angleria, Peter, 171–2
Mata, Francisco Martínez de, 60
Matheu y Sanz, Lorenzo, 181
Mathieu, Pierre, 34
Mazarin, Cardinal, 47, 231
Medina, Pedro de, 86, 138
Melo, Francisco de, 293
Mena, Juan de, 74–5
Mendo, Andrés, 67
Mendoza, Francisca de, 107
Mendoza, María de, 108
Mercader, Gaspar, count of Buñol, 202, 204–5
merchants, 104–5, 114, 123
Mérida, 87
Mexico, 200, 246, 258, 263, 296–7, 299, 300, 305–10, 312, 330
Mira de Amescua, Antonio, 40, 44
Molino, Miguel de, 167, 169–70, 176–7
Molinos, Pedro, 177
Moluccas, 245, 255
monarchy, concepts of, 130
monarch, Spanish
    chamber of, 36–7
    ideal friend of, 31, 42
    privacy of, 34–5
    responsibility of, 39
    and theory of two persons, 30, 32, 44
    see also royal favourite; Spanish monarchy
Moncada, Sancho de, 60
Montaigne, 29
Montesquieu, 325–6, 329–30
Monzón, Francisco de, 143
Morales, Ambrosio de, 78, 86, 138
Moret, José de, 99

moriscos, 110, 115, 202–3
Moura, Cristóbal de, 32
Mur, Luis de, 182–3, 187
Murcia, 91–2, 95, 115, 120, 122–3, 190
Murillo, Diego, 93
Muslims, 78, 89, 90, 190–1, 201, 202–3, 255
Mut, Vicente, 66–7

Napoleonic invasion, 336
Narbona, Eugeniuo, 59, 66
nation, 125–6, 158–9, 162, 230, 233, 235–7;
    see also national identity; *patria*
national identity, 229–30, 236–7, 239–42
Navarra, 133–4, 137, 169, 181, 230
Navarra, Pedro de, 76
Nebrija, Antonio de, 77
Netherlands *see* Low Countries; *see also*
    Spanish Netherlands
New Castile, 154
nobility, 94–5, 174, 191–3, 196–8, 202–3
    debts of, 209–10
    and lure of the court, 205–7

Ocampo, Florián de, 77, 138
Oihenart, Arnald, 181
Old Castile, 154
Old Christians, 104–5, 111
Olivares, count-duke of, 3, 5, 7, 8–9, 14, 15–16, 22, 55, 64, 69, 81, 207, 294, 318
    aimed to restore Spain in Netherlands, 273
    and attack on Dutch, 274–7, 279, 286
    and attack on France, 270–2, 282–4
    fiscal reforms of, 49, 68, 181
    as royal favourite, 43–6
    and royal history, 83
    and Spanish unity, 146–8
Orense, 151–2
Oropesa, count of, 197
Orrente, Pedro, 204, 207
Ortiz, Elvira, 112
Ortiz, Leonor, 114
Ovando, Juan de, 303
Ovando, Nicolás de, 298
Overseas Provinces
    central control of, 346–9
    equal rights for, 336–40
    and postponement of special laws, 334–5
    representation in Cortes, 341–7

Paéz de Castro, Juan, 77
Pagden, Anthony, 50
Palafox, Juan de, 146–7
patria, 19, 20, 125, 155, 162
    in Aragon, 163
    in Castile, 127, 130–1, 132–3

patria (cont.)
  in Cerdanya, 235
  and good government, 189
  new concept of, 157–9
  in Valencia, 189, 197, 208–9
Peace of the Pyrenees (1659), 228–9, 230–1, 267
Penyafort processions, 214
Pérez, Antonio, 170
Pérez de Oliva, Hernán, 15
periphery *see* centre and periphery
Peru, 200, 258, 296, 300, 305–6, 309, 310, 314, 330
Peter II of Valencia, 198
Philip II, 19, 21, 32, 51, 54, 68–9, 83, 86, 119, 140, 142, 166, 172, 198, 200–1, 314, 327, 329, 330
  banned studies of Indians, 303–4
  consulted theologians and jurists, 50, 52
  criticism of, 146
  crowned King of Portugal, 245
  and divine providence, 248, 258–60
  empire of, 246
  failures of, 261–6
  inaccessibility of, 34
  integrated Portugal with Spain, 250–1
  and liberty, 173, 175
  and taxes, 58
  and religious orders, 302
  and history, 76, 78
  universal monarch of, 247–9, 254–6
  and war with England, 253, 256–7, 260–3
Philip III, 17, 44, 46, 50, 54, 140, 142, 144, 152, 154, 192, 198, 201–2
  death, 43
  favourite of, 33, 40, 42
  gave key role to Lerma, 38
  inaccessibility of, 34–5
  and royal history, 78–9
Philip IV, 6, 8, 16, 21, 66, 97, 140, 148, 152, 154, 183, 192, 197, 202, 207, 270, 330
  aimed to restore Spanish Netherlands, 273
  and attack on Dutch, 274–7, 279
  consulted theologians on tax policy, 50, 51, 72
  debated attack on France, 288
  and new concept of royal favourite, 43–7
  reinforced Netherlands, 291–2
  and royal history, 79–82, 83
Philippines, 23, 247–8, 254–6, 261, 263, 330, 334–5, 346, 348–9
Piccolomini, Octavio, 271, 279, 280–1, 283, 287, 289, 290
Pizzaro, Gonzalo, 297, 304–5
political theory, 51, 56, 69–71, 320–1
Porcar, Joan, 195, 198, 201–2

Portalegre, count of, 37
Portugal, 21, 143, 195, 258, 264–5, 267
  administration of, 250–2
  disaffection of, 141
  empire of, 245–6
  English attacks on, 252–3
  map of, 251
  revolt of, 3, 22, 45, 149, 150, 182–3, 185, 187–9, 290–1, 292
  supported Spanish universal empire, 245–6
  unification with Spain, 248–51
Potosí, 306–7, 310–11
privado see royal favourite
Ptolemy, 84
Puerto Rico, 23, 334–6, 348–9
Puigcerdà, 235, 237–8
Pujades, Jeroni, 20
  diary, 213–16, 222–6
  history of Catalonia, 212, 223
  legal background of, 215
  life and works, 211–12
  and politics, 214, 224
  religious beliefs, 216, 224
  xenophobia of, 215–16
Pulgar, Hernando de, 76, 135–6
Pyrenees
  French–Spanish conflict in, 227–8
  and political boundary, 228–34
  village disputes in, 237–8
  see also Cerdanya

Quevedo, Francisco de, 43–5

Ramos Arispe, 343–4
'reason of state', 180–1, 320–2
regidores, 105–6, 117
religious orders, 299, 301–3, 312
Rheinberg, 273, 285–6, 289, 293
Rhine valley, 274–5, 277, 283, 286, 293
Ribadeneira, Pedro de, 249, 265
Ribalta, Juan, 203–4
Ribera, Juan de, 204, 207
Ricci, Matteo, 254–5
Richelieu, Cardinal, 8, 9, 281–2, 291–2
Rioja, 154
Rioja, Francisco de, 81
Roa, Martin de, 94
Roa Dávila, Juan, 57, 59, 68
Rocaberti, Ramón Dalmau de, 183
Rocroi, battle of (1643), 22, 270, 292, 294–5
Roermond, 273, 275
Rohan, duke of, 45
Roig i Jalpi, Gaspar, 85
Rois Soares, Pero, 253
Román, Fray Gerónimo, 91

Román de la Higuera, Gerónimo, 89, 106
Roman empire, 316–17, 320, 324
Ronquillo Peñulosa, Gonzalo, 254
Roussillon, 228–30
royal favourite, 27, 31–3, 38–9
  changing role of, 46–7
  justification of, 39–42
  new concept of, 41–2
  opposition to, 39, 42–3, 45
  types of, 43–4
  see also friendship

Saavedra Fajardo, Diego, 60, 66, 127, 130,
  140–1, 145, 323–25
Sahagún, Fray Bernardino de, 303
Salamanca, 151, 157
Salamanca, Gerónimo de, 120
Salamanca, Miguel de, 283, 292
Salamanca, School of, 17, 50, 56–60, 62, 68
Salazar, Domingo de, bishop of Manila, 254
Salazar, Fray Juan de, 146
Salazar y Castro, Luis de, 84
Sallagosa, 236
Sánchez de Avila, Díaz, 119
Sánchez de Cisneros, Juan, 113–14
Sánchez Doria, Rodrigo, 69
Sande, Francisco de, 247
Sandoval, Fray Prudencio de, 79, 144
Santa Cruz, marquis of, 256
Santa María, Fray Juan de, 42–3
Santiago de Compostela, 136
Santos, Francisco, 156
Sanz, Cristóbal, 96
Saragossa, 93, 97, 141, 161, 166, 173, 175,
  178, 184
Schenck, 274–7
Sebastian, king of Portugal, 248, 265
Segovia, 53, 54, 90, 94, 97
Seville, 53, 55, 87–8
Sicily, 195
silk trade, 108–9, 113, 115–16, 120–23; *see
  also* tax farming
silver, 306, 308, 310–11
Smith, Adam, 332–3
Sobrarbe, legend of, 164–6, 169, 174, 181–2,
  184
Soto, Domingo de, 318–20
Sotomayor, Fray Antonio de, 50
South America, 296, 299, 300, 305–6, 314,
  336; *see also* America
Spain
  attacked Dutch at sea, 287–8
  and colonial representation, 341–7
  concepts of community in, 128
  confederal concept of, 73–4, 96
  conquest of America, 296–7

decline of, 15–16, 262–4, 329
and difficulties of preserving empire,
  322–5
and domination of America, 298–302, 314
and doubts about empire, 316–20
exploration of America, 305–7
fiscal theory in, 56–66
and free trade, 328–31
growth of provincialism in, 153–5
and history, 6, 9–10, 17–18, 74–99, 154
and legal equality for colonies, 336–40
liberalism in, 239, 336, 341, 343, 344, 349
local patriotism in, 130
map of, 251
military organization of, 153
new patriotism in, 157–9
new provincial administration in, 151–2
and opposition to royal favourite, 39,
  42–3, 45
postponed special overseas laws, 334–5
pure blood ethos in, 124
and Pyrenean boundary, 227–34
reform of, 326–7
relationship to Castile, 126–7, 130, 137–41
sought to retain control in colonies, 346–9
spiritual autobiography in, 220
and taxation, 49, 51–2
theology in, 50–1, 56
and tribute payments, 304–5, 310
unification with Portugal, 248–9
unity of, 145–51
and war with England, 253, 256–7, 260–1
see also Spanish monarchy; Spanish
  Netherlands
Spanish Burgundy *see* Franche-Comté
Spanish monarchy, 16, 73, 246
  Aragonese support for, 182–3, 185–7
  and concept of community, 129
  court of, 30–1, 36–7, 205–7, 214
  crisis of, 141–5
  decline of, 325–6
  and disputes with clergy in America,
    302–3
  and divine providence, 258–60
  external threats to, 149–50
  failed to reform, 331–2
  fiscal administration in, 152
  and growth of centralized state, 156–9
  inaccessibility of, 34–5
  and interests of Castile, 131, 132, 137
  and liberty, 174, 175
  naval organization of, 152–3
  opposition to, 318–20, 327–8
  respected rights of non-Castilians, 140
  and right of taxation, 61, 62–3, 64–5,
    68–70

Spanish monarchy (*cont.*)
and royal history, 74–84, 96
strategic base of, 267, 269
suppressed Aragonese liberties, 162
survival of, 15, 24
and universal monarchy, 247–9, 254–6, 317
and Valencia, 198–201
see also Spain; Spanish Netherlands
Spanish Netherlands, 269–70, 324
and attack on Dutch, 274–7, 279, 285–7
and attack on France, 270–2, 278–80, 282–4, 293–5
failure of grand assault on France, 284–5
Franco-Dutch offensives against, 273–4, 290
reinforcement of, 291
restoration of, 273
see also Low Countries
Stow, John, 90
Suárez, Francisco, 39, 129
Suárez de Figueroa, Cristobal, 67, 130, 145, 147
Sumatra, 255
Sweden, 278–9, 289

Tacitus, 320–1, 323
Tarragona, 150
Tavara, marquis of, 198
taxation
in Catalonia, 232
consent for, 58, 59, 61–2, 66, 70
constitutionalist argument for, 58, 60–2, 63–4, 66
debates on, 68–71
discourses on, 54–5
justification of, 52, 61
literature on, 59–60
and monarch's right to, 61–6, 68–70
opposition to, 53–5, 66–7
and political theory, 69–70, 71
and social justice, 57–9, 62
and theology, 48–9, 51–2, 71–2
in Valencia, 194, 200–1
see also tax-farming
tax-farming, 104–5, 109–21
Teresa, St, 144–5
theatre, 204–5
theology, 48, 49–54, 56, 71–2
Thirty Years' War, 269, 270
Tiberius, Emperor, 35
Toledo, 18–19, 51, 54, 64, 88, 90, 106–7, 136
conversos in, 104–5, 111, 123–4
growth of, 103
middle class in, 103–4
and pure blood law, 123–4

silk artisans in, 120–2
silk trade in, 122–3
Torre family in, 116–17
Toledo-Zapata, Fernán Alvarez de, 106, 109, 118
Toledo-Zapata family, 106–8
Toreno, count of, 344–5
Torre, Alfonso de, 109
Torre, Alonso de la, 111–12, 115, 117, 119–20
Torre, Juan de la, 109–12, 114–15, 116–19, 123
Tortosa, 150
Tubal, 77, 89, 99
Tudela, 98–9
Turgot, A.R., 331–33
Turks, 248, 264

Uceda, duke of, 41
Union of Arms, 147–8
universal monarchy, 247–9, 254–6, 258–9, 317, 319
Urgell, bishopric of, 232
Uztarroz, Juan Andrés de, 84, 181

Valencia, city of, 87–8, 98, 134, 137, 190–93, 196; *see also* Valencia, kingdom of
Valencia, kingdom of, 20, 84, 153, 181, 218
arts in, 204
Corts of, 209–10
early history of, 190–1
expulsion of *moriscos* from, 202–3
language of, 206
laws of, 197–8, 208–10
and lure of the court, 205–7
nobility of, 191–3, 196–8, 202–3, 205–10
patriotism in, 189
people and character of, 195–6
political economy of, 194–5
popular celebrations in, 196–7
relations with monarchy, 198–201
religious conflicts in, 203
silk trade in, 113, 115, 122
taxation of, 194, 200–1
towns in, 192–3, 195
Valladolid, 52, 135, 151, 154
Vargas, Tomás Tomayo de, 81, 97
Vázquez de Menchaca, Fernado, 318–20
Vega, Lope de, 81, 204
Velasco, Juan Fernández de, 82
Vélez de Benaudalla, 118, 119
Vélez Malaga, 93
Venezuela, 336, 338, 346
Venlo, 273, 275, 285
Vicens Vives, Jaume, 4, 6
Vich, Diego de, 202–5, 207

Index

Viciana, Martin de, 191, 195, 200, 203, 205–6
Vilar, P., 158n, 159
Vincent Ferrer, St, 196, 203
Vincent the Martyr, St, 196
Vitoria, Francisco de, 50, 129–30, 320
Vitrián, Juan de, 45–6
Vitrián de Biamonte, Felipe, 183–4
Vives, Juan Luis, 37, 203
Vizcaya, 153–5

War of Mantua, 273
War of the Spanish Succession, 326
Ward, Bernardo, 326–8, 331

Zamora, 98, 143
Zapata, Fray García, 107
Zapata, Luis de, 32–3, 138
Zúñiga, Baltasar de, 44
Zurita, Jerónimo de, 82, 165